Beyond the Basilica

University of Chicago Geography Research Paper no. 237

Series Editors
Michael P. Conzen
Chauncy D. Harris
Neil Harris
Marvin W. Mikesell
Gerald D. Suttles

Titles published in the Geography Research Papers series prior to 1992 and still in print are now distributed by the University of Chicago Press. For a list of available titles, see the end of the book. The University of Chicago Press commenced publication of the Geography Research Papers series in 1992 with no. 233.

Beyond the Basilica

Christians and Muslims in Nazareth

Chad F. Emmett

The University of Chicago Press

Chicago and London

Chad F. Emmett is assistant professor in the geography department at Brigham Young University.

The University of Chicago Press, Chicago 60637
The University of Chicago Press, Ltd., London
© 1995 by The University of Chicago
All rights reserved. Published 1995
Printed in the United States of America
04 03 02 01 00 99 98 97 96 95   1 2 3 4 5
ISBN: 0-226-20711-0 (paper)

Library of Congress Cataloging-in-Publication Data
Emmett, Chad F. (Chad Fife), 1956–
    Beyond the basilica : Christians and Muslims in Nazareth / Chad F. Emmett.
        p.   cm. — (University of Chicago geography research paper ; no. 237)
    Revision of author's thesis (Ph.D.—University of Chicago, 1991) under the title: The Christian and Muslim communities and quarters of the Arab city of Nazareth.
    Includes bibliographical references and index.
    1. Nazareth (Israel)—History.   2. Christians—Israel—Nazareth.
3. Muslims—Israel—Nazareth.   4. Neighborhood—Israel—Nazareth.
5. Nazareth (Israel)—Religious life and customs.   I. Title. II. Series.
DS110.N3E48   1995
956.94'5—dc20
                                                                        94–28395
                                                                             CIP

♾ The paper used in this publication meets the minimum requirements of the American National Standard for Information Sciences—Permanence of Paper for Printed Library Materials, ANSI Z39.48-1984.

For Mom and Dad

Thou shalt love thy neighbor as thyself.
—Jesus of Nazareth

Contents

Tables

Figures

Preface

During April of 1989, three religious holidays, representing the three major religions of the Middle East, all occurred at the same time. From a Friday-morning vantage point in a Christian Arab's shop, in the heart of Nazareth's market, I saw families from all three religions making preparations for these holidays. Several Greek Orthodox families were buying new clothes and feathery angel wings for their children to wear the next Sunday for Orthodox celebrations of Palm Sunday; a Muslim family from a village in the Triangle had come to Nazareth to buy, among other things, a new shirt for their young son to wear during '*Id al-Fitr* celebrations at the end of the fasting month of Ramadan; and Jewish residents from Upper Nazareth had descended into the Arab market to shop while stores in their own town remained closed for Passover.

This convergence of Muslims, Christians, and Jews in the holy town of Nazareth is symbolic of the convergence of Islam, Christianity, and Judaism in the region known today as the Middle East. This region has for millennia been identified as a land of conflict and a land of accommodation. The all too frequent conflicts have often had their origins in political, strategic, economic, historical, and ethnic differences, but religion has been the most frequent source of the contentions. In 1869, Mark Twain made the following observation about the connection between religion and conflict while visiting the Church of the Nativity in Bethlehem: "The Priests and the members of the Greek and Latin churches cannot come by the same corridor to kneel in the sacred birthplace of the Redeemer, but are compelled to approach and retire by different avenues, lest they quarrel and fight on this holiest ground on earth" (Twain 1966, 436).

This contention between the two Christian sects is not one of theological differences, but rather geographical. It is the land, deemed holy by both groups as the birthplace of Jesus, that is the source of conflict. While this conflict is very site-specific, it indicates rivalries and conflicts between religious groups in the Middle East not only for control of places of worship, but also for access and control of their own quarters, cities, lands, states, and regions.

Central to the religious conflicts of the Middle East is the land of Israel/Palestine—a holy land to Jews, Christians, and Muslims alike. This holiness has prompted all three religious groups to settle in the land and to fight for control of it at various times. Jerusalem is at the core of the conflict, but there are other holy sites and cities in which multiple religious communities have settled and where conflict is always a possibility.

One of these communities is the Galilean town of Nazareth. Priest, pilgrim, refugee, and merchant have gathered in this holy town, not always for religious reasons, but nevertheless representing a variety of religious allegiances. Here they have created a religious landscape of segregated quarters centered on religious institutions. The communities of Nazareth experienced conflict during the Crusades, but since then most incidents of communal conflict have been relatively minor.

In August 1988 I journeyed to Nazareth for a year of field research, with an additional visit in April 1994, to better understand how Christians and Muslims have managed to live together for centuries in relative peace in a region known for its ethnic and religious conflicts, and to determine to what degree they have remained segregated in religious-based quarters. In order to assess adequately patterns of segregation and integration and to ascertain levels of conflict and accommodation, I spent the year traversing the winding, up-and-down roads of the town. I attended religious services and ceremonies, searched through local newspapers, supervised a three-hundred-household survey, and interviewed (mostly in English, but also in Arabic when necessary) a broad cross section of willing Nazarenes, from religious and civic leaders to greengrocers, teachers, unemployed youths, and the many hospitable families who welcomed me and my surveyors into their homes. Most questions were answered without hesitation, especially those about refugee experiences or government injustices. Some respondents were very open even when talking about communal rifts, while for many others, religion and communal relations were the most sensitive issues, and answers to questions were offered with caution or not given at all. In some instances I have included the names of persons interviewed, but at the request of some individuals and for the sake of protecting others, I have left some statements anonymous.

I lived just beyond the limits of Arab Nazareth in a mixed neighborhood of Christian and Muslim Arabs called Hakramim in the predominantly Jewish city of Upper Nazareth. Here I picked up the local Palestinian dialect from fun-loving neighborhood youths, and I witnessed first-hand the friendships that exist among the many religious communities. These same feelings of brotherhood were evident through the year and throughout the town. There were those who expressed contempt for others, but in most cases this was the direct result of political preferences. Some resented the involvement of Communists in their religious councils and the municipality, while others feared the divisive prospects of the entrance of an Islamic party into local politics. For the most part I found people who had friends, neighbors, workmates, and classmates from opposing communities, and while they did not mix in marriage or in some quarters of the city, they genuinely felt as if they were one in spite of their religious and political differences. This unity stems from several different factors: they are all Arabs who speak Arabic and enjoy Arab culture; they all consider Nazareth their home and revere it as a holy town; they follow religious teachings of tolerance and love; and they are all part of an Arab minority within the state of Israel joined together in striving for equal rights as citizens of Israel and in supporting the aspiration of their Palestinian brethren in the occupied territories and diaspora who are striving for statehood.

The year was not without its challenges. Telephones were uncommon and appointments were often broken. In a city where street numbers and the few street names exist only on maps and where unposted house numbers are known only to postmen, finding homes without a guide was next to impossible. As a result, interviews often had to be arranged at restaurants rather than in homes. The lack of house and street numbers made survey organizing a lesson in improvisation. Unable to send surveyors to addresses obtained from telephone books or voter registration rolls, houses had to be randomly selected from town planning maps. A request for information on the settlement of refugees in Nazareth and land compensation offers was denied by the Israel Lands Administration office in Upper Nazareth. Acquiring base maps of Nazareth from the Survey of Israel office in Tel Aviv required multiple visits, and the maps were then obtained only with a promise that the 1:10,000 scale maps not be reproduced (the base map of streets used in most of the maps in this work is based on these maps). A request for companion maps of Upper Nazareth was denied. Municipal archives were in such shambles, owing to the overcrowded, run-down municipal offices, that requests even to sort through the mostly boxed materials were denied. Some parishes had excellent records, while in others they were significantly lacking. For the most part, my being a Christian from the United States was no problem. However, one sheikh was concerned that I might be with the CIA or Mossad; and one household, in reading the introduction to the survey, assumed that I was Jewish because my surname, Emmett (an English name), when transliterated into Arabic, resembles the Hebrew word *emet* (truth).

Nazareth has a future full of challenges. The municipality constantly struggles to keep up with uncontrollable growth while disgruntled residents complain of the lack of municipal services. It also struggles to obtain fair funding and treatment from the national government. Residents complain of unfair treatment as an Arab minority in a Jewish state, including such frustrations as restricted access to certain jobs and other opportunities, expropriation of lands, and a lack of progress toward peace between Israel and the Palestinians. There is concern that the rise of an Islamic party might antagonize and politicize the Christian community, and thereby divide the two communities of Nazareth. The Christian community worries that ongoing emigration will leave them further weakened in a town that has a rich Christian heritage.

In spite of these challenges, there is still hope. The Nazarenes I met are a resilient people. They have the capacity to endure and to overcome. Their strength comes from their family and friends, their communities, culture, and religion, and from their strong ties to the land. These strengths will continue to sustain them.

Many people have supported this project and I would like to thank them all. First and foremost are my parents, John and Norda Fife Emmett, who have always cared, supported, and helped. When funding fell short, they were the ones who came to my aid. The Emmett clan has provided welcome respites in the form of quarterly family letters, skiing and mountain biking vacations, and visits to Chicago and Israel. Noted among that clan are Uncle Martin and Aunt JoAnn Emmett Hickman, who by chance happened to be living in Jerusalem (where he served as director of the Brigham Young University Jerusalem Center) while I was living in Nazareth. They opened their hearts and home to me and provided welcome support.

Throughout the process I have also been sustained by the interest and encouragement of Mormon communities (members of the Church of Jesus Christ of Latter-day Saints) wherever I have happened to land, whether it be the multiracial community on Chicago's South Side; the small, linguistically mixed community of the Galilee, which gathers for weekly Sabbath (Saturday) services in Tiberias; or the more homogeneous communities in Logan and Provo, Utah, there have been kind souls who cared. Noted among the Mormon community in the Galilee is friend and brother Ehab Abunuwara, a Palestinian Israeli Arab Christian Mormon from Nazareth, who has rendered tremendous help throughout the process.

In Nazareth, the Samir and Su'ad Abunuwara family and their extended families adopted me as one of their own. The families, and especially children, of the Hakramim quarter warmly welcomed me into their midst. Every family, sheikh, priest, principal, party leader, community leader, municipal official, librarian, and merchant that I met was willing to offer help, which often included lengthy and multiple interviews. This book could not have been, without their interest and help.

Ghazi Falah and the Galilee Center for Social Research provided welcome help with the survey, as did six willing students, Rawiya, Enaya, Nesreen, Rula, Sawsun, and 'Alaa, who ventured into unknown quarters and ended up working more than they bargained for. Adib Daud of the municipal planning office readily supplied town planning maps used for the surveys. Amin Qudha provided meticulous election results and lists of precinct boundaries, which I then used to create the election maps. There are far too many more to name here, but as you read on you will come to know many by name.

Professor Marvin Mikesell, of the University of Chicago, has been most helpful throughout the long process with insightful advice and trust in my abilities. Professors Michael Conzen and Chauncy Harris have also been of great assistance. Chicago colleagues Shaul Cohen, Maura Abrahamson, Alexis Papadopoulos, Kelly Hayford, Alec Murphy, Jane Benson, and Mary McNally, as well as friends Lauri Hlavaty, Mark Ellsworth, Troy Scotter, and Curtis Thomson, have all provided encouragement and advice amid the fun times and good food. Special thanks to Stephen Daw and Jeff Bird for their cartographic computer skills in creating the maps, and to Carol Saller and Don Norton for their editing skills.

While once living in Indonesia, I was intrigued with a custom of publicly apologizing beforehand for any offense that might result from a speech or publication. I think it would be beneficial to invoke that practice here. My initial attraction to Nazareth was a deep interest in and concern for Christian and Muslim Palestinians and an admiration for their being able to coexist in a region where religious tolerance is not always practiced. I journeyed to Nazareth not to criticize or find fault, but to learn and understand. Many Nazarenes opened up to me, and in the process I learned of problems and pain, frustrations and fear, and tolerance and hope. Propositions and perspectives differed, but everyone responded to my questions out of a sincere desire to improve Nazareth and its communities. In documenting what I learned, both positive and negative, I hope that no offense is given or taken, either from what I have written or what others have said. If there is offense, then I offer a sincere apology. Much good comes out of Nazareth, and I consider the many Nazarenes I met to be my friends.

1
Introduction

Rising from the heart of the Arab city of Nazareth is the Basilica of the Annunciation with its towering inverted cone-shaped cupola. This imposing structure commemorates Nazareth's most noted claim to fame—the annunciation to Mary that she would bear a son named Jesus. The religious structures built to commemorate this and other holy events and to accommodate nuns, priests, and pilgrims dominate the landscape of Nazareth. To these holy sites have come pilgrim, tourist, and scholar. Their written records and studies most often center on the holy events and places, but beyond the basilica is a seldom considered city inhabited by both Christian and Muslim Arabs.

The residents of Nazareth are very much aware of the sacred nature of their city, but the daily chore of living means that their lives are often dominated by more secular matters. Still, in Nazareth the sacred and the secular are never far apart. This mix is noted not just in the holy structures and the travelers they attract, but in the variety of residents who have come to live in the city, in the way they have or have not chosen to segregate according to religious communities, and in the way religion influences their participation in local and state politics. This complex mixing of the sacred and secular renders Nazareth a fascinating and in many ways unique city.

The earliest known map of Nazareth is an 1868 work of Titus Tobler of Germany (reproduced in English in figure 1). It shows the small Galilean village of just a few thousand inhabitants divided into three distinct religious quarters: a central Muslim quarter centers on the White Mosque; a Latin quarter expands westward from the Latin Monastery at the site of the Annunciation; and a Greek Orthodox quarter surrounds the bishop's compound and then stretches northwestward, almost reaching the Greek Orthodox Church of the Annunciation and Mary's well. A 1914 map in Arabic by Anglican pastor As'ad Mansur (fig. 4) shows the town divided into the same three, but expanded, quarters. The role of religion in determining patterns of segregation is clearly evident, because religion served not only to unite each community into its own quarter, but also to divide, not just Christian

1

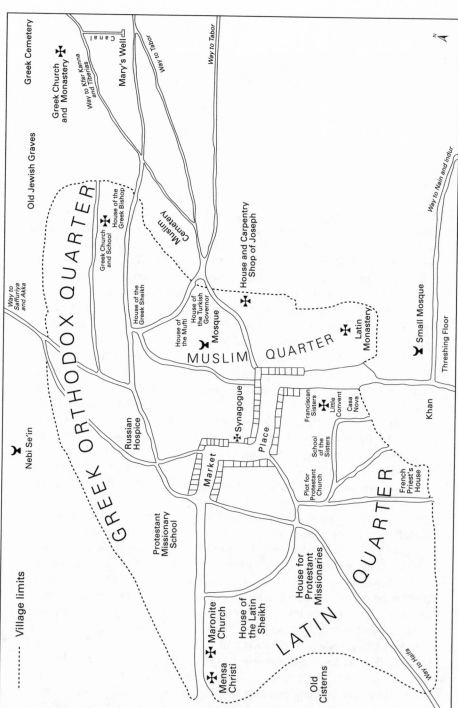

Fig. 1. Map of Nazareth, 1868, by Titus Tobler of Germany.

Village limits

Greek Cemetery

Old Jewish Graves

Greek Church and Monastery

Way to Kfar Kanna and Tiberias

Canal

Mary's Well

Way to Tabor

Way to Tabor

GREEK ORTHODOX QUARTER

Way to Saffuriya and Akka

House of the Greek Bishop

Greek Church and School

House of the Greek Sheikh

Muslim Cemetery

Nebi Se'in

House of the Mufti

House of the Turkish Governor

Mosque

MUSLIM QUARTER

House and Carpentry Shop of Joseph

Way to Nain and Indur

Russian Hospice

Synagogue

Place

Latin Monastery

Small Mosque

Market

Franciscan Sisters

Little Convent

Threshing Floor

Protestant Missionary School

School of the Sisters

Casa Nova

Khan

Plot for Protestant Church

French Priest's House

Maronite Church

House of the Latin Sheikh

House for Protestant Missionaries

LATIN QUARTER

Mensa Christi

Old Cisterns

Way to Haifa

and Muslim communities, but also the differing Christian communities.[1]

The phenomenon of segregated quarters is most often attributed to the traditional Islamic city and is always mentioned in the literature on that subject as one of its key elements and primary indicators.[2] Segregation has persisted as a common characteristic of cities in the Islamic world. It typifies a complex pattern of relationships in which the communities of the region found that, in spite of ethnic and religious tensions, coexistence was and is possible. Quarters helped to insure that conflict gave way to accommodation as communities found strength within their quarters. Here extended family relationships, holiday celebrations, similar origins and customs, and shared municipal functions of defense and tax collection all helped to keep each community unified and in a position where it was not so threatened by other communities. Nazareth was no exception.

That so many communities came to exist in such a small and obscure village is also a direct influence of religion. Nazareth's sanctity to Christians as the site of the Annunciation and the childhood home of Jesus meant that it attracted a variety of Christian communities to its holy sites. The mention of Nazareth in the Quran as the home of Mary and the prophet 'Isa (Jesus), along with its location within the Islamic world, meant that it was also home to a Muslim community. Both of these communities have lived together in the town for at least the past four hundred years.

The Nazareth of today presents a more diverse array of communities and a much more complex pattern of distribution than the original three quarters. The village of Tobler's day has expanded from its traditional core in an isolated basin up and over the surrounding hills to become the largest Arab city in Israel, with a population of 60,000. Dotting the hills of the now sprawling city are several score of quarters. In addition to the Latin and Greek Orthodox quarters, there are also Greek Catholic, Coptic, and Maronite quarters. There is even an American quarter named for the half dozen American and Arab Baptist families who have clustered there. The original Muslim quarter, having been crowded out by the central market and Latin religious institutions, has since spread to the eastern slopes of the town, where it is

---

[1] In discussing the relationship of culture and cities, Agnew, Mercer, and Sopher (1984, 8) note: "In their form and in the lives of their inhabitants, cities have reflected the working of dominant, residual, and emergent cultures. To study the city in cultural context therefore requires us to acknowledge that cities are cultural creations and that they are best understood as such." This is indeed the case with Nazareth.

[2] For an overview of the various characteristics attributed to Islamic/Middle Eastern cities and the ongoing debate associated with this field of study, see, for example, Grunebaum 1955; and Abu-Lughod 1987.

Fig. 2. City core, central market, and site of the original village. White mosque (center), Greek Catholic Church and synagogue (right center), Basilica of the Annunciation (top right)

now known as the Eastern quarter. Newer Muslim quarters also cover the northern and southern hills of the town. In addition to these religious quarters, there are quarters where religious separation has taken second seat to more pressing and contemporary matters, such as housing availability and affordability, thus attracting a mixed population. There are also quarters where refugees from surrounding villages have gathered out of loyalty to family and friends and a shared heritage of village life and then exile (figs. 2, 3).

The persistence of the original religious quarters and the evolution of new religious, refugee, and mixed quarters typify patterns and relationships that go beyond residential segregation. They speak of a city in which communities of Greek Orthodox, Greek Catholics, Roman Catholics, Maronites, Copts, Anglicans, Baptists, and Muslims have all chosen to live. They also speak of a city in which early and continuing patterns of separation speak of underlying tensions where Christian-Muslim relations can be strained, and where Christian-Christian relations have not always been cordial. This separation is also indicative of a much more complex set of relationships in which the many communities of Nazareth have been able to ensure a relatively peaceful coexistence in a region where communal conflict is often the norm. The gradual change in patterns, resulting in more mixed quarters, also suggests greater communal accommodation, where religion no longer serves as the primary dividing line.

This century-long transformation during turbulent times from village into city raises some interesting questions. What communities make up the community of Nazarenes? Does religion still serve as a dividing line among the communities? Has segregation persisted, or is integration more common? How have the quarters changed in size, number, and composition? How does the level of segregation typify other aspects of communal relations? And if religion has been a primary factor in determining residential patterns, how influential has it been on other aspects of communal life in Nazareth? To answer these and other questions, this study focuses on the degree to which these quarters have maintained earlier patterns of residential segregation among the communities of Nazareth and the degree to which patterns can be used to better understand community relations in general.

Nazareth's quarters are not unique to the region. Groupings by religion have long been associated with settlements in the Middle East. In the first centuries A.D. in Palestine, the Galilean village of Baina had separate sectors for its Judeo-Christian and Jewish communities, and similar patterns perhaps existed in other villages in the region (Bagatti 1969, 19). In Iraq before the advent of Islam, Nestorians, Jacobites (both Christian sects), Jews, and Mandeans chose a separated existence in or-

Fig. 3. Nazareth today; Greek Catholic high schools and quarter (center hill top), Anglican apartment building (lower right), Baptist school (lower left), Coptic Church and Salam Mosque (behind Baptist school)

der to preserve liturgical and legal life for the Jews and in order to prevent intermarriage between the rival Christian communities (Morony 1974). Similar patterns persisted and even expanded under Islam. English (1973, 147) notes that "the pattern of differentiation on the bases of race, religion and common origin" and "small cohesive urban groupings were preeminent features" of the traditional Middle Eastern city. For example, Christian neighborhoods were part of the original plan of the city of Baghdad, which was founded in A.D. 756 (Lapidus 1973, 30), and Jewish quarters once existed in cities spreading from Morocco to Iran. These quarters most often were located next to the palace of the ruler so that security for the Jewish communities could be guaranteed.

Boal (1976) identifies four general functions of residential quarters or neighborhoods: defense, avoidance, preservation, and attack functions. These characteristics were formulated primarily in regard to urban patterns in Western cities, and while they can also be applied in part to urban patterns in the Middle East, several characteristics are unique to the region. For example, Abu-Lughod (1987) identifies several variables peculiar to Islam which were influential in the development of segregated quarters in the traditional Islamic city. These include the juridical distinctions between Muslims and non-Muslims or outsiders, and the decentralized form of government that required neighborhoods to determine land use and adjudicate mutual rights. She then adds that in addition to these Islamic influences, several other factors are involved in the establishment of quarters, including the levels of internal strife and of internal and external security. Using information from two studies that describe ethnic mixing in Beirut prior to the 1975 outbreak of hostilities and the ethnic segregation that followed, Abu-Lughod notes that it "was not segregation that gave rise to inter communal tensions; rather, it was tensions that gave rise to labels which were then partially translated into reality, as population resifted and resorted itself to share a common fate" (166).

The Beirut example shows quarter formation and transformation as an ongoing process that still persists in Middle Eastern cities. In Tripoli, Lebanon, Gulick (1967, 66) identifies sectarian clusters in the city, accompanied by either homogeneous class interests, such as the lower-class Alawite cluster, or by place of origin, such as the cluster of Maronites from the same village. Since their expulsion from Anatolia, Armenian refugees have congregated into quarters in cities scattered throughout the Levant. Greenshields (1981) describes several factors which led to the creation of these quarters, including security, the desire to preserve cultural and community structure, and a low economic status, which forced the refugees to live in camps or shanty towns on the edge of cities. Coptic Christians in Cairo have continued to live in separate neighborhoods, even as they have moved from their quarters in the central city out to new suburban neighborhoods. They also are identified as maintaining some degree of commercial segregation, as illustrated by the distribution of Copt-owned shops on the gold merchants street (Chitham 1986).

Quarters in the land of Israel/Palestine are the topic of several studies. The coastal city of Jaffa in the nineteenth century included Muslim, Christian, and Jewish quarters, and a colony of Egyptian Copts outside the city walls (Kark 1981, 105). Jerusalem has four traditional quarters to accommodate its diverse communities. Within its walls are the Muslim quarter, which spreads out from the Haram al-Sharif (noble sanctuary) where the Dome of the Rock and al-Aqsa mosque now stand; the Christian quarter surrounding the Basilica of the Holy Sepulchre or Church of the Resurrection (the term used by Christian Arabs); the walled Armenian quarter centered on the ancient Church of St. James; and the Jewish quarter to the west of the Western or Wailing Wall, the holiest site for Jews. Historical studies of these quarters indicate that the boundaries between them were permeable and changeable, and that subquarters based on Christian sect (Latin, Greek, Syrian) or place of origin (the Maghrebia quarter for North African Muslims) have often existed within the larger quarters.

As Jerusalem expanded, so too did its quarters. In the late nineteenth century, Christian, Muslim, and Jewish residents of the town moved beyond the walls and into new religious-based quarters (Ben-Arieh 1975; Hopkins 1971). Today the Ultra-Orthodox Jewish quarters in Jerusalem are expanding into Secular Jewish neighborhoods. This process has resulted in conflict between the two Jewish groups, the Secular Jews feeling that their way of life is being threatened by the stricter observances of the Orthodox Jews (Shilhav 1983).

Romann and Weingrod (1991, 61), in a study on Jewish-Arab segregation in Jerusalem, suggest that there are a variety of factors which influence that city's high degree of ethnic segregation: "Jews and Arabs prefer to live separately in order to better preserve their own group identity as expressed by religion, language, cultural norms, and lifestyle. In addition, this permits the two communities to conserve and develop their own public institutions and various sector oriented commercial activities. Voluntary spatial segregation also serves a common desire to prevent interethnic frictions which might otherwise arise from different religious practices or severe national conflicts."

Segregation between Jews and Arabs in the other mixed towns of Israel also continues. In cities like Haifa and Akka (also Akko, Acco, or Acre), an increasing percentage of Arabs live in and around the city

center with its Arab core, while Jews choose to move out to new neighborhoods. Kipnis and Schnell (1978, 178) describe the still vital enclaves
as constituting "a territorial community whose members attach a
meaningful value to their cultural, national and institutional resources." In the village of Rameh, Nakhleh (1973, 76–77) identifies five
quarters with the majority of Druze living in the Upper quarter, Roman and Greek Catholics in the Eastern quarter, Greek Orthodox in the
Lower and Western quarters, and refugees on the western periphery of
the Lower quarter.

   While segregation has long been a factor in the urban Middle
East, it has not always been complete. Integration has also persisted as
part of the pattern. The Geniza documents indicate that in twelfth-
century Egypt, the predominantly Jewish neighborhoods were not ex-
clusively so, and in one town Jewish homes bordered on Muslim
homes (Goitein 1971, 290). In Kirman, Iran, the Zoroastrian quarter located outside the walls of the city was once very homogeneous, but
through a variety of modern forces it has gradually become mixed as
Zoroastrians move out and Muslims move in (English 1967). In
Jerusalem, the Christian quarter is now sometimes referred to as the
Hebronite quarter, owing to the influx of Muslim merchants from Hebron (Tsimhoni 1983, 57).

   The persistence of segregation in Middle Eastern cities, even as
cities expand beyond the traditional Islamic city core, remains an important factor in understanding the distribution and relations of ethnic
groups. Ehlers (1992, 91) notes that most studies of cities in the Middle
East concentrate primarily on the traditional city (*madina*), and that
there is "hardly any attempt to comprehend the city of the Islamic
Middle East as a composite of the madina *plus* its modern extensions."
Greenshields (1980, 135), who provides an interesting overview of the
historical development of quarters and of works done on the subject,
concludes his study by noting the need for more detailed work on "the
formation and development of ethnic clusters both in the past and in
the present." "Ethnic quarters," he writes, "are by no means a dead subject."

   Quarters in Middle Eastern cities are a product of the ethnic and
religious diversity found in the region. While perceived by many to be
solely the land of Islam and of Arabs, the Middle East is actually a
mosaic of communities resulting from millennia of migration and religious innovation. Ethno-linguistic groups include Turks, Kurds, Persians, and Arabs. Religious groups include Shi'i and Sunni Muslims,
Ashkenazi and Sephardic Jews, Greek, Latin, and Armenian-Rite
Christians (to name just a few), and others such as Druze, Zoroastrians,
Mandeans, Alawites, Bahais, Samaritans, and Yazidis.

Roderic Davison (1954, 844) describes the influence of religion on relations in the Middle East: "In the Near East until very recent times the major boundary between groups and therefore the principal barriers to a homogeneous society of equals, have been religious. Although today social and economic disparities in the Near Eastern society have vastly increased as modern technology and finance have provided greater opportunities for getting and spending and although nationalist rivalries now challenge the primacy of religious rivalries, it is still true that religion is the dividing line and that a man's creed is his distinguishing mark."

The much contested land of Israel/Palestine illustrates the divisiveness among the religious communities of the Middle East. The interaction of Judaism, Christianity, and Islam, with their competing claims and strong religious ties to this holy land, is of continuing interest and importance.

The spatial distribution of these three religious groups is complex. Within this small strip of land are found Jews, Muslims, and Christians who are further divided into various and often competing sects and denominations. This diversity is complicated by the fact that the groups are scattered throughout the land in cities, towns, and villages, some of which are homogeneous and others very heterogeneous. Their close proximity serves to make conflict more common and accommodation more evasive.

Most studies on ethnic relations in the land of Israel/Palestine focus primarily on the division between Arab and Jew (Newman and Portugali 1987; Yiftachel 1992). Only occasionally are these groups viewed in terms of the ethnic division between Sephardic and Ashkenazi Jews, or the religious division between Muslim and Christian Arabs, or Orthodox and Secular Jews, all of which have resulted in tension and conflict. Even fewer studies look at the divisions among the Christian sects, which are known for their ongoing conflict for control of holy sites in Bethlehem and Jerusalem.

Several general works exist on Arabs in Israel and on relationships between Arabs and Jews in Israel. Such works, however, tend to treat the Arab community as a single unit, not examining its religious parts. Smooha (1978, 4) in his study on pluralism in Israel notes that "whereas some works on each of the three Arab religious communities (Druzes, Christians and Moslems) are available, there is virtually none on the relations among them." In their bibliography of works on Arabs in Israel, Smooha and Cibulski (1987, 17) identify certain subpopulations of Arabs that are underrepresented in social research, including Christians and the Arabs of Nazareth. Al-Haj (1985, 105) writes that "those few scholars who studied the communal structure of the Arab population did so without analyzing the internal dynamics of Arab inter-ethnic relations." Waterman notes that in regard to urban studies in Israel, little work has been done on the Arab urban population (Waterman 1985, 204).

A few works concentrate on Christian Arab communities in the Middle East. Betts's (1978) work on Christian Arabs is a valuable resource for understanding the whole picture of Christianity among Arabs; it includes a description of the many communities, their doctrinal differences, histories, and contemporary status. Joseph (1983) looks more at inter-Christian rivalries and relationships in the Middle East, paying particular attention to the Jacobites (Syrian Orthodox), while Joseph and Pillsbury (1978) focus on examples of contemporary Muslim-Christian conflicts in a variety of locations.

Closer to Nazareth, Colbi's work (1988) on Christianity in the Holy Land provides a good general history. Its primary focus, however, is at the institutional and ecclesiastical levels; there is little mention of the Christian Arabs as a people or of their interaction with Muslim, Jewish, and Christian neighbors. Tsimhoni (1983, 1984a, 1984b, 1993) has published several interesting works on Christian Arabs, but most deal either with Christians during the British Mandate, or with those in Jerusalem and the West Bank. Christian Arabs are most often mentioned in connection with holy sites, institutions, and organizations, but beyond these imposing structures are an indigenous people whose heritage and culture are rich. Cragg's work (1991) on Christian Arabs includes a chapter on Arab Christianity and Israel which describes how Palestinian Christians have sought to find an acceptable balance between a theology closely associated with Judaism and Israel, and the aspirations of a stifled nationalism.

The Muslim Arabs of Israel receive some consideration in studies of Bedouin or rural villagers, but like the Christian Arab communities, they are most often categorized within the more inclusive term of Israeli/Palestinian Arab. This classification is necessary for studying the Israeli-Palestinian conflict, or Palestinians in general, but it denies the existence of its differing parts. A few works look at the diverse parts which make up the Arab whole, including Rubin's work (1974) on group relations in Acre (Akka); al-Haj's monograph (1985) on ethnic relations in the Arab town of Shefar 'Am among its Muslim, Christian, and Druze communities; and Nakhleh's dissertation (1973) on communal conflict among Christian communities and between Druze and Christian communities in two Galilee villages. Nazareth and its communities are noticeably absent from any of these or other studies.

Few studies on settlements in the Middle East have focused on towns or small cities like Nazareth. Most of these studies are devoted to either large cities or villages. Studies on the large urban centers have been used in developing a typology of what is referred to alternately as the Islamic, Muslim, or Middle Eastern city. As a city located in the Islamic Middle East, Nazareth has certain elements common to the traditional urban model, such as religious- and ethnic-based quarters, a central market centered on a central mosque, and *waqfs* (religious endowments); but it also exhibits differences and variations noted by the central presence of Christian structures and the absence of fortifications. These divergences from the traditional model owe partly to the fact that Nazareth's emergence as a city came much later than the more frequently studied larger cities and partly becasue the city's morphology has been strongly influenced, not just by Islam, but also by Christianity.

This study attempts to fill several of these noted gaps. It describes a smaller city of the Middle East with characteristics common to other urban centers in the region, but also with unique characteristics. It documents the growth of Nazareth from a small, segregated village core to a city whose peripheral quarters are both segregated and integrated. It adds to the literature devoted to Islamic cities not just by describing urban morphology, but by analyzing the peoples and processes—cultural, political, and economic—that have influenced the formation of quarters. It identifies and describes the many communities represented among the Arabs of Nazareth, in more specific categories than the usual Palestinian or Israeli-Arab. It analyzes historical and contemporary relations between the Christian and Muslim Arab communities and between the several different Christian communities. It also attempts to examine the relatively neglected experience of internal refugees in Israel and the rise and political involvement of Islamists in Israel.

With a central theme of quarters and communities in an Israeli-Palestinian-Christian-Muslim-Arab town, this social geographical study of Nazareth is an integrated study which includes topics pertinent to historians, sociologists, anthropologists, and political scientists. Chapter 2 traces the history of Nazareth from earliest times to the present, emphasizing the communities and their relations. It describes the growth of Nazareth from a village to a city, and the position and problems of Nazareth as an Arab municipality within the Jewish state of Israel. Chapter 3 deals with the many Christian communities of Nazareth—their churches, institutions, landholdings, holidays, clergy, and parishioners. It also describes intersectarian cooperation and conflict, and in the case of the Greek Orthodox community, intracommunal conflicts. Chapter 4 is devoted to the Muslim community and its gradually changing status as the community becomes more active. It also identifies the refugee communities that congregated in Nazareth following the 1948 war, the budding community of Arabs in the mostly Jewish municipality of Upper Nazareth, and the Communist party, which in many ways functions as a separate community. Chapter 5 focuses on the quarters of Nazareth, their origins, development, and communal composition, and on the levels of segregation (congregation) and integration that exist in the city. Chapter 6 looks at community relations, including areas of conflict and accommodation. The final section of the chapter analyzes the rise of Islamic parties and their influence on communal relations. Chapter 7 is devoted to concluding comments.

Throughout the study, data collected from a survey will be used. This survey was conducted in the last week of August and first week of September 1989. Six university students (five women and one man, four Christians and two Muslims) were each assigned an average of fifty homes to visit. The three hundred households consisted of twenty-five clusters of eight homes and one hundred separate homes. The households included in this stratified random sample were selected from town planning maps in proportion to the population percentages for each census subdistrict. In order to obtain a good cross section of communities, several households were selected on the basis of their locations in areas known to be inhabited by Baptists, Copts, or Anglicans.

Respondents were generally very cooperative. Only one household (Muslim) refused to answer the survey. The wife started to answer, but when her husband returned he asked the surveyor to leave. An alternate home on the street was then selected. Some respondents objected to questions regarding religion, because of its sensitive nature in Nazareth, but in only a few isolated incidents did they refuse to answer (in particular, when asked the religion of their dentists and insurance agents).

The survey took longer to administer than expected. One of the problems stemmed from the social nature of Arab visits. Stains on several of the surveys indicate visits lengthened by the requisite drinking of coffee. Custom required that visits to Muslim homes by men when only the wife was home required a return visit in the evening when the husband was present. Most of the surveyors had never looked at a map of their city (the only one readily available was a small tourist map that does not show the outer quarters), and so it took extra time to orient themselves to the detailed town planning maps of Nazareth, which identified the houses they were to visit.

Survey respondents included 123 men and 177 women at an average age of 48 for the men and 44 for the women. Muslims represented 54 percent of the group, and Christians, 46 percent (results from the 1983 *Census of Israel* identified Nazareth as being 60.4 percent Muslim and 39.4 percent Christian). The Christian respondents were divided as follows: 35 percent Greek Orthodox, 30 percent Greek Catholic, 27 percent Roman Catholic, 4 percent Maronite, 2 percent Copt, 1 percent Anglican, and 1 percent Baptist. Their levels of education included 8 percent with none, 19 percent with elementary school, 26 percent middle school, 29 percent secondary school, and 17 percent university. The 281 men in the households surveyed included construction workers (22), metal workers (20), drivers (19), merchants (15), laborers (13), painters (11), mechanics (10), and teachers (9). Those with professions included four attorneys and three each of engineers, bankers, and doctors. Most women (79 percent) indicated that they were housewives, teaching (25) being the main source of employment for those who worked. Sixty percent of the households surveyed owned a car. The average household size was 5.5 (6.2 for Muslims and 4.6 for Christians), ranging from one to fifteen members, the average length of household residence being 17.5 years.

This project considers only a small part of the mosaic of ethnic and religious diversity in the Middle East and Israel/Palestine. Nonetheless, it provides a needed addition to the often neglected studies of Christian and Muslim communities in the Middle East, of religious quarters, and of midsize Middle Eastern towns. Understanding how the various communities have arranged themselves spatially into religious and ethnic quarters and clusters, and analyzing to what extent barriers are starting to bend and break through increased interaction and integration, are a beginning toward understanding how the followers of diverse religious traditions can find accommodation in cities, states, and lands they all call home.

2

The History of Nazareth and Its Communities

Beginnings

The history of Nazareth is a history of its communities. Canaanites, Israelites, Jews, Judeo-Christians, Christians, and Muslims have come and gone, and some have come again. Because its history has been so influenced by religion and religious communities, it seems fitting that the first known reference to Nazareth comes from a religious text. In the New Testament, Nazareth enters the pages of history as the town of Gabriel's annunciation to Mary,[1] and the town where Jesus "increased in wisdom and stature." From that point on it has been primarily the religious pilgrims, scholars, and skeptics whose written accounts of visits to and studies of Nazareth's holy places have left a chain of references about the town and its communities (LeHardy 1905). Many of these references were only incidental to religious purposes and as such reveal prejudices, inaccuracies, and rough estimates. Still they provide a fragmented history that is more complete than that of the many other obscure Galilean villages.

Nazareth's existence before its first mention in written text is verified by excavations in the vicinity of the Latin churches of the Annunciation and St. Joseph. The original village must have been located here because excavations have revealed pottery dating from the Middle Bronze Age (2200–1500 B.C., during the time of the Patriarchs); ceramics, silos, and grinding mills from the Iron Age (1200–586 B.C., after the conquest of Israel and before the Babylonian exile); and tombs and

---

[1] As with just about every other Christian holy site, there are conflicting views over the authenticity of the site of the annunciation. Jerome Murphy-O'Connor, in his archaeological guide to the Holy Land writes: "The evangelists do not agree as to where Mary and Joseph lived before the birth of Jesus. Matthew implies that it was Bethlehem (Matt. 2), but Luke says that it was Nazareth (Luke 2:4–5). It is more probable that Matthew was correct. Joseph belonged to a Judaean family. Were Nazareth their home it would have been more natural to return there when Herod menaced the family than to go to Egypt. . . . If she lived near Jerusalem it would have been natural for Mary to visit and stay with Zachary's wife Elizabeth (Luke 1:39–40); no young Jewish girl would have been permitted to make the three-day journey from Nazareth alone" (Murphy-O'Connor 1986, 309).

homes built of masonry, with back rooms of natural or rock-hewn caves from the Roman era (63 B.C.–A.D. 324) (Ludwig 1986, 112). In light of the archaeological data gathered, it seems that the earliest inhabitants of Nazareth would have included first Canaanites, then Israelites (part of the tribal allotment of Zebulun), and then Galilean Jews during the Roman period.

While little is known of Nazareth from these early periods, references to neighboring locales are a reminder that beyond the inner ring of its encircling hills, Nazareth was in the midst of a region where prophets, kings, and generals enacted many of the familiar events of the biblical world. Pilgrims to the hometown of Jesus would often climb to the top of the hills of Nazareth, just as they imagined the boy Jesus to have done, to look out and remember what had happened before. In the 1890s, biblical geographer George Adam Smith (1966, 282) climbed the hills of Nazareth and wrote:

> The position of Nazareth is familiar. The village lies on the most southern of the ranges of Lower Galilee, and on the edge of this just above the Plain of Esdraelon [Jezreel, Armageddon or Marj Ibn 'Amr]. You cannot see the surrounding country, for Nazareth rests in a basin; but the moment you climb to the edge of this, which is everywhere within the limit of the village boys' playground, what a view you have! Esdraelon lies before you, with its twenty battle-fields—the scenes of Barak's and of Gideon's victories, of Saul and Josiah's defeats, of the struggles for freedom in the days of the Maccabees. There is Naboth's vineyard and the place of Jehu's revenge upon Jezebel; there Shunem and the house of Elijah; there Carmel and the place of Elijah's sacrifice. To the east of (sic) the Valley of Jordan, with the range of Gilead; to the west the radiance of the Great Sea, with the ships of Tarshish and the promise of the Isles. You see thirty miles in three directions. It is a map of Old Testament history.

Scenes from the New Testament also unfold to view from the hilltops. To the east, the rounded top of the Transfiguration's Mount Tabor peaks above closer hills; to the southeast in the Jezreel valley at the foot of Mount Moreh is Nain, where the widow's son was raised; and to the north is Cana (Kfar Kanna), where water was turned to wine. On a clear day even Mount Hermon (also a possible sight of the Transfiguration) can be seen far to the northeast across the Galilee hills and the depression where the Sea of Galilee lies hidden.

Specific references to Nazareth in the New Testament are limited and reveal relatively little about the village or its people. References in Matthew and Luke relate that it was located in the Galilee (Luke 1:26); that Joseph, one of its inhabitants, was of the house and lineage of David and therefore Judah and his ancestral home was Bethlehem (Luke 2:4); that his wife was named Mary and their children included

five sons and several unnamed daughters (Matthew 13:55); that the village was located on the brow of a hill (Luke 4:29); that there was a synagogue in the village (Matthew 13:54); and that the people were initially
not receptive to the teachings of Jesus (Matthew 13:57).

Nazareth in the First Millennium of the Christian Era

For the first few centuries A.D., little is known of Nazareth other than
that relatives of Jesus lived here as well as Christians and Jews. The
Jewish community is mentioned in reference to Nazareth until the
seventh century (Bagatti 1969, 18). Nazareth became known as a Jewish
center in the second century when, following the Bar Kochba revolt,
the priestly family of Hafizaz moved to Nazareth along with other Jewish families who sought refuge in the north (Stendel 1973, 5). Scholars
have suggested that the Christians living in Nazareth during the first
centuries were more specifically Judeo-Christians, who, as former Jews,
still adhered to the Mosaic law in varying degrees (Briand 1982, 10). Archaeological evidence suggests that before the building of the Byzantine
basilica at the site of the house of Mary in the middle of the fifth century, there existed a pre-Byzantine synagogue church with Judeo-
Christian symbols carved into the stone and plaster (Ludwig 1986, 28).[2]
Since the Jews of Nazareth were not expelled until the seventh
century, they most likely were still using the original synagogue of
Nazareth, whereas the Judeo-Christians would have needed to build
their own place of worship, most likely at the site of Mary's house.

It is interesting to note that during this same period, the Galilee
village of Baina (Bu'eina) had two separate parts—Jews living in one
part and Judeo-Christians in the other. In addition, several other villages of the Galilee, including Kfar Kanna near Nazareth, had two synagogues, which Bagatti uses as evidence to suggest that separate quarters for the two religious communities might have also existed elsewhere in the region (Bagatti 1969, 19). Ludwig also suggests that Judeo-
Christian and Gentile-Christian communities might have lived separately. After explaining how Judeo-Christians had been ostracized by
the Jews, he writes: "Should those banished in this way not wish to
lose their national identity or religious and cultural heritage by becoming assimilated into the foreign Gentile Christians, they had no choice
but to live in separate communities and gather in their own houses of

---

[2] The fourth-century Byzantine basilica is attributed by some to Empress Helena,
who while on a pilgrimage to the Holy Land identified several holy sites, including
those of the nativity and crucifixion, and initiated the construction of places of worship
to commemorate those spots. Her anonymous biographer writes that "the empress
Helena . . . turned to Nazareth and having sought the house where the Mother of God
. . . received the hail of the Archangel Gabriel, thereat she raised the temple of the
Mother of God" (Hollis and Brownrigg 1969, 103).

worship. They thus led a shadowy existence between the Synagogue and the Church" (Ludwig 1986, 30).

Fourth-century writings about Nazareth are distinctly Gentile-Christian, as evidenced by several Gentile-Christian writers. Eusebius, for example, makes the distinction between Nazarenes, as Jesus was called, and the Nazarenes (Judeo-Christians) of his day who called themselves Christian, but whom he did not consider to be true followers of Christ (Bagatti 1969, 20). Likewise, Epiphanius, out of either ignorance or contempt for the Judeo-Christians, describes Nazareth as a city of only Jews until the time of Constantine, who ordered that churches be erected in "the towns and villages of the Jews in which before that time no one had been able to build them for the reason that neither Greeks nor Samaritans nor Christians had been admitted into them." Nazareth was one of the cities designated for church building, which seems to have taken place after A.D. 352 (Meistermann 1923, 480).

Diversity among Nazareth's inhabitants still existed in the sixth century. An anonymous pilgrim of Piacenza visiting Nazareth in 570 wrote that "there is no love lost between Jews and Christians" in Nazareth (Murphy-O'Conner 1986, 310, 313). In reference to the anonymous pilgrim's observations that the Jewesses of Nazareth boast of being relatives to Mary, Bagatti suggests that they could "very well be Judeo-Christians." He also mentions that the contempt of the Hebrews toward the Christians could be toward Judeo-Christians who resent the Gentile-Christian's occupation of the holy place (Bagatti 1969, 22).

The Persians invaded Palestine in 614, but there is no mention of their attacking or passing through Nazareth. Throughout the land, Samaritans and Jews allied themselves with the Persians in opposition to Byzantine Christian rule. When Emperor Heraclius reestablished Byzantine control in 629–30, he expelled the Jews from Nazareth, perhaps because such Jews might have turned upon the Christians and Christian shrines during the Persian invasion. The expulsion of the Jews, and perhaps the Judeo-Christians, turned Nazareth into a Christian village, but not for long.

Muslim invaders conquered the land of Palestine in 638, but had no immediate impact upon the Christians of Nazareth. When the Gallic Bishop Arculf visited Nazareth during a pilgrimage thirty-two years after the invasion, he noted two large churches in the unwalled village, one at the site of the house of Joseph where Jesus was reared, and one at the site of the house of Mary where the Annunciation took place. Arculf does not mention a synagogue, which may by then have been taken over as a mosque.

Christian-Muslim relations took a turn for the worse in 722 when Yazid II ordered the destruction of all images in churches, following the Islamic prohibition of depicting the human form. Perhaps as a result of this decree, the Church of St. Joseph was also destroyed, for when the pilgrim Willibald visited Nazareth in 724–26, just forty years after Arculf and two years after the decree, he found only the Church of St. Mary in the village and recorded that "the Christians have to repurchase it from the Pagan Saracens every time they decide to destroy it." The Church of St. Joseph remained in ruins for many years, while the Church of St. Mary continued to be mentioned in a variety of accounts, including that of the Muslim geographer Mas'udi, who in 943 mentions "a church greatly honored by the Christians" (Bagatti 1969, 24–26; and Ludwig 1986, 109).

The Crusades and After

When the crusaders, under the leadership of Tancred, entered Nazareth in 1102, they found the city and its churches in ruins, as recorded by the traveler Saewulf, who writes: "The city of Nazareth is entirely laid waste and overthrown by the Saracens; but the place of the Annunciation is indicated by a very noble monastery" (Wright 1848, 46). The city had been destroyed, then abandoned, by its Muslim inhabitants (Mansur 1924, 41). Within a decade, Daniel of Russia wrote that the Church of the Annunciation was being rebuilt by the Franks (i.e., Europeans) and that a "very rich" bishop lived at the monastery (Wilkinson 1988, 164). During this same period the Greeks built the Church of St. Gabriel near Mary's well (Meistermann 1923, 481). Nazareth became the seat of an archbishop in the mid-twelfth century, and by the 1170s it was described by travelers as a large village or even a town.

When the crusaders were defeated by Saladin at the Battle of Hittin in 1187, the inhabitants of Nazareth, as well as Nablus and Haifa, fled to Tyre or Jerusalem (Maalouf 1984, 195) or, as Michel of Syria records, to "cities in the north." Mansur writes that the army of Saladin did not kill or destroy in its conquest of Nazareth, but only expelled the crusaders (Mansur 1924, 42). Nakrizi,[3] however, writes that the city was pillaged and the women and children taken into slavery (Bagatti 1984, 12). Nazareth was again under Muslim control.

In 1192, pilgrims were given permission to visit the holy places freely. To facilitate these visits, two priests and two deacons were allowed to return to Nazareth. Then in 1204, al-'Adil, the son of Saladin, signed a treaty which lasted until 1211, formally recognizing the right of pilgrims to visit the holy places (Bagatti 1984, 12). The Mamluks of Egypt, under the leadership of Baibars and in battle with the crusaders,

---

[3] An alternative and unannotated version of the 1187 fall of Nazareth is found in Benvenisti 1970, 166, in which the author writes that the Frankish inhabitants "sought refuge in the Church of the Annunciation, but were butchered by the Moslems."

entered Nazareth in 1263, destroyed the churches and convents, and killed those Christians who would not convert to Islam. Prince Edward reconquered the city in 1271 and started to rebuild the churches, but in 1291 the Muslim armies regained control and killed all Western Christians (Mansur 1924, 43). The killings during the Crusades were by the invading foreign armies and not the result of Nazarenes turning upon each other.

The Muslims who took up residence in Nazareth after the Crusades were described in 1322 by Sir John Maundeville as "very cruel and wicked" and "more spiteful than in any other place" (Conder 1878, 141). A German pilgrim who visited the village in 1350 described how the Saracens attempted to fill in the fountain and defiled the remains of the church by using it as a dumping ground for the carcasses of camels and other dead animals (Von Suchem 1895, 125). Cotovicus, who visited at the end of the century, described the Muslim inhabitants as the "worst he had seen" and declared that his party was "treated only with insult." He noted that there were only two or three Christians in the town (Robinson 1970, 343).

Muslim control did not keep all Christians away; in fact pilgrims and priests came to Nazareth from a variety of places. In the midfourteenth century an Italian pilgrim named Niccolo of Poggibonsi visited Nazareth and wrote of the black Nubian Christians who inhabited a "beautiful monastery," which included a church called St. Mary of Fright, and of Indians of Persia who held the "beautiful monastery" of St. Gabriel. In addition he wrote "the city is in great decay, with no walls, and to enter there is a payment of XII dirhems" (Niccolo 1945, 64). Bagatti adds that these Nubians came to Jerusalem and Nazareth from Egyptian-controlled Nubia in 1347 in search of religious freedom. A century earlier Armenians and Greeks were reported living near the Mount of Precipice (Bagatti 1969, 14).

Ottoman Rule

Nazareth and all of Palestine came under the control of Ottoman Turks in 1517. An interesting account of Nazareth during the first century of Ottoman control comes from the Ottoman Tapu registers,[4] which enu-

---

[4] The register lists the amounts of crops received from the assessed tax of one-quarter of the crop. Wheat was the largest crop for all four listings, followed by barley, cotton, and sesame, with smaller harvests of *duraa* (probably sorghum) and beans. Taxes on olives and olive presses as well as goats, bees, and brides are also recorded. The final tax listed is the *jizye* (poll tax) which is levied in Islam for all Christians and Jews. The Christians of Nazareth paid the lowest of the three rates allowed by law, one gold piece (Lewis 1965).

merate the residents of the village and describe their revenues and products. These registers show that in 1525–26, there were forty-three Muslim households listed by name and six Christian households, and that by 1574 there were 215 Muslim households and seventeen Christian households (Lewis 1965).[5]

Other accounts from this period show that while a few Christians were living amid the Muslim majority, relations between the two indigenous groups or between Muslims and Christian pilgrims fluctuated. One report from the sixteenth century describes how, once Christian pilgrims had entered the churches, the local Muslims would shower stones through the windows until the pilgrims offered money for relief (Tobler 1868, 56). However a report by an Italian pilgrim in 1524, shortly after the start of Ottoman control, records that in the village reduced to eighty homes, the holy chapel in the center of the Church of the Annunciation "is held in great veneration by all Christians and Moslems" and that "on the Feast of the Annunciation all Galilee gathers to this chapel and this most holy house, both Christian and Saracens, and on that day they make a great fair and great rejoicing and they feast in honour of the Blessed Virgin" (Suriano 1949, 160).

In 1620, Emir Fakhr al-Din, the Druze ruler of the Galilee, granted permission for the Franciscans to enter the Grotto of the Annunciation, and a group of priests moved in to protect their holdings. The emir, a sworn enemy of the Turks, had lived in Italy for several years and was an ally of the Grand Duke of Tuscany. By allowing the Franciscans to return, he was able to insure that the Duke would continue to assist the emir in his struggle against the Turks (Colbi, 1988, 88). The Franciscans moved quickly to establish their presence. A 1664 drawing of the village by Franciscan Brother Roger shows the dormitory and refectory of the Franciscans to be the largest building in Nazareth. This imposing, two-story rock building, which stands adjacent to the house of Mary and close to the village mosque with its tall minaret, is surrounded by a garden and a wall. The illustration also identifies the grotto near Mary's well, which "is used by the Greeks as a church" (Bagatti 1969, 5).

The return of the Latin priests after an absence of several centuries was not without incident. In 1624 the sanctuary was pillaged and three priests were battered. Village officials took compassion and came to their aid. Then in 1636, priests were incarcerated by Muslims, who insisted that the church must remain the same as in ancient times. Meanwhile an ongoing feud between Nazareth and neighboring Saffu-

---

[5] Mansur writes that Christian families came from the Huran region of Syria in the middle of the fifteenth century in search of livelihood and refuge from the Muslim Arabs (Mansur 1924, 205).

riya resulted in a 1639 burning of the convent altar to prevent the priests from remaining in Nazareth. Apparently the people of Saffuriya felt that if priests were present in Nazareth, then the Nazarenes would become stronger and they would be able to attack Saffuriya. Further problems erupted later in the century when in 1696, in the face of persecution, the Christians of Nazareth were forced to flee, only to return the next year.

Henry Maundrell, who visited Nazareth in 1697, wrote that at the place of the Annunciation were "seven or eight Latin fathers, who live a life truly mortified, being perpetually in fear of the Arabs, who are absolute lords of the country" (Wright 1848, 477). Two years later, other pilgrims offered an opposing view. Beaugrand records that when his group of pilgrims had barely reached the houses on the outskirts of town, Muslim men, women, and children came out and greeted them, kissed their hands, and then escorted them to the church (Tobler 1868, 57). In 1708 there was a brawl between the Christians and Muslims of Nazareth; the convent was pillaged again and abandoned for a year (Bagatti 1984, 22).

The presence of Franciscans in Nazareth took a turn for the better in 1730, when Bedouin sheikh Dahir al-Umar, the regional ruler, granted them permission to build a small church dedicated to the Annunciation. The structure they built had to be very modest because construction time was limited to six months—the time it took for a pilgrimage from Nazareth to Mecca to be completed. The Franciscans were even required to pay the cost of the pilgrimage for the official who issued the building permit (Nazareth Today, 17). Al-Umar also allowed the Franciscans to buy in 1741 the traditional site of the synagogue where Jesus taught and in 1754 the traditional site of Joseph's workshop. In 1767, Dahir al-Umar also granted permission to the Orthodox bishop of Akka to reconstruct the Church of St. Gabriel over the ruins of the octagonal crusader church at Mary's well (Colbi 1988, 89).

One of al-Umar's wives was from Nazareth, so he made sure that the residents of the village were well protected. This protection increased immigration of both Muslims and Christians. Like Fakhr al-Din, al-Umar favored the settlement of Christians in Nazareth, partly because maintaining good relations with the Franciscans ensured good relations with France (Kana'na 1964, 47).

With sympathetic leaders and the increase in Christian-owned holy sites, the Christian population of Nazareth continued to grow. The Franciscans bolstered the Christian presence by asking the Maronite patriarch to send some Maronite families from Lebanon. During this same period, a Greek Orthodox priest and family settled in Nazareth from Transjordan. In 1762, twenty Roman Catholic families left

Bethlehem and moved to Nazareth because of either a severe famine (Colbi 1988, 89) or years of feuding with the residents of Hebron (Kana'na 1964, 48). One report from around 1750 indicates fifty-four Muslim houses, four Maronite houses, and two Greek Orthodox houses in the village; another from 1767 mentions Roman Catholics and Greek Orthodox living together with Muslims in Nazareth; and "anything in the past that has been said bad about the inhabitants, one could now say the opposite" (Tobler 1868, 57, 68).

Life for the Christians in Nazareth had its ups and downs, depending on the graces of regional rulers. When al-Umar was assassinated in 1775, Ahmad Pasha, an Albanian soldier known as *al-Jazzar* (the butcher) for his cruelty, began to rule in Akka. Nazarene Yakub Farah noted that, unlike the reign of Dahir al-Umar when Christians and Muslims in Nazareth lived in harmony, al-Jazzar's reign made conditions for the Christians bad. Farah said it was especially bad on Fridays after prayer when Muslims, often villagers in town for the Friday sermon, would riot and attack Christians; al-Jazzar did nothing to prevent such incidents (Mansur 1924, 66–67).[6]

The Nineteenth Century

The nineteenth century saw a steady stream of pilgrims and travelers visiting Nazareth and writing of their adventures. Most of the accounts deal primarily with visits to the holy places, but some provide additional information about the town and its people. Reports vary considerably and can be contradictory in content, depending on the disposition and intent of each writer.[7] One of the first in the nineteenth century to file a report was John Lewis Burckhardt, who wrote in the 1820s of the "industrious" inhabitants of Nazareth, two-thirds of whom were Turks (or more specifically Muslim), and one-third Christian. He divides the Christians into about ninety Latin families and "a congregation of Greek Catholics and another of Maronites." It is interesting that

---

[6] In 1799 Napoleon Bonaparte failed in his siege of Akka, which would have removed al-Jazzar from power, but he did go on to defeat an Ottoman army at Afula in the valley of Esdraelon. After the battle he retired to the Franciscan monastery in Nazareth, where he spent the night (Colbi 1988, 89).

[7] Selective use of these accounts could depict a very one-sided view of Nazareth, as evidenced by Friedman (1982), who quotes only negative references about Nazareth. They may also convey inaccurate information. A visitor to Nazareth at the end of the last century writes of services in the Latin church "where wild figures in the rough drapery and the rude rope-fillet and kefeyeh of the Bedouin dress, join in the responses of Christian worship, and the chants of the Latin Church are succeeded by a sermon addressed to these strange *converta* in their own native Arabic with all the earnestness and solemnity of the preachers in Italy" (Stanley 1895, 531, italics added). His account suggests that the Arabs were converts to Christianity, when in fact they descend from some of the earliest Christians.

no mention is made of Greek Orthodox inhabitants or congregations even though both existed at the time. He also notes eleven friars in the convent of the Annunciation, whom he identifies as being primarily Spaniards. These monks and the Christian residents enjoyed a much improved situation over the previous decades. Burckhardt records that "the Christians of Nazareth enjoy great liberty. The Fathers go a shooting in their monastic habits to several hours distance from the convent without ever being insulted by the Turks" (Burckhardt 1922, 337–41).

Still there were occasional incidents in which Christians and Muslims clashed. In 1828, a Christian was accused of robbing the mosque. When the ruling pasha came to investigate, he noticed that the Christians and Muslims of Nazareth were all wearing the same style and color of head coverings. This was very unusual for a region where Christians and Jews were required to differentiate themselves in their attire from the Muslims. The Pasha ordered Christians to stop wearing black headdresses, then ordered the Muslims to attack and kill Christians. The Muslims protested with the argument that a man does not kill his milking cow. The Pasha rescinded his order and instead ordered the Muslims to rob the Christians, which they did during Easter services, when they entered the churches and took jewelry from the women.

That same year, a Christian girl, in rebuffing advances from a Muslim boy, was accused of blasphemy against the prophet Mohammad. Her sentence was to either convert to Islam or die. She chose to die, and execution was carried out by tying her to a horse and dragging her through the streets.

The situation, however, soon improved when in 1832, Egyptian ruler Ibrahim Pasha brought Palestine under his control and instituted reforms that improved the situation for Christians. So good was Ibrahim to the Christians that some Muslims accused him of being a Christian in disguise. When there was a revolt against Ibrahim, the Christians of Nazareth sided with him (Mansur 1924, 65–66).

When Edward Robinson traveled to Nazareth in 1838, he wrote of visiting with an "Arab-Greek Christian" of Nazareth named Abu Nasir, whom he described as being "mild, friendly and intelligent." This resident of Nazareth told Robinson that the current population of Nazareth was about 3,000, composed of five main sects (table 1).

Abu Nasir was concerned with improving the "moral condition of the Greek-Arab community around him." In travels to Beirut he had been impressed with the mission schools there, so on returning to Nazareth he had established perhaps the first school in Nazareth. This school had fifty students and a second school had an enrollment of twenty. His daughter became the first female student and is said to

TABLE 1. 1838 Population of communities by family and by taxable men

Community	Families	Taxable men
Greek Orthodox	160	260
Muslim	120	170
Roman Catholic	65	120
Greek Catholic	60	130
Maronite	40	100
Total	445	780

have been the first young woman in Nazareth for centuries who learned to read and write. Support for the schools, which still did not have books, was limited and depended on the resources of the mission in Beirut and its sponsoring society. When support from Beirut decreased, Abu Nasir had to close down the schools (Robinson 1970, 337–39).

Tobler, in his monograph on Nazareth, quotes Ali Bei's description of intercommunal relations in Nazareth. He writes: "The most perfect harmony existed at the beginning of the present century [nineteenth] among all religious parties: at their festivals, at play, and in any merry moments there was no difference in how their race and religion was regarded." Tobler confirms this account when, following his 1846 visit to Nazareth, he writes of finding "untainted harmony" among what he calls a "very loveable people." However, his praise for the Nazarenes was tempered by comparing them to the Bethlehemites—both of whom could be "easily provoked." He also mentions that while relations were generally good, "from time to time there were always occasional dark spots." Tobler, a Christian, insightfully writes that while the Muslims of Nazareth had been called "heathens" by earlier writers, this was not the case in the traditional meaning of the word, because they were also monotheistic (Tobler 1868, 57–59).

The intercommunal conflicts that plagued areas in Lebanon and Syria in 1860 had no effect on peaceful relations in Nazareth. One of the reasons for this was the willingness of Bedouin chief 'Aqila Agha al-Hasi to enforce peace in the region under his control. To emphasize the point, he was known to withdraw his sword and threaten, "Woe to him who takes offense against a Christian" (Kana'na 1964, 60). During this period of conflict in the region,[8] the Muslim and Christian com-

8 During this time, Christian-Muslim relations, which for years had been relatively calm under the Ottoman millet (recognized and organized non-Muslim communities) system, became strained in other regions of the empire as Tanzimat reforms gave expanded freedoms to the Christian and Jewish minorities. This in turn gave cause for Muslims to fear that the Islamic nature of their state and their dominant position in

munities of Nazareth cooperated in protecting their village; Muslims stood guard on the surrounding hills, while the Christians stood guard in the town (Mansur 1924, 93).

Tobler estimates that Nazareth had added over 3,000 people to its population during the first half of the nineteenth century, then cites estimates of the population for three different years, as shown in table 2. The great fluctuations in numbers over a short period probably reveal the crudity of the estimates rather than real change.

One year before the 1867 estimate, the Roman Catholics had indicated that there was a total of only 680 in their community, which led Tobler to believe these estimates perhaps too high. He added an appropriate caveat about such estimates by explaining the inability of most pilgrims who write about the communities of Nazareth to distinguish between "Arabs, Turks and Moors," all lumped together under the general classification of Muslim, and between "Franks, Greeks, Maronites, and Greek Catholics," often all classified solely as Catholics.[9]

Tobler predicted that the population of Nazareth would never become large because of its distance from the sea and main trade routes, and because even with the help of cisterns, the local water supply was not plentiful enough to support a large population (Tobler 1868, 67–68). Other problems also kept the population from increasing. For example, in 1865, Nazareth suffered a cholera outbreak, the plague, drought, deadly disease among its livestock, and a locust invasion so devastating that stories about it were passed on for generations (Kana'na 1964, 61–62).

In the late 1860s two "irreverent pilgrims" (Walker 1974), who both happened to be noted authors, visited Nazareth. J. Ross Browne, visiting in 1868, described Nazareth as follows: "It is a mere village of

---

the government might be weakened. As Christians asserted their new-found privileges, conflicts often resulted, as in the 1860 massacre of Christians by Muslims in Damascus (Ma'oz 1982; and Salibi 1968).

[9] Tobler includes an overview of the makeup of Nazareth's communities. He makes many historical references, illustrative of the uncertainty and variability of pilgrims' estimates. A sample of the various communities cited as living in Nazareth follows: 1627, Muslims and Franciscan monks; 1650–58, only Muslim farmers; 1666, besides Christians, Arabs and Turks again; 1668, Muslims mixed with Greek Orthodox and a single Roman Catholic family; 1681, Arabs and Turks among Greeks and Maronites; 1699, some Christians and some Turks; 1738, Roman Catholics, Greeks, and Turks, each a third; 1756, Turks, Arabs, Greeks, and Roman Catholics; end of the 1800s, the majority of the inhabitants Christian; 1807, mostly Roman Catholics; 1812, two-thirds Turks and one-third Christians; 1814, Muslims in the minority again; 1819, only a few Greeks, most of the inhabitants being Roman Catholic; 1827, Christians with the upper hand, but Muslims multiplying and having a fleeting lead. Tobler than adds that from 1827 on, all reports say that Christians were in the majority (Tobler 1868, 61–63).

TABLE 2. Estimates of the population of Nazareth's communities, 1856–67

Community	1856	1862	1867
Muslim	2,300	680	2,000
Greek Orthodox	1,000	1,040	2,500
Greek Catholic	250	520	180
Roman Catholic	500	480	800
Maronite	200	400	80
Protestant	100	—	100
Total	4,350	3,120	5,660

SOURCE: Tobler 1868, 67–68

square flat-roofed houses, situated on the side of a hill, with a mosque and some large buildings, occupied by the monks, in the lower part. The valley is well wooded with olive trees, which extend up beyond the houses towards the top of the hill. A few palm trees present a picturesque outline near the mosque. The general appearance of the valley of Nazareth is similar to that of most of the valleys through which one passes in Syria."

Distance for Browne was deceptive, for when he actually entered the village he formed a different view. He describes Nazareth as "one of the worst specimens of a Syrian town; it abounds in abominations of all kinds, and is the abiding-place for as dark and villainous a population as we had yet seen. The difference was striking between the inhabitants of this part of the country and those about Tripoli and Mount Lebanon." He goes on to compare the people of what is known today as Palestine with those further north by describing the people of the northern Levant as "polite and affable," having a "frank and cheerful expression that was very pleasing," while those of environs around Nazareth and Jerusalem are described as having a "scowling and morose cast of countenance." He also mocks the holy places, calling them "mere catch-penny shows," which depend on the contributions of pilgrims and visitors for the support of the convents built upon the holy sites. The convents then depend on the "the skill of the monks in maintaining the authenticity of the localities." But he also writes about the school at the convent, where Christian children are educated for free, and the infirmary run by the religious establishments (this time primarily Italian monks). "Whatever may be objected to these institutions throughout Palestine, their effect is beneficial to the poor people; and, in general, the monks who occupy them are kind and humane to all who need their assistance." Browne, like nearly every other visitor to Nazareth, notes that the women of Nazareth were "extremely beautiful" (Browne 1868, 330–34).

Mark Twain, as an "innocent abroad," visited Nazareth the year after Browne. He is less critical of the town and its people, but more harsh on holy places and pilgrims. He makes light of the fact that the site of the Annunciation is conveniently adjoined by the "Virgin's kitchen, and even her sitting room" which were all situated "under one roof, and all clean, spacious, comfortable 'grottoes.'" The Catholics are, however, praised because they have preserved the location of the holy sites through the construction over the grottoes of "massive— almost imperishable—church[es]." He comments that if the Protestants had been left to do the work, "we would not even know where Jerusalem is today." Twain then turns on the pilgrims he is traveling with, whose "chief sin is their lust for 'specimens,'" They chipped off portions of the rock wall remaining from the synagogue of Nazareth as they did in just about every other holy place they visited. Twain diverges from the usual and describes the young girls of Nazareth he sees at the well as being "homely," with "large lustrous eyes" but not "pretty faces." In his final view of the "city," Twain describes it as "clinging like a whitewashed wasp's nest to the hillside." Then he descends into the valley of Esdraelon along a bridle path, "fully as crooked as a corkscrew" and "as steep as the downward sweep of a rainbow" (Twain 1966, 381–89).

Four Mormon pilgrims visited Nazareth in 1873. In a letter to the local newspaper in Salt Lake City—with its wide, straight streets—Paul Schettler wrote after a walking tour of the town that his group came to the conclusion that "of all the narrow and dirty streets of the Palestine cities we have visited, the beautifully situated Nazareth could boast the most crooked, the steepest and the filthiest" (Smith 1977, 289). Eliza R. Snow, one of few women pilgrims to leave a record of her visit to Nazareth, confirms Schettler's description, writing of the "narrow, crooked and indescribably filthy streets." In her next letter back to a magazine for Mormon women, she adds that in contrast to the dirty streets and the "intolerably negligent and uncomfortable-looking houses," she had noticed the "personal cleanliness" of the people and described seeing women dressed from head to toe in "really white" clothes come out of the "most untidy and forbidding-appearing dwellings" (Smith, 264, 277).

Writing about Christian monks in the Holy Land, who had been portrayed by earlier writers as being persecuted, Jacob Freese states: "There is no persecution, no martyrdom; all around these retreats there is a Christian population, ready for the service and orders of the monks of the convents. The Turks annoy them in no respect whatever; on the contrary they protect them. They are the most tolerant people on earth." While impressed with the respect that the Muslims exhibit toward the Christian clergy in the towns he visits, Freese is less impressed with the relations between the monks of Nazareth, where the "Spaniards decry the Italians, and the Italians the Spaniards" (Freese 1869, 187).

A few years after Freese's account, J. P. Newman offers a contradictory description of the status of Christians in Palestine, while explaining why the Christians of Nazareth are different. He notes that of a population of 4,000, about three-fourths are Christian, and it is under the "enlightened influence" of the Christians that "Nazareth is increasing in wealth and numbers." He continues: "As if conscious of their superior numbers, intelligence, wealth, and piety, the Christians assert and defend their rights. In nearly all other parts of Palestine the Christians are cringing and fearful, but the Nazarenes are not afraid either to measure swords or creeds with the followers of the Prophet" (Newman 1876, 424).

Occasional conflicts still arose, such as in 1881, when an incident that occurred in Egypt against Egyptian nationalist Arabi Pasha incited some Muslim notables in Nazareth, whom Mansur (1924, 100–101) describes as having "big dreams and little minds," to meet and demand the slaughter of the Christians. The local sheikh rebuked those who proposed the slaughter, and no action was taken. The leader of the group was Judge Abu Sa'ud. A Christian who had been at the meeting (apparently incognito) reported the plan of Abu Sa'ud to the archbishop, who told the patriarch in Jerusalem, who then told officials in Istanbul. Charges were filed, but no one would ever come forward to testify against the judge. While never convicted, he was dismissed from his position.

Throughout the century, Nazareth continued to grow. William Thomson suggests that this was partly a result of raids and attacks by Bedouin from beyond Jordan, which made it unsafe to live in Beisan and in the valley of Esdraelon. These threats prompted local Arabs to desert many places and move to the safety of Nazareth, or toward the coast. He concludes by saying that if the government would drive the Bedouin back across the Jordan and keep them there, then "the population and importance of Nazareth would decline." Nazareth's function as a place of security is suggested in Thomson's idyllic description of its location. He writes, "The view of Nazareth, when first seen from the north, with its encircling hills giving the idea of protection and repose; its green vale, its olive-orchards and fields of waving wheat bespeaking peace and plenty, and the town itself reflecting the golden light of the setting sun, awakened thoughts of security and quiet home life" (Thomson 1882, 310, 313). Nazareth would again become a place of refuge in the middle of the next century.

Early Twentieth Century

As Nazareth entered the twentieth century, its size and outward appearance continued to change. One estimate from 1912 puts the population of the town at about 15,000, which included 5,000 Muslims, 5,000 Greek Orthodox, 2,000 Roman Catholics, 1,000 Greek Catholics, 250 Protestants, and 200 Maronites; but in light of later enumerations in 1922 and 1931, this estimate seems to be grossly exaggerated. Contradictions in size aside, the growth of Nazareth prompted Karl Baedeker to refer to it as a "small town" rather than its usual designation of village. He refers to it as a "charming town," especially in the spring when "its dazzling white walls are embosomed in the green cactus-hedges, fig-trees, and olive-trees" (Baedeker 1912, 246).

This isolated Nazareth eclipsed its surrounding villages, developed into a small town, and grew eventually into the bustling city of today as a result of several factors. First, its central location in the lower Galilee helped it emerge as the regional economic and political center. Secondly, its sanctity attracted Christians, both foreign and Arab, who wanted to live in a holy city. The foreign Christians brought much needed schools, hospitals, and opportunities for employment, which also stimulated population growth. Writing in 1909, Ernest Masterman noted how religious factors influenced not only population patterns, but also transportation networks in the region.

Today a high road passes through Nazareth, but this is clearly not a natural route to anywhere. The ancient high roads passed from west to east, one along the foot of the Galilean hills to the south, and another through Sepphoris and the Battauf to the north. It is the sanctity of the spot alone which has dragged the road out of its natural route to mount the steep hills of Nazareth (Masterman 1909, 134).

The main east-to-west road connecting Haifa with Tiberias continued to pass through Nazareth until just recently. The State of Israel has now constructed highways that bypass the city to both the north and south (fig. 6), as well as an alternative route through town that skirts the city to the east as it winds between Nazareth and Upper Nazareth. Even with these improvements, the main street through Nazareth still slows to a crawl on most days, owing to increasing population pressures and Nazareth's continued status as a regional center.

Frederic Scrimgeour, who lived in Nazareth for several years as a doctor at the English hospital, describes Nazareth at the beginning of the century as "attractive and prosperous." He notes that the landscape of the town changes with the seasons. He describes it at its best in spring, when "all is green," for it is then that the "early crops of wheat and barley cover the hill-sides" and the fig, almond, and apricot trees are in leaf. Only after the harvest in May did the hillsides become "brown and bare," a state in which they remained until the rains of November turned the hills green again. Only the olive groves and scattered carob and cypress trees gave the hills any lasting touches of green. Land utilization was intensive, the patches of uncultivated land being "few indeed" (Scrimgeour 1913, 2).

With the absence of a city wall, Nazareth is described as spread out, with many scattered houses in the outskirts surrounded by gardens and trees. Houses in the purely Muslim quarter are described as being in the old style, with flat roofs and usually one or two rooms, which are divided into two levels: the lower level where the camels, horses, donkeys, goats, and sheep are kept at night; and the upper level where the family lives.

In the Christian quarters and larger homes in the central Muslim quarter, the use of the low-maintenance red Marseilles tiles had replaced the older flat roofs, which were made of a thick layer of lime, gravel, and cinders and needed repair every few years. When these mostly double-storied houses with whitewashed walls received their new orange tops, the Nazarenes called it "putting on the Fez" (Scrimgeour 1913, 4, 11). Mansur confirms the sharing of houses with chickens and livestock and the replacing of clay roofs—which needed to be daubed with mud each year to prevent leaks—with first the lime and gravel roofs and then the red tiles (Mansur 1924, 15). Today central Nazareth is still distinguished by its many large old houses with faded orange roofs. Newer houses have resorted to flat roofs, but with more durable covers.

The narrow streets of the town center were noted as having gutters two and a half feet wide running down their centers. These gutters, then and now, carry the heavy winter rains off the hills of Nazareth and serve as refuse heaps. Today, municipal workers clean out the gutters daily and load the refuse into large containers strapped to the sides of donkeys (municipal garbage trucks cannot negotiate the narrow streets). But at the beginning of the century, the "half-dozen donkey boys" who acted as scavengers and removed some of the garbage were too few for the town of 11,000, so it was only when the winter rains rushed down the gutters that the streets became "really cleaned" (Scrimgeour 1913, 3). Mansur describes the force of this street-cleaning torrent as being able to carry away "dirt and pebbles and even large trees and children as happened in the winter of 1905" (Mansur 1924, 14).

In *Nazareth of To-Day*, Scrimgeour provides interesting descriptions of daily life and customs in Nazareth. While this is not the place to rerecord his observations on life in Nazareth, some aspects of the Nazareth he observed are similar to the Nazareth of today. Scrimgeour made note of the quarters of Nazareth which were divided into Greek

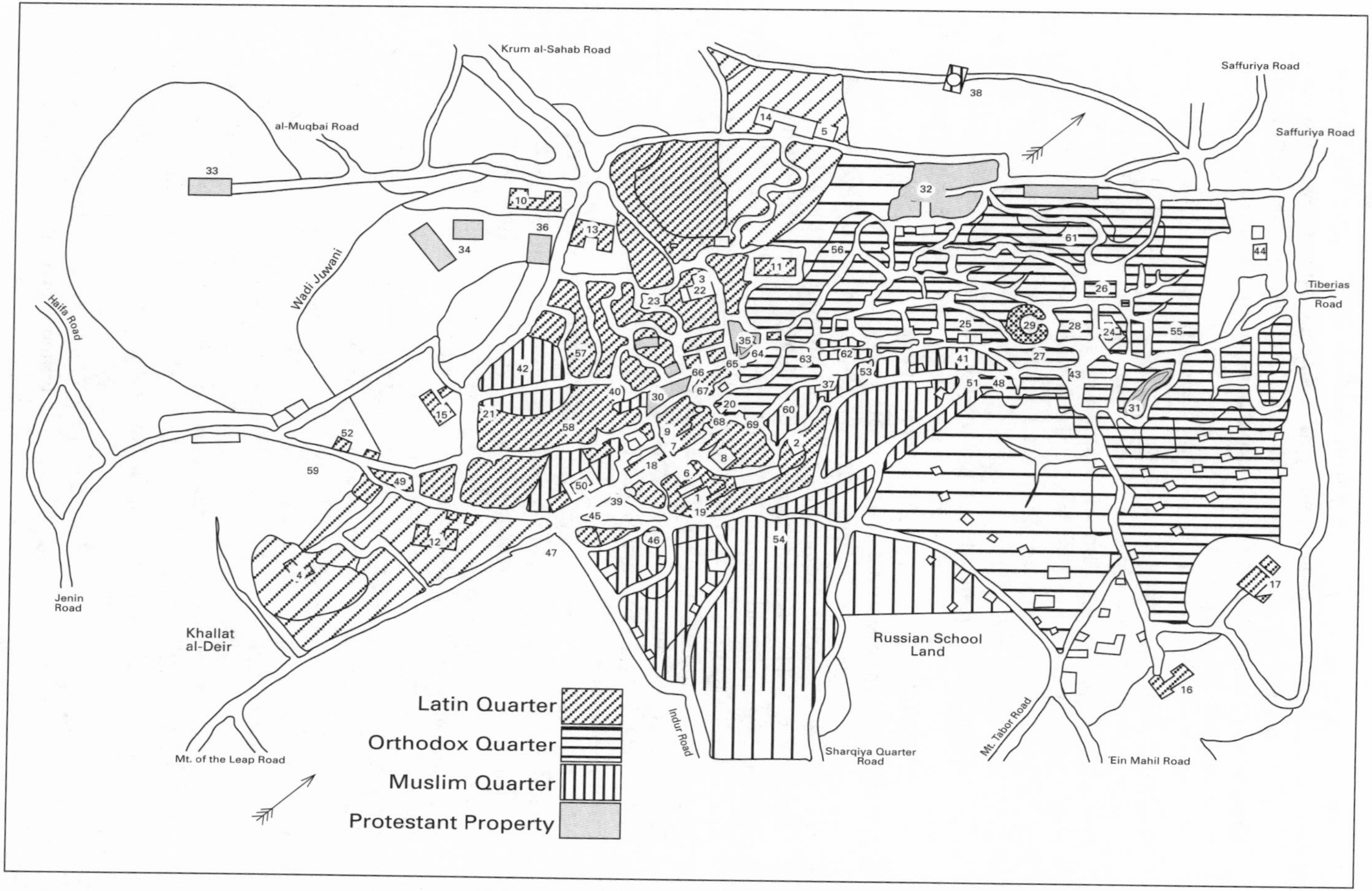

Fig. 4. Mansur's map of Nazareth, 1914

Latin Quarter

Orthodox Quarter

Muslim Quarter

Protestant Property

Orthodox, Latin, and Muslim sectors. He also noted that each religious community had its own cemetery, and that the Muslims had two (1913, 70). Each community also had its own schools. The Muslim school was described as teaching "nothing very thoroughly, with the exception of the fluent recitation of the Koran, which is achieved through endless repetition." There were several schools run by the various Catholic orders, as well as Protestant, Greek Orthodox, and Russian schools. The Catholic schools emphasized the French language, but also taught English in response to increased emigration to America, while the Greek and Protestant schools emphasized English. Russian was "zealously taught" to both the girls and boys who studied at the Russian school, and no other European language was allowed (1913, 86). Today the Russian, Greek Orthodox, and Muslim schools are no longer in operation.

TABLE 3. Places identified on Mansur's map (70 of 91 places)

Roman Catholic

1. Latin Church
2. St. Joseph's Church
3. Mensa Christi Church
4. Church of the Trembling
5. Salesian Church
6. Latin Monastery
7. Latin School
8. Sisters of St. Joseph Convent
9. Sisters of Nazareth Convent
10. White Fathers Monastery
11. Freres School
12. Poor Clares Convent
13. Carmelite Convent
14. Latin Orphanage
15. Sisters of Mercy Hospital
16. Austrian Hospital
17. St. Joseph's Hospital
18. Casa Nova
19. Latin and Greek Catholic Cemetery

Greek Catholic

20. Greek Catholic Church
21. Greek Catholic Waqf

Maronite

22. Maronite Church
23. Maronite Cemetery

Greek Orthodox

24. Greek Orthodox Church
25. Greek Orthodox Bishop's Compound
26. Orthodox Cemetery
27. Orthodox Waqf
28. Orthodox School
29. Muscobi (Russian Compound)

Protestant

30. Protestant (Anglican) Church
31. Protestant Waqf
32. St. Margaret's Orphanage
33. Schneller Orphanage
34. English Hospital
35. Protestant School
36. Protestant Cemetery

Muslim

37. White Mosque
38. Nebi Se'in Tomb
39. Shahab al-Din Monument
40. Sheikh 'Amer Monument
41. Muslim Cemetery
42. Muslim Cemetery (for strangers)

Public

43. Mary's Well

44. Police Station
45. Public School
46. Municipal Dump
47. Threshing Floor
48. Flour Mills
49. Hotel Galilee
50. Khan of the Pasha
51. Municipal Khan
52. Abu 'Assal Khan
53. Serai

Selected Quarters

54. Sharqiya
55. Khanuq
56. Farah
57. Shufani
58. Mazazwa
59. Maidan
60. Jami' (mosque)
61. 'Araq

Selected Markets

62. Arcade of the Sheikh
63. Dyers
64. Protestant
65. Vegetable
66. Coffee
67. Goldsmith
68. Blacksmith
70. Shoemaker

Religious separation in life, learning, and death created little difference when it came to daily life. According to Scrimgeour, "The family life of the Nazarene varies somewhat with the social position of the household, the occupation of the head of the house, and, to a less extent, with the religion of the family; but the variation is less than one would expect" (1913, 25). Today, as then, Arab culture and customs transcend religious differences. For example, the Islamic practice of veiling women became a practice accepted by the "well-to-do" Christians, as well as Muslims. Scrimgeour describes the practice of wealthy women wearing an outer garment made of silk called a *malayeh* when making visits. If the visit were to another quarter and the women had to pass through the market, then they also wore a heavy patterned veil called a *mandeel*. He goes on to explain that "to a stranger it seems as if all the well-dressed women are Moslems owing to this custom, but it is by no means so, and is only a mark of social superiority" (1913, 94).

A look at municipal services reveals that some things have changed while others have not. Scrimgeour notes that Nazareth had "no parks, public gardens, picture galleries, museums, libraries, municipal music or children's playgrounds" (1913, 48). Today there are modest successes in each of these categories. The municipality provides most of the services, but the Latin Church provides the only museum and an additional library. In regard to taxes, Scrimgeour offers the observation that "if all the money collected for local purposes was spent in the way it ought to be, our roads would be less like river beds and our streets less resemble manure heaps" (1913, 99). Similar complaints are still heard today, and have had a significant effect on local politics.

An account of the mostly congenial intercommunal relations comes from Scrimgeour's description of the gossip among the women and girls who gathered daily at Mary's well: "Moslems, Catholics, Greeks, and Protestants all mingle in one throng. They chatter and laugh together, and sometimes they quarrel. Here it is that any special news spreads like wildfire, and from here a rumor is carried in a few minutes to every quarter in the town" (1913, 30).

Mansur, however, records a few incidents in which Christians and Muslims clashed, or nearly clashed. In 1901, a fight between the two communities erupted during the Feast of the Assumption when drunk Christians from Haifa started name-calling. In 1913, tensions created by the fighting between Christians and Ottomans in the Balkans led to rumors that the Muslims in Nazareth were conspiring to kill the Christians. The rumor was apparently started by the principal of the Russian school, who, upon her return from a trip to Haifa, announced that on Orthodox Easter, which also happened to be the anniversary of the crowning of the sultan, the Christians would be killed. This caused considerable commotion in the city, which subsided only when the Muslim governor denounced the rumor. Two years later, sealed letters from Istanbul were delivered to the Muslim *mukhtars* (leaders) in town. This started rumors that the letters contained instructions for the massacre of Christians. The rumor was not without basis, because in Anatolia, Armenian Christians were in fact being persecuted and killed. However, once again in Nazareth there was no fighting or killing. In the end it was discovered that the letters contained only instructions for the impending war (Mansur 1924, 105).

During World War I, some Christians from Nazareth, including women and priests, were imprisoned and whipped because of accusations from Muslim Nazarenes that they were spying for the British. A committee sent from Beirut eventually acquitted most of the sixty-six prisoners, but a few were sent to prison in Ankara (Mansur 1924, 110). Christians were further warned that if they revealed the movement of Ottoman troops, they would be hanged. Worried Christian leaders met with the military commander, convincing him that they were a loyal minority. The commander believed them, then ordered the imam of Nazareth to neither harm nor submit false reports about the Christians (1924, 113).

In the final years of the Ottoman Empire, the *dhimmi* (non-Muslim minorities), who had been exempt from military service, began to be conscripted. Fu'ad Farah noted in a 27 August 1989 interview that this conscription began in Nazareth in 1908. Because conditions in the military were very bad and only worsened during World War I, many Christian young men of Nazareth sought refuge elsewhere. According to Farah, these Christians were educated in foreign languages, were not tied to landholdings, and had relatives living abroad. Since they saw the Ottoman army as an Islamic army fighting a *jihad*, many chose to emigrate. Fu'ad's four uncles emigrated to Cuba during this time, while his father remained in Nazareth to take care of his father. One of the four later returned to Nazareth, but to this day there are Farah clans in both Cuba and Nazareth.

British Mandate

Nazareth entered a new era with the fall of Ottoman and rise of British control in Palestine in 1917. For the first time since the Crusades, a Christian power ruled over the land. This changed the status of Christians in Nazareth. With the coming of the British, the Christians were not as likely to leave. The new government looked to the educated Christians to staff its bureaucracy. These and other job opportunities motivated Christians to stay and to migrate to the urban centers where jobs were more available.

One of the first things the British set out to do was to enumerate the population of its mandate. In the 1922 census the population of Nazareth was 7,424. Muslims composed 33 percent of the population at 2,486; Christians 66 percent at 4,885; and 53 Jews lived in Nazareth. The ratio of male to female Muslims was almost equal—1,234 male and 1,252 female; but there were fewer male Christians (2,321) than female (2,564). This is perhaps indicative of migrations during the last years of Ottoman rule. The Christian denominations were divided as follows: 2,054 Greek Orthodox, 1,165 Roman Catholics, 995 Greek Catholics, 297 Anglicans, 200 Maronites, 49 Syrian Catholics, 39 Protestants, 31 Copts, 25 Presbyterians, 9 Lutherans, 9 Armenian Catholics, 7 Armenian Orthodox, 1 Abyssinian, 1 Templar,[10] and 3 others.

The diversity of the religious communities was the result of both the desire of each religious community to have a presence at a significant Christian holy site, and the presence of foreign Christians who lived in Nazareth in a variety of capacities, such as missionaries, mandatory officals, and church, school, and hospital workers. These workers no doubt increased the totals for the various Protestant sects. Nine years later in the 1932 census, the population had grown to 8,756: 5,445 Christians (62 percent), 3,226 Muslims (37 percent), 79 Jews, 5 Bahais, and 1 Druze woman. While the male-to-female ratio among Muslims remained almost equal (1,624 male to 1,602 female) the male-to-female ratio for Christians shifted to include more men (2,733) than women (2,712) (*Census of Palestine* 1931). This increase seems to signal the developing administrative and economic role of Nazareth, and the resulting increase in jobs for men, both Christian and Muslim, who migrated to the city.

An interesting portrait of Nazareth from its earliest times up to and including the early years of the Mandate comes from As'ad Mansur's *Tarikh al-Nasira* (History of Nazareth). He describes the quarters of Nazareth and notes the concentration by religion in each of those quarters. He also describes the many *suqs* (markets) of the town, which, like the quarters, cluster together on the basis of similarities. These quarters and markets are also detailed in Mansur's 1914 map (replicated in figure 4 with the original Arabic labels now in English and with only 70 of 91 places identified).

The variety of goods sold in the markets, including such goods as sickles, saddles, seeds, shoes, drugs, cloth, and coffee, shows the diversity of Nazareth's commercial activities as of 1914 and helps to identify it as a regional center where neighboring villagers came to shop. Other

---

[10] A group of Templars arrived in Nazareth in 1870 to establish a presence, but were thwarted in the attempt after most of them died of malaria (Kana'na 1964, 63).

sources also refer to the economic activity of the town. Frances Newton, who worked as a teacher and supervisor for the Christian Mission Society in the Nazareth region, noted in her memoirs of fifty years in Palestine that at the time of her arrival in 1905, Nazareth was "a prosperous thriving little market town with its blacksmiths' 'souk' or street, and its grocers', jewelers', and saddlers' 'souks,'" and that peasants from "scores of villages resorted to its shops for the supply of their needs." However, after World War I, Nazareth "lost its importance as a market town for dozens of the Arab villages were supplanted by Jewish colonies, especially in the plain of Esdraelon" (Newton 1948, 30).

In addition to the many markets and quarters, Mansur's map and history of Nazareth also describe the many institutions and buildings which dotted the hills of Nazareth. The most prominent of these buildings were those that crowned the hilltops, such as the police station on the northern hill, the Salesian orphanage on the western summit, the Schneller orphanage and the English hospital near the crest of the hills to the southwest, and the Latin Church of the Trembling on a southern hill. Mansur's map of Nazareth identifies nine churches, seven monasteries, one mosque, five tombs or monuments of Muslim saints, five orphanages, four hospitals, seven cemeteries, one hotel, one hospice, three khans, two flour mills, and the large Russian complex.

The next published maps of Nazareth were a great improvement over Mansur's 1914 freehand approximation. The British-sponsored Survey of Palestine published maps of Nazareth in 1930, and again in 1946. Figure 5 shows the approximate inhabited limits of Nazareth as indicated on these two maps. It also shows the size of the small village of Nazareth in Tobler's time as well as the sprawling city of today. In the 1930 map, Nazareth's landscape still shows signs of its rural origins, as evidenced by the many orchards and planted fields surrounding the town and interspersed among the houses, beginning to spread beyond the compact town center. New to the town were a Baptist church, a municipal garden near Mary's well, a police station housed in the Turkish serai near the mosque, and a playground near the slaughterhouse to the south of the growing Muslim Sharqiya (Eastern) quarter.

The 1946 British map shows an extended municipal boundary that included new neighborhoods such as Maidan, Maslakh, Khanuq, and Nimsawi, as well as many more houses gradually filling in the older quarters and lying scattered among the threshing floors and still plentiful fields and orchards. The town's economy and political status had been bolstered by the addition of two cigarette factories, a tile factory, two cinemas, and a tobacco store. It also had expanded government buildings that included a new police station on the southernmost hill, an office for the district commissioner—complete with tennis

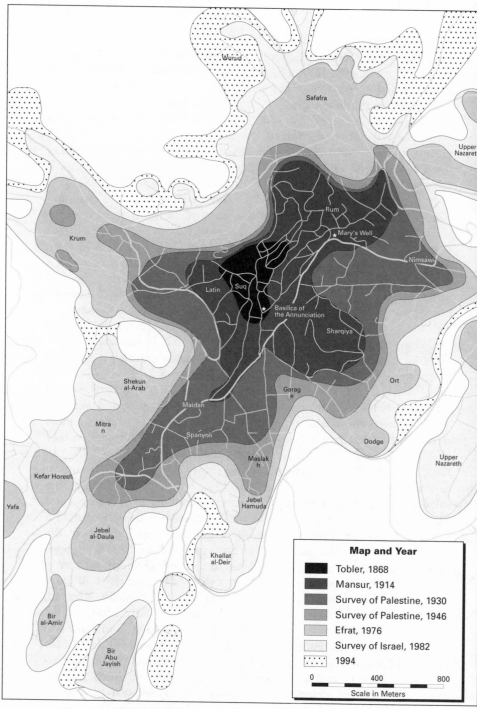

Fig. 5. The inhabited limits of Nazareth, 1868–1994

court—perched on the northern hill where the old Turkish military barracks were located, and offices for the Department of Survey and Settlement, and the Department of Agriculture located near the Greek Orthodox Church. Government offices were also now housed in the former Russian compound. The Turkish serai turned police station had become the new residence for the municipality (this crowded and crumbling building served as municipal offices until 1991). The British also constructed several watchtowers on encircling hilltops and two new reservoirs on the northwestern hills beyond the Salesian orphanage to augment the water supplied by the one spring (Mary's), many cisterns, and one small reservoir already in place to the north.

Nazareth's image as an obscure village in the Galilee began to change during the Mandate. With the influx of Jewish immigrants and increasing protest from Arabs, Nazareth became an active participant in outside events. In 1919 a delegation from Nazareth attended the First Palestine Congress, and in 1920 a letter of protest was issued from Nazareth denouncing Zionism while at the same time acknowledging as "brothers in humanity" the "Jews of our country" and even "all the Jews of the world." In a meeting that preceded the presentation of this petition, As'ad Mansur, the Anglican priest, explained that because the Jews had rejected the Messiah, the land had been taken from them, and the Talmud taught the Jews to prevent strangers from entering the land as long as they had the power to do so (Porath 1974, 61). This last interpretation of Jewish law was evidently used by Mansur to suggest that while the Arabs had the power, they should prevent the strangers, or Jews, from entering into the land.

Further involvement in rising Palestinian nationalism came in 1922, when a branch of the Muslim-Christian Association (MCA) was organized in Nazareth. This association was organized in 1918 in other urban centers in protest of Zionism and the first anniversary of the Balfour Declaration. The main support for the MCA came from the al-Zu'bi family. Representatives from Nazareth did not attend the Third and Fourth Palestine Congresses, but began to attend again with the Fifth Congress (Porath 1974, 278). The MCA tried to present a united front of Christian and Muslim Nazarenes, but not always with success, as evidenced by the creation of two Muslim organizations in the 1920s: the National Muslim Association (in Nazareth and other cities of the north), which was organized partly in reaction to Christian dominance in government administration; and a Nazareth chapter of the Organization of Muslim Youth, which was formed by the Supreme Muslim Council (Porath 1974, 303).

As the Arab revolt increased in intensity, Nazareth's involvement took a back seat to the cities of the south and even to neighboring villages. Of the 281 officers identified by Porath as participating in the Arab revolt, only two were from Nazareth: Fu'ad Nassar, a Christian Communist, and Tawfiq al-Ibrahim, a cigarette seller in Nazareth who was originally from Indur. Both served as band leaders in the revolt. Neighboring Saffuriya had seven men participating as leaders and Mujeidil two (Porath 1977, appendix B).

Nazareth was not totally excluded from activities of the revolt. In 1937, Nazareth was selected by the leaders of the Arab revolt as the site to protest the intended inclusion of the Galilee in the Jewish state, and to prove that the Galilee was no less nationalistic than the population of historical Judea and Samaria, as the royal commissioner had suggested. The act of protest chosen was the assassination of Lewis Andrews, acting district commissioner of the Galilee, as he walked to church on Sunday morning, 26 September (Porath 1977, 233; and Samuel 1970, 139).

War and Refugees

The revolt turned to war when the United Nations recognized the State of Israel. Originally the Arabs of Nazareth were not concerned with possible annexation into the Jewish state. One resident at the time said that people were not worried because they "believed that Nazareth, a holy city, like Bethlehem and Jerusalem, would be internationalized," and that it would be "part of Arab Palestine as stated in the United Nations partition plan" (Nazzal 1978, 78). This was not to be the case. Within a matter of months, Nazareth found itself occupied and annexed into the state, and swollen with a teaming population of urban and rural Arabs who had sought refuge in the city.

The first Palestinians to seek refuge in Nazareth were those of Haifa. Fighting between the Jews and Arabs of the port city started in November 1947 and escalated until 22 April 1948, when Jewish forces of the Irgun gained complete control of the city. Most of the Arabs fled in the few days just before the fall. Many fled to Lebanon via boat or overland, while others sought refuge in nearby villages, Akka, or Nazareth. The Arab Emergency Committee and private entrepreneurs helped those fleeing by organizing daily convoys, under the protection of British armored vehicles which took hundreds of Arab families to Akka, Nazareth, Jenin, and Nablus (Morris 1987, 86). In the growth years of the Mandate, many Arabs from Nazareth had moved to Haifa to work. During the months of tension and fighting which led up to the final exodus, many of these transplanted Nazarenes sought safety with relatives back in their hometown.

The next group of refugees to come to Nazareth were those from Tiberias, who on 18 April left the city after several days of fighting, during which eight Arab houses were blown up by Jewish troops of the Haganah. The British brought in buses and trucks and transported the Arabs to either Transjordan or Nazareth (Morris 1987, 71). The effect on Nazareth of this influx of refugees from Haifa and Tiberias is described in a 12 May 1948 *Jerusalem Post* article: "picturesque Nazareth of the twining streets is unrecognizable today. With all quarters packed to capacity, hundreds are simply parked out-of-doors. The buses and lorries, all of which are idle now, serve as hotels." The author goes on to describe that with no room or food in Nazareth, refugees were forced to move on, many toward Jenin or Beisan. But Beisan would no longer be a destination, because the day the article was published, it too fell.

Naim Ateek (1989, 10), now an Anglican priest in Jerusalem, tells of the fall of his hometown of Beisan (now Beit Shean). When Beisan was occupied, many residents fled across the Jordan River while other families remained. The seventeen members of the Ateek family remained, including a sister who had recently fled from Haifa with her husband and two little daughters. Two weeks later, on 26 May, those notables of the town who had remained were called to meet with the military governor, who told them they must evacuate Beisan. The remaining Arab families quickly packed necessities and gathered in the center of town where the Muslims and Christians were separated. The Muslims were sent to Transjordan, while the Christians were put on buses and transported to the outskirts of Nazareth.

The influx of refugees from Haifa, Tiberias, and Beisan compounded as residents from several villages near Nazareth fled to the security of the city. In July 1948, Jewish troops converged on predominantly Arab Galilee in what was termed "Operation Dekel." Among those villages to fall were Saffuriya, Mujeidil, and Ma'lul (fig. 6), which were occupied along with other Galilean villages between 15 and 18 July by the Israeli Defense Force (IDF). By occupying Ma'lul to the southwest of Nazareth, the Israelis were able to connect the isolated kibbutz of Kefar Ha Horesh—located between Nazareth and Ma'lul—with other Jewish-controlled land in the Jezreel valley. Mujeidil and Saffuriya came under attack because both villages had strongly supported the Arab uprising in the thirties. Many of the inhabitants from Mujeidil and Ma'lul fled to Nazareth in anticipation of an attack by Jewish troops. They were supported by only a few Arab soldiers or volunteers and were without many arms. According to Morris (1987), the primary reason for leaving their villages was fright caused both by knowledge of what had happened to Arabs in Deir Yassin and Haifa and by actual attack.

Those in Mujeidil who offered resistance were eventually driven toward Nazareth. One resident of Mujeidil related in a 2 May 1989 in-

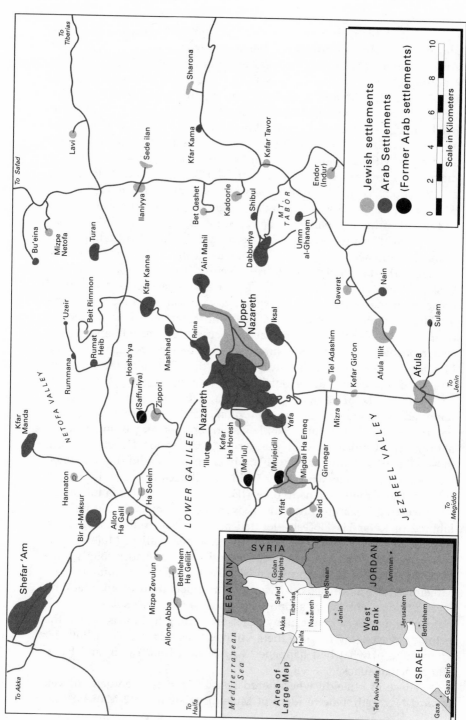

Fig. 6. Nazareth and environs

terview that the defense of the village was entrusted to only ten Arab soldiers from Jordan and Iraq. The villagers had no guns and were frightened. Another resident related how in 1948, he, his wife, and their young sons fled Haifa, where he worked, and returned to live with family in the village. They fled a second time to Nazareth just a few days before the occupation of their village. He said that he went to Nazareth to protect his family, with the intent to return to the village after the fighting stopped. A woman who fled Mujeidil as a thirteen-year-old remembers running into the olive orchards for protection, and when the Jewish soldiers arrived, they blew up ten homes as a warning; the rest were blown up over the next few weeks (Schwarz 1959, 32).

Saffuriya put up greater resistance. At the time, the village was inhabited by 4,330 Muslim Arabs. During the night of 14 July 1948, the town of Shefar 'Am fell to the Israelis, and as many as 2,500 people fled eastward to Saffuriya. The people of the village now realized that war was at hand. They hoped they would be able to resist for several days until the Arab Liberation Army (ALA) could come from Nazareth and save the village. But during the night of 15 July, three Israeli planes bombed Saffuriya. Additional shelling continued through the night, and residents fled into the surrounding orchards for protection. The next day, most of the villagers opted to flee to nearby villages or northward to Lebanon (Nazzal 1978, 74). Some families remained, only to be evicted several months later. Unlike the villagers of Mujeidil and Ma-'lul, most refugees from Saffuriya did not go immediately to Nazareth. It was only over the years that many gradually congregated in what was to become Nazareth's Safafra (Saffuriya) quarter.

These three villages were later destroyed by the Israeli government (except for two churches and a mosque in Ma'lul, two churches in Mujeidil, and a convent and Ottoman fortress in Saffuriya) in order to keep those refugees who had stayed within the borders of the expanded State of Israel from returning. Those who had come from the mixed Jewish and Arab cities were also forbidden to return, under harsh, military-enforced travel restrictions.

The residents and refugees of Nazareth fared much better during the conquest of the Galilee, partly because of the steadfastness of town leaders, and partly because of unique treatment by the Israeli government and military. On 15 July, the day before the fall of Nazareth, David Ben-Gurion cabled his military commander in the north and ordered him to prepare a special administrative task force to oversee the occupation of Nazareth, with strict orders to ensure that there be no looting or desecration of religious buildings. A commander of one of the brigades that took Nazareth explained why there was a different policy for Nazareth: "The conquest of Nazareth had a political importance. . . . Because of its importance to the Christian world—the behavior of the [Israeli] occupation forces in the city could serve as a factor in determining the prestige of the young state abroad" (Morris 1987, 201).

These instructions, although specialized, still called for the occupation of the town holy to Christendom. On 16 July 1948, Nazareth became the next target as Israeli troops moved to surround it from all sides but the east. Many local militia men refused to join in fighting with the ALA troops because, with the fall of Saffuriya, the situation looked hopeless, and because when Qawuqji's Arab forces entered Nazareth on 9 July they had apparently ill-treated some of the Christian inhabitants and clergy. Therefore, there was little support from local residents to join in with the ALA in defense of the town. Mayor Yusef Fahum even urged that all resistance be stopped, owing to the weakness of the Arab troops and volunteers and the perceived strength of the Israeli troops. He thought resistance would only end in defeat and the destruction of the city.

The willingness of the mayor and other councilmen to remain in Nazareth, even though they had little hope of fending off occupation, helped to allay fears among the populace that there would be atrocities committed by the Jews. Most of the city's 170 municipal policemen also stayed put. This willingness to stay among the leaders and police prompted most of the residents of Nazareth, as well as the new refugees in town, not to flee. Although some residents tried to flee out of fear of battle and possible occupation, most of those were turned back by ALA troops who feared that a mass exodus would hinder the defence of the city. On the morning of the attack, "a few people were able to flee, . . . but the majority of the people remained and hid in the various convents in the city" (Nazzal 1978, 79).

When the attack came, Nazareth was defended by only two or three hundred Arabs scattered in units on the hills to the north, west, and south. Those to the south and west encountered Israeli shelling, while those to the north faced an advancing armored unit. The resistance collapsed shortly after the shelling began, when the police officer in charge at the embattled police station put out a white flag of surrender. Soon afterward Nazarene notables, including the Muslim mayor and two Greek Orthodox priests, met with the Israeli military leaders and signed the terms of surrender. As ordered, there was no looting or damage to property by the occupying forces, and few soldiers entered the town. This helped to prevent the exodus of Nazarenes (Nazzal 1978, 78; *Jerusalem Post* [hereafter referred to as *JP*] 18 July 1948).

When an Israeli officer entered the town, a refugee asked if they had come to turn them away again, to which the officer replied: "No, not in Nazareth. Nazareth is a holy place, a holy town. The world is watching us. You will not be a victim here." This special treatment prompted one local businessman to suggest that Nazareth had always been a "pro-Catholic town" and that "any conqueror would have to think twice before causing a mass expulsion which would invoke the wrath of Rome" (Palumbo 1987, 123). The next day, Saturday 17 July, the bells of the Greek Catholic Church summoned the residents of Nazareth to surrender their firearms to the Israeli army. Men and women, old and young, brought forth their shotguns and machine guns (*New York Times*, 18 July 1948).

In 1946 the British figure for the population of Nazareth was 15,540—6,290 Muslims and 9,250 Christians (McCarthy 1990, 69). Christians were still the majority at 60 percent. Following the upheavals of 1948, the population and religious mix of Nazareth underwent significant changes. In the initial days after the conquest upward of 20,000 refugees were crammed into the city. In the days thereafter, refugees from villages and towns like Shefar 'Am, Kfar Kanna, and Dabburiya returned home, while those of Saffuriya, Ma'lul, Mujeidil, and the larger mixed cities of Tiberias, Beisan, Haifa, and Akka were prevented by the military from returning (Morris 1987, 202). Those refugees who had no choice other than to stay in Nazareth were predominantly Muslim. The neighboring villages of Reina, Kfar Kanna, and Yafa, which like Nazareth had strong concentrations of Christians, had not been targeted for expulsion, while those villages where expulsions and mass exodus did take place had been active in the revolt and were predominantly Muslim. In 1945, Saffuriya had a population of 4,320 Muslims and 10 Christians (probably residents of the convent and orphanage of St. Anne). Mujeidil had 1,640 Muslims and 260 Christians. Ma'lul had 490 Muslims and 200 Christians (*Village Statistics* 1945, 8). Not all these villagers ended up in Nazareth, but these figures show that a greater percentage of the refugees who did go to Nazareth would have been Muslim.

Charles Kamen lists by place of origin the following numbers of refugees in Nazareth at the end of the hostilities: 1,185 from Mujeidil, 560 from 'Illut, 241 from Beisan, and 120 from Qumiya. Refugees from the following towns and villages are listed as having sought refuge in Nazareth, as well as several other places inside Israel: at least 527 from Tiberias (also to Mughar), at least 303 from Hadatha (also to eight other villages), at least 201 from Saffuriya (also to seven other localities), 165 from Balad al-Sheikh (also to two other villages), and 2,585 from Haifa (mostly in Nazareth, but also to twenty-six other localities). The estimate of 20,000 refugees in the town in mid-July 1948, when added to the estimated population of 17,000 at the beginning of 1948, means that

as many as 35,000 people could have been living in and around Nazareth that summer. However, an army census conducted in July 1948
showed a population of 17,118, which included 12,640 residents and
4,478 refugees, evidence of an almost even exchange of refugees leaving Nazareth and refugees coming to Nazareth. Estimates for 1948 indicate that perhaps 20 percent of Nazarenes left the town for other countries. Not all the refugees enumerated remained in Nazareth. Some
moved to other villages, and some returned to their former homes (for
example, some of the refugees from Haifa and 'Illut). By 1951, Kamen
records 5,154 refugees in Nazareth and an increase in total population
from 15,540 in 1946 to 20,300 in 1951. Refugees represented 25 percent of
the population of Nazareth in 1951 (Kamen 1987 and 1988).

The diversity of refugees who stayed in Nazareth is shown in the
results of the survey in which fifty-four of the husbands and fifty-one
of the wives, or 18 percent of the 573 adults surveyed, indicated that either they or their parents were refugees of 1948.[11] Twenty-seven people
indicated that they came from Mujeidil, followed by twenty from Saffuriya, sixteen from Tiberias, twelve from Haifa, nine from Ma'lul,
four from Indur, two each from Beisan, Hadatha, Qumiya, Yajur, and
Meithalun, and one each from Sirin, Sulam, Jaljulia, Dabburiya, Zba-
bda, 'Araba, Dahi, Sejera, Bal'a, Bir'am, Mansi, 'Illut, Ijzim, Abu Gosh,
Iksal, Maghar, and Tayba.[12]

With the increased population, refugees ended up living in a variety of places. Christian schools, hospitals, hospices, and convents
provided housing for both Christians and Muslims. Many refugees
stayed with relatives, while others stayed under trees, in tents, in caves,
in abandoned or rented houses, in hastily constructed tin shacks called
tanaks, in the abandoned barracks of the Royal Engineers, or with

---

[11] Smooha suggests that about 20 percent of Israeli Arabs are refugees, or had
parents who were refugees (Al-Haj and Rosenfeld 1990, 53). Kamen (1987, 469) estimates that between 8 and 10 percent (12,000–15,000 of 163,000 total Arabs) of the post-
1948 Arab population excluding the Bedouin were internal refugees.

[12] Of these villages, Morris identifies the following as having been demolished
by the Israeli government, giving the primary reason for and the date in 1948 of the
Arab exodus from the village: Qumiya, fear of Jewish attack or of being caught up in
the fighting, 26 March; Hadatha and Sirin, abandonment on Arab orders, 6 April;
Mansi, military assault on the settlement by Jewish troops, 12–13 April; Yajur, military
assault and influence of the fall of, or exodus from, a neighboring town, 25 April; Indur,
military assault and influence of the fall of a neighboring town, 24 May; Ma'lul and
Mujeidil, military assault, 15 July; Saffuriya, military assault, 16 July; Ijzim, military
assault, 24–26 July; and Bir'am, expulsion by Jewish forces, November 1948. Military
assault prompted the exodus of Arabs from Tiberias, Beisan, and Haifa, in addition to
fear incited by the exodus of a neighboring town, for Beisan, and abandonment on Arab
orders, for Haifa (Morris 1987, xv). Tiberias and Beisan were abandoned, but not demolished, while 7,500 of Haifa's 71,200 Arabs remained (Kamen 1987, 465).

friends, employers, or charitable strangers. Many families from Tiberias were able to stay in the rooms of the Roman Catholic hospice, the Casa Nova. Two families surveyed said they came from Tiberias in 1948 and lived in homes they owned. The seventeen members of the Ateek family from Beisan stayed in two rooms of a friend's house near Mary's well. At the end of the summer, the family was able to rent a small house belonging to the waqf of the Anglican Church (Ateek 1989, 11).

Ahmad, from the Muslim village of 'Illut—several miles to the west of Nazareth—told of staying in the Salesian school for five months until his family could find a home in the suq to rent. He reported that about one-third of the inhabitants from his small village fled to Nazareth in July 1948. Most returned after the fighting, but about twenty to thirty families remained in Nazareth, mostly at the Salesian school. One of the reasons for staying was that those who returned to 'Illut were allowed to return only to their homes, not to their farmlands. Ahmad, a Muslim from Mujeidil, explained that his family stayed with relatives in Nazareth, while others less fortunate from his village stayed in tents pitched on Jebel al-Daula, the government hill surrounding the police station. Nimer, another man from Mujeidil, told of staying in two rooms of a house abandoned by Nazarenes who fled to Jordan. One Muslim woman from Mujeidil told in the survey how her family stayed at first under the olive tree in the garden of a Christian family. A Christian woman, whose childhood home was in a large house in the suq, told of her father allowing seven Muslim families from Mujeidil to stay in the lower level of their two-story home in the rooms where grain and seed were normally stored. These families had all worked land in Mujeidil owned by the Christian family.

The refugees from Saffuriya often took a circuitous route to Nazareth. Most families surveyed or interviewed from Saffuriya told of first going to villages like Reina, Kfar Manda, Mashhad, or 'Illut, and only later coming to Nazareth. At first scattered throughout the city in temporary lodgings, these refugees over the years gradually moved out, first to any available and affordable housing, whether rented or purchased and then gradually, as in the case of Mujeidil, Ma'lul, and Saffuriya, as if drawn together by a sense of community with their fellow refugees, into quarters with others from the same village. This process forced Nazareth to expand faster than resources could provide and gradually shifted the 60 percent Christian majority to a 60 percent Muslim majority, two of the chief contributing factors for current political rift in Nazareth.

An early 1949 report from the Ministry of Minorities sums up the conditions in Nazareth:

Conditions of poverty and congestion were widespread because of the refugees who poured in from every direction . . . The refugees comprise some 30% of the population. They live in the monasteries and anywhere else they can find a place. The great majority of them suffer from unemployment, from hunger, cold and want. Food prices are high. Nazareth is neither an industrial nor a commercial town, and it is unable to provide jobs for its residents. Even in normal times part of the population found work elsewhere in Acre, Haifa and Jaffa. Nazareth is fortunate in being a town with many monasteries and convents supported by foreign philanthropic organizations. (Kamen 1988, 80)

Nazareth in Israel

The absorption of refugees into occupations, living quarters, schools, and society was not the only challenge Nazareth had to contend with. As the largest all-Arab municipality within the new state of Israel,[13] Nazareth had to endure along with the other Arabs of Israel an ongoing struggle to gain equality as an Arab minority within a Jewish state. It was within the context of this struggle that the Muslim and Christian communities of Nazareth joined together as a community of Nazarenes who now began to identify with a new and larger community of Israeli Arabs. For many residents, particularly the refugees, old community ties of family and village no longer existed in the traditional sense, and so it was within the framework of shared sufferings and aspirations that new and larger communities were forged.

Much has been written about the status of Arabs in Israel, and while it is not within the scope of this work to treat their status as a whole, specific examples from the first forty years of Nazareth as a city in Israel illustrate the challenges the community of Israeli Arabs have had to face. Perhaps the most enduring and sensitive of the issues facing Nazarenes, and all Israeli Arabs, is the continual influence of Arab/Palestinian nationalism, which has manifested itself in a variety of ways over the years. At the regional level, this nationalism results in support for Arab causes and for leaders of Arab nationalism like Gemal Abdel Nasser, or more recently Saddam Hussein. At the state level, this nationalism either supports a return of all the land of Israel/Palestine to the Palestinians, or supports an independent Palestine in part of the land alongside a state of Israel. Since the State of Israel now includes

---

[13] While classified as urban, Nazareth has maintained rural roots. In 1952, a small notice in the *Jerusalem Post* announced that traffic had been blocked for thirty minutes when a cow calved in the middle of Nazareth's main street (*JP*, 4 September 1952). A 1989 spring walk on the western slopes of Nazareth's hills revealed a Maronite resident of the town grazing his flock of several dozen goats, sheep, kids, and lambs, and a resident of the Bir Abu-Jayish quarter on the southern edge of town indicated that she did not own a car, but that she did have a horse.

and probably will always include Nazareth, the local brand of nationalism, in addition to the call for a state of Palestine in the West Bank and Gaza, calls for equal rights for the Arab citizens of Israel.

Support for these differing levels of nationalism has united the various communities of Nazareth into a community of Nazarenes and with the overlapping communities of Israeli Arabs, Palestinian Arabs, and Arabs as a nation. This overlapping of communities is experienced by all. For example, Archimandrite Nathaniel Shahada, of the Greek Catholic community in Nazareth, is an Arab, a Christian, and a citizen of Israel who describes the Christian Arabs of Nazareth, Israel, as being "one hundred percent Palestinian" (al-Fajr, 23 October 1985).

Absorption of the Arab community into the State of Israel was not warmly accepted, and opposition to the state has continued to this day, although in decreasing numbers. In the early years of the state, there was continual pressure for Arabs to remain united in their opposition to the state. During the fasting month of Ramadan in 1950, the Friday sermon, delivered by the qadi (judge) of Nazareth from the White Mosque, was broadcast over Voice of Israel radio. When the qadi failed to use the opportunity to denounce the State of Israel, Damascus Radio responded by denouncing the qadi as a traitor and calling on all faithful Muslims to boycott prayers at which he was present (JP, 12 July 1950).

While the Arabs were trying to remain united in their opposition to the state, the government was working to keep them fragmented, as summarized in a top-secret memorandum: "The government's policy . . . has sought to divide the Arab population into diverse communities and regions. . . . The municipal status of the Arab villages, and the competitive spirit of local elections, deepened the divisions inside the villages themselves. The communal policy and the clan divisions in the villages prevented Arab unity" (Segev 1986, 65).

In those first years, the settlement of the internal refugee problem claimed much of the attention of the Nazarenes, who sought permission for the refugees either to return to former homes, or to receive an equitable compensation for lost land. They also focused on ending the oppressive military occupation, with its travel restrictions and curfews, and on stopping the confiscation of Arab lands. There was also the continual effort to solve the lingering Arab-Israeli conflict.

The frustration of making no progress in the resolution of these problems came to a head ten years after the creation of the State of Israel in the form of a May Day rally. With limited political access, as well as restrictions on the creation of Arab parties, many Nazarenes found that the Communist party was the only political medium which addressed Arab needs. As a result, the Communist party has always had

strong support among Israeli Arabs, particularly in Nazareth. In anticipation of the 1958 May Day parade, officials sought permission for a
morning march. The permission was denied because two other organizations, the *Histadrut* (labor federation) and the United Workers party,
had already been granted permission. The Communists were given
permission for an afternoon march, but opted to march illegally in the
morning. On the evening before the march, Communist leaders drove
through town announcing by loudspeaker the morning parade, but
during a year of ten-year anniversary celebrations, government leaders
had hoped to show its Arab populace at its best as they marched behind
the banner of Ben-Gurion's Mapai party. In order to prevent a Communist rally, the government arrested about a dozen leaders whom the
police defined as "known Communist and nationalist activists." Still,
on the morning of the march, the planned Histadrut procession turned
into a "moving battleground," with stones being thrown and young
protesters being arrested. The banners carried during the march were
very nationalistic, not communistic, in their content. They read:
"Return the refugees," "Self-determination for Palestinians," "Stop the
Land-grabbing," and "Free Algeria."

Walter Schwarz attributes the riot to two primary causes: first
"the malaise of a conquered minority—a listless, smouldering disaffec-
tion, systematically fed through radios that could blare forth Cairo,
Damascus, Baghdad, or Amman as loudly as the Arabic broadcasts of
the Voice of Israel"; second, "military rule, imposed in war-time but
lingering, like a tedious guest, through the years of peace" with its
"system of travel permits, its queues, formalities and occasional sudden
arrests" which were "a nagging inconvenience and a daily affront."
Additional reasons were offered by a disgruntled Nazarene who is
quoted as saying, "They take our land. Why? For security reasons! They
take our jobs. Why? For security reasons! And when we ask them how
it happens that we, our lands and our jobs threaten the security of the
State—they do not tell us. Why not? For security reasons!" (Schwarz
1959, 15–18).

Part of the frustration resulting in the 1958 May Day protest
stemmed from the fact that there were few other avenues for venting
anger or seeking change. Arabs could vote, and there had always been a
handful of Arab members in the Knesset (parliament), but tight controls limited their effectiveness in the democratic process. This control
of political and other activities has gradually loosened over the years,
allowing for the emergence of Arab parties in the last few years, and an
improvement in government policies toward its Arab citizens. Ian Lustick summarizes how the government succeeded in controlling its
Arab minority for so long:

An important element in Israeli political life has been the absence of independent Arab political activity. For 18 years, a military government, established by Israel during the 1948 war, closely regulated many aspects of life in Arab areas of the country. Fledgling attempts to form political organizations, newspapers, and protest movements were thwarted relatively easily during this period by military governors who used their power, not only to prevent independent Arab political activity, but to deliver larger majorities of the Arab vote to the dominant Labor Party and its "Affiliated Arab Lists."

The military government was abolished in 1966, but its functions continued to be performed by a network of ministerial Arab departments, the Arab department of the Histadrut (Israel's dominant trade union organization), and the Office of the Adviser to the Prime Minister on Arab Affairs. This later bureau worked closely with the internal security services and the police. The primary objective of the policies carried out by this bureaucratic array was to prevent independent Arab political organization. Through policies which kept the Arab minority internally fragmented, economically dependent, and bereft of credible leadership, this overall objective was reliably achieved at relatively low cost. (Lustick 1989, 100)

One of the major concerns of Nazarenes during this period of strict governmental control was the struggle to keep hold of their land. Land was taken by the government in two general ways: first, by not allowing refugees to return to their village homes and lands, and second, through the expropriation of Nazareth land. Starting in the latter half of 1948, the Ministry of Justice began working on the Absentees' Property Laws. An initial draft of the law declared that all persons no longer present in Israel would be declared absentee and thereby lose title to their land. This met with objection from the Ministerial Committee, which proposed that absentee status be expanded to all who left their homes after 29 November 1947, regardless of whether or not they left the country. Committee member Moshe Sharett drew attention to the thousands of refugees in Nazareth who, if not defined as absentees, would be allowed to return to their village homes. The law was thus modified to include all who had abandoned their "usual place of residence" (Segev 1986, 80).

Knesset member Saif al-Din al-Zu'bi of Nazareth challenged this seizure of Arab lands belonging to legal residents of Israel who carried identity cards and participated in elections. He stressed that many of those declared absentee were refugees who had left their villages, but not the country, for only a few days during the fighting. He explained that some of the refugees now living in Nazareth and Turan had left their villages for only a few hours, yet were still declared absentee (Peretz 1958, 153). One survey of Arabs in Israel estimates that 52 percent of all Israeli Arab families lost land during the period of 1948 to 1967, representing a total of 40 to 60 percent of all Arab-owned lands

(Smooha 1989, 152). The government offered compensation to the internal refugees for the lost land in the form of either small plots of land in Nazareth or money, but most rejected the offers because it meant they would have to relinquish their right to ever return.

The expropriation of Nazareth land began in 1954 with a government announcement that 1,200 dunams (one dunam is equal to one quarter of an acre) of land in the northeast section of town were being "requisitioned" in order to build administrative offices. Residents of Nazareth opposed the plan because it deprived them of land in one of the main areas targeted for expansion, while the government offered "full compensation" to those families who were going to lose land (*JP*, 25, 26 July 1954). Then in 1957, the government announced that in addition to the planned governmental offices, the land would also be used to establish a new Jewish town to be called Natzerat 'Illit (Upper Nazareth). The new town would serve as a counterbalance to the Arab municipality of Nazareth, which as the largest Arab town in Israel had become a center of Arab nationalism. There were also many Arab villages in the Nazareth region, so the government hoped a Jewish city would serve to break up this large concentration of Arabs (Jiryis 1976, 107).[14]

The first 1,200 expropriated dunams were gradually added to, not only from Nazareth's land, but also from neighboring villages of Reina, Mashhad, and 'Ain Mahil. By 1961, Upper Nazareth controlled 6,000 dunams, and by 1984 had increased its landholdings in successive expropriations to 19,300 dunams. In the meantime, Nazareth's original 15,000 dunams had diminished to 8,300 (Rosenfeld 1988, 47). In 1959, landowners of the expropriated land questioned the legality of the action and petitioned (in vain) for a return of their land, citing the fact that the land had been requisitioned only for the purpose of building government offices and housing for government employees, not for the units constructed, which housed 2,000 settlers, of which only 100 of the families included government employees. In addition, a chocolate factory had been built, and there were plans to build other factories, a cinema, a shopping center, and more housing units (*JP*, 15 January 1959).

In 1959, one writer describing the new town noted that "the angular apartment blocks on the bald hill" give "the impression of a scab on the gently contoured landscape—a rash, rather, because it grew month

---

[14] The establishment of Upper Nazareth preceeded by only a few years the formation of a government policy referred to as "the Judaization of the Galilee," in which Jewish settlements and cities, like Upper Nazareth, were established on hilltops and adjacent to Arab settlements in an attempt to offset the strong Arab majority in the mountainous north of Israel.

by month on compulsory purchased land" (Schwarz 1959, 31). With this growth, governmental offices were gradually transferred from Arab Nazareth, Tiberias, and Afula to the new city. Today, Upper Nazareth serves as the governmental seat for the Northern District, the domineering Government House towers above the Sharqiya quarter, and large apartment blocks skirt the Arab town of Nazareth on the hills to the north and east. The municipality of Upper Nazareth even includes an exclave on the southern hill of Nazareth composed of a hotel and a large police complex which are surrounded by Arab residential neighborhoods. With a population that nearly doubles that of Upper Nazareth, the cramped Arabs of Nazareth continue to resent the loss of their land.[15]

From as early as the master plans of the 1940s, the intended and natural area of growth for Nazareth had been to the north and east, owing to the location of Yafa and Kefar Ha Horesh to the southwest, 'Illut to the west, and Reina to the north. With the development of Upper Nazareth to the north and east, the only areas left for expansion were to the northwest and the south. The harsh topography to the south limited development in that direction, so the northwest area along the road to the former site of Saffuriya became the major area of expansion. These lands to the south and northwest were Mandate lands of the British high commissioner, and became State of Israel lands in 1948. They were not originally included within the municipal boundaries of Nazareth, and according to a 15 August 1989 interview with In'am Zu'bi, wife of the former mayor, it took a "fierce fight" in the Knesset and with the Ministry of the Interior to have the lands included within the city's boundaries.

A more recent land battle, according to a 6 September 1989 interview with a municipal clerk, has resulted from the government's attempt to graft the village of 'Illut into the municipal boundaries of Nazareth. Both the village and city have opposed the unification, because they see it as an attempt by the government to cut back on municipal funding. The Nazareth municipality wants 'Illut to be a separate municipality with its own council and budget.

---

15 The population of Upper Nazareth boomed in the early 1990s with the influx of Russians. Population estimates in 1994 indicate an increase to upward of 35,000 residents (1983 census figures placed Upper Nazareth's population at 23,360). Ties between the two Nazareths have been increasing as Russian immigrants have sought employment in Arab Nazareth. In a 25 April 1994 interview, Musa Jamil of Nazareth's sanitation department indicated that of seventy-five employees, about thirty Russians from Upper Nazareth and other Jewish towns now work cleaning Nazareth's streets. For the most part they replace West Bank Palestinians, who frequently are denied entry into Israel.

The 1982 census includes 'Illut as one of the thirteen statistical areas within Nazareth, and in the last two municipal elections the village has been included with Nazareth. However 'Illut voters boycotted the 1983 municipal election with only one of 1,164 eligible voters voting. In the 1988 national election, 'Illut voted as part of Nazareth with a 68 percent voter turnout, but the 1989 municipal election was still boycotted, with only 18 percent of the voters participating. Of those who voted, 80 percent voted for the new Islamic party. In March 1991, the Ministry of the Interior decided that 'Illut would be granted independent municipal status and would no longer be included in the Nazareth municipal zone (*Arabs in Israel*, 26 March 1991).

Another frustration for the municipality has been the lack of government approval for a town plan. According to a January 1989 interview with city planner Adib Daud, no municipal plans have been approved since 1942. The most recent plan, submitted in 1982, still awaits approval by the Ministry of the Interior. Compounding this frustration is the fact that many residents of Nazareth do not actually live on municipal lands. The complex land policies of the state, with its various authorities and jurisdictions, have left several sections of Nazareth in limbo. When the upper part of the Sharqiya quarter was expropriated for the building of the regional government office, the land came under the jurisdiction of the Upper Nazareth municipality. As the quarter has expanded up the hill and onto the expropriated land, Arab residents have had to go to Upper Nazareth for building permits, while voting and receiving municipal services from Nazareth. Some houses in the Jebel al-Daula quarter which sit next to the military installation are also within the bounds of Upper Nazareth and are in a similar situation.

Most of the Bilal section of the Safafra quarter is located beyond the municipal boundaries on land that technically belongs to the village of Reina and comes under the jurisdiction of a regional planning commission. Until 1993, inhabitants of this quarter considered themselves to be residents of Nazareth in that they voted in Nazareth municipal elections and relied on Nazareth for services. Obtaining building permits, however, was a bit more complicated. City planner Daud confessed that the unclear status of the Bilal quarter meant that the municipality could not issue building permits as it does to everyone else who lives, votes, and pays taxes in Nazareth. The result of this complex mess, according to Daud, was that the residents of the Bilal quarter had to "go to God for permits," or they were forced to build without them, which most of them did. This problem was resolved in 1993 when the Ministry of the Interior decided that residents of the quarter living on Reina land should participate in Reina elections. This now means that Reina has jurisdiction over the quarter and is responsible for municipal services. However, water and sewer lines, if connected, are still hooked into the Nazareth system.

Since the loss of land to Upper Nazareth and the lifting of military control, there have continued to be reasons for protest in Nazareth. Each March since 1975, on what has become known as Land Day, Nazarenes have joined with Israeli Arabs to protest the continued expropriation of Arab lands in the Galilee. Rallies are held in selected Arab towns and villages throughout the country, so the streets of Nazareth are quiet for the most part, with shops closing for the day and workers staying at home. Land Day in 1989 found extra police vehicles along the main street and young men with nothing else to do but cruise through town in cars or mill around the streets in front of Mary's well and the Communist party building, hoping for but never seeing any excitement.

A more active day of protest is May Day, when Nazarenes take to the streets to air their grievances (figs. 7, 8). Each year, thousands (many coming from surrounding villages) parade through town carrying red banners of communism, and banners protesting the expropriation of lands, demanding equal rights, calling for two states for two peoples and, most recently, supporting the *Intifada* (Palestinian uprising). The parade begins at the municipal secondary school on the southeast side of town, proceeds north through the industrial section, and then continues along the main street to the Communist party's House of Friendship where a rally is held.

In addition to these two annual days of protest, there are special days of strikes and protest called by the the the municipality, Communist party, Christian community, and the National Committee of Arab Local Council Heads. For example, on 13 May 1989, the Nazareth soccer team and many of its fans traveled to the coastal city of Nahariya for a game crucial to advancement into a higher league for both teams. Tensions were high among the players and fans of the Arab and Jewish teams. Late in the game, with Nazareth leading 2 to 0, a riot broke out. In the ensuing melee, one Jewish youth was stabbed and fifty-four people were arrested, primarily Arabs. Police accused the Arab fans of starting the riot by throwing bottles and stones at the Nahariya fans, while the Arabs accused the police of using excessive violence and provoking the incident, perhaps to get the game canceled in order to prevent Nahariya from losing.

Several days latter on 19 May, several thousand Arabs took to Nazareth's main street to protest what they viewed as a "racist attack" against the Arab fans at the game, and a general policy within the Israeli government that discriminates against Arabs. Following the pro-

Fig. 7. May Day parade down Pope Paul VI Street

test parade, a rally was held (*JP,* 16, 21 May 1989; *al-Fajr,* 22 May 1989). Toward the end of the hour-long rally a group of about twenty Israeli border police appeared in the distance. Merchants hurriedly secured their shops in anticipation of a confrontation. Mayor Tawfiq Ziyad went out to talk with the police, then came back and addressed the anxious crowd, saying, "This is Nazareth and not Nahariya and we will make this a peaceful demonstration." The crowd disbanded and the border police left.

Other protests include the 15 November 1989 general strike throughout the Arab sector in protest of the demolition of Arab houses in the Israeli town of Tayba. In March 1990, a thousand residents of Nazareth joined 4,000 other Israeli Arabs in signing a petition demanding a halt to the increasing influx of Soviet Jews. One Nazareth resident complained that the new immigrants would only make a bad sit-

Fig. 8. Beit Sadaqa (house of friendship), headquarters of the Jebha (Communist) party, during a May Day rally

uation worse by causing unemployment rates to climb and prices to increase (*JP*, 4, 9 March 1990).

Israeli Arabs are also very mindful of their fellow Palestinians' situation in the West Bank and Gaza. The success of the Communist party is partly a result of its willingness to support rights for Palestinians in both Israel and the Occupied Territories (fig. 9). There is also quiet support among many for the PLO.[16] For example, Anglican pastor Riyah Abu 'Assal, as a representative of the *Taqadumia* (Progressive List for Peace) party, traveled to Tunis in February 1985 to met with PLO chairman Yasser Arafat (*al-Senara*, 15 February 1985).

The Arabs of Nazareth often take to the streets, ballot boxes, and press, to protest not only their less than equal status as Arab citizens of Israel, but also the oppression that their fellow Palestinians have experienced in the West Bank and Gaza since 1967. Several events in par-

[16] Not all Nazarenes support the PLO or the establishment of a Palestinian state alongside Israel. One extreme example is Azem Espagnoli, a 24–year-old Christian Arab of Nazareth, who said in an interview while serving as a volunteer in the Israeli Defense Forces that he considers himself to be a Christian Zionist who supports the existence of the state of Israel based on its biblical boundaries. "Everyone thinks the people of Nazareth all support the PLO but that isn't true. Those who do support the PLO say they want a Palestinian state instead of Israel, not alongside Israel, but not all of us agree. We Christian Zionists don't want any Palestinian state at all" (*JP*, 19 November 1989).

Fig. 9. Jebha campaign poster during the 1988 national elections urging Israeli Arabs to support their fellow Palestinian Arabs, not by throwing stones, but by throwing votes for Jebha

ticular have incited the wrath of Nazarenes to go beyond their usually peaceful methods of protest. One such incident was in response to the September 1982 massacre of Palestinian refugees in the Sabra and Sha- tilla camps in Beirut. A week after the massacre, a planned strike, memorial service, and mourning procession erupted into a full-scale demonstration in which Pope Paul VI Street was blocked by rocks, logs, barrels, and burning tires. Passing cars were stoned, and one tourist bus was burned by the mob. Apparently two busloads of tourists had been warned by locals that it was not safe to enter the city. One busload left, while the other ventured into the city center to visit the Basilica of the Annunciation. These tourists, on a day trip to the Galilee, became stranded in the church as fighting in the streets escalated. During the riot, their bus was set afire. After nine hours in the church the group of tourists were evacuated in minibuses provided by an order of nuns. Those injured by the demonstration included thirty-nine Arabs, twenty-five policemen, and six Jewish motorists; more than a hundred Israeli Arabs were arrested (*JP*, 23, 29 September 1982).

Five years later, the beginning weeks of the Intifada prompted the Israeli Arabs of Nazareth to show support for the Palestinian Arabs in the occupied territories by holding a strike and a midday moment of si- lence, announced by church bells and calls from the minarets, to commemorate those who had died in the violence.[17] Border police were on patrol in the city throughout the day while youths roamed the streets throwing stones and looking for trouble. Strike leaders had managed to squelch most outbursts of violence, but following the moment of silence, the already tense atmosphere erupted into a riot as youths erected barricades along the main street. Police responded in full riot gear with tear gas and a high-pressure water cannon as they moved through the streets and tried to disperse the stone- and bottle-throwing crowd (*JP*, 22 December 1987). Other reactions to the Intifada have included additional demonstrations,[18] the appearance of pro-Palestinian graffiti on walls around town and even in Upper Nazareth, makeshift Palestinian flags pasted on government buildings, the throwing of petrol bombs at the main department store in town, and occasional stones thrown at passing Egged buses (*JP*, 24 January; 4 March 1988; 14, 24 April; 3 November 1989). One of the rallies held in early 1988 was organized by Archimandrite Nathaniel Shahada of Nazareth's Greek Catholic community, in cooperation with spiritual leaders representing Druze, Muslims, and Christians in the the Galilee (*JP*, 26 January 1988).

When, during the Easter season of 1990, Jews moved into the St. John's hospice in the Christian quarter of Jerusalem, Nazareth's Christian community joined in the worldwide protest by closing churches for the day, ringing church bells, and holding vigils in front of the churches (*al-Fajr*, 30 April 1990). The Hebron massacres in March 1994 prompted two large demonstrations in Nazareth. The first demonstration was a spontaneous display of anger in which youth and police fought it out with stones and tear gas (*JP*, International Edition, 5 March 1994). Several weeks later, the Islamic movement organized a more peaceful rally in which several thousand paraded through town behind a large banner showing blood streaming from the Tomb of the Patriarchs in Hebron (*Salt Lake Tribune*, 20 March 1994).

---

[17] Christian and Muslim communities have not always been united in their support of fellow Palestinians in the occupied territories. In 1983, in response to the deaths of Palestinians in an attack by Jewish settlers against the Islamic College in Hebron, the committee of Arab council heads called for a day of mourning and prayer, which was to include the noon ringing of church bells. Christian leaders in Nazareth failed to heed the call, and when criticized for not supporting the protest, they replied either that they were not asked to participate, or that the churches should not become involved in political matters (*al-Anba'*, 31 July 1983).

[18] Estimates of the number of people who participate in such demonstrations can vary, as illustrated in two 24 January 1988 articles about a previous day's demonstration. The *Jerusalem Post* reporter described the demonstrators as "thousands of chanting, banner-waving Israeli Arabs," while Nazarenes interviewed in the article described it as the "town's biggest demonstration ever" with "nearly 20,000" people. Larger still was the estimate of the Communist Arabic daily, *al-Ittihad*, which estimated the number demonstrating at "about 50,000."

Each year for Christmas the municipality distributes a leaflet in which it offers holiday greetings and invites attendance at an ecumenical gathering. The event is sponsored by the municipality and is preceded by the annual scout parade. The 18 December 1987 leaflet, issued shortly after the beginning of the Intifada, included an announcement of the municipal meeting and offered Christmas greetings, but most of its text was devoted to condemning the "oppressive occupation" of the Israeli government and praising the "heroic opposition" of the Palestinian people. During the height of the Intifada, Muslim and Christmas feast-day festivities were more subdued. The Christmas scout parade was canceled the first year, and the traditional strings of colored lights were replaced with regular lights or not put up at all. Shopping was also curtailed. One Roman Catholic merchant, referring to the decline in sales, said, "People are upset because of the situation in the territories and they have answered the calls by leaders of the community to celebrate the holiday in a quiet manner" (*JP*, 23 December 1988). The next year the same merchant noted that there "is no Christmas atmosphere and all festivities are being confined to people's houses out of respect for what is happening in the territories" (*JP*, 24 December 1989). Buoyed by the prospects of the Madrid peace talks, the municipality reinstated the hanging of colored lights and the holding of the annual reception for the 1991 Christmas season (*Herald Journal*, 25 December 1991).

While increased incidents of nationalist activities such as demonstrations and graffiti indicate a renewed solidarity of Nazarenes with Palestinians on the other side of the green line, the fact remains that most residents of the city are in Nazareth to stay. The foremost loyalty of Nazarenes is to their homes and hometown. Representative of most Nazarenes, Su'ad Abunuwara, when asked if she would remain in Israel or move to the West Bank if a State of Palestine were established there, emphatically replied that Nazareth was her home, and it was where she was going to stay. Atallah Mansour, who lives in the neighboring village of Yafa, writes that the platform of most Israeli Arabs is to "pursue a struggle for equality within Israel," while at the same time supporting the "right of self-determination" for the Palestinians. He says that those Arabs "who live in Israel are Israeli citizens and on the whole have no aspiration to change this status" (Mansour 1988, 265).

Economic Problems

Political problems have been compounded by economic problems. One of the continual challenges of Nazareth has been to achieve financial stability and acquire sufficient revenue to properly run a city. Several contributing factors continue to inflict financial strain on the city. First,

Nazareth as an Arab municipality continues to receive a lower amount of funds from the national government than Jewish municipalities of similar size. Second, up to one-third of the land within the municipality is church-owned and therefore tax free. Finally, the municipality has often avoided increasing the local tax rate, has been negligent in collecting taxes owed by residents, and has experienced problems of inexperience, ineffectiveness, and corruption. In April 1974 when Saif al-Din Zu'bi resigned as mayor of Nazareth, he explained that he had done so in the face of severe economic strain on the municipality—the municipal council had refused to raise "rock bottom" rates, residents had been unwilling to pay the already low taxes, and the government had failed to offer sufficient aid to the ailing city (*JP*, 23 April 1974). One government report assigned part of the blame for the financial crises in Arab towns and villages to local administrators "who perform poorly because they have never been trained for their jobs," while a reporter, speaking specifically about Nazareth, accused the Communist-run municipality of having produced a "run-of-the-mill maladministration" (*JP*, 27 February 1980).

The issue of low government expenditures for Nazareth and other Arab municipalities has been a continual source of contention, not just over discrepancies between Jewish and Arab municipalities, but also over whether there actually are inequalities. For example, following the resignation of mayor Zu'bi, Interior Minister Hillel announced that Nazareth received more aid for its budget than Jewish towns like Upper Nazareth and Hadera, and that it had also received more money per person in the form of loans and grants (*JP*, 24 October 1974). Several years later, however, an article in the Communist party Arabic daily, in reference to a slash in the municipal budget by the Interior Ministry, reported that Nazareth had requested a budget of IL 122 million, or about 3,000 lira per person, but had only been offered a budget of IL 82 million, or about 2,000 lira per person. This was less than half the average allotment for Jewish municipalities, where the average per capita expenditure was about 5,000 lira per person (*al-Ittihad*, 7 July 1978, in *Journal of Palestine Studies* 8 [Autumn 1978]: 134). The disparity between Jewish and Arab municipalities is also shown in figures supplied by the municipality in a mimeographed document for the 1984 volunteer work camp which cites 1960 budget allotments of IL 2.61 per capita for Arabs and IL 14.30 per capita for Jews, and 1982 allotments in Nazareth of IS (Israeli sheqels) 243 per capita while neighboring Upper Nazareth received IS 843 per capita.

Low levels of revenue have resulted in many municipal strikes and shutdowns over the years. In 1981, municipal workers went out on strike for thirty-two days after not receiving salaries for two months. A government payment of IS 10 million finally brought the strike to a halt, returned basic services like street cleaning and garbage collection, and reopened schools (*JP*, 2 December 1981).

In 1987 Arab municipalities staged a strike "to protest against the government's 'apartheid' polices." Arab workers from Nazareth who worked in the Jewish sector complained that their Jewish employers pressured them to ignore the strike (*JP*, 24 July 1987). In early 1990 Nazareth and forty-seven other Arab municipalities were paralyzed by a twenty-day strike in attempts to get the government to bail out their debts and increase their regular and development budgets. Lack of municipal funds prevented Nazareth from paying its bill to *Mekorot*, the National Water Company, and as a result the city went without water for a day (*JP*, 21, 25 February 1990).

The struggle with the budget is exemplified by a statement of Mayor Ziyad, who, in a July 1981 article in *Ha'aretz* said that he and "his deputies had been employed, since their election to office [in 1975], as clerks in every respect, being endlessly required to see to it that the municipal employees' salaries arrived on time" (al-Haj and Rosenfeld 1990, 147). More recently, the owner of a photo store in Nazareth complained in an 18 August 1989 interview that as a result of the Intifada the government has directed all of its funds toward putting the uprising down rather than developing cities like Nazareth. He also noted that there were no factories in town and that unemployment was very high.

In an effort to compensate for lagging budgets, the municipality has undertaken several self-help projects. In 1978, it published a fourteen-page pamphlet entitled *Nazareth of Peace Calls!* With text in English, French, German, and Arabic, the introduction speaks of the deteriorating situation in Nazareth caused by "governmental policy which deprives the city from the necessary development budgets," and lists matters such as "housing projects, parks, industrialization, cultural centers, libraries, stadium, sport centers, art galleries, tourism, and hygienic projects" that need attention. The publication then singles out education and school buildings as the "most unbearable problem which must be given priority," and describes the planned improvements in education. These plans are illustrated with architectural drawings of the planned schools, day-care facilities, and an institute for the mentally handicapped, as well as photographs of several schools under construction and classrooms full of pupils. The assumed intent of the pamphlet was to bring attention to the financial plight of Nazareth and to solicit support from outside sources.

A second attempt at self-help has been the annual volunteer work camp, held each August since 1976. The camp is organized by the

Communist-dominated municipal government. For one week, thousands of volunteers come from around the world to help in a variety of projects such as widening and paving roads, painting schools, repairing water lines, laying sewer lines, and cleaning streets and parks. A listing of the quarters in which projects were performed in 1989 issued by the municipality shows that all the quarters of Nazareth benefited by the project assignments. This strategic assigning of projects is done in part to ensure that the Communists do not alienate any supporters or potential supporters. The thirteenth work camp included 1,250 citizens of Nazareth, equal numbers of Israeli Arabs, as many as 3,000 Arabs from the occupied territories, some 300–400 Israeli Jews, and 96 foreigners from eighteen countries including the United States, USSR, and Eastern and Western Europe. Mayor Ziyad estimated that the 1988 work camp saved the municipality U.S.$500,000, double the amount of the annual development budget Nazareth receives from the government. In explaining why the Communist-led municipality organizes these work camps, the mayor noted the continuation of "economic discrimination against Arab municipalities," which per capita receive only "20–25 percent of what their Jewish counterparts get" (*JP*, 20 August 1988) (fig. 10).

Another source of economic frustration has been continual high rates of unemployment. In 1986, Mayor Ziyad noted that nearly 30 percent of the work force in Nazareth was unemployed, three times the national average. The deputy director-general of Employment Services for Israel noted that in 1980 there were only 600 unemployed in Nazareth, while six years later, that amount had risen to 3,166. The head of the Nazareth Labor Council, in response to the severe lack of jobs, said, "The unemployed Arabs of Nazareth cannot help feeling that they have lost their jobs because they are Arabs. Most of them have large families of which they are the sole breadwinners" (*JP*, 5 June 1986). Additional setbacks include a drop in construction and increased competition for jobs with immigrants from the former Soviet Union, who Deputy Mayor Suheil Diyab suggests are hired over Arabs for patriotic reasons (*Ha'aretz*, 9 September 1992).

A letter written in Hebrew from Mayor Ziyad to the Minister of Labor and Welfare on 22 June 1989 quotes Nazareth's unemployment rate as 3.5 times the national average. The letter was followed up by a letter to the central committee of the Histadrut, suggesting several ways to reduce unemployment, such as encouraging large corporations to invest in Nazareth and changing the status of Nazareth to that of development town. Since unemployment is not an isolated issue, the municipality felt that the lack of government support for economic incentives and industrial development was at fault and that a change in

Fig. 10. Jebha-sponsored work camp in which narrow streets in the suq are being repaved

municipal status could help remedy the frustrations of unemployment and economic stagnation. In order to stimulate economic development, the Israeli government has passed a law for the encouragement of capital investment, which has created three economic zones: zone A, which includes development towns, is assigned the highest priority and given the best incentives; zone B, which includes Upper Nazareth, is given reduced rents for industrial buildings, grants for industrial developments, and lower rates for working capital; zone C, or the central zone, is offered no incentives (al-Haj and Rosenfeld 1990, 124). Nazareth was put in zone C until 1994, when the government changed its status to a more preferred zone B.

Classification within zone C kept industrial development in Nazareth at a minimum, while Upper Nazareth has become the site of many large factories, the result being lower unemployment rates. Of the 1,230 industrial and commercial licenses issued by the municipality of Nazareth in 1984, only 111 were for manufacturing enterprises, while 130 were for car repair garages, and 989 for small commercial, professional, public, and private services (Khalidi 1988, 176).[19] Upper Nazareth, on the other hand, has upward of seventy plants and work-shops, the four largest (metal, automotive, textiles, and sweets) each employing five to seven hundred persons, including some Arab Naza-renes (Rosenfeld 1988, 50).

Minority Problems

Nazarenes also experience day-to-day frustrations as a minority within a Jewish state. Because there is no mandatory conscription for Israeli Arabs, as there is for Israeli Jews and Druze, many benefits derived from military service, such as government assistance for education and housing and greater access to jobs—especially those related to defense or security—are denied to Israeli Arabs. This means, for example, that newlyweds are not eligible for subsidized housing, and that job prospects for engineers and computer scientists are very limited. As a result some Christian young men in Nazareth have started to volunteer for military service in order to gain access to these benefits.

Lack of access to higher-education opportunities is also a frustration. To meet this challenge, the Greek Catholic St. Joseph's school has developed a competitive educational program in which students graduate at a level comparable to those from Jewish schools. Emile Shufani, principal and priest, explained that a higher level of education was needed in Nazareth so that Arab students could pass college entrance exams and thus diminish their need to leave the country in order to gain a higher education. University entrance exam scores have risen, but now the challenge, as explained by Shufani, is for the government to find a way to integrate the students into the state with jobs befitting their university degrees (*JP,* International Edition, week of 26 May 1990).

Living as Muslims and Christians in a Jewish state can also have its challenges, and even lighter moments, when it comes to holidays. Independence Day passes without note in Nazareth, except for the few flags flying from government buildings. There have been, however, the obligatory observances for political and religious leaders, especially

---

[19] The industrial licenses issued included factories or shops in the following categories and amounts: metal products, thirty-nine; wood products, twenty four; paper and printing, eight; clothing and textiles, eight; chemicals, seven; food products, seven; and blocks and stone, six. The smallness of the enterprises is illustrated by the fact that almost all of these shops are staffed by ten or fewer workers (Khalidi 1988, 176).

in earlier years. For instance, in 1962 "several thousand residents of Nazareth and Arab villages in the Galilee" called on the military governor at his office in Nazareth "to extend greetings on the 14th anniversary of the State" (*JP*, 8 May 1962). On Yom Kippur, the Jewish Day of Atonement—a day in which the Jewish community comes to a halt—Arabs in Nazareth drive without guilt.

Since the Jewish and Arab communities each have their own holidays, celebrations are usually separate; however, there can be problems when holidays overlap. In 1983, the Muslim holiday of 'Id al-Adha (The Great Feast of the Sacrifice) coincided in a rare occurrence with Yom Kippur. For twenty-five years, Muslim scouts had paraded through town in celebration of their day of sacrifice, but because of the Jewish holiday, the police rejected their request (*al-Senara*, 23 September 1983). During Passover, the Nazareth branch of the Mashbir department store chain adorns its windows with Passover themes—an odd display for a Christian-Muslim town, but another of the many reminders that Nazareth is indeed part of a Jewish state. The mezuza placed on the doorpost of the main entrance to the branch of Bank Leumi during its opening ceremony is another unique example of Judaism in an Arab town (*JP*, 23 February 1958).

One enterprising Jewish-owned company has found it good business to acknowledge non-Jewish holidays. Telma food company distributes, via newspaper inserts, Ramadan calendars in which all five prayer times for each day of the month are listed. The back of the calendar includes favorite Ramadan recipes using Telma brand products.

Other problems have included bans on most theatrical productions of a political nature. In 1981, for example, a play with a central theme of Palestinian history scheduled to be performed at the municipal cultural center was canceled on the pretext that the text of the play had been altered from the text originally screened by the Film and Theater Censorship Board even though the play had previously been performed in East Jerusalem and in the West Bank (*JP*, 18 January 1981)

These common experiences of dealing with the many problems of being a minority within a Jewish state have forged the people of Nazareth not only into a local community of Nazarenes, but also into a larger community of Israeli Arabs. As citizens of Israel, the people of Nazareth have had to decide how and to what extent they choose to join in with what at times seems to be an almost nonexistent community known as Israelis, and not the more familiar Israeli Jewish or Israeli Arab communities. In some instances there have been attempts, successful and unsuccessful, to blend the two communities.

Religion has often been cited as one of the primary causes of division in the land deemed holy by Jews, Christians, and Muslims, but it has also occasionally helped to bring the differing religious groups together. The Jewish mayor of Upper Nazareth has on occasion, more so formerly than recently, attended holiday religious services and celebrations in Arab Nazareth. The Upper Nazareth municipality annually offers, via the local Arab newspaper, holiday greetings to Christians and Muslims. Government officials, mostly from the Ministry of Religion, also attend religious celebrations and dedications of new religious buildings. Because of its role as a religious center, Nazareth has attracted occasional ecumenical conferences in which representatives of Israel's religious communities gather. For example, in January 1984, Jewish, Christian, and Muslim religious leaders gathered in Nazareth at the invitation of Greek Catholic Archbishop Maximos Salum for a meeting under a slogan of "harmony and acquaintance between all mankind" (al-Anba,' 20 January 1984).

Language is perhaps one of the most common bonds. Since Hebrew has been a required subject in Arab schools since the founding of the state, the majority of Nazarenes know how to read and speak both national languages. Many of those who are too old to have learned Hebrew in school have still learned it to varying degrees out of necessity for work, travel, or shopping. Store and street signs throughout the town are written in both languages, and most residents listen to both Hebrew and Arabic television and radio as well as read newspapers in both languages.

Higher education is another link between the two peoples. Many students from Nazareth go on to attend university, the majority commuting from Nazareth to the University of Haifa, and others attending Hebrew University in Jerusalem or the University of Tel Aviv. Here they find access to and friendship with Jews, often for the first time. The intermixing of Jews and Arabs in higher education is partly the result of a government-thwarted initiative from the municipality in the early 1980s to establish an Arab university in Nazareth, to be called Galilee University. Instead of opening an Arab university, an extension office of Haifa University was built in Upper Nazareth.

Economic activities have also been a main catalyst by which the Arab and Jewish communities have mixed. Since Mandate times, the Arabs of Nazareth have had to look outward to find sufficient employment. As old patterns of employment came to a halt in 1948 when Arab and British endeavors in Haifa and elsewhere became casualties of war, new patterns emerged with Arabs working for Jews. Following the 1948 war, the Israeli government attempted to ameliorate the high rate of unemployment among the Arabs of Nazareth. Many of the Arabs, who were refugees with only farming backgrounds, were hired as unskilled workers, harvesting crops on Arab lands now controlled by the Custodian for Absentee Property and constructing army fortifications and public works projects (Kamen 1988, 93).

By 1959, one source noted that of Nazareth's 4,700 working population, 1,400 worked locally, 1,700 commuted daily to work outside town, and the rest were either on emergency work (140), unemployment (160) or not registered (1,163) (Schwarz 1959, 34). Through the years, the work projects have changed, but the pattern of Arabs working for Jews or in Jewish communities continues. According to a 1974 report from the Nazareth Labor Exchange, 47 percent of the 12,750 registered workers from Nazareth worked outside the city, 11 percent worked in Upper Nazareth, and 41 percent worked in Nazareth (Bar-Gal and Soffer 1981, 56). The deputy mayor estimated in 1986 that more than 60 percent of the wage earners in Nazareth worked outside town (*JP*, 29 July 1986). Results from the 1989 survey show that of the 197 employed men surveyed, 31 percent work in either a Jewish town (including 5 percent in Upper Nazareth and some as far away as Eilat), a kibbutz, or a mixed Jewish Arab town like Haifa; and 57 percent work in Nazareth, 6 percent in another Arab town, and 5 percent in no specific locale (mostly truck or taxi drivers). Similarly, of the sixty-eight adult children surveyed, 32 percent work in Jewish locales, while of the forty-nine working women surveyed, only 8 percent indicated working outside Nazareth in Jewish communities, half of those in Upper Nazareth. Not all Jewish Arab commercial endeavors require that Arabs commute out of town; one Nazarene works at home welding large coils of tubing for a kibbutz that manufactures solar heaters.

Nazareth's role as a regional center brings not only Arab villagers for Saturday shopping and services, but also Jews from Upper Nazareth, other towns, and kibbutzim in the region who know of Nazareth's many garages, fine produce shops, and exciting markets.[20] A physical therapist from Safad has kept her road-weary Volkswagon Beetle running through regular visits to her favorite garage in the

[20] A 1986–87 listing of commercial establishments in Nazareth indicates the diversity of the city's economic activity. It includes stores, shops, and establishments in the following categories: food-related establishments included 138 grocery, 57 cafes, 47 produce, 31 restaurants, 31 meat, 24 coffee beans, 20 wholesale food, 20 sweets, 13 fish, and 1 supermarket (Hypermarket). Retail stores included: 57 electrical goods, 56 clothing, 47 books and office supplies, 45 shoes, 30 souvenirs, 28 fabric, 22 jewelers, 21 car parts, 20 household goods, 20 furniture, 13 pharmacies, 11 watches, 8 sewing machines, 6 photo supplies, 5 flowers, 5 bicycles, and 1 department store (Mashbir). Service-related establishments included: 70 financial, tax, and accounting services, 54 barber and beauty salons, 16 banks, 10 taxi stations, 10 gas stations, 7 printers, 4 driving schools, 4 bus and travel, 3 hotels , 3 dry cleaning, and 2 cinemas. Industries included: 97 garages, 16 food, beverage, and tobacco plants, 14 lumber and carpentry shops, 10 ceramic, glass, and nonmetalic goods, 5 textile plants, 3 quarries and cement factories, and 3 leather shops (*Strategy for Economic Development* 1988, 32–34).

Garage quarter of Nazareth. While waiting, she enjoys hummous, kebab, and pita bread at a nearby restaurant. A couple from a moshav north of the Sea of Galilee comes for dental work. The Arab bus company, which services both Nazareth and Upper Nazareth, shuttles Jewish women of Upper Nazareth, with their plastic baskets and conversations in Spanish or Russian, to the markets of Nazareth for weekly shopping. A Christian yarn merchant in the suq and a Muslim produce vendor in the Khanuq switch easily from Hebrew to Arabic depending on who the shoppers are. Ahmad, the Muslim produce merchant, is the son of refugees from Saffuriya, and is therefore not very fond of the Israeli government; but when it comes to business, he is as friendly and receptive to his Jewish clientele as he is to the Arabs. Business also goes in the reverse direction. Arabs from Nazareth will go to Haifa to shop or Tiberias for weekend recreation. Upper Nazareth's better municipal facilities attract Arab youths to the swimming pool, tennis courts, and cinema. Different Sabbaths find Jews shopping in Arab Nazareth on Saturday and Arabs using the post office of Upper Nazareth on Sunday.

This intermixing took a turn for the worse during the Intifada, when most Jewish shoppers stayed out of Nazareth. An owner of a Nazareth garage noted that in the first six months of the Intifada his business declined 30 percent because Jewish customers from throughout northern Israel stopped coming, some out of fear of violence and others, who make no distinction between Israeli Arabs and Arabs from the occupied territories, for nationalist reasons (JP, 10 June 1988). One cloth merchant from the heart of Nazareth's suq lamented that the Intifada had brought a decline in sales because Jews, who make up 40 percent of his clientele, had stayed away (JP, 19 May 1989).

Nazareth's role as a destination for pilgrims and tourists from around the world has also suffered from the political instability of the region. Whenever there is war or the threat of war in the Middle East, visits to Nazareth plummet and its economy suffers. Rula Tabar indicated in an interview on 8 September 1989 that the Grand New Hotel, which her family operates, had experienced a 50 percent decrease in occupancy since the start of the Intifada. Also suffering are the other hotels, taxi drivers, and souvenir shops. According to Nazarenes, the Israeli government also serves as an impediment to tourism. Rula Tabar related how the hotels in Nazareth held a one-day strike in December 1986 in protest of the government's lack of concern for the decline in tourism in Nazareth and because of inequitable tax rates. She explained that the hotels in Tiberias pay a lower hotel tax than those in Nazareth and therefore can attract more occupants.

Stimulus to Nazareth's tourist industry and overall economy may result from citywide improvements associated with the Nazareth

2000 development plan—the first government-sponsored tourism project in Nazareth since 1948. Municipal secretary Abdallah Jubran explained some of the proposed changes to Nazareth in a 25 April 1994 interview. These include: long-awaited street signs, a tourist center, lookout points on the northeastern and northwestern summits, improved roads and sidewalks, museums, art and music festivals, development of a tourist site at the precipice—including perhaps a bell garden and amphitheater, restoration of the central market, a pedestrian mall linking two new town squares near the basilica and Mary's well, and new hotels.

These proposed changes are made possible in part by a change in government policies toward Nazareth. Nazareth has been designated a class A tourist site, which means the government will provide 30 percent financing for hotels and other tourist-related projects. Nazareth is also part of a "point development" program in which government funds will be provided to help finance the many proposed projects. According to Jubran, the sudden shift in government interest in Nazareth is partly the result of the ongoing peace process. With the possible inclusion of Christian holy sites in Bethlehem and Jerusalem in a Palestinian entity, Israel will need its own center for Christian pilgrimage. In addition, the possible return of the Golan Heights will leave tourist-friendly Tiberias on the periphery of the country. This means that tourists who once bypassed Nazareth's hotels for Tiberias may be attracted to a more central Galilee location. Nazareth 2000 has brought increased hope to Nazarenes—hopes that improvements in the tourist sector will bring more pilgrims, more revenues, more jobs, and more incentives for Nazarenes to remain in Nazareth.

The history of Nazareth and its communities does have its share of comings and goings, conflicts and strife, but it is important to remember that more often than not the disturbances have been the result of outside intervention as Christian crusaders, Muslim Mamluks, and Jewish soldiers have all battled for control of the city. The volatile nature of communal relations in the region has obviously had an influence on communal relations among Nazarenes, but for every recorded incident of contention there are many years of calm and coexistence. Far removed from ruling kingdoms, dynasties, and empires, Nazarenes have concerned themselves more with day-to-day living than with the affairs of foreign powers, and have found their identity not as Ottomans, British, or Israelis, but as Muslim and Christian Arab families of Nazareth.

3

The Christian Community
and Communities

When asked to define who they are, Nazarenes may give a dozen or more varied answers.[1] They might say that they are either Arab, Palestinian, or Israeli Arab. If pressed further they may identify themselves as either Muslim or Christian. Christians, particularly among fellow Christians, may further identify themselves by one of the many sects. Further identification comes from place or former place of residence, such as Nazareth or Saffuriya. Nazarenes might describe themselves as an Israeli Arab Maronite from Nazareth or as a Palestinian Arab Muslim from Mujeidil. Anglican Pastor Riyah Abu al-'Assal, in a 2 December 1988 fund-raising letter for a book he plans to publish on Palestinian identity, refers to himself as an "Arab-Palestinian-Christian-Protestant-Israeli priest."

Identification with these communities is usually determined by birth. Scrimgeour, in writing about a family of Nazareth who "belong, as regards to religious persuasion, to the Greek Catholic community," notes: "They are Catholics because Mousa's father and grandfather are Catholics. Had these ancestors been Moslems, Druses, or Protestants, the present family would have continued in the faith of the parents. Religious conviction rarely decides the particular creed to which a Syrian adheres" (Scrimgeour 1913, 49). Salibi offers a similar, but somewhat more contemporary view: "Religious sects, in their social behaviour, may be described as tribes in disguise. What holds a given sect together, and keeps it in existence down the generations, is instinctive group solidarity rather than reasoned religious conviction. In the modern Arab East, . . . existing Christian and Islamic sects are in fact tribes, not only in social behaviour but also by historical origin" (Salibi 1988, 15).

---

[1] A 1970 psychological study of religious affiliation and ethnic identification among eleventh-grade boys in Nazareth revealed that when asked, the Muslim boys identified first with the classification Arab, followed by Lebanese Muslim, Israeli Arab, and finally Lebanese Christian, while the Christian boys identified first with Lebanese Christian, followed by Israeli Arab, Arab, and Lebanese Muslim (Hofman and Debbiny 1970, 1014).

Identification with a community is important because it usually determines where most people will be married and later buried, where they will worship and attend school, where they live, and how they interact with those from other communities. Under Israeli law, religious communities are responsible for issuing birth, marriage, and death certificates, for granting divorces, and for settling other disputes. Consequently, Nazareth is home to Greek Orthodox, Roman Catholic, Greek Catholic, Maronite, and Muslim religious courts (Stendel 1973, 10). All must identify with a religious community, whether or not they are actually believers, to obtain civil services. This also makes conversions more difficult, because it requires dealing with the religious courts, and it makes intersectarian marriages impossible unless one of the parties consents to adopt the religion of the other, or the marriage is performed outside Israel.

The importance of community status is evidenced by the fact that all the major political parties in Nazareth make a concerted effort to include a mix of all the communities in their lists of candidates. It is important that each community feel that it is represented in the municipality, so party lists read like a shuffled roster of Nazareth's communities, with Muslims alternating between Greek Orthodox, Roman Catholics, Greek Catholics, and sometimes Copts, Maronites, or Anglicans. Also included are representatives of Nazareth's prominent families and clans, as well as representatives from the several refugee communities.

All the religious communities have increased in numbers over the years (table 4), but the most dramatic shift has been among the Muslims, who as a result of the influx of the 1948 refugees and a higher birthrate, no longer constitute the minority. Among Christians, the Greek Catholics have shown a significant growth, partly because of added refugees.

Figures representing population increases are not always accurate. The 1961 *Census of Israel* does not include any Copts living in Nazareth, even though in 1949 the community dedicated a Coptic church in its quarter. They were probably included under the category of another sect or an unknown sect listed here as "other Christian." The 1922 *Census of Palestine* also shows inaccuracies. The enumerations for the neighboring village of Ma'lul list all 250 of its Christians as Greek Orthodox even though many of its former residents who now live in Nazareth are Greek Catholic. Similar errors must also have occurred among the communities of Nazareth. Part of the problem stems from terminology and the lack of understanding of sectarian differences by the enumerators: the Greek Catholics and Greek Orthodox share the term *Rum* (Greek); the Greek Orthodox and Coptic Orthodox share the

TABLE 4. The religious communities of Nazareth by population and year

Year of census	1922	1931	1946	1961	1972	1983	1989*
Muslim	2,486	3,226	6,290	12,045	18,295	25,236	36,000–42,000
Christian (total)	4,885	5,445	9,250	12,939	14,933	16,445	24,000–28,000
Greek Orthodox	2,054			4,927			12,950–14,000
Greek Catholic	995			3,433			6,500
Roman Catholic	1,165			3,286			5,500
Maronite	200			568			1,200
Copt	31						500–600
Anglican	297			410			320
Other Christian	143			315			400–600
Other religion	53	85		43	58	42	
Total	7,424	8,756	15,540	25,027	33,286	41,723	60,000–70,000

*Estimates of community leaders

term "Orthodox," and Greek Catholics refer to themselves as Catholics, while Roman Catholics refer to themselves as Latins.

The Christians of Nazareth consider themselves a minority within a minority. As Arabs, they are a minority among the Israeli Jews and as Christians they are a minority among the Muslim Arabs. Just as minority status within the State of Israel has helped to mold a community of Israeli Palestinian Arabs, so too has being a minority within the Muslim-dominated Arab world helped to unite the many sects of the Christian Arab world into a community of Christians. Part of this unity stems from a very real concern among Christians that they must unite in order to keep from being absorbed within the larger Muslim Arab community. They are also concerned that the Christian nature of the town is being threatened by a growing Muslim population and the recent entrance of an Islamic party into local politics.

One of the reasons for these concerns lies in the fact that until recently, Christians in Nazareth were primarily the doctors, traders, and merchants, while the Muslims were the laborers and farmers. This occupational separation is gradually disappearing as more and more Muslims move into those occupations once dominated by the Christians. The Christians are worried about this trend, not because they do not want Muslims to make advances, but because it is a sign of their own weakening control and influence in the city. This has left many Christians feeling more vulnerable and in a more precarious situation.

Another real concern is demographic. Greek Orthodox Ernest Farah estimated in his monthly religious publication that the population of Nazareth had jumped from 15,000 in 1948 to an estimated 75,000 in 1988, and that the Muslim percentage of the population had increased from 34 percent to 60 percent (al-Bishara, September 1988). These concerns about surviving in an Islamic region and a Jewish state continue to forge a united Christian community.

Common beliefs and customs have also helped to establish a common bond among Christians. As Christians they all follow the teachings of Jesus, consider the Bible to be scripture, are baptized and married in a church, worship the Trinity as well as Mary,[2] and acknowledge the holy nature of Nazareth as the place where the Annunciation took place and the holy family lived. The preeminence of Christian devotion to Nazareth is symbolized by one of the Arabic words for Christian—Nasrani, a derivative of the Arabic name for Nazareth, al-Nasra (the other common word for Christian is Masihi, from the same root as the Hebrew word Messiah).

In spite of the shared name of Nasrani, differences among Christians naturally exist. Original theological divisions stem from fourth- and fifth-century disputes over the nature(s) of Christ. While these differences have persisted, the lay Christians of the many sects of the Middle East would find it difficult to explain what those differences are. Sectarian loyalty is much more a matter of tradition, of historical and political divisions, as in the case of the Greek-Latin split of 1054, and of ethnicity, as in the case of sects like the Maronites (centered in the mountains of Lebanon), Copts (Egyptian Christians), and Armenians (from eastern Anatolia).

The Roman Catholics, Greek Catholics, and Maronites all find common bonds in their allegiance to the pope in Rome, but differences arise from liturgical languages (originally Syriac for the Maronites and Latin for the Roman Catholics, but now primarily Arabic), marital status of priests (Maronite and Greek Catholic priests, like Greek Orthodox priests, can be married), and the format of the mass (while affiliated with Rome, the Greek Catholics still use the Byzantine rite of Greek Orthodoxy). As members of larger Christian communities, the Christians of Nazareth also receive varying degrees of financial and moral support from religious hierarchies and institutions.

The Christian communities all celebrate in similar ways the same holy days, such as Palm Sunday, Good Friday, Easter, Annunciation

---

[2] This adoration for Mary is manifest not only in the statues, icons, and pictures of Mary which adorn almost every Christian home in Nazareth, but also by the evening services held each day during the month of May at both the lower level of the Basilica of the Annunciation, and at the Shrine of the Virgin, located in the heart of the Greek Catholic-sponsored housing project called Shekun al-Arab, and by the Feast of Mary (Assumption) celebration, held in mid-August. For this feast, Christians from throughout the town gather in the Shekun al-Arab quarter for the festivities.

Day, and Christmas. Palm Sunday finds each community celebrating with palm branch processions and festive gatherings inside and out of the churches. Adults wear their finest new clothes; children are dressed as angels, priests, and little Marys.[3] All communities share similar holiday treats and decorations. Intermarriages have joined couples from differing communities, so families will often participate in several community celebrations, those of the wife's former sect and those of the couple's present sect.

The difference in calendars between Eastern (Greek Orthodox and Coptic) and Western (Roman Catholic, Greek Catholic, Maronite, and Protestant) churches means there are always two Christmas celebrations in Nazareth and usually two Easter and Palm Sunday celebrations. Since these holidays are not on competing days, Greek Orthodox celebrations are attended not only by Greek Orthodox families, and Latin festivities by Roman Catholics, but also by former community members and youths from other sects who, given the absence of many other forums for meeting or associating with members of the opposite sex, enjoy attending several of the celebrations.

Most Christians also participate in adorning their homes, inside and out, with religious markings. Of the 139 Christian homes surveyed, 96 percent had such markings. Of those homes, 120 have at least one religious decoration inside, 11 have decorations inside and out, and 2 homes have only statues of Mary on the outside. Many of the homes display several religious items. Mary was the most popular item, with 73 percent of the Christian homes surveyed having a statue of Mary inside, 70 percent having a picture of Mary inside, and 7 percent having a statue of Mary outside the home. Other popular items include crosses, pictures of Jesus, and pictures of St. George. Other less common items included a picture of the Last Supper, and pictures of several different saints, including a patron saint (Tanous) of the Maronites, whose picture was found in three homes, Maronite, Roman Catholic, and Greek Catholic.

This outward display of Christianity is practiced by all segments of the community, even those who care little for religious practice. For example, 83 percent of the twelve homes in which the wife never at-

---

[3] Holidays and Sundays have always been days for dressing up. Nowadays during feast days the churches are the place to show off, but an account from the nineteenth century describes how on Sunday mornings at Mary's well the women would gather for water and visiting "in their best attire" because "the well is the place for its exhibition" (Ashworth 1869, 182). In 1913 Scrimgeour wrote: "New clothes are obtained once a year, and are donned for the first time on Easter day, an occasion when the poorest Christian Nazarene strives to possess at least one new garment. The crowd of women and girls coming out of church on an important feast day is a brilliant scene" (Scrimgeour 1913, 51).

tends church or attends only for baptisms and weddings have a statue of Mary. This is similar to the 83 percent of the twenty-three homes in which the wife attends church weekly or at least several times a month that have a statue of Mary inside. One of the surveyors noted that when she asked about religious items in the homes, all, including those who were not religious, were proud to show their icons and statues.

For nonpracticing or seldom practicing Christians to display religious items openly in their homes may seem unusual, but for Nazarenes it is perfectly acceptable, because the great majority of them claim to be believers, even if their actions do not always suggest it. As a means of ascertaining religiosity among Christians, survey respondents were asked how often they attend church (table 5). Of the 258 respondents, only 10 percent indicated that they never attend church. Of those who do attend, 56 percent indicated that they attend only for holidays, weddings, or baptisms; and women attend more regularly than do men. Among sects, the Greek Orthodox attend least frequently and the Roman Catholics most frequently. Still, most of those who seldom or never attend respect religion, have a basic belief at their core, as demonstrated by their display of religious items, their attendance at church on holidays, their identification with a Christian community, and through such actions as one exhibited by a Greek Orthodox women, who attends church only on holidays, but regularly crosses herself as she drives by her community church and has her home decorated with a fluorescent green statue of Mary, a large picture of the Last Supper, and a painting of St. George.

There are many possible reasons for the lack of regular church attendance. Zahi Nasser, assistant pastor of the Anglican Church, sug-

TABLE 5. Percentage frequency of church attendance by gender and sect

Sect: (N):	Men				Women			
	All (121)	G.O. (44)	G.C. (34)	R.C. (34)	All (137)	G.O. (48)	G.C. (41)	R.C. (37)
Weekly	10	2	12	15	19	6	22	24
Several times/ month	5	4	9	3	10	6	12	11
Several times/year	12	11	9	17	13	12	15	14
Holidays only	53	50	59	53	40	44	42	38
Baptisms and marriages only	10	16	6	9	12	21	7	8
Never	8	16	6	3	7	10	2	5

gested in a 22 May 1989 interview that the decline in practice and belief among Nazareth's Christians is caused by: (1) a laxness in the people who, because of relative financial security, feel that they do not need the church; (2) the necessity for working on Sundays, for many who must work outside Nazareth in the Jewish sector; (3) negligence of community leaders who "are not true shepherds," in that they do not offer Sunday school classes or other religious training; and (4) the political situation associated with the Arab-Israeli conflict which has resulted in Arabs no longer having a strong trust in God. In reference to the half that attend only for special occasions, Father Arturo Vasaturo, a Roman Catholic parish priest, explained in a 13 July 1989 interview that they still have an "outstanding faith," which means "they believe in their hearts," but attend only on holidays. He suggested that many do not attend because of "the difficulties associated with being a Christian in the Middle East."[4]

Christians from Nazareth also participate in pilgrimages, but not to the same extent as Muslims. The most frequented site of pilgrimage is nearby Mount Tabor, a mountain "set apart" in the Jezreel valley and the traditional site of the Transfiguration. In earlier times, during the August Feast of the Transfiguration, "most of the Christians living in and around Nazareth used to go up to Mount Tabor, a two-hour walk from the village. The pilgrimage was the occasion for great rejoicing: the people were in the habit of drinking and dancing on the mountain" (Carrouges 1956, 130). Of the Christians surveyed, 79 percent indicated that they had gone to Tabor for religious reasons—a baptism, the Feast of the Transfiguration, or both.

Bethlehem and Jerusalem are also pilgrimage destinations, but not to the same degree; 37 percent of Christian respondents indicated that they had visited Bethlehem and 25 percent had visited Jerusalem for religious reasons. The inaccessibility to these two holy sites for Israeli Arabs from 1948 to 1967 provided an additional reason to make the pilgrimage during those years; it was one of the only ways to gain permission to travel into Jordan. Each year a specific number of Christian pilgrims were allowed to cross over into Jordan to visit Bethlehem at Christmas and Jerusalem at Easter.[5] Once over the border into Jor-

---

[4] Scrimgeour made a similar comment about Ottoman times. He described how matters such as taxation, conscription, the Turkish systems of government, and "the deadening effects of Islam" have "handicapped the enthusiastic adoption of the faith" and caused the Christian communities of Nazareth to have "church-going observance of fasts and feasts, and other outward symbols of loyal attachment," while in actuality possessing a "passive respectability rather than active virtue" (Scrimgeour 1913, 64).

[5] In 1960, for example, 2,500 Israeli Catholics crossed through the Mandelbaum gate into the West Bank for a two-day Christmas stay in Bethlehem, and two weeks

dan, Israeli Arabs took advantage of the opportunity and used the few days not only to visit holy sites, but also to travel about and visit relatives, both refugee and others.

Nazareth is also a destination for countless pilgrims every year. Each day, pilgrims and tourists visit the Latin Basilica of the Annunciation and the adjacent Church of St. Joseph. Individuals or groups with more time then visit the Greek Catholic synagogue church and the Greek Orthodox Church of the Annunciation, while the more adventuresome will wander into the maze of the market, try some local sweets, or arrange to visit the excavations under the convent of the Sisters of Nazareth. Much to the frustration of local hotel proprietors and food and souvenir vendors, most tourist groups stay only a few hours and then hurry on to visit other sites in the Galilee such as neighboring Kanna, Mount Tabor, or Tiberias and the Sea of Galilee.

The international nature of tourism in Nazareth can be observed in front of the Basilica of the Annunciation, where souvenir hawkers adroitly guess the nationality of each group and offer greetings and sales pitches in the appropriate language, whether it be English, Spanish, German, French, Italian, or Hebrew. The Feast of the Annunciation celebration at the Greek Orthodox Church in 1989 included dozens of pilgrims from Greece, Cyprus, and Romania (al-Senara, 14 April 1989).

From 1948 to 1967, Nazareth served as the showpiece of the travel promotions Israel directed toward Christian pilgrims. Even before the Basilica of the Annunciation was completed in 1969, its inverted cone-shaped dome adorned Israel travel posters, which encouraged Christians to visit Israel's half of the Holy Land. In order to accommodate these pilgrims, many of whom descended on the city at Christmastime, Nazareth started to organize special Christmas week activities, complete with a Christmas Eve ecumenical reception held at Cinema Diana, a scout parade, special stamps and postmarks for Christmas mail, and Christmas Eve services in the Western Rite Churches. In 1967, Nazareth's preeminence as the holiest Christian site in Israel was surpassed when the occupation of the West Bank brought Bethlehem and the old city of Jerusalem under Israeli control. With Bethlehem now easily accessible to Christmas pilgrims, Nazareth's weeklong celebrations, which had been attended by upward of 25,000 people, almost came to a halt.

To attract more pilgrims and secular tourists to Nazareth, the municipality has considered various proposals for improving tourist

---

later, 1,500 Israeli Greek Orthodox made the journey for their Christmas celebration. That same year Nazareth expected over 1,000 foreign pilgrims to celebrate Christmas in their town (JP, 19 December 1960).

sites and facilities. The most recent (1994) and most comprehensive of the plans is the Nazareth 2000 project. In 1993 the municipality, under the recommendation of a UNESCO advisor on municipal restoration, began developing plans to restore historic structures in the central city (*JP*, International Edition, 9 January 1993). This is in sharp contrast to 1965, when the municipality seriously considered a multimillion dollar scheme proposed by an American doctor to raze the old houses of the central market area in order to create a landscaped area where pilgrims could walk barefooted while viewing the sites (*JP*, 2 March 1965).

The lament over the decline of Nazareth's importance as a destination for Christmas pilgrims is only one of many concerns facing the Christian community. Other concerns include declining church attendance, emigration, insufficient resources, domination by foreign clergy, intersectarian squabbles, and declining power at the expense of the Muslim community. One of the strongest proponents for preserving and strengthening the Christian community is a former leader of the Greek Orthodox community who describes the decline as the result of several causes, including neglect from the foreign-dominated clergy and hierarchy who do not care about the local Christians; isolation caused by a lack of connections with Christians of the outside world; the increased power of Muslims through political, educational, numerical, and economic advancement; and the fear of local Christians that any actions they might take to promote the Christian community will be interpreted by their Muslim brothers as divisive to the unity of the larger Arab community.

Feeling very strongly that Nazareth needs to remain a Christian town, which means it must maintain a Christian presence, this leader suggests that Christians develop their own infrastructure (partly because he sees Mayor Ziyad as being more interested in establishing a state of Palestine than in helping his own city). Such an infrastructure would promote visits by more pilgrims, attract more Christian institutions (which might prefer a less politicized Nazareth to a very politicized Jerusalem), and encourage Christians to remain in Nazareth by providing more housing and job opportunities. Specifically, he suggests a new Christian quarter, new Christian schools, a Christian pilgrim center, and activities such as a week-long celebration for the Feast of the Annunciation and a Christian music festival. He hopes that the international church will step in and help by establishing and strengthening new institutions and making Nazareth a Christian center. He notes that when the Franciscans first arrived, they built a church, then a school. These institutions provided employment and education, and the Christian presence flourished. He said his proposals of a new school or Christian quarter would not antagonize Muslims, and suggested that they too would benefit from increased tourism, from which they are "already making good money."

While some want to increase the Christian presence in Nazareth, others feel that the churches already have too much power, specifically when it comes to land. According to most reports, up to one-third of Nazareth's land is owned by its many churches and their institutions. This land, like that of mosques, synagogues, and charitable institutions, is tax exempt, as established under Ottoman rule and perpetuated under British and Israeli rule. This presents a problem in a city that has always been plagued with insufficient funds and a lack of municipal services. At several different times during the 1950s and 1960s, there were proposals to start taxing churches, or at least have them pay for services such as garbage collection and help in the financing of footpaths, roads, and drainage in and near the church lands, in order to rescue a floundering municipal budget (*JP*, 7, 28 November 1968). One of the earliest proposals to tax the churches was supported by Greek Orthodox councilman Yacub Farah, but Muslim Councilman Majid Fahum rejected the tax proposal, noting that the Christian institutions bring "great benefits to the town" and "take a great load off the shoulders of any council" (*JP*, 18 March 1954). Later proposals also met with opposition, especially from the churches. In a 1966 letter to the editor, Greek Catholic Archbishop George Hakim wrote:

> It is true schools are not paying "for services, like garbage collection," and it is true that such a fee would count for less than one-tenth of one per cent of the school's budget. . . . But would we not expect the municipality to appreciate the work done for it for hundreds of students and exempt the school of this tax and offer other grants to help us improve the standard of our schools? It is time Nazareth churches cease to be used as a scapegoats for all the Municipality's troubles, clearly indicated in your reporter's article, such as "arrears in tax collections, waste, nepotism and lack of initiative." It is also time the government did its duty toward Nazareth, the neglected Arab city of the Galilee, which is one of the biggest tourist and pilgrim attractions in the country. If tourism is yielding $60–$70m. a year, could we not expect part of this amount to be used in the improvement of this Holy City whose churches and holy places attract the biggest number of pilgrims? (*JP*, 10 November 1966)

Complaints are still heard. A 16 May 1989 evening visit with young men with nothing to do but hang out on a street corner in their neighborhood near the Carmelite convent revealed their contempt for the many Christian institutions. These Maronite, Roman Catholic, and Greek Catholic young men, some of them unemployed, complained, while pointing to the high walls of the convent, that the churches own plenty of vacant land. They suggested that part of that land be used to build neighborhood clubs, which would give youth like them something to do. Others, however, point to the fact that the only remaining vacant land and patches of green in Nazareth are church properties, and building on the land would only add to the congestion and overcrowding in the city.

The Christian community as a whole shares many similarities and faces many of the same challenges, and while there is a general feeling of unity among the community, there still exist differences among its various sectarian segments.

The Greek Orthodox Community

The largest of the Christian communities is the Greek Orthodox. Locally, the Greek Orthodox refer to themselves as Rum Orthodox *(orthodhoksia)*, Orthodox or, more commonly, just plain "Rum" (pronounced like "room"). The use of the word "Rum" hearkens back to the community's Byzantine roots, and hence their claim to being the original Christians in the land. Rum, a derivative of "Rome," is the Arabic term used for Romans, Byzantines, and adherents of the Greek Orthodox Church. Anything to do with Greek Orthodoxy is identified officially with the term "Orthodox," as in Orthodox Church or the Orthodox council, and colloquially with "Rum," as in Rum Church, Rum community center, Rum quarter, Rum cemetery, and Rum scout troop.

The community and its quarter center on the Greek Orthodox Church of the Annunciation *(Bishara)*, or Church of St. Gabriel. The church is at the foot of the hills at the northern end of the town's basin (fig. 11). In Nazareth's smaller days, this location was beyond the inhabited portion of the village. The church was built at the site of the only constant source of water for the village. This spring, which nows bears the name of Mary, is where millennia of Nazareth's women have gone daily for water and where, according to Greek Orthodox belief, the Angel Gabriel made his first annunciatory visit to Mary. According to the Apocryphal Book of James, or the Protevangelium, Mary took a "pitcher and went forth to fill it with water." There she heard a voice saying, "Hail, thou art highly favored; the Lord is with thee: blessed art thou among women." Mary then "looked about . . . to see whence this voice should be: and being filled with trembling she went to her house and set down the pitcher." There the Angel of the Lord stood before her and told her that she would conceive and bear "the son of the highest," whom she was to name Jesus (James 1924, 43).

In commemoration of the annunciation at the spring, various churches have been built over the site. The first church to be built was probably in the later Byzantine period. A second church, round in structure, was built during the Crusades period (Murphy-O'Conner

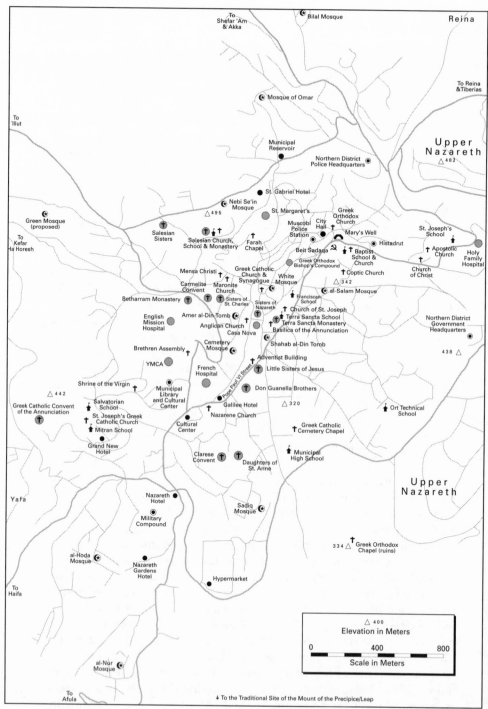

To
Shefar 'Am
& Akka

Bilal Mosque

Reina

To Reina
&Tiberias

Mosque of Omar

To
'Illut

Municipal
Reservoir

Northern District
Police Headquarters

Upper
Nazareth
△482

St. Gabriel Hotel

Nebi Se'in
Mosque
△495

St. Margaret's

Greek
Orthodox
Church

Green Mosque
(proposed)

Muscobi
Police
Station

City
Hall

Mary's Well

St. Joseph's
School

To
Kefar
Ha Horesh

Salesian
Sisters

Salesian Church,
School & Monastery

Farah
Chapel

Beit Sadaqa

Histadrut

Baptist
School &
Church

Apostolic
Church

Holy
Family
Hospital

Greek Orthodox
Bishop's Compound

Coptic Church

Church
of Christ

Mensa Christi

Greek Catholic
Church &
Synagogue

White
Mosque

△342

Carmelite
Convent

Maronite
Church

al-Salam Mosque

Betharram Monastery

Sisters of
St. Charles

Sisters of
Nazareth

Franciscan
School

English
Mission
Hospital

Amer al-Din Tomb

Church of St. Joseph

Terra Sancta School

Northern District
Government
Headquarters

438 △

Anglican Church

Casa Nova

Terra Sancta Monastery

Basilica of the Annunciation

Brethren Assembly

Cemetery
Mosque

Shahab al-Din Tomb

YMCA

French
Hospital

Adventist Building

Little Sisters of Jesus

Shrine of the Virgin

△442

Municipal
Library
and Cultural
Center

Don Guanella Brothers

△320

Greek Catholic Convent
of the Annunciation

Salvatorian
School

Galilee Hotel

Nazarene Church

Ort Technical
School

St. Joseph's Greek
Catholic Church

Mitran School

Cultural
Center

Greek Catholic
Cemetery Chapel

Grand New
Hotel

Clarese
Convent

Daughters of
St. Anne

Municipal
High School

Upper
Nazareth

Yafa

Nazareth
Hotel

Sadiq
Mosque

Military
Compound

334 △

Greek Orthodox
Chapel (ruins)

al-Hoda
Mosque

Nazareth
Gardens
Hotel

Hypermarket

To
Haifa

△400
Elevation in Meters

0   400   800

Scale in Meters

al-Nur
Mosque

To
Afula

↓ To the Traditional Site of the Mount of the Precipice/Leap

Fig. 11. Places of interest in Nazareth

1986, 313). According to a history of the church published by the Greek Orthodox Council in its Easter 1989 booklet, this church was reconstructed over the ruins of the first church between 1109 and 1113 by members of the Greek Orthodox sect, and it remained in use until 1263, when it was destroyed by the forces of Baibars. Franciscan monks built a third church, actually a small chapel, from 1628 to 1631, with the intent of it becoming Roman Catholic (al-Fusuh al-Majid, 1989). According to a 27 August 1989 interview with Fu'ad Farah, the very fact that the Franciscans built a chapel at the site of Mary's well seems to indicate that they too believe that the well is the site of the first Annunciation.

Following the return of the Franciscans in 1620, Greek Orthodox families began moving to Nazareth. This growing Orthodox community asked the Franciscans if they could use the church at the well. The Franciscans agreed, but later rescinded the agreement because of a growing schism between the Roman Catholic–backed Greek Catholics and the Greek Orthodox. Without access to a church, the Orthodox community appealed their case to Dahir al-Umar, the ruler of the region, who, under the urging of the patriarch in Akka, turned over the keys to representatives of the Greek Orthodox community in 1741. During the subsequent fifteen years, the Orthodox constructed a larger church alongside the smaller chapel. At the time, the Orthodox community numbered two to three hundred, so the community built a church large enough to hold them all.

This centuries-old church includes an even older crypt which runs perpendicular to the main chapel. This crypt served as the original chapel and has wall tiles dating back to the crusader church. Here pilgrims and parishioners can lower a tin cup down into the flowing water of Mary's spring and bring it back up for a drink. This water originates from three springs farther up the hill and is channeled into the church to where the Orthodox community believes the original village well was located. With the building of the several churches at the site, the water was eventually channeled fifty yards beyond the church to make it more accessible to villagers.

The structure built over the terminus of the water supply has a distinct shape, resembling five sides of an octagon standing on end. Several decades ago, the municipality, which owns Mary's well and uses its image on the municipal logo, tore down the centuries-old structure and replaced it with a larger limestone structure in the same five-sided shape. Fu'ad Farah noted that the Orthodox community supported replacing the structure, because then pilgrims and tourists could note that because of its newness it was not a traditional site. Farah took action to further ensure that pilgrims visited the correct site by personally cutting the pipes leading down to Mary's well. Hygiene was also a factor in redirecting the flow. The pipes were not under anyone's control, and the cleanliness of the water could not be controlled as it now can within the church. Today Mary's well runs dry, and pilgrims must descend into the grotto of the Orthodox Church if they want to drink the holy water. Excess water from the spring is diverted into the municipal water supply.

A scandal in 1994 revealed that the water for the church well was actually connected to the Israeli water grid and not to the original springs. According to a 24 April 1994 interview with Fu'ad Farah, the council made the change about five years ago with the belief that once the water entered the church it still became holy water. Members of the community attacked the executive committee of the council for lying about the source of the water and have petitioned that water from the springs once again flow into the church.

In the 1970s this church at the well was refurbished. Part of the process was supported by the Romanian Orthodox Church, which sent two brothers to paint the walls and ceilings with images of holy men and women on a sky-blue background. The Greek Orthodox community has long since outgrown this church. The chapel is large enough to hold the Sunday faithful, but for feast days and larger weddings, people overflow into the large courtyard, with its surrounding stone wall and towerlike entrance. For Palm Sunday, Good Friday, Easter, and Annunciation days, the roundabout in front of the church as well as the streets surrounding the church block are crowded with worshipers and revelers who come to watch the procession of clergy and scouts (figs. 12, 13).

There have been a few unsuccessful attempts over the past few years to remedy the problem of overcrowding in the church. Several years ago, an older woman donated to the community 3 dunams of land in the Khanuq quarter with the stipulation that the land be used only for the construction of a new church, but the ongoing feud between the Greek clergy and Arab council has prevented the implementation of the plan. Fu'ad Farah explained that when Father Sim'an drew up the agreement he failed to heed the warnings of Farah and had the deed signed over to the Greek Orthodox Church rather than to the Greek Orthodox Community Council. As a result, the council lost the right to the land in a court case. Thus if a church is ever built on the land it will come under the control of the metropolitan and patriarch.

Other obstacles to the building of a new church include objections within the Orthodox community that a second church would divide the parish into two, and, at least according to some, greater interest in building youth clubs than a new church. There has also been a suggestion that Orthodox services be held in the Shekun al-Arab quarter,

Fig. 12. Greek Orthodox Church (left center) and quarter during Palm Sunday procession

Fig. 13. Bagpipe band of the Greek Orthodox scouts during Palm Sunday procession

where about a hundred Orthodox families live. Father Barnaba said in a 23 August 1989 interview that the plan involves renting a house and making it fit for worship, but that it will just have to remain a plan for the time being, because of a shortage of priests in Nazareth to conduct the services.

In addition to the church, the Orthodox community owns a variety of buildings and lands. Located on the same block as the church are two buildings which compose the Greek Orthodox community center known as *nadi* (club) Rum. The older and smaller building to the northeast of the church houses a kindergarten and a seniors club, while the newer three-story building towering on the west side of the church contains youth and women's clubs, Sunday school classrooms, recreational and sports facilities, and a large banquet hall on the top floor which is leased by the Shebun brothers, who rent it out for catered weddings and other parties. The playground of the nadi is used free of charge during the week by the children of the nearby Middle School B. The east side of the church block includes a row of shops which are waqfs of the church.[6] The two newest buildings in the complex surrounding the church include a building for scouts to the northeast across the street and a hall crowding in against the eastern end of the church which is used for community gatherings such as funerals. Located on the block to the west of the church is the Greek Orthodox cemetery.

Southwest of the church are two blocks of waqf land where the Orthodox council, with the financial support of investors, has built several multistoried buildings which house a variety of establishments, including restaurants, bakeries, stores, newspaper offices, beauty salons, and law offices. Orthodox council head Adib Hazan noted in a 4 August 1989 interview that the investors get almost all of the rent during the first ten years, after which time the waqf gets full rent. The council regulates what kinds of businesses can rent the offices. One renter turned his three offices into a gambling restaurant. When the council found out about it, it revoked the contract, returned the deposit, then rented the offices to the government for a health clinic. Some of the renters are Muslims or members of other Christian sects, but most are Greek Orthodox, primarily because they prefer to rent offices and shops close to their homes in the Rum quarter. One waqf building in the vicinity of the church is rented to the municipality for use as new municipal offices. Waqf properties also include homes scat-

---

[6] A waqf is a Muslim institution of property donated to the community for religious and charitable purpose. It is not limited to Islam, however. Islamic law entitles other religious communities to create religious endowments, and Jewish and Christian communities in the Islamic world have adopted the practice (Tsimhoni 1984b, 174).

tered throughout the Rum quarter and several shops in the suq, where one street is known as suq al-Rum because of the Orthodox waqfs located there. These waqf lands have been donated to the church and are administered by the council. None of the land, houses, or offices can be sold, so they are rented. Revenue generated from these waqfs is used for all nonreligious needs of the Orthodox community, including the building, remodeling, and maintenance of the church, cemetery, waqf buildings, and nadi complex; salaries and benefits for the priests (as opposed to other Orthodox parishes where the priest's salary comes from donations); and the running of the several clubs and scout organization. Several of the waqf properties are assigned to the Greek Orthodox Charitable Society, whose volunteer members use the revenues to help the poor of the community. According to Hazan, there have been few donations to the waqf in recent years, besides the land for a new church.

In addition to these lands which are owned by the local Orthodox community and administered by their council, the Greek Orthodox patriarch also owns land in Nazareth. Halfway between the church and the central suq is a walled complex that contains the office, living quarters, and chapel of the Orthodox metropolitan (or in former times, a bishop) of Nazareth. At one time nuns, deacons, and monks also lived here and assisted the bishop, but now the metropolitan lives alone. South of town, rising out of the flat plain of the Garage quarter, is a hill known as *Qasir* (castle or palace) Mitran (patriarch), which is also owned by the patriarchate and is crowned by the ruins of a small Orthodox chapel. Hazan explained that the council had proposed that the chapel be repaired and the lands be used for some combination of a new school, neighborhood (either Greek Orthodox or public), shopping center, bus terminal, and expanded industrial zone, but nothing concrete has been decided. Part of these lands were expropriated from the patriarchate by the municipality for the construction of the municipal high school.

In 1983, a committee made up of members from the Ministry of the Interior recommended that this land belonging to the patriarchate be expropriated and joined to Upper Nazareth. Since three of the five-member committee had convened without the presence of its sole Arab member and without one other Jewish member, the Nazareth municipality was able successfully to protest to the high court of Israel the proposed expropriation on the grounds that the committee had met illegally. According to a 17 March 1983 municipal leaflet, part of the expropriated land was to have been used to build a new main road connecting Upper Nazareth with the Jezreel valley and in so doing bypass Arab neighborhoods and congestion on the narrow, winding road which now descends into the valley.

Unlike most of the other Christian communities, the Greek Orthodox community does not currently operate any schools. However, Tobler's 1868 map of Nazareth shows a school located in the bishop's compound, presumably for boys. In 1876, the Greek Orthodox bishop also started a school for girls in Nazareth. This school was established partly as a rival to a girls' orphanage founded in 1874 by the English "Ladies' Society for Promoting Female Education in the East," in conjunction with the Anglican Church in Nazareth. Perhaps because most of the boarders at the school were Greek Orthodox, the bishop felt it better that the girls be educated in their own religious tradition rather than learn from Protestants, who taught "the elements of domestic and social education, Bible history, and Christian hymns" in hopes that the young women would then influence "their future husbands and children, and indirectly prepare the way for evangelical Christianity" (Schaff 1977, 327).

Early education for the Orthodox community was also provided by the Russian Society of Palestine, which, during the second half of the nineteenth century, built a large complex called *Muscobi* near the Greek Orthodox Church. This complex housed boys' and girls' schools, a dispensary, a hospital, and a hospice for pilgrims (Hoade 1984, 702). Its services ceased during World War I and since then it has been used by the British and Israeli governments for offices. It now houses the police and post office.

Since the closing of the Russian schools, the Orthodox community has operated an elementary school, but according to Hazan, it was shut down because elementary schools are expensive to run, and the community members did not want to use waqf money to support a school. The community would still like to run a secondary school, which would be eligible for financial support from the government; for without a school of their own, Orthodox children are scattered among the other Christian schools as well as the public schools, where they represent the dominant Christian sect among the large Muslim majority (table 15). There has been talk of setting up a joint school with the Anglicans at St. Margaret's, former home of the Anglican orphanage, but nothing has ever materialized, and now the Anglicans are planning to use the complex for their own needs.

The body organized to administer the needs of the community is the Greek Orthodox Council. The council was first organized in 1949 after the ceasefire lines of the 1948 war left the Nazareth community separated from the patriarch in East Jerusalem and for the first time it had to take care of all the needs of the church and its community. The Orthodox community in Haifa responded to the crisis by organizing a council and adopting a constitution which the Nazareth community then used as a model. The nine-member council is elected by a thirty-five member committee, who are elected by the adults of the parish. According to Hazan, in the June 1988 election about 4,000 of the 5,000 eligible voters voted. In addition to paying the salaries of the priests, administering the waqf properties, running the nadi, clubs, and boy scouts, and maintaining the physical facilities of the church, the council also is in charge of registering baptisms, weddings, and deaths—a task originally performed by the priests. Hazan described the council in a 25 August 1989 interview as the "second largest organization providing services to Nazareth after the municipality."

The Greek Orthodox community finds unity through its religious and community functions which are centered in its church, council, and clubs and through communal clustering in the Rum quarter surrounding the church. Baptisms, weddings, funerals, religious holidays, Sunday and daily mass, and the clubs all serve to unite the community, and while not all Orthodox live in the quarter, most have friends or relatives who do, and this helps to perpetuate a central gathering place for the Orthodox and to maintain community ties and cohesiveness. Still, of all the Christian communities in Nazareth, the Orthodox community has found itself the most divided in what has evolved into a mess of interrelated disputes concerning ethnicity, religiosity, and politics.

The longest lasting of these disputes is an issue not only for the Orthodox of Nazareth, but for all Orthodox Arabs: they all resent the continued dominance of Greek clergy in their churches. The congregation and parish priests of Nazareth are local Arabs, but the local metropolitan is Greek, as is the patriarch in Jerusalem. This frustrates the Christian Arabs, who feel that they lack representation within the hierarchy of the church. This frustration with Greek dominance fostered a movement in the 1920s which, among other things, called for greater Arab participation within Greek Orthodoxy. One of the events that lead to the birth of this Arab movement within the Orthodox Church was the appointment, against the wishes of the local Arab Orthodox community, of a metropolitan in Nazareth who could not speak Arabic (Porath 1974, 297). The movement also sought the installation of an autocephalous Arab patriarch, or some form of a joint patriarchate, in which an Arab and a Greek share the position. But according to one prominent member of the Nazareth Orthodox community, the effort was about to succeed when war and the flight of many of the Greek Orthodox Arabs in 1948 brought the movement to a halt. He said that any attempts since then to establish an Arab hierarchy have been thwarted by the Israeli government, which finds it easier to deal with Greek than Arab leaders.

An incident in 1954 reveals the intense feelings resulting from the split. After years of Greek-Arab strife, a group from the Orthodox community of Nazareth decided they wanted to make a conciliatory gesture to the shunned Greek hierarchy. One hundred fifty heads of Orthodox households submitted a petition requesting that Archimandrite (later Metropolitan) Isidoros, who is Greek, be elevated to the position of archbishop. The Communist faction, and certain others in the Orthodox community, opposed the proposal and went so far as to suggest that the Nazareth community be brought under the control of the Russian Orthodox patriarchate in Antioch rather than remain under the control of the Greek Orthodox patriarch in the Old City of Jerusalem. When an Arab priest mentioned the Greek patriarch in Sunday prayers at church, a number of the anti-Greek element left the church in protest (*JP*, 15 January 1954).

This division along ethnic lines is heightened by the fact that neither the patriarch and the metropolitan, the patriarch and the parish, nor the metropolitan and the parish have good working relationships. It is true that on feast days they cooperate and parade together, but when it comes to taking action for the community, the lack of cooperation among the three different ecclesiastical levels hinders efforts.

The ineffective relationship between Metropolitan Isidoros, who died in 1992, and the parish led some members of the community to refer to him as a puppet of the local council; others confessed that he was a "very weak person" who did little for the community. A former council chairman related in a 27 August 1989 interview that the council resents the involvement of religious leaders, from Arab priests up to the Greek patriarch, in the affairs of the council and said that they should stick to religious matters and not interfere in the business of the council.

This rift is exacerbated by desires from both Greek and Arab church leaders to wield control of properties. When Dahir al-Umar granted control of the church near Mary's well to the Orthodox, he granted it to the local community and not to the patriarch in Jerusalem. Several years ago, the patriarch set out to survey all patriarch lands in Israel, at which time it was discovered that in Nazareth all that he controlled was the bishop's complex and the hill of Qasar Mitran south of town and not the Church of the Annunciation or waqfs, which are controlled by the local council (not the local church). According to Hazan, the patriarch wanted control so that he would receive the revenues generated from the church and its properties and so he could dictate the affairs of the church on such matters as appointment of new priests. He threatened to take the issue to court, saying that he had documents to prove ownership, but no documents were ever produced, and the Nazareth church remains an anomaly because it is locally controlled, having never been registered with the patriarch. Since the church falls outside of the control of the patriarch, local jurisdiction remains in the hands of the Orthodox council, but the patriarch still tries to exert control over the local affairs of the church.

Fu'ad Farah told how the metropolitan had once asked for a copy of the church keys, but he and the council had denied the request. Farah said he told the metropolitan that he would fetch the keys from the caretaker anytime they were needed by the metropolitan. Prior to this event, the patriarch had informed the council that he would announce during a Feast of the Annunciation reception and banquet that he was going to contribute U.S.$5,000 toward the construction of the nadi and that he would send two young men from the Nazareth community to study theology in Greece. However, when the patriarch heard that the council would not give the keys to the metropolitan, he rescinded the offer.

Problems at the parish level also beset the Greek Orthodox Arabs of Nazareth, because the community is in conflict over what some perceive as an attempt by the Communist party to control the council, and thereby the community. The problem dates back to the days when the Russian Orthodox Church, as protectorate of the Greek Orthodox Arab Church, established schools throughout Palestine. The schools in the imposing Muscobi building created an educated generation of Greek Orthodox who were at the vanguard of the Arab nationalist movements, who found favor during the Mandate as skilled employees, and who have been the stalwarts of the Communist movement since its early days, increasing its membership since the establishment of the State of Israel. One reporter estimated that in 1950, 90 percent of Communists in Nazareth were Greek Orthodox. The influence of the party on the church was made manifest when, on June 25 of that year, a special service was held in the Orthodox Church in support of a Communist peace petition. In reference to the Greek-Arab split, the reporter also noted that a local Arab priest chosen by a committee of Arab elders officiated at the service and not the Greek archimandrite of Nazareth (*JP*, 12 July 1950).

Communist dominance of the Greek Orthodox community became a clear reality in the early 1960s. Until that time, Khalil Khouri, secretary of the Israel-USSR society in Nazareth, had been the only Communist on the community council. When the council decided to hold elections in April 1961, seven hundred of the nine hundred registered Orthodox participated in the election (with an estimated six hundred more Orthodox not registering) and, partly owing to the involvement of Khouri, they elected twenty-two supporters of the Communist party to the thirty-five-member council. On the nine-member executive committee, two members were Communist, and two others were affiliated with the party through family ties. Eight months later, the council elected Sim'an Nasser as the officiating priest of the community. Nasser's brother had been secretary of the Communist party in Palestine and at the time was leader of the Communist party in Jordan. While no mention is made of Nasser himself being Communist, his sympathies, if not loyalties, to the party made him an acceptable choice.

Nasser was a respected and well-liked bookseller in town, but was not known for his religiosity. A reporter noted that "his apprenticeship in how to conduct a religious service was received mainly after he became vicar." Many in the community objected to Nasser's appointment, noting that he did not always wear the traditional garb of a priest, and that he refused to grow a beard and leave his hair uncut, as is the tradition for Greek Orthodox clergy. In spite of the protest by some members of the community, Metropolitan Isidoros, who had ordained the priest, issued a statement in which he asserted that the council represented "the whole Orthodox community in Nazareth" in electing Nasser, and that "at no time whatsoever" has the community been "so united around its council and clergy as it is nowadays" (JP, 6, 18 January 1963).

Ernest Farah, a member of the community who has long opposed Communist domination, noted in a 17 August 1989 interview that Nasser—a friend of his—was "a public relations man who was very cooperative in social life, but totally unorthodox as far as religion was concerned." He said that Nasser came from a prominent Orthodox family who were known for being Communist and that he was "pushed into the priesthood at an advanced age at the request of the Communist party"; that they "could control the church." According to Farah, Nasser was ordained only because the metropolitan was "a yes-man of the Communist party." Farah justified his contempt of the whole situation by noting that following the death of Nasser in the early 1980s, Metropolitan Isidoros finally admitted that Father Sim'an "never crossed himself the right way." In defense of Si'man, council head Hazan noted that some people consider him to be the best priest to have served in Nazareth because he was liberal in his views and was an avowed nationalist. He explained that the people did not see Sim'an's ordination as an attempt by the Communists to influence church activities, but rather as a popular choice by the community to select a leader with positive leadership qualities.

Fu'ad Farah (from a different Farah clan than Ernest), who served as head of the council from 1967 to 1984, said during this period that there was a gentleman's agreement that the chairman would be from neither the Communist camp nor the Communist oppostion camp centered on the Farah and Debini families; the secretary would be from the Communist group; and the other members of the council from the noncommunist group. This system worked well until the *Taqadumia* (Progressive) party emerged in the early 1980s in opposition to the dominant Communist party. Farah said that when some members of the council became candidates in the municipal elections for Taqadumia, the Jebha members of the council tried to have them dismissed from the council. According to Farah, this is when the real split began, politics being the cause. As a result, Farah and others resigned from the council. Farah, with the caveat that he belonged to no party, said, "It is true, no doubt about it, that the Communists are trying to control the council."

The rift in the community widened during the 1986 council elections when, according to one faction of the Orthodox community, twenty-five of the thirty-five council members elected were affiliated with the Communists either as party members, or as members of the Communist-dominated coalition called *Jebha* (front), and that all nine of the executive committee members were from Jebha. In a 6 May 1989 interview, Sami Debini, of the opposition group, accused Jebha of distributing cards telling party members whom to vote for and that "those who believe in God and are educated were not elected." He then added that because of the Communist rise to dominance in the Orthodox council, the Roman Catholics and Greek Catholics canceled their council elections out of fear that the Communists would gain control in their councils too.

Suheil Diyab, the executive secretary of the Communist party in Nazareth, explained the situation differently in a 3 May 1989 interview. He said that only three members of the Greek Orthodox Council were actual Communists, while seven were from Jebha, and fifteen others were simply men who agreed with Jebha ideas and actions in the council meetings. Among those fifteen were one council member, Zahi Jubran, who refused to come to a council meeting scheduled to be held in Jebha party offices, and another, Sa'id Khalil, a member of the Labor party. In reference to the politics of the nine-member executive council, Hazan explained that only one was a member of the Communist party, and that he attended church and was not an atheist; six of the members were from Jebha (including Hazan, who until 1988 represented the academic faction on the Jebha council); and two were not from Jebha. In defense of the Communists, Hazan explained that they have "a different character" in Nazareth; many are Communists because it is the "only way to confront oppression of Arabs in Israel." The fact that Communists are on the council is certain, but the extent to which they intentionally try to influence Orthodox community policies and actions through mixing religion with politics will always be a matter of debate.

One of the more noted schisms between the two orthodox factions centers on the unfortunate Father Romanous, who unwittingly became the center of both the Greek-Arab and the non-Communist–Communist conflicts within the Orthodox community. During the 1980s the Orthodox parish in Nazareth was served by two Arab priests, Fathers Barnaba and Bishara, and the Greek Metropolitan Isidoros. The workload for the priests was heavy, with daily services, baptisms, funerals, and weddings to officiate at (up to five a day on Saturdays and Sundays during the summer), as well as administering to any other needs of the community. To lighten the load of the two priests the Orthodox community decided to hire a third priest—not always an easy task because of the scarcity of men entering the priesthood. Enter Father Romanous from Haifa, who after having graduated with a bachelor of arts degree in Orthodox theology from a White Russian seminary in New York and then being ordained a deacon by the patriarch in Jerusalem, was assigned to the Nazareth parish in about 1984. Romanous indicated that he came to Nazareth with the intent to help with the many duties of the parish. He also hoped to reestablish the practice of conducting the full mass without cuts and to teach children the correct way of worship. This was not to be the case. After only a few weeks at work, Father Romanous was told by one of the other priests that he was not allowed to serve in the parish; he should go back to his hometown of Haifa.

Father Romanous was rejected in Nazareth partly because he was sent to the parish by the patriarch, without prior consent of the church council, which resents any attempt by the patriarch to meddle in council affairs. Unfortunately, Romanous was very loyal to the patriarch. When Romanous arrived, the council wanted him to sign a contract of employment which, according to the explanation of Father Romanous in a 25 June 1989 interview, said that he must answer to the council members and do their bidding. According to Romanous, the Nazareth parish is the only Greek Orthodox Church that requires such a contract. Romanous refused to sign the contract. The patriarch was pleased that Romanous would not give in to the council, and shortly after Romanous found out that the Nazareth council would not accept him, the patriarch invited him to Jerusalem to be ordained a priest in a special ceremony.

Romanous continued to live in Nazareth. At first he served the community but not within the official bonds of the church. He taught religion at several of the government schools, conducted engagement ceremonies in peoples' homes, visited members of the community, and liturgized at a family-owned chapel in Nazareth and for the Greek Orthodox parish in Shefar 'Am. Liturgizing in the Nazareth parish church, however, was restricted to only those functions performed by visiting priests. Father Romanous noted in a 28 August 1989 interview that on St. Romanous day in 1985 the council ordered the church to be locked so that he would not be able to liturgize there on his saint's day. Some members of the parish complained and for several years after that he was allowed to liturgize in the church on a limited basis. When he did liturgize he said he brought his own robes and crosses so that he did not have to use those in the church and that the local priests refused to officiate with him.

Romanous was never certain why he was not originally accepted by the council. He said it could have been because he would not sign the contract, or was considered a danger to the church, or was thought to have been assigned elsewhere, or because his appointment was viewed as interference from the patriarch. A 1993 change in policy by the council allowed Romanous to serve as a parish priest.

Explanations for the Romanous fiasco are many. One prominent member of the Orthodox community, who is active in the Jebha rival Taqadumia, explained in a 6 May 1989 interview that Romanous had gone to study in New York at the urging of the Orthodox council before it was dominated by Communists. When he returned, he was interviewed by the now Communist-dominated council and "found to be a true believer" who "refused to take orders from Jebha—only from the Patriarch." The supporter of Taqadumia accused the council of spreading rumors about the priest, saying he was not fit to serve as a priest, his ideas were old fashioned, and he was better suited to serve as a monk. He said that the council influenced the metropolitan, whom he described as being "very weak and passive," to send a letter to Romanous telling him to be a priest outside Nazareth.

One source told how a group from Nazareth approached the Holy Synod (the highest authority in the Orthodox Church) and the patriarch seeking a settlement of the Romanous conflict. The Synod issued a *firman* (decree) proclaiming Romanous a parish priest with the right to liturgize in Nazareth, but when the decision was sent to Metropolitan Isidoros in Nazareth, he told the council about it, but did not order them to accept it.

Adib Hazan, in presenting the council side of the dispute, explained that the council objected to Father Romanous because he was

appointed to serve in Nazareth at the same time the patriarch was su-
ing the council for control of the Orthodox Church and lands in Nazareth; "the patriarch considered Father Romanous as a test case of his
hegemony over the Nazareth church." Hazan explained that it was the
tradition in Nazareth that new priests be approved by the leaders of the
community (notables in former times and the council in modern
times), and then be ordained in Nazareth. This did not happen in the
case of Romanous, who was approved by the patriarch and then ordained, first as a deacon and then later as a priest, in Jerusalem. He also
explained that even before the appointment, there had been contact
with Romanous, and they had explained to him that if he came to Nazareth, he would be an employee of the council and thereby must sign a
work agreement, noting that the agreement did not give the council
the right to interfere in religious matters. He thinks Romanous refused
to sign the agreement only on orders from the patriarch, who felt that
he should be the one to decide on priestly appointments. Finally,
Hazan explained that once the patriarch dropped his claim to the Nazareth church, Romanous was no longer needed in Nazareth, so he was
assigned by the patriarch to the small Orthodox community in Shefar
'Am.

The Romanous's theology was also an impediment to his being hired.
Several community leaders suggested that Nazareth needed a more
modern priest rather than one who had studied with "the most reac-
tionary Orthodox in the world" and one who was "very fanatic in his
belief."

The most divisive of the conflicts within the Greek Orthodox
community are centered on these differing theological views. One of
Father Romanous's most ardent supporters is Ernest Farah. The devout Farah has taken upon himself the task of restoring the Orthodox
Church to orthodoxy. He explained in a 17 August 1989 interview that
in order to do this, he and others from the community formed the al-
Nur (light) Orthodox Society in 1983 with a membership that Farah
identifies as all of the "non-Communist Orthodox" in Nazareth, but
with no official membership roster, because the society does not want
to provoke the parish council. The society is governed by a five-
member board of directors and a twenty-member executive council.
The purpose of the society, as explained by Farah, is to bring about a
"revival of spirituality among the Orthodox" and to "fill the gap resulting from the constant negligence and indifference of the ecclesiastical
authorities." Farah said: "We are not against anybody, we are for something; we want to revive and keep alive our identity." In order to
achieve these goals, the society started the St. Gregory Palamas Library
and Christian Orthodox Information Center. It also publishes the

semimonthly *al-Bishara* (The Annunciation) magazine, which includes articles in both English and Arabic about community and church history, theology and doctrine, occasional calls to repentance for the misguided—including unrighteous priests and despotic leaders, and warnings of Greek Orthodox Council wrongdoings. As a watchdog of the community, the society has condemned Communist control of the council and supported Father Romanous.

Farah and his followers' fervor for reform resulted from their contempt for the late Metropolitan Isidoros's[7] lack of orthodoxy and his subordination to the Communist elements in the community. They are also concerned that many of the members of the Orthodox community are not being properly taught church doctrine as a result of indifference, low church attendance, and the lack of either Orthodox-run schools or Orthodox education in the public schools. They attempt to overcome what Farah calls the "three curses of the century: ecumenism, communism, and conformism." Farah estimated that while only 10 percent of the Orthodox were believing Christians, upward of 50 percent of the Western-Rite Church members were believers. In commenting on the parish priests, Farah noted that Father Barnaba was the "worst of all," that he had become a Baptist at one time and had never been readmitted into the Orthodox Church, and that the young Father Bishara, while a believing Orthodox, was a "slave to the Communist party," partly because his wife had been given a job by the Communists. He added that the aging Father Demitri had left the Nazareth church because of the bad situation and now liturgizes in neighboring Yafa. Farah criticized the council for mixing "a billion percent in spiritual matters" of the community while it claims to be concerned only with financial and physical matters.

Those who oppose the goings-on in the parish not only have chosen to separate themselves from the Orthodox community on spiritual grounds, they also have been able to separate themselves physically. In 1982, Farah had a small chapel built to the side of his home in memory of his parents. Farah said this had been a dream of his since childhood. The chapel is dedicated to St. Charalampos (the Greek equivalent of Farah, which means joy or happiness), and can seat about thirty people. Farah said the private chapel was built before the divisions in the community developed; it was never intended to be a rival to the parish church. However, for several years during the height of the schism, dissatisfied parishioners came to the Farah chapel for services; thus creating for a time an unofficial second parish in Nazareth. When Fa-

---

[7]Metropolitan Isidoros passed away in 1991. Metropolitan Kyriakos became the new ecclesiastical leader of the Orthodox community following his official consecration as metropolitan on Annunciation Day 1992.

ther Romanous became a parish priest he no longer felt able to officiate in the Farah chapel, thus bringing to an end the services.

In response to some of the accusations from the Farah-led opposition, Hazan explained several matters. He said that "Ernest and his people are responsible for the division" in the community, that "everything Romanous did was with prior consultation with Ernest and his group," and that Romanous "came to us with prejudices influenced by Ernest." Concerning the allegations of Communist influence in the council, he explained that while each member of the council has his own personal political beliefs, those beliefs have nothing to do with council responsibilities. "The first motivation of the council is national service above religious service," most of its work being geared to social and national affairs, including keeping the youth off the streets, serving the community with clubs and adequate finances, and promoting the welfare of the Arab community at the national level (also one of the main platforms of Jebha).[8] It is these responsibilities the opposition objects to.

Hazan expressed disappointment in the accusations of communist dominance in the council made by Sami Debini in a local newspaper. Hazan called the attack on the council an attack on communism; and Debini and others from the Farah camp, who accuse council members of being Communists, "don't want to recognize the work we are doing" or "how we are serving the community." To illustrate his point, Hazan described how before Jebha gained control in the council, "everything was neglected," the youth center was empty because of no planned activities, the cemetery was crumbling with a mess of beer and liquor bottles on the graves, the new office buildings were empty (the investors having gone bankrupt), and even the church was run-down. Since then, he said, the council has sought to remedy these problems. It has provided new chairs, liturgical books, and an altar for the church; it also prints and distributes a weekly gospel reading. Fu'ad Farah, under whose leadership the nadi and most of the waqf office buildings were constructed, saw it differently. He said that since the Communist-dominated council came into power, "they haven't done one single thing." He mentioned initiating the project of building a new cemetery near the road to 'Illut, but said that nothing more had been done by the new council.

[8] This concern of the Orthodox community with affairs of the larger Arab community is a result of its longtime identification as a church indigenous to the Arab world. Tsimhoni notes that the Greek Orthodox community has the "widest residential dispersion and greatest integration in Muslim society" of any of the Christian communities; and this has helped to give them a distinct Arab nature with which both Christians and Muslims can identify (Tsimhoni 1986, 413).

Hazan acknowledged that the accusation of the council not being religious is at least partially true, in that some of the members "are not churchgoers." In order to clarify why some council members were not religious (and why in fact many members of the community are not religious in an Orthodox sense), he explained that in the mentality of the Greek Orthodox community of Nazareth, "people consider religious activity more out of social feelings than piety"; and this "feeling of belonging to the church and the parish" means that parts of the community come on feast days for social, not religious motives, and some "celebrate by drinking rather than praying."

Hazan further illustrated this identification with the community, but not the religion, by describing one newly elected member of the committee who started coming to church following his election, but who stopped after only a few weeks because he was not able to make the sign of the cross correctly and did not want to be a hypocrite. Hazan added that in spite of this councilman's lack of religious adeptness, he was still very much a part of the Orthodox community. The Communist members of the council "see no contradiction between being a member of a religious community and of a political party."

Jebha leader Suheil Diyab said that most people in Nazareth, including himself, want to separate religion from politics, and that Jebha "has no interest in interfering in religious life," but that it does have to interfere when "some people, groups and priests, under the cover of religion, want to attack our [Jebha] position and to have a political position against communism." He noted that during the 1960s when Communist Khalil Khouri served on the council (part of the time as its chairman) there was a policy of friendship with all council members; politics was never an issue. The council worked to stop the confiscation of Orthodox lands in Nazareth and to establish good relations between Muslim and Christian groups. Now, he said, the opposition wants the council to be concerned only with Orthodox religious matters. They want an Orthodox council for the Orthodox, while the Jebha contingent wants to continue Khouri's efforts of the 1960s in being involved with all of Nazareth, in making nadi Rum available to all people and in strengthening Muslim-Christian relations. "Jebha also wants noninterference by council members in Nazareth political life." He cited the example of George Debini, who entered the municipal election of 1983 for Jebha rival Taqadumia one year after being elected secretary of the Orthodox council. Diyab accused Debini of using his influence on the Orthodox council to further the work of Taqadumia, while noting that the Jebha members of the council were "not involved politically."

The debate continues as each side accuses the other of meddling in the affairs of the community for political and religious gain. Part of the problem stems from the fact that there are two differently perceived objectives of the community council. One contingent believes that the council's role is to deal primarily with Orthodox matters and to strengthen the religious commitment of the community; the other contingent sees the council in more of an ecumenical light, in which it would use the council's influence and waqf revenues for the benefit not only of the Orthodox community, but also for the larger community of Nazarenes. Stubbornness persists on both sides, with little hope of compromise. Father Barnaba cited invitations to Ernest Farah and the Nur contingent to sit together with the council and "cooperate for the benefit of the church, but they won't listen." Nor will the council listen to the Nur society's call for a return to the fundamentals of their religion.

The Roman Catholic Community

The Roman Catholic community of Nazareth holds the longevity record for sustained occupancy in the town, thanks to the persistence of the Franciscan fathers, who in 1620 were the first Christians to gain permission to return to the Muslim village. In addition to longevity, they also excel over the other communities in landholdings and religious institutions. At present they lag behind the Greek Orthodox and Greek Catholics in numbers, but their presence is still strong and their Basilica of the Annunciation remains the focal point of the town and first destination for most pilgrims. The Roman Catholic community is referred to colloquially by the term Latin—hence the Latin quarter and the Latin Church.

Latin-speaking pilgrims had long visited the city before the Crusades, but this was before the division in 1054 of Christendom into Greek-east and Latin-west. It was not until the crusader period that a separate Latin entity emerged in Nazareth with the conquest of the city in 1102 by Tancred, the subsequent construction of a new Church of the Annunciation over the ruins of the Byzantine church, and the establishment of a bishopric and then archbishopric in the growing town. The presence of the Latins in the Holy Land was short-lived. In fact, the church in Nazareth was never fully completed. Excavations in 1909 revealed five well-preserved Romanic capitals for the crusader church. These capitals were carved by artists from northern France and had not yet been put into place when news of Saladin's victory at Hittin in 1187 reached the city; thus the capitals were hidden for protection (Murphy-O'Connor 1986, 311). Saladin granted permission for Franciscan priests to remain in Nazareth in order to officiate at the Church of the Annunciation, but in 1260, Baibars and his Mamluk army attacked Nazareth and destroyed the church (Colbi 1988, 54, 62).

Franciscans remained in the city until the fall of Akka and Naz-areth in 1291.[9] The Latin presence in Nazareth was sporadic during the next three centuries, with the Franciscans coming and going, depend-ing on the local political situation, in which changes in leadership, Bedouin raids, and persecutions prevented a permanent presence. Franciscan accounts of these years tell of their expulsion in 1363 and re-turn in 1468, and of a massacre of some of their members in 1542. In spite of these difficulties, Franciscan and other Latin pilgrims still man-aged to visit the site of the Annunciation and home of Jesus, which were at times cared for by local Christian families with the support of the Franciscans (*Nazareth Today*, 17).

As the designated Custody of the Holy Land, the Franciscans were eager to reestablish a presence in Nazareth. That opportunity arose in 1620 when Emir Fakhr al-Din granted permission for their return to the ruins of the church, where a small structure was built to enclose the holy grotto that is venerated as the house of Mary and therefore the site of the Annunciation. Then in 1730, Dahir al-Umar granted permis-sion to build a new church. This hastily built Church of the Annuncia-tion became the central focus and gathering point for the Latin com-munity in the Latin quarter to the west of the church. The church was enlarged in 1877, then torn down in 1954 to make way for a large basil-ica, completed in 1969. The basilica is used by the Latin parish, but is under the control of the Franciscans.

The Custody of the Holy Land has also entrusted to the Francis-cans control over a variety of other sacred sites, including the Church of St. Joseph—also known as the Church of the Nutrition, built over the site of Joseph's house; the Terra Sancta Monastery and High School, which connects the two main churches; the Casa Nova Hospice for pil-grims to the west of the Basilica of the Annunciation; the dilapidated Mensa Christi chapel adjacent to the Maronite Church, where, accord-ing to tradition, the resurrected Jesus and his apostles dined on a large rock now enshrined within the church; and the Chapel of Fright on the Deir al-Banat hill south of the Latin quarter, where Mary stood in fright as Jesus was taken to be thrown off the precipice. They also have stew-ardship over the Sanctuary of St. Anne, one of the few buildings left standing in the village of Saffuriya; the Chapel of St. Gabriel in Mujei-dil, also left standing after the rest of the village was demolished; and the Chapel of St. James in Yafa.

---

[9] During this period of uncertainty for the Christians of Nazareth, religious tradition tells of the miraculous transfer of the holy house of the Virgin Mary on 9–10 May 1291 from its endangered location in Nazareth to Tersatto (near Rijeka) in Croa-tia, and then on 10 December 1294 to Loretto (near Ancona) in Italy, where it remains to this day (Colbi 1988, 62).

During the nineteen-year partition, the Latin patriarchate in Jerusalem was separated from the Latin community in Israel, so it established a vicariate in Nazareth to handle its affairs. The offices of the
vicar are located behind the Casa Nova in a structure relatively new to
the central part of town. Nazareth is also home to an impressive as-
sortment of Roman Catholic religious orders who gradually followed
the Franciscans into the holy town (table 6). Two of the orders are cloistered convents with almost no outside contact, but the majority of orders function within the community and serve the people of Nazareth
through their schools, hospitals, and other institutions. Interviews in
1989 with representatives of several of the orders show that the priests
and nuns come from a variety of places. For example, in 1989 the Holy
Family Hospital was run by four priests and two nuns from Italy and
eleven nuns from India; the Poor Clares had four sisters in contact
with the outside, three from Lebanon and one from France, with an
undisclosed number cloistered inside; and the brown-robed Franciscan
brothers included six from Italy, four from Spain, two from Belgium,
and one each from Poland, Germany, the United States, and Israel (an
Arab from Kfar Kanna). The Salesian brothers included seven from
Italy, one from Poland, and one from Damascus, Syria.

  These religious orders of the Roman Catholic Church have had a
significant impact on the landscape of Nazareth. The large cupola of
the Basilica of the Annunciation, the square steeples of the Church of
St. Joseph and the chapel of the Sisters of Nazareth, the Salesian school
and beautiful Church of Jesus the Adolescent just beneath the summit
of the western hill, and the high, imposing walls surrounding the
Carmelite convent and other church properties all signify the extensive
commitment of the Roman Catholic Church to maintain a presence in
Nazareth and serve its peoples and pilgrims.

  The Roman Catholic community, however, is more than just institutions and churches built to commemorate holy happenings and
the mostly foreign priests and nuns who staff them. Beyond its basilica
are more than 5,000 Roman Catholics who call Nazareth home and
who find part of their multifaceted identity within the Latin community. The arrival of the first member of the community was a domestic
of the Franciscans named Yamini, who arrived from Lebanon in 1620
(Pena 1986, 11). He was followed by other migrants, some of whom
were attracted to Nazareth by the security of the Latin convent and the
opportunities for employment by the Franciscans. The details of the
origins of the community are debatable. Samir Rok, of the Latin community, explained in a 30 May 1989 interview that the original Latins
were actually Maronites who came from Lebanon at the request of the
Franciscans shortly after their arrival in order to bolster the Christian

TABLE 6. Roman Catholic orders and institutions in Nazareth

Order	Function	No.	Year est.
Priests:			
Franciscans	Monastery, secondary school, Casa Nova, and Custody of Holy Sites	13	1620
Salesians	Don Bosco Technical School	7	1906
Brothers of St. John of God	Holy Family Hospital	4	1879
Brothers (Freres) of the Christian Schools	School	3	
Fathers of the Holy Heart of Betharram	House of hospitality and prayer	3	1907
Order of Don Guanella (Servant of Charity)	School for disabled adolescents	3	1974
Sisters:			
Clarese (Poor Clares)	Convent	16	1884
Carmelites	Convent	14	1910
Franciscans of the Immaculate Heart	Secondary school and Casa Nova	12	
Sisters of Maria Bambina	Holy Family Hospital	12	1984
Sisters of St. Vincent de Paul	French hospital and nursing school	10	1898
Salesian Sisters	Primary school and kindergarten	9	1950
Sisters of St. Joseph	Primary and secondary school	8	1887
Salvatorian Sisters	Greek Catholic school	8	1958
Sisters of Nazareth	School for the deaf and blind, hospice, and hostel	6	1855
Daughters of St. Anne	Rest home for aged women	6	1949
Sisters of St. Charles Borromeus	Hospice	5	1934
Sisters of Charity	Service at the Terra Sancta Monastery	4	1910
Little Sisters of Jesus	Community service	3	1949
Sisters of the Cross of Chavanod	Reception at Betharram hospice and service	3	1986
Sisters of the Madonna of Fatima		3	1990

SOURCE: *Annuaire de l'Eglise Catholique en Terre Sainte,* 1993

presence in the town. Colbi also writes of the Franciscans' request that the Maronite patriarch send families to settle in Nazareth (Colbi 1988, 89). Rok said that these original Christians were referred to as the "bucket sect" because they would go to the Franciscan monastery to request food, which they would then carry home in a bucket. Yusef Nakhleh, a prominent member of the Greek Catholic community, also indicated in a 17 May 1989 interview that the original Latins in Nazareth were Maronite Catholics from Lebanon who converted to the Latin rite in order to receive Franciscan protection.

Father Arturo Vasaturo, a Franciscan and the parish priest, said that the Maronites came not out of invitation from the Franciscans, but hoping to find security in Nazareth from persecution in Lebanon. While it is certain that Maronites were among the first members of the Latin community, it is not certain whether they came at the request of the Franciscans or on their own initiative, seeking safety. Perhaps it was both. Once they were in town, it is evident that some switched sects, with possible motives of receiving food and employment from the Franciscans.

As news spread that Christians once again lived peacefully in Nazareth, others came to join them. Rok related how his family came to live in Nazareth. His ancestors were Italians who came during the Crusades to serve as translators. Afterward they remained in the land, living first in Ein Karim near Jerusalem, then Bethlehem, and finally settling in Nazareth. Another prominent Latin family, the Spanyoli clan, have European roots from Spain. The Latin community is therefore mixed, with origins from a variety of sects and places. Through immigration and natural increase the community has continued to grow over the years (table 7). Records from the Latin parish show steady growth of the community to a 1989 estimate of upward of 5,500 members.

Like the other Christian parishes in town, the Latin parish is made up almost entirely of Arabs, but unlike the other parishes, the priests of the Latin parish are not Arab. When asked about this difference, Father Arturo noted that it is the hope of the Franciscans, who are entrusted with presiding over the parish, that in the future they will have enough Arab members of their order to serve in all their pastoral duties. He noted that currently there are Franciscan Arab parish

TABLE 7. Number of Roman Catholic parishioners in Nazareth

Year	Number	Year	Number
1620	1	1900	1,335
1691	24	1950	2,017
1715	85	1970	3,650
1734	150	1974	4,090
1755	355	1984	4,500
1832	379	1989	5,500
1856	689		

SOURCE: Pena 1986, 11; Latin parish records

priests in Bethlehem, Jerusalem, and Jaffa, but not yet in Nazareth. Arturo is fluent in Arabic and conducts mass and parish duties in that language. Former parish priest Gennaro De Robertis, when asked if having a foreign priest in a parish of Christian Arabs presented any problems, replied that he had spent the first nineteen years of his life in Italy and the next twenty-five in the Holy Land. He continued: "I have learned Arabic and tried to adapt to the oriental mentality. Who would consider me a foreigner in the Holy Land?" (Pena 1986, 16).

Unlike the Greek Orthodox community, the Latin community does not have waqf land. All the land is in control of either the Franciscans or the other religious orders. The Basilica of the Annunciation is under the custody of the Franciscans, who see the church as having dual functions. First, it is a church for the world, as evidenced by the many beautiful artistic renderings of Mary, Jesus, and the Annunciation adorning the walls of the church and the portico of the courtyard. These large mosaics were donated by Roman Catholic communities from around the world and include such diverse depictions as a black, rust, and cream-colored mosaic from Cameroon which shows African women bringing gifts in head-borne baskets to the outstretched arms of Mary and the boy Jesus, a mosaic from Japan showing a beautiful Japanese Madonna and child dressed in traditional Japanese kimonos, and Canada's terra-cotta depiction of Mary as an Indian maiden. The worldwide nature of the church is also seen in the faces of countless pilgrims who come to reflect on the sacred events that the church commemorates and to worship silently or during a mass conducted in a babel of languages by priests traveling with the pilgrim groups.

Second, the large church serves as the parish church for the local Latin community. This is manifest in the ceramic stations of the cross on the central pillars of the church, which are written in Arabic, and by the Arab Latins who worship at three Sunday masses conducted in Arabic by Italian Father Arturo. A fourth mass using both Arabic and Latin in the liturgy is also conducted each Sunday. Local Latins flock to the church in even greater numbers for the daily masses held on the lower level surrounding the grotto during the month of May (Mary's month) and for main feast days, when the church and courtyard are full. Father Gennaro estimated that about 25 percent of the community participates in weekly mass, while during the Easter week services, about 80 percent attend. He related that many Latins who are employed in the Jewish sector must work on Sunday, whereas in Nazareth most of the town shuts down on Sunday. In order to accommodate those who work on Sundays, one of the masses is held on Sunday evening, while a Saturday evening mass started by Gennaro had little response (Pena 1986, 13).

The main basilica is not the only place of worship for members of the Latin community. About a quarter of the Latin respondents to the survey indicated that they usually attend a Roman Catholic church closer to home, with the Salesian and St. Joseph churches and the chapels in the Clarese and Carmelite convents being the most frequented of the alternative places to worship. One resident of the Krum quarter indicated that she prays each week at the Carmelite convent, which is within easy walking distance just below the quarter, along with fifty to a hundred others. She said that the Latins from the upper section of Krum prefer to worship at the Salesian Church, which is closer to their homes. For feast days, however, most of the community chooses to attend the larger basilica, with its greater pomp. Father Arturo estimated in a 13 July 1989 interview (which was continued at a later date because he had to go visit Muslim notables for the Feast of al-Adha) that on regular Sundays 700–1,000 Latins pray at the main parish church, with a total of about 1,500 praying there or at one of the other churches. He added that the parish stresses that the sacraments be performed at the Basilica of the Annunciation.

The Franciscans are financially independent of the local community and thus do not depend on revenues from waqf properties like the Orthodox community. Since they are an international order, their policy is to keep property from local ownership. This has caused some problems, because local Latins would like the church to help finance commercial buildings, as the Orthodox and Greek Catholic communities have done, in order to help local merchants and businesses. Muslim mayor Zu'bi even proposed that Franciscan-owned land, located along the main street on the lower perimeter of the large Basilica of the Annunciation and Terra Sancta Monastery complex, be converted from a neglected garden area, separated from the main street by a tall rock wall, into a row of shops like those found on the opposite side of the street. The Franciscans rejected the proposal, because, according to Arturo, "the people aren't ready" for it. He explained that if the Franciscans built the shops with the intent to rent to members of the community or others, they would never be able to please everyone and it would only incite jealousy among the members of the community. However, the Franciscans have for the last fifty years rented some of their land near the Don Guanella complex (former Poor Clares convent) to the Holy Land Restaurant, which has facilities to accommodate large busloads of pilgrims. This project was approved in order to stimulate tourist development in Nazareth.

Franciscans also approved the tearing down of the southern end of the protective wall surrounding the former Poor Clares convent so the municipality could pave a road across Franciscan land between the restaurant and the convent and connect the Garage quarter with the main street. The Franciscans also own a large tract of land beyond the Krum quarter on the road to 'Illut. Arturo said that the Franciscans would eventually like to use this land to build a housing project with the intent to help alleviate the housing crunch and as an incentive to keep Christians in Nazareth. The catch is to figure out how the Franciscans can maintain ownership of the land and yet not be involved as landlords. Arturo thought they might have a contractor build and sell the apartments, but have the ownership of the land remain in the hands of the Franciscans. Plans have also been suggested that part of this land be used for a new cemetery.

The Latin community does not have a council to run its affairs, as does the Orthodox community, primarily because the normal duties of a council are carried out by the Franciscans. However, when the need arises, the parish priest will convene a meeting with prominent parish members. When, for example, Michel Sabah, the Latin patriarch of Jerusalem, planned to come to his hometown of Nazareth for a visit, Arturo invited about fifty parish members to help plan the event and to make proper arrangements. He cited efforts to get parishioners to serve more within the Latin community, but said there is no established tradition of service. Community organizations include a choir, a committee in charge of upkeep of the cemetery, and a scout troop, which was reorganized in the early 1980s after being disbanded for a number of years. The scouts meet in the Catholic Action building across the street from the church next to the Sisters of Nazareth compound. The building was formerly a school, but now provides meeting and recreational facilities for the scouts. There is no nadi for the community. Although there are plans to build a nadi on Franciscan land near the Holy Land Restaurant, Arturo said that the Franciscans are hesitant to take on total responsibility for its financing and construction because "Nazareth's Latins must first help themselves."

Unity among the community has been strengthened by the momentous events of the 1963 visit of Pope Paul VI to Nazareth, and the ordination of Nazareth native Michel Sabah as Latin patriarch of Jerusalem on 6 January 1988. But there have also been times of dispute. In the early 1940s, for example, a group of Latins became angry at the Franciscans, who, during the construction of the Terra Sancta Monastery, opted to buy lower-priced building stone from Muslim and Greek Catholic stonecutters, rather than the Latins, who had expected to be the suppliers, out of recognition of their loyalty to the community. The disgruntled group stopped coming to church, and eventually the feud became so heated that the patriarch intervened and assigned a new priest to the group, who then held mass in a private home. This group became known as "the Angry Church," although eventually their anger subsided and the group disbanded and returned to the main parish church.

A second item with which the local community has little concern, but which affects the Franciscans and Sisters of Nazareth, stems from a brotherly-sisterly disagreement over the site of the house of Joseph, where Jesus would have been raised. The Franciscans, supported by long-standing tradition, believe that the Church of St. Joseph marks the spot. The Sisters of Nazareth, on the other hand, quietly believe that ongoing excavations (1884–1963) beneath their convent have revealed the ruins of the church with a fresh fountain and two arches which Arculf described in A.D. 670 as marking the "place where once was the house in which the Lord, our Saviour, was brought up." A well-preserved Roman-period tomb, complete with a rolling stone door, was also discovered in the excavations (Livio 1982, 26–34). In deference to their Franciscan brothers and the older tradition associated with the Church of St. Joseph, the Sisters of Nazareth do not actively promote news of their exciting find, and as a result, few tourists, or Nazarenes for that matter, know of the excavations or of an alternative site for the home of the holy family.[10]

The Greek Catholic Community

The Greek Catholics currently represent the second largest of the Christian communities in Nazareth. They surpassed the Roman Catholics in numbers as a result of the influx of the 1948 refugees, many of whom were Greek Catholics from throughout the Galilee, where they represent the largest of the Christian sects. The official designation for the sect is Melkite Greek Catholic, Melkite being the common term used throughout the Middle East. But the everyday designation is simply Catholic, which is the term used to identify adherents of the sect as well as their churches, schools, and scouts. This can cause confusion for those accustomed to calling Catholic anything associated with Roman Catholicism. For example, when the still uncompleted Basilica of the Annunciation was first opened for Christmas mass in 1965, some foreign tourists asked the locals for directions to the Catholic church and were directed to the Greek Catholic Church in the heart of the market instead of to the Roman Catholic Church, which is known locally as the Latin Church (JP, 26 December 1965).

[10] Those who want to see the excavations can do so by making an appointment with the sisters for a guided tour and a persuasive presentation of their claim to holy ground. Because the sisters do not promote their discovery, access to the ruins has not been upgraded to accommodate large numbers, which discourages visits from large tourist groups, most of whom plan to spend only a few hours in Nazareth.

The Greek Catholics' arrival on the scene was more momentous than the gradual immigration to the village by the Greek Orthodox and Roman Catholics. They arrived en masse and already as residents, but the actual details of the events surrounding the birth of the Greek Catholic community are sketchy and still a matter of debate. According to a 31 August 1989 interview with Father Nathaniel Shahada, parish priest of the Greek Catholic community, in 1741 "a misunderstanding between families" divided the Orthodox community in two. The two parish priests then ended up taking opposing sides, based on which families they had been serving. One of the groups and its priest, feeling that reconciliation was impossible, decided to leave the established community and start their own. The natural choice was to become Greek Catholics with their similar liturgy and customs. A second explanation comes from a short, undated mimeographed history of the sect, in which the author, Father Shahada, contradicts himself and explains that the split was caused by a "dispute between priest and priest." In a 17 May 1989 interview, Yusef Nakhleh, a prominent member of the Greek Catholic community, seconded the story of disputing priests, in which one of the priests led 220 people away from the Orthodox Church. He said that the group found refuge at the Franciscan convent and they were given the old synagogue by the Franciscans to use as their first church.

Shahada's history notes that in 1741 the Greek Catholics "took possession of the old Gabriel's Orthodox Church with the support of the Franciscan Fathers" by paying 301 piasters in an auction. The Greek Orthodox leaders protested to al-Umar; he reversed his decision and returned rights to the church to the Greek Orthodox community. Without a place to worship, the Greek Catholics then asked al-Umar for permission to use the abandoned synagogue, which was granted. Persecution by the Orthodox soon drove the Greek Catholic families to seek refuge in Safad for about thirty years. While they were gone they entrusted the keys of the church to the Franciscans out of fear "that the Muslims might put their hands on the shrines." When the Greek Catholics returned to the city, the Franciscans refused to return the keys. The Greek Catholics sent a petition to Rome, which sided with the Greek Catholics over the Franciscans, but the Franciscans failed to heed the edict. Although they did allow the Greek Catholics to pray in the church, the Franciscans also insisted on using the church for their own services as a statement of their control. The two groups continued to use the synagogue church jointly for about a hundred years, a situation which Shahada describes as causing "annoyance, confusion, problems, and feuds." All the while the Greek Catholics continued to petition Rome, but with no success. Finally they issued an ultimatum.

They wrote to Rome saying that if they were not granted control of the church, they would abandon Greek Catholicism for another sect, presumably one not in allegiance to Rome. Leaders in Rome listened to the ultimatum, and on 13 February 1846 the Franciscans were ordered to grant control of the church to the Greek Catholics, which they did. Shahada noted that some Franciscan historians have written opposing accounts which claim that the Franciscans bought the church first and then agreed to allow the Greek Catholics to use it. When retelling this story in the interview, Shahada concluded by describing current relations with the Franciscans as "very good."

In 1887 the Greek Catholic community moved into its new church constructed to the side of the synagogue, which had to be reduced in size to make way for the new church. The church is in the heart of the marketplace. From a distance its two rounded gold cupolas can be seen, but from within the maze of the market it is easy to miss the church, whose perimeter is surrounded by shops. A metal gate leads into a small courtyard with entrances to the synagogue (now primarily a destination of tourists),[11] the parish church, and stairs leading up to the home of the parish priest. Other holdings of the Greek Catholic parish include several waqfs composed of seven shops near the church, and a commercial building on the main street near the central bus stop. This building houses such establishments as the al-Fahum coffee store, the Farah pharmacy, the Galilee Bus Company, and *al-Senara* newspaper offices. Part of the church complex also includes a meeting place for the scouts and several rooms used by the Bishara library, which is operated by the papal mission and staffed by Roman Catholic lay sisters, two of whom are from the Philippines.

The parish also has a small chapel in its section of the joint Christian cemetery in the Garage quarter. Funeral services are held here, as are several masses during the year. The chapel is also used by the Latins, while the Maronites and Copts each have an altar in their sections for conducting funeral services. Parish services have also, in times past, been held near the junction of the roads to Haifa and Afula, at the Wasifiya elementary school which is run by the Greek Catholics and feeds into St. Joseph's (Mitran) school. A small chapel here—now a classroom—served the Catholics in the neighborhood until 1960, when services were moved to St. Joseph's Church in the Greek Catholic complex. In addition, Father Shahada indicated that before the Copts built

[11] Tourists and pilgrims come to the post–Roman period synagogue to read the accounts in Mark 6 and Luke 4 of Jesus preaching in the synagogue and his subsequent rejection by the villagers. For first-time visitors without an experienced guide, access to the synagogue can be a challenge, because the keeper of the keys is usually to be found visiting in one of the shops surrounding the church.

their own church, they were baptized in the Greek Catholic Church and prayed at a Greek Catholic chapel near Mary's well. This chapel has since been converted into a store, which is located in the lower level of the building that houses the Greek Catholic–sponsored *Sadaqa* (friendship) scouts.

The holdings of the Greek Catholics in the central part of town are limited in comparison to the two other main Christian sects, but with its rapid growth, the community has been able to expand its holdings to areas beyond the city core. The focus of this expansion is on the southwest hills of town where the community has sponsored a housing development called Shekun al-Arab with a shrine dedicated to Mary at its center, and where many Greek Catholic institutions have emerged. Here, on land acquired in the early 1950s, sit two schools, scout headquarters, a church, convent, seminary, Christian center, and the Grand New Hotel. These are not parish lands, but lands of the Greek Catholic archbishop in Haifa. Emile Shufani, principal of the St. Joseph school, who, along with Father Laham, presides over the complex, described these Greek Catholic enterprises in an 11 July 1989 interview. The junior seminary of St. Joseph (also called Mitran) was completed in 1956. It prepares youth for entrance into seminaries, with twenty-eight prospective candidates enrolled in 1985, but mainly functions as one of Nazareth's better schools for students in grades four through twelve.

Adjacent to the seminary/school is the Church of St. Joseph, dedicated in 1961. Originally built for the use of seminarians and students, the nonparish church, with an interior decor of mustard-colored walls and sky-blue trim (which matches the blue robes of the officiating priests), has become an additional gathering place for the city's Greek Catholics, many of whom live in surrounding neighborhoods and find it more convenient for Sunday worship than the church in the suq. Since the church is accessible to cars, many of the weddings and baptisms for the parish are conducted here by Father Shahada. Also in the complex is the Christian Training Center, completed in 1982, which houses a kindergarten, library, and conference rooms. The *Mukhalis* (Salvatorian) school, just to the west of St. Joseph's school and seminary, is the other Greek Catholic school in Nazareth. It was opened in 1961 and is run by the Salvatorian Sisters, or more formally the Sisters of the Divine Savior. Principal Margaret Ann from Grand Rapids, Michigan, related in a 23 May 1989 interview that the six sisters in charge of the school are all Roman Catholics, two from Austria, three from Germany, and one from the United States, who at the request of Rome now assist in the Greek Catholic school. They participate in Greek Catholic rites held at the school, but since the Greek Catholics do not have daily mass, they usually attend early morning mass in the Latin Basilica of the Annunciation. Just below the two schools is the new (1985) headquarters for the Greek Catholic scout organization in Israel. To the east of the St. Joseph's school is the Grand New Hotel. The hotel was built in 1957 as a joint project between the Greek Catholics and Tabar family. These institutions crown the hill now known as *Jebel Mitran* (mount of the archbishop), after Archbishop Hakim, who instigated the purchase of the lands and the construction of most of its buildings.

On the back side of the hill is the secluded Convent of the Annunciation–St. John the Baptist. Completed in 1966, this convent, with its small, white domed chapel (1978), is the home of nine semicloistered nuns and the resident father John Leonard and his wife. Leonard, from Grand Rapids, Michigan, is a former foreign service officer for the United States government who decided to enter the Melkite priesthood.

The Little Sisters of Jesus, while a Roman Catholic order, choose to be affiliated with the Greek Catholics in Nazareth because they feel it is a more indigenous church. They serve by visiting people, working with handicapped children, and assisting at a day-care center, and include three sisters from Vietnam and one from France,

The archbishop also owns property behind Mary's well between the Greek Orthodox Church block and the municipal garden. A large building houses shops, scouting facilities, and a new restaurant, with vacant land behind it planned for more commercial buildings and a youth hostel. Additional vacant lands are owned south of town near the Hypermarket, near the Salesian Church, and adjacent to the French hospital. According to Shufani, the land near the hospital is the property of Greek Catholics from Lebanon, who formed a congregation in Nazareth before 1948, but then left during the war. In April 1993 the Greek Catholic Church purchased the Franciscan Sisters of Mary convent and in cooperation with the Saffuri brothers inagurated the St. Gabriel Monastery Hotel, with its spectacular hilltop view.

Unlike the Greek Orthodox and Roman Catholic communities, the Greek Catholics pride themselves on having a hierarchy that is entirely Christian Arab, from the parish priest up to Archbishop Salum in Haifa. Father Shahada,[12] who described his work as keeping him "busy

---

[12] Father Shahada passed away in August 1991. Finding a suitable replacement has been a challenge. He was first replaced by Father Elias Chacour, one of the first graduates of the St. Joseph seminary in Nazareth. While serving in the small Ibillin parish, Father Chacour devoted much of his time to broader activities associated with achieving reconciliation among Israeli Jews, Muslims, and Christians, and with strengthening the Israeli Christian community (Chacour 1992, 208). Shortly after his

night and day," served the community as its single priest for thirty-two years. (Before that there were two parish priests.) He said that the community was in great need of additional priests. He did not drive, yet his parishioners lived scattered throughout the town. Many were homebound, which meant that he visited about forty homes every month to offer communion to the aged. He noted that those who came to church were mainly the elderly and that the parish sponsored no Sunday schools or youth classes. In the 1970s he would conduct three masses on Sunday and one on Saturday evening, but now there is only one mass at 9:30 on Sunday morning. This decline is caused in part by parishioners who now attend St. Joseph's instead, but it is also caused by more and more Greek Catholics moving out of the Latin quarter and no longer living within easy walking distance of the church. According to Father Shufani, St. Joseph's Church holds about 700 people and has an average weekly attendance of about 200, with 2,000 or more attending on feast days.

The parish priest presides over the parish council. Originally the parish council was elected by the community, with each family or clan electing their notable to represent them. However, in the last election, Father Shahada became frightened by the inroads of Jebha (Communists) in the Orthodox council and by an announcement from Jebha that they were planning to name a list of candidates from their party for the council, so he decided to forego elections and appoint the twenty-one council members himself. He said he selected those people who would be the most productive workers. The council is in charge of the schools, the synagogue, and the church buildings. Ten of the council also serve on the pastoral committee, which helps the priest in visiting families and preparing church ceremonies.

According to Father Shahada, various clubs have been a part of the community, but only the Charitable Society of Jesus of Nazareth—which helps the poor of the community—still exists. Former clubs, all of which were discontinued in the 1970s, included the Galilee Knights for both men and women; a chapter of the Society of Mary for men, women, and adolescents; and the Society of Women and Girls for the Decoration of the Church. An earlier organization was the Greek Catholic Club, with a membership of thirteen prominent men of the community whose stated goal in 1944 was to raise the moral and educa-

---

appointment to the larger Nazareth parish, Chacour realized that he did not have enough time or energy for both the parish and his other projects, so he asked to be relieved of his duties in Nazareth. He was succeeded by Father George Khouri, who soon asked to be reassigned because of hierarchical disputes. His successor was Massoud Abu Hatum, who was shortly thereafter rejected by the parishioners. As of April 1994, Archimandrite Emile Shufani and Maroun Tannous are serving as parish priests.

TABLE 8. Number of Greek Catholic parishioners in Nazareth

Year	Number	Year	Number
1741	220	1948	3,000
1854	750	1961	3,750
1912	1,067	1972	4,000
1946	2,500	1989	6,500

tional levels of the young men of the community (Israel State Archives [ISA] 27, N–583, 2662).

Community members include both descendents of the original splinter group and more recent immigrants. Yusef Nakhleh traces his family roots back to Lebanon, which they left in about 1790, coming first to Akka and then in 1830 to Nazareth. More recent members of the community arrived in 1948. Several of the Greek Catholic families living in Shekun al-Arab and other quarters indicated in the survey that they were refugees from Haifa, Tiberias, Beisan, and Ma'lul. Growth of the community is shown in table 8.

The Maronite Community

The Maronite community had its beginnings in Nazareth with the invitation from the Franciscans to the Maronite patriarch to send some Lebanese Maronites to Nazareth to bolster the Christian presence there. Father Yusef 'Isa, the parish priest of the Maronite community, explained in 5 April and 31 August 1989 interviews that Maronite families did come at the request of the Franciscans, but they became Latin, partly because the Latin priests gave money to the poor Maronite families. Gradually, however, other Maronite families settled in Nazareth and maintained their religion. Eventually there were enough to support a priest, who arrived in 1760, and to build a church. The Maronite Church of the Annunciation (also known as the Church of St. Anthony), built in 1770, is several hundred yards to the northwest of the Latin Church at the base of the hill. One suggested reason for its location here at the edge of the village is that it was located near the precipice where the offended villagers took Jesus to cast him out of town. In 1879 a visitor to Nazareth wrote:

> We found in the rear of the Maronite church the precipice, still forty or fifty feet high, which Robinson, Tobler, Hackett, and others well regard as perhaps more probable than any other. The Traditional Mount of Precipitation is two miles away from the town. An anger so hot as to attempt his violent death, and yet so cool as to travel two miles for a good place for the assassination, may not tax the credulity of a monk, but it is difficult for an Anglo-Saxon to accept. (Bartlett 1977, 482)

Growth in the community came from ongoing immigration from Lebanon, especially during times of ethnic and political strife, and from Maronite refugees from Ber'am, a Maronite village near the Israel-Lebanon border which the Israeli government forced them to abandon in 1951 for supposed security reasons. Four families came directly to Nazareth, but many others initially settled in nearby Jish. In 1964, a half dozen more of those families left Jish and came to Nazareth. Most of the Maronites chose to settle near the church in what became known as the Mawarna (Maronite) quarter; however, since the 1950s, families have started to move out to newer neighborhoods and are now scattered throughout several quarters. Father Yusef estimates about 1,200 Maronites now in the parish.

On nonfeast days about a hundred attend services, which until fifteen years ago were conducted in Syriac, but now are mostly performed in Arabic. Greek Catholics and Roman Catholics in the neighborhood of the church also attend services, while Maronites attend services of other Western-Rite churches in their neighborhoods.

Located in the church compound are two other buildings belonging to the parish. The older of the two buildings houses a kindergarten with fifteen to twenty students, mostly Maronite, and the priest's residence and office. A newer building completed in 1982 houses the scouts and a recreation hall as well as a still uncompleted residence for the priest. There are also plans to bring several nuns from Lebanon to serve in the community, and they would also take up residence in the parish buildings. The parish cemetery was originally located behind the church on the hill, but has since been moved to the joint cemetery in the Garage quarter. The community waqf includes four homes, which were donated to the church by families of deceased Maronites. These are rented to families for only a few sheqels a month based on rents established years ago, which cannot be increased until the present occupants either all die or move out.

Church activities are governed by a nine-member council who are selected by the priest and the bishop in Tyre, Lebanon. Organizations include a women's committee, who help clean and organize the church and visit families; the choir; and the scouts, who have the only marching band in town. An earlier organization, in existence during the mandate, was the St. Antonius Maronite Charitable Association, organized with the purpose of providing "material assistance to the needy" (ISA 27, N–616, 2662).

The Coptic Community

Nazareth's Coptic community originated when a Coptic man named Suleiman visited Nazareth in 1840 with an Egyptian military expedition and then returned several years later with his wife and children to settle permanently (an alternative account says he stayed in Nazareth and married a local girl). The five or six hundred Copts who now live in Nazareth all descend from this one family and go by the family name of Qupti (Copt). Munthir Qupti related in a 21 August 1989 interview that he is the fifth generation (Suleiman-Hannah-Saleh-Azat-Munthir) descendent of Suleiman and that children in some Coptic families are the seventh generation. According to a 17 April 1989 interview with Yusef Nakhleh, Suleiman was given Ottoman land in Nazareth by Ibrahim Pasha, the ruler of Egypt who, at that time, ruled the land of Palestine. The family settled on the land to the southeast of Mary's well and eventually a family quarter emerged, which is now known as the Aqbat (Coptic) quarter.

For years the Copts had no church of their own, so they worshiped with the Greek Catholics or a few with the Greek Orthodox. Then in the late 1930s, the Coptic families donated part of the family land in the quarter for the construction of their own church. The cornerstone was laid in November 1949, at which time a reporter numbered the Coptic community in Nazareth at 150 (JP, 23 November 1949). At the September 1951 dedication, the Coptic Church of the Annunciation with its orange dome and two pyramid-topped steeples was "crowded to capacity by the 300 members of the Coptic community in Nazareth." During the service, the Coptic archbishop (a citizen of then enemy Egypt) thanked the government of Israel for their help in providing building materials (JP, 10 September 1951).

Since the dedication, the community has also constructed a building next to the church with living quarters for the parish priest and a reception hall. The reception hall walls are adorned on one side with pictures of Coptic patriarchs and on the other with a brass plate engraved with a picture of the White Mosque, which was presented as a gift in 1986. According to a 27 July 1989 interview with Father Sidrak from Egypt, this building and the church along with a playground are on parish lands, but to the south of the church complex between the church and the Salam Mosque lies a large vacant plot of land which was purchased by the Coptic patriarch from a Muslim family with the intent to build a school for the Coptic community. The plot is now used mostly as a parking lot for mosque attenders with plans eventually to build a commercial center.

The Anglican (Protestant) Community

The final Christian sect that functions as a community is what is known locally as Protestant and more formally as Episcopalian or Anglican. Members of the community worship at the Christ Evangelical

Episcopal Church, which is independent of the Anglican Church of England, but still has roots and ties to the Anglican sect of Protestantism, including the Anglican Bishop of Jerusalem. For years it was the only Protestant church in Nazareth and hence the colloquial designation of Protestant, but today there are several other Protestant churches in Nazareth, and so the term Anglican will be used.

The Anglican community got its start in Nazareth in 1848 when the Christian Mission Society started work there. The society opened a school in 1851 where members and local residents held Anglican services. Then in 1862, Prince Edward visited Nazareth and, seeing the need for a more appropriate place for worship, donated ten pounds toward the construction of a church. Additional funds were raised and land was purchased to the west of the Latin Church in 1866. A firman of approval was issued by the Ottoman sultan in 1868, construction began in 1869, and the church was dedicated in 1871, when Edward, now the king, returned for the dedication. Originally called the Church of the Redeemer, it later became known as the Church of Christ, becoming the second Anglican church to be built in Palestine (the first was built in Jerusalem in 1848) (Abu al-'Assal, 1971).

The rapid rise of Protestant edifices in Nazareth during this period can be seen by comparing Tobler's 1868 map of Nazareth, which identifies only a Protestant mission school and a home for missionaries, and includes a drawing of the planned Protestant church in its lower right corner, to Bartlett's 1879 map—an anglicized and updated version of Tobler's—which identifies the addition of the new Protestant church, as well as a parsonage, mission hospital, and an orphanage for girls. The only other identified addition to the religious landscape is the new quarters of the Latin convent, now known as the Casa Nova (Bartlett 1977, 483).

Growth in the community was primarily the result of conversion in which, according to an 8 September 1989 interview with pastor Riyah Abu al-'Assal, members of the four main religious communities of Nazareth joined the church for various reasons. As with the other communities, reasons for change are often based on intracommunal disputes, or because of perceived opportunities in a new community. No doubt the Anglican school and the opportunities for employment attracted some of the earlier converts. A more recent convert, Zahi Nasser, who currently serves as assistant pastor and religion instructor at the church-run school, suggested several other reasons for religious conversion. He explained in a 22 May 1989 interview that he left Greek Orthodoxy for the Baptist Church while still a student at the Baptist school, primarily for theological reasons. Then upon his return to Nazareth from studying theology at a Baptist college in Switzerland, he decided to become Anglican because the Anglican Church in the Middle East is an independent church and at the local level is considered to be a Palestinian church with a Palestinian bishop, while the Baptists in Nazareth are still tied to the Southern Baptists from the United States and are perceived as a missionary church. Fu'ad Farah made a similar observation. He explained that "Anglicans are a bit more tolerable to us," because they are "considered more Christian than the Baptists" and because they are "seen more as an Arab church."

Whatever the reasons for entering the Anglican Church and its community, only 320 Nazarenes belong to the Anglican community after a presence of more than a hundred years. Emigration has also taken its toll on the community, whose emphasis on education and strong ties to the West have provided greater opportunities for educated youth than they can find in Nazareth or Israel.

In spite of its smaller numbers, the Anglican community has significant landholdings and institutions. The church compound includes offices, a reception hall, and a two-story elementary school. The old mission school further into the suq now serves as a kindergarten and youth club (nadi). St. Margaret's, the former orphanage on the hill below the Salesian property, is now a home for the mentally handicapped (which in the mid–1980s enrolled its first non-Arab resident), a kindergarten, a small school for expatriate children, and a hospice. Reverend Abu al-'Assal indicated in a 25 April 1994 interview that the community also has plans to build a secondary school on the property. Waqf properties include seventeen shops in the suq and Latin quarter and several houses. The community cemetery is located near the English hospital.

The community waqf also includes land located near the Orthodox Church, which was donated in 1893 with the intention that it be used as a community cemetery. The land was never needed for a cemetery because the cemetery near the hospital has never filled, so the land lay vacant. In the late 1960s, a neighbor planted fruit trees on the Anglican land and even started to build temporary housing, claiming the property to be his. The Anglican community, fearing it might lose the land, took the matter to court, which reaffirmed the property as belonging to the Anglican waqf. With ownership guaranteed, Abu 'Assal set out to utilize the land to the benefit of the community which, like other communities, was experiencing a housing shortage and emigration. The Anglicans decided to build a housing complex on the property. The multistory structure was completed in 1984 with fourteen two-and three-bedroom apartments. All fourteen of the apartments are currently occupied by Anglicans who purchased the apartments at cost, with no monetary gain for the community. There are still several other parcels of waqf lands which are also being considered as future housing development sites.

The Baptist Community

Whether the Baptists should be considered a community is a matter of debate. They have their own church, school, cemetery, and even a quarter, but unlike the other main Protestant group, the Anglicans, they have not been established in Nazareth for as long a period of time, nor have many entire family units converted. This means that those who do convert, mainly young singles, many of whom are students or former students of the Baptist school, do so while still maintaining ties to their families and community. Thus, while religiously they may be believing Baptists, they return to the community of their families for feast days, family baptisms, weddings, and funerals, and even their own weddings and funerals.

According to an 8 March 1989 interview with Reverend Fu'ad Sakhnini of the Baptist congregation, the Baptists got their start in Nazareth in the early 1920s when Shukri Musa, a native of Safad who had become Baptist while studying in Texas, came to Nazareth and started preaching. By 1928 there were enough believers to warrant the construction of a church. Musa died shortly thereafter, and his nephew took over as pastor of the small Baptist group. Sporadic missionary service, interruptions from World War II, and the political unrest that came with the establishment of the State of Israel resulted in rather slow growth. Then in 1950, Dr. Dwight Baker, a Southern Baptist missionary, came, and by 1953 had organized the Nazareth Baptist Church. He resigned in 1959, and Reverend Sakhnini became the new pastor. Now the work is entirely under the control of Arabs and is the only self-supporting Baptist church in Israel.

While functioning as an independent Baptist church they still have ties to the Southern Baptists. During the British Mandate, the Southern Baptists bought land to the north of the Coptic quarter where they established a school in 1948 and have recently completed construction of a church. In 1956, the Southern Baptist mission purchased 15 dunams, some of which was absentee land, in the Nimsawi quarter. The Baptists purchased the land anonymously in a magistrate court auction through the help of an Arab friend. Four Arab families then bought parcels of the land from the Baptist mission; along with the two expatriate Baptist families, the Registers and Hellers, they live in a Baptist cluster in what has become known as the American quarter after the two American Baptist families who live there. During the Mandate, the Baptists also purchased land for a cemetery nestled just below the main road to Reina on the edge of the Safafra quarter, which they share with the Brethren Assembly. At present there are only three grave markers in the cemetery, because many of the Baptists return to their former communities for burial. Since there are no nonsectarian cemeteries in Israel, it is important that each community have its own cemetery.

On Sunday the Baptists hold Sunday school, followed by a morning worship service, with only adults who are true believers remaining afterward to take communion. There is also a Sunday evening worship service, a Thursday evening service, and a Wednesday home visitation program in which interested people are taught about Baptist beliefs. While this is not technically proselytizing, which is strongly discouraged in Israel and is a criminal offence if conversions are the result of offering the convert monetary or other gain, it is how the Baptists are able to spread the word in addition to the work of the Baptist school. Services were held in the auditorium of the school until a new church was finished in the early 1990s. A Sunday morning in September 1989 found about 150 in attendance, many of whom were young men and young women of high-school or college age; a dozen or so were foreigners who could listen to a translation of the service via headphones. During the service an announcement was made of an upcoming course on Islamic studies so that Baptists would be able to have a meaningful dialogue with Muslims. The announcer said it was necessary for the Baptists to "use what the Quran teaches to bring them to Christ," adding that since they live among Muslims, it is important to know what they believe.

Missionary work is not directed only toward Muslims. Most members of the Baptist community are from other Christian sects. As part of the missionary movement, the Baptist community of Nazareth serves as the mother church for Baptist centers now established throughout the Galilee in Yafa, Kfar Kanna, Turan, Rama, Akka, and Haifa. Reverend Sakhnini noted that these centers are for the most part led by former members of the Nazareth community. In his anthropological study of the village of Rama (Rameh), Khalil Nakhleh writes of several members of the village who, beginning in the early 1960s, became Baptists under the tutelage of Baptists from Nazareth. Some of the converts moved to Nazareth and others stayed in the village. In explaining why conversions take place, Nakhleh writes: "Whereas the Baptist Minister in Nazareth hopes that conversions are fuelled by divine ulterior motives, those Arabs who consider conversion do so apparently for personal maximization." He then explains that the Baptist phenomenon is for the most part "resisted by the traditional sects mainly because of its foreign character" and because of the "generous monetary rewards the Baptists offer." Nakhleh suggests that conversions take place not because of "differences in religious doctrine, as the Baptist minister in Nazareth would like to believe," but rather because it supplies "the villagers with one more alternative to express their dissatisfaction not of the traditional sects, but of the people . . . who run them" (Nakhleh 1973, 103).

Other Christian Groups

In addition to the seven main Christian religious communities already mentioned, there are several other Christian groups in Nazareth, some of which are gradually gaining community status. One common problem for most of the new groups—especially those not established in the land prior to the establishment of the State of Israel—is that they are not officially recognized by the government of Israel and as such cannot perform weddings, grant divorces, or issue birth and death certificates.

Another problem of the new groups is that even though members of a religious community may not be satisfied with the doctrine of their own church, few are willing to step out from the security and comfort of the traditions of their community. There is also pressure from within the community to remain a part of it. When Evangelist Billy Graham visited Nazareth in 1960, he held a service in a wooded area on the grounds of the English hospital. During the service, he asked those who would like Christ to come into their hearts to raise their hands. A reporter noted that many of the Greek Catholics in attendance "seemed hesitant as they looked back towards where Archbishop George Hakim sat in his car," but that about two hundred of those in attendance did eventually raise their hands (*JP*, 21 March 1960). In spite of the difficulties, several Protestant sects are present in Nazareth. Most of the leaders of these Protestant sects admit that the greatest number of their followers have come out of the Greek Orthodox community.

The Brethren Assembly became established in Nazareth in the 1930s when followers from New Zealand and England came to town and started to testify. Originally the group met in homes; then in the late 1960s they purchased the Bathgate Clinic of the English hospital, located near the Greek Orthodox bishop's compound, where until recently they held their Sunday morning services and Tuesday and Friday evening Bible studies. Baptism is not required to join the Brethren and no formal list of followers is kept, but according to a 25 July 1989 interview with longtime believer Farah Khalil, Sunday services average twenty to fifty in attendance. The group has recently built a meeting place (the Brethren do not refer to it as a church) just above the YMCA and below the English hospital on land purchased from the English

Mission. The building also houses the Emmaus Bible School. Khalil said that believers come from all of the traditional Christian communities and that there are even Jewish believers who come from Upper Nazareth and Haifa to attend the services. There are no Brethren missionaries, but each believer witnesses to friends.

The Nazarenes came to Nazareth in 1952, when they built a church in the Maidan quarter on land purchased from a family moving to Lebanon. In 1982 they added a kindergarten behind the church which has an enrollment of 120 pupils, a quarter of which are Muslims. According to a 3 April 1989 interview with Pastor Chris Grubb, current membership is made up of forty-nine Arabs who have been born again. He estimates that about 60 to 70 percent of the believers are women, many of whom eventually leave the church when they marry; about 80 percent are former Greek Orthodox; one of the believers is a Muslim boy who has accepted Jesus; about 50 percent of the members seldom attend. A Sunday meeting in April 1989 found about thirty-five people in attendance, ten of whom were expatriates living in Nazareth. The Arab congregants included seven young girls, nine teenage girls, four teenage boys, an older couple whose son is a Nazarene pastor in Jerusalem, and several adult women, one of whom was formerly associated with the Brethren, but now attends the Nazarene Church, where she serves as translator during the services and works during the week in the kindergarten. Two of the teenage girls came late and were dressed in scout uniforms. They were members of the Latin scout troop and had participated with their troop in Annunciation Day services at the Latin Church earlier that morning. In July 1989 Chris Grubb left Nazareth for a new assignment in Cyprus in an attempt by the mission director to pull all missionaries out of Nazareth. He was eventually replaced by Butrus Gharib, a native of Nazareth who will serve concurrently as pastor for both the Haifa and Nazareth parishes.

The Church of Christ was established in Nazareth in 1960. Church membership increased rapidly, with upward of three hundred being baptized over the next three decades, although many of these conversions have not been permanent. Bill Clark, who currently serves as a missionary and acting pastor, related in a 9 May 1989 interview that now there are only about fifty practicing members; attendance each week ranges from a handful to several dozen. Clark explained that many of the people were converted to the foreign missionary, most of whom served in Nazareth for two-year periods, and not to the teachings. He said that when the missionary couples return to visit, the chapel is full of the people they converted, but when they leave, so do their converts. Many of the early converts were young men who saw the church as a way of escaping Nazareth and life in Israel. Clark knows of twenty-nine young men from Nazareth who have gone to the United States to study at Christian colleges with the support of the church, but knows of only one who has returned and remained faithful. Some have remained abroad; others have returned to Nazareth but stopped coming to church.

The church building is located in the Nimsawi quarter. During the week it is used as a church-run daycare center. A sign on the perimeter fence identifies the building as the Church of Christ; an added warning in English, French, and Hebrew says: "This is not a historical site. It has importance only to the Christians who worship here." Clark said this was posted to prevent the trespassing of Christian pilgrims, many of whom figure every church in Nazareth is built to commemorate the site of a sacred event.

The Church of Christ operates a high school in the Arab village of 'Eilabun. The largest of the eight congregations in the Holy Land is also located there. Several of the members from Nazareth work at the high school, one as principal and another as its business manager. The church is not officially recognized and owns no cemetery, so its members are encouraged to maintain ties with their former churches so that marriages and funerals can be held there. When Bill Clark's wife passed away, she was buried in the Anglican cemetery in Ramla because their son-in-law, who is Arab, had relatives in Ramla who were Anglican. Johny Jahshan related in a 5 July 1989 interview that he left Greek Catholicism for the Church of Christ, but had to return to the Greek Catholic Church to be married. He said that until the Church of Christ is officially recognized, he will also have to return there to be buried. He knows of one wedding that was performed in the Church of Christ, but it was done only after exerting much pressure on the government to issue a certificate of marriage. Now that a precedent has been set, he hopes the Church of Christ might be able to perform more marriages.

The Seventh Day Adventists began work in Nazareth in 1980 when they purchased the third floor above St. Joseph's Restaurant in the Barclay's Discount Bank building. This location serves as the gathering place for Saturday church services and for Bible, health, and language courses taught during the week. An Adventist couple from Finland is in charge of the language classes and the health center (complete with aerobic and stop-smoking classes and studies on obesity, high blood pressure, and the risk of heart attacks). They also assist native Nazarene Emil Nasser in his duties as the local pastor. In 1989, the English courses were taught by two college-age brothers from Maryland who volunteered to serve their church for one year as English teachers. In a 26 April 1989 interview, Nasser told of how he originally belonged to the Church of Christ, which sent him to a Church of Christ college in Tennessee to study theology. While there he became interested in the Adventist Church, converted, switched to an Adventist seminary in Michigan, served with the Jerusalem parish for three years, and then returned to Nazareth to open up a new parish. As of 1989, he said there were only eight adult members and six children. All members of the parish are converts: the Finnish couple from another Protestant sect, Nasser from Roman Catholicism via the Baptist School and Church of Christ, three from Greek Catholicism, one from Greek Orthodoxy, and one from Islam. They live scattered in Reina, Yafa, Upper Nazareth, and Nazareth. A Muslim young woman also attends regularly. Her family approves of her association with the Adventists, but does not approve of her being baptized. One of the adult members is currently studying at an Adventist college in London. Most of those who join are attracted initially to the language courses. According to Nasser, they have experienced "very slow growth"—only four baptisms in the past five years.

The Apostolic Church started efforts in Nazareth at about the same time as the Adventist, but with significantly better results. Headquartered in Germany, the Apostolic Church sent representatives to Nazareth to preach. Converts were then enlisted to visit others in spreading the word. Within a decade the group claimed membership of about three hundred. Riyad Hassan, a deacon in the church who had been a member for three years, explained in a 29 August 1989 interview that converts are not expected to separate themselves from their previous churches, but simply to come to the Apostolic Church to "hear the right word." He said that his papers are still with the Latins and that he attends church there as well. This makes it easier for new members to join, for in doing so they are not required to be baptized and they can maintain ties with their former community. In October 1989 the Apostolics were able to move from a family home in the Krum quarter, where they held their meetings, to a new church in the Nimsawi quarter just below the American/Baptist quarter and behind the Church of Christ. The large, two-story church, the first Apostolic church in Israel, was built with financial help from headquarters in Germany and is the first local structure to be faced with locally processed, polyester-fortified limestone, called St. Michael's stone by its Nazarene developer Michel Tabri (JP, International Edition, week ending 1 September 1990).

The Church of Jesus Christ of Latter-day Saints (Mormon) has had to limit its activities in Israel because of strong opposition from some Orthodox Jewish groups toward the church-sponsored Brigham Young University Center for Near Eastern Studies in Jerusalem. There are three Jewish/Mormon families living in Upper Nazareth who came as immigrants to Israel from Uruguay and, like many of the more recent immigrant Russian Jews, have some family members who are Jewish and others who are Christian. These Mormons travel to Tiberias every Saturday for Sabbath services attended by a score of Mormons who live scattered throughout northern Israel.

The Edinburgh Medical Missionary Society (EMMS) started activities in Nazareth in about 1863. They constructed a hospital in 1914, which also includes a small chapel where Sunday services are held, primarily for the expatriate and local staff at the hospital.

In addition to these Western sects, there are several longtime Eastern sects that do not maintain places of worship in Nazareth, but do have community members living there. According to Agob Bogosian, who runs a photo shop in the center of town, about thirty-five Armenians live scattered in Nazareth and Upper Nazareth. This number does not include the Armenians who have become completely Arabized to the point of even changing their names, such as the Bitar family who took on their Arab name during the Mandate and are now Greek Orthodox. Bogosian explained in an 11 September 1989 interview that his father came to Nazareth in 1948 from Tiberias, and that other Armenians came from Turkey via Lebanon or Haifa. He said that most of these Armenians attend the Coptic Church and that marriages are performed there by Armenian priests who come from Jerusalem. Baptisms are also performed by visiting priests either in the home or in the Coptic Church.

There are nineteen Syrian Orthodox (Jacobites) in Nazareth, according to a 28 August 1989 interview with George Afram. He related how his father's family came from northern Iraq and settled in Jerusalem,[13] where his father was born. Afram's father worked for the YMCA in Jerusalem, then transferred to the YMCA in Tiberias. In 1948 he came to Nazareth as a refugee. The small group of Syrian Orthodox is made up of four households, all related. While most similar to the Maronites, who also use Syriac in their liturgy, they associate most closely with the Greek Orthodox Church, where the grandmother prays and where the children will marry in a ceremony officiated by a Syrian Orthodox priest who comes from Jerusalem. The Syrian archbishop came from Jerusalem to baptize the children at home.

Rivalry and Cooperation within the Christian Community

With so many distinct Christian communities, it stands to reason that there would be divisive elements as well as ecumenical efforts. Theo-

---

13 There are larger Syrian communities in Jerusalem and Bethlehem. In Jerusalem many have congregated into the area around the Syrian convent of St. Mark in the Armenian quarter, while in Bethlehem they remain scattered (Tsimhoni 1984, 361).

logical differences would seem to be one of the main sources of contention, but in fact they are seldom an issue, differences in doctrine
rarely being mentioned or even considered. Allegiance is more a result
of family and ethnic tradition than belief. They do not conflict over
holy places, as happens in Jerusalem's Basilica of the Holy Sepulchre or
Bethlehem's Basilica of the Nativity.[14] Nazareth has been spared this
rivalry, in part because the two dominant sects, the Greeks and the
Latins, both have their own site of the Annunciation. Rather, division
comes from concern over conversion, intermarriage, where and with
whom to build cemeteries, and on what days to celebrate holidays.

Christian-Christian conflicts are seldom mentioned in the traveler accounts, as Muslim-Christian relations are. Mansur, however,
does mention several incidents from the nineteenth century. In 1855,
the Franciscan monks held a large celebration in which they gathered
in the courtyard of the church and burned all the religious books of the
Protestants. Then they attacked the Protestant missionaries in their
home, killing one. In 1875, the Roman Catholic and Greek Catholic
communities, who were still at odds over rights to the synagogue
church, came to blows when the Latin priests wanted to share appointments to the religious court in rotation with the Greek Catholics.
During Easter services, Latin youths entered the Greek Catholic Church
and started a fight. As the brawl moved outside, more Latin youths lay
in wait to join the ruckus. When the government stepped in to punish
the Latin youths, the Franciscan priests sent them to their monastery
on Mt. Tabor for sanctuary (Mansur 1924, 87, 100).

Two travelers from the first part of this century provided interesting but conflicting accounts of inter-Christian relations. Fredrick
Treves described Nazareth in 1913 as follows:

> As is the case with other sacred towns in Palestine, Nazareth is the
> scene of acute religious competition. If one Christian sect erects a palatial
> convent it is incumbent upon some other Christian sect to found an oppo-
> sition building of still greater pretence. These arrogant buildings provide an

[14] The Greek Orthodox, Roman Catholic, and Armenian sects share control of
these two churches (other sects have nominal rights), which are regulated down to who
cleans what window, repairs what roof, or hangs extra lamps. This status quo was established centuries ago. Conflicts result when there are any threats to extend control
beyond that which has already been established and regulated by successive ruling
powers. There is a long history of conflict over these holy places. An example of its continuation comes during preparation for Christmas services at the Basilica of the Nativity, on general cleaning days held jointly by the three sects, which have erupted in
recent years into actual fights between the competing clergy over who cleans what,
because cleaning constitutes ownership. Colbi (1988, 82) writes that "the annals of
Christianity in the Holy Land are little more than a chronicle of quarrel after quarrel
between Latins and Orthodox for possession of the Holy Places."

unedifying spectacle of that bitter civil warfare which engages the world of Christendom. . . . Nazareth is not a Christian town because the followers of Christ are apparently more concerned in discomfiting their co-religionists than in bettering the state of the people about their doors. (Treves 1913, 181)

A contrasting view was filed in 1921 by Whittingham:

> I found Nazareth very interesting, and impressive in its peaceful calm. . . . I have seen it stated in books that 'the people of Nazareth are extremely turbulent in disposition'; perhaps they were in the days of perpetual conflict. . . . To-day a great peace would seem to have descended upon this lovely valley, a peace that could be felt in the streets, on the hills, by the fountain, and in the church. Although there are Greek Orthodox and Greek Catholics, Maronites and Latins, and a small number of Moslems, there is no religious conflict, for the Holy Places belong exclusively to the Franciscans. (Whittingham 1921, 263)

A similar dichotomy might be found today, for there is indeed conflict, but for the most part it is between the leaders of the religious sects, while among the lay members of the Christian communities, little distinction is made among sects.

When asked to rank inter-Christian relations, the 139 Christian survey participants indicated a very positive view. On a scale of one to five (one being very good and five very bad), 22 percent ranked relations as very good, 61 percent as good, 11 percent as average, 4 percent as bad, and 1 percent as very bad, for a mean of of 2.014. When asked why relations were good or bad, sixteen people ventured a response. The most common response was that the failure to celebrate holidays on the same day divided the Christian community. Two complained of a lack of intersectarian associations or understanding; three identified politics as being influential, one of those saying that since the rise of the Islamic party, inter-Christian cooperation has improved; and three indicated that relations are good with no real factions existing.

A notable from the Greek Orthodox community offered his views of inter-Christian relations: "In Nazareth the atmosphere has always been very good between the Christian communities. Why? Because the Orthodox community is the largest and the Latins are weaker and couldn't do much about it." He then added, "The Latins are the ones who have caused the inter-Christian rivals in the holy land," maintaining that this was the result of the Latin clergy differentiating between Christians of the various sects through such methods as hiring only Latins or requiring their pupils to attend Latin services. The lay Christian people on the other hand "never cared or never saw the differences between them."

While not mentioned by the respondents as a contemporary cause of intersectarian strife, conversion continues to be a sensitive issue. As early as 1823, Protestant missionaries from the American-based Church Missionary Society were distributing scriptures, including Arabic Bibles, in Nazareth. One of the missionaries reported that among the Christian communities, "the Greeks make no objection," while "the Latins are the principal objectors" and "the instigators of all the opposition that is made" (Jowett 1827, 40). More recently, when a watchman at St. Joseph's Church was asked about inter-Christian relations, he said that the main problem was between "Christians and Protestants" because the "Protestants are trying to convert the Christians rather than the Muslims." Ernest Farah's concern with conversion stems from the continual demographic decline of the Orthodox community, which in 1948 made up 36 percent of Nazareth's population, but today makes up only an estimated 18.5 percent. Part of this decline is the result of low birthrates among Christian Arabs, Muslim refugee migration to Nazareth, and Christian emigration, but it is also the result of "movement to the Western churches." He writes: "Were it not for the 'slide' of Orthodox Christians toward the other denominations, Nazareth's Orthodox community should number today 18,555 (instead of 12,950, —a loss of 5,666)" (al-Bishara, September 1988, 3).

As already illustrated, conversions resulted when migrant Maronites became Roman Catholics in order to gain the food, money, employment, and protection offered by Franciscan monks and when disgruntled Greek Orthodox families left the fold for Greek Catholicism. Similar motives are still found today. Maronite Father Yusef 'Isa explained that conversions to the Anglican or Baptist church have resulted when these two Protestant sects have offered help to a person or family. Johny Jahshan related two accounts of how complications surrounding weddings resulted in a change of sect. A member of the Greek Catholic Shufani clan married a French woman who was Roman Catholic. When they later wanted a divorce, the Catholic Church disapproved, so he became Greek Orthodox, where divorce was allowed. The second incident involved a local member of the communist party from the Greek Catholic community who became Orthodox in order to get married because the Greek Catholic Church refused to perform the ceremony. Father Arturo explained that in former times, older parishioners often felt that the church was obliged to them and that if they did not get what they wanted, they would change rites.

One Greek Orthodox explained that until recently there had been active proselytizing on the part of most religions and that because the Orthodox were neglected spiritually and had no schools or religious education, "they were easy prey for the wealthier Latins and Catholics."

He explained further that conversions to the Protestant sects are still more difficult because even the "indifferent Christian" can see the difference between Protestantism and the more traditional Catholic and Orthodox churches. He added later that most of the Baptists, Anglicans, and Greek Catholics have come from the Greek Orthodox community, but that he personally has never felt uneasy about people leaving the Orthodox Church. He explained that he refers to the Greek Catholics as the "liberals" of the Orthodox Church "because they didn't want the tyranny of the Greek priests" and that he "admires the Baptists who left because they had the guts to make the change."

The most common cause of conversion is intermarriage. Until several decades ago this was also a major source of intersectarian contention. The intensity of feelings that existed is illustrated by a story related by a prominent member of the Greek Orthodox community who reported that only six years ago his cousin had been told by a clergy member of a Western-Rite Church that "it is better to take a Muslim to the church for marriage than an Orthodox." Father Barnaba explained that up until the mid-twentieth century, intermarriage between a member of the Greek Orthodox community and members of one of the three Western-Rite communities often resulted in excommunication, one of the problems being that the Western-Rite churches did not encourage the wife to follow her husband's religion. Then in the 1950s people started to complain to their priests. They wanted to marry beyond their own family and community and at the same time wondered why such a policy existed when all it did was foster enmity between the Christian sects. Gradually the churches began to grant permission for intersectarian marriages, the end result being an unwritten agreement that the woman automatically follows the religion of the man when they get married. In order to facilitate this policy, the woman is required to obtain a baptismal certificate from her family church, which is then submitted to her husband's church prior to the marriage. This guarantees her baptism, grants permission for her to enter into the new sect, and fulfills Israeli laws which require that all changes in religion be recorded. Commenting on the changed policy, Zahi Nasser noted that the once tense relationships between the Christian sects are now friendly and that resolving the issue of mixed marriages has helped.

This relaxed marriage policy has resulted in many mixed marriages and many changes of sects. In addition, there is greater harmony between the once conflicting groups, primarily because most members of the many Christian communities are now interrelated through marriage to members of the other communities. Records from the Latin parish indicate that of the fifty-two marriages performed by Father Arturo in the Roman Catholic Basilica of the Annunciation in 1988, eighteen of the brides were Roman Catholic, twenty were Greek Catholic, thirteen were Greek Orthodox, and one was Maronite. Marriage forms from the office of the Greek Orthodox bishopric indicate that of the ninety-seven marriages performed at the Greek Orthodox Church in 1988, fifty-six were to Greek Orthodox brides, nineteen to Greek Catholics, sixteen to Roman Catholics, three to Maronites, and three to Anglicans. Of the 139 Christian wives surveyed, 50 percent indicated that they had changed religion when they married, while only 3 percent of the 136 husbands who responded indicated that they had changed religion, including one Orthodox man from the village of Turan who became Baptist when he married his Baptist wife in the early 1980s and an Orthodox man who became Roman Catholic when he married his Latin wife in the early 1960s.

The extent to which marriage and conversions are interrelated is illustrated by the genealogy of Rawiya Abu Hanna, a university student who is Anglican, as related in a 24 August 1989 interview with her and her mother, Julia. Rawiya's maternal grandfather was raised Orthodox. He married a Maronite who became Orthodox. Rawiya's paternal grandfather was an Anglican who married a Greek Catholic in 1932. The bride's father consented to allow the marriage only if the Anglican man would become Catholic, which he did. Rawiya's father Anis was therefore raised as a Greek Catholic. When he married Julia, who was raised Orthodox, she became Greek Catholic too. Anis provided attorney services to his church for many years and was a member of the church council, but when a dispute arose between Anis and the church treasurer over accounting procedures, Anis decided he would return to the childhood religion of his father. Julia had attended the Anglican school as a child, so the change was an easy one for the family. One of Rawiya's sisters married a Maronite and followed his religion, while a brother's wife became Anglican when they married.

A marriage in the Greek Orthodox Church ran into difficulty several years ago when Father Romanous objected to performing a marriage between an Orthodox groom and his Latin-turned-Orthodox bride because he thought the bridesmaid (the Roman Catholic sister of the bride), who was to play a role in the marriage ceremony, should also be Orthodox. According to council chairman Adib Hazan, the council had to explain to Father Romanous that it was all right to have other Christians participating in the ceremony and that they were happy that mixed marriages were now allowed because it gave Nazareth the feeling of being one large parish.

The mixed-marriage problem and the tensions it helped to create kept the religious communities more separated than they are today. Kamil Asfur, a Greek Orthodox, explained in a 4 February 1989 interview that as a child he would go to the Latin Church for holidays, but that he never felt welcome there because of the sectarian rivalries. Now he said he feels welcome in any church.

The greatest intermixing of church attendance occurs within the three Western-Rite churches. The Roman Catholic churches are well attended on a weekly basis by members of all three Western-Rite sects because they are scattered throughout town and are therefore more accessible than the Maronite and Greek Catholic churches located in the narrow streets of the market. Holidays, however, find most Roman Catholics at the main basilica and the Maronites and Greek Catholics back in their parish churches.

Attempts to forge stronger intercommunal relations have come primarily from an ecumenical council, organized in Nazareth in 1975 by the seven major communities—Orthodox, Latin, Greek Catholic, Maronite, Copt, Anglican, and Baptist. Each community is represented at the monthly meetings by a priest and two lay people. Interest in the council has waxed and waned throughout the years with little success resulting from the many meetings. The few successes have included the implementation of an annual ecumenical week of prayer, visits to other churches, an agreement not to proselytize members of other sects (a gesture of goodwill from the sponsoring Western-Rite churches that had been gaining converts from the Orthodox community), and an ongoing interest in creating Christian fellowship and unity.[15] But other concerns and topics, such as unifying the celebration of Christian holidays, creating a common cemetery, and standardizing Christian education, have met with little success.

The concern over holiday celebrations stems from the difference in calendars used in the Western and Eastern-Rite churches. Christmas is always celebrated on 25 December by the Western churches and on 7 January by the Eastern churches. This thirteen-day difference between

[15] The Nazareth version of ecumenism is concerned more with cooperation than promoting any form of theological unity. Father Arturo noted in a seminar on the Arab Christian communities of Israel, which was sponsored by the Israel Interfaith Association, that the ecumenical activities discussed in Nazareth should not be concerned with converting the Orthodox to Catholicism, but rather with striving to make the Orthodox truly Orthodox and the Catholic truly Catholic. He stressed that "tolerance is the basis of the movement," then noted that although Christians usually say that the differences between sects "are unfortunate," he himself thinks the "differences are wonderful, and a source of joy." He feels that "the liturgy of the Eastern Churches, so rich and marvelous, is a treasure for the whole church" (Carse 1985, 29). Ernest Farah, on the other hand, writes: "I do not believe in to-day's ecumenism. It is soothing but not healing. It keeps the faithful away from thinking about the real reasons of the schism, and thus indirectly contributes to its continuation. I need a dialogue between brothers facing the 'sins and heresies' committed by either part" (al-Bishara, February-April 1990, 4).

the Julian and Gregorian calendars also means that Easter, which is celebrated on the first Sunday after the first full moon following the spring equinox, coincides only on occasion between the two groups, and is usually celebrated a week, five weeks, or occasionally four weeks apart (Colbi 1988, 296). This can be helpful to couples coming from two different communities, for they can celebrate with both of their families and at both churches without a conflict of time and interest, but it also causes problems when it comes to school vacations, municipal holidays, business closings, town decorations and celebrations, and tourism. It also serves to separate the communities by singling out the Greek Orthodox and Copts, who most often celebrate on different dates.[16]

The problem of holiday dates has been solved in several Middle Eastern countries where the Christian communities have decided to celebrate Christmas according to the Western Julian calendar and the holy week at Easter according to the Eastern Gregorian calendar. In an attempt to unify holiday celebrations in Israel, the ecumenical council of Nazareth sponsored a 1982 conference held in nadi Rum and attended by 150 representatives from all Christian sects and from Christian communities representing eighteen cities and villages in Israel. The conference, directed by Fu'ad Farah, endorsed a proposal that the Christian communities unite holiday observances in the same manner as in other Middle Eastern countries (al-Anba', 14 November 1982). Father Shahada, who attended the conference, noted that "unifying the Christian holidays is a religious and secular necessity" (al-Ittihad, 16 November 1982). The final approval for this monumental effort rested with the Greek and Latin patriarchs, who in the end refused to support the plan. Father Arturo noted that "it is not so easy to change tradition," and that to make such a change both patriarchs need to agree. Such an agreement has not yet been made. The lack of support from the patriarchs has caused many in Nazareth to lose hope, including those involved with the ecumenical council and members of the Christian community who see this issue as their single most divisive issue. They feel they have no control over the situation and that the ecclesiastical rivalry in Jerusalem adversely influences their attempts at unity.

On occasions when the two Easters do fall on the same day, the ecumenical council has proposed that joint processions be held, but ac-

---

[16] In 1913, Scrimgeour offered his comments concerning separate feast days: "To any impartial thinker, as well as to the sharp Moslem observer, it appears to be a most deplorable fact that two sections of the Christian Church in the town where Christ Himself lived cannot agree together even so far as to allow them to celebrate the feasts of Christmas and Good Friday on the same day of the year" (Scrimgeour 1913, 96).

cording to Greek Catholic Yusef Nakhleh, the Greek Orthodox patriarch in Jerusalem rejected the idea. Fu'ad Farah offers an alternative
account. He says the plan for a united procession was stopped not by
the patriarch, but by the Jebha-dominated Orthodox council, who
turned down the proposal from Farah because they said a joint celebration would offend the Muslims. The ecumenical council had also
agreed to open a Christian information center, but this too was rejected
by the Greek Orthodox Council. Farah thinks that politics may have
been the motive on this occasion, for Anglican minister Abu al-'Assal,
who is a leading figure in the Taqadumia party, actively supported the
plan, and the Jebha members of the Greek Orthodox Council did not
want to support an opponent even on a nonpolitical issue.

   Attempts by the ecumenical council as well as separate negotiations and discussions to cooperate on a joint Christian cemetery have
also been stalled by intersectarian problems. Cemetery space is rapidly
filling up in both the Greek Orthodox cemetery near the church and
the quartered cemetery of the Western-Rite and Coptic communities.
In recognition of the need for a new cemetery, Fu'ad Farah issued a
memorandum on 5 September 1982 in which he proposed that a new
joint cemetery be established on land to the west of Nazareth near the
road to 'Illut. Citing population projections he estimated that by the
year 2030, the deceased of Nazareth's Christian community would require about 38 dunams of land for burial. In anticipation of this cemetery crisis, the Greek Orthodox community had been able to obtain a
long-term lease from the government for 18 dunams of land by threat-
ening, if their request for land was not granted, to bury their dead in
the Orthodox cemetery in the former Arab village of Mujeidil in what
is now the Jewish town of Migdal Ha Emek. Farah then proposed that
this land be joined with at least 20 dunams from a large plot of land belonging to the Custody of the Holy Land (Franciscans), which is located
next to the Orthodox-leased land.

   The municipality and all parties involved agreed to the proposal,
but when it came down to its implementation, the project fell apart.
The problem was that no one could decide who was responsible for the
financing of such necessities as an access road, parking lot, wall, chapel,
and toilet facilities. They were also concerned about whether to partition the cemetery into separate sections for each community. Farah's
wife was formerly Anglican and his two daughters have married a
Latin and a Greek Catholic. He would therefore like to see the cemetery
used jointly by the entire Christian community, now intertwined
through marriage, so that mixed families like his can be buried in the
same plot rather than in separate sections according to sect. Farah criticized the Latins for wanting a separate section for the Latin deceased.

Riyah Abu al-'Assal, whose Anglican community still has plenty of burying space near the English hospital, accused the Orthodox of bringing a halt to the project. He said that the forty-nine-year lease was issued to the Orthodox council, but the other community leaders did not want to invest in a cemetery they did not have any control over. They also did not want to cooperate with the Orthodox council, which they felt was being manipulative. From the Latin side of the issue, Father Arturo explained that the Franciscans were willing to cooperate, but since they were contributing their own land—unlike the Orthodox who were contributing government-donated land—they felt it should be the responsibility of the Orthodox to finance the building projects and maintenance. He indicated that the Latins were also waiting for concrete plans, which never materialized, before they approved the project. The land is yet to be developed and there has been no further discussion on the cemetery issue in the last several years.

Whether it be religious, political, or monetary squabbles, the ineffectiveness of the ecumenical council prompts harsh criticism. One Greek Orthodox accused the Latins of being "a big dam in front of us which prevents us from moving." He then turned on his own and described the Orthodox patriarch in Jerusalem as one who "doesn't give a damn about the people" and of being "even worse" than the Latin hierarchy in terms of supporting the objectives of the ecumenical movement.[17] Adib Hazan said the council "doesn't do very much, but it does keep the people in touch." Riyah Abu al-'Assal noted that it worked very well in the beginning, but that over time its effectiveness declined owing to the lack of support from the patriarchs (including the Orthodox patriarch's outspokenness against the council), a lack of interest from Nazareth's Christians, and the tendency for each to blame the other when progress was not made. Because of these problems, the council did not meet for several years in the 1980s, but there has recently been a revival and many of the same topics have reemerged in the meetings.

[17] In 1989 the Greek Orthodox patriarchate announced that it would no longer participate in an ecumenical dialogue with representatives of other Christian sects. The patriarch indicated that such dialogues had been used by other Christian denominations to "steal members of his flock." He then stressed that the Orthodox tradition has the "fullness of Christian truth." Observers suggest that this statement was directed to the many Roman and Greek Catholics who have left the Greek Orthodox Church (Eldar 1990, 3). Soon after the announcement, the Greek Orthodox patriarch consecrated a new church in Beit Sahur near Bethlehem. On such occasions, representatives from all of the other Christian communities usually attend, but on this occasion none did. Some observers interpreted this act as a sign that the tensions between the Orthodox and Western-Rite sects continue (*JP*, 10 August 1989).

4
Muslim and Refugee Communities

The Muslim Community

The Muslim community is Nazareth's largest and has the longest record of continual occupancy in the town. When Muslim inhabitants first settled in the town is unknown, but it would have been in the century following the A.D. 638 Arab-Islamic conquest of Palestine, for mention is made of Saracens (Muslims) in Nazareth by the early decades of the eighth century. It appears that there were no Muslim inhabitants in the village during the crusader period (1102–87), but from the time the crusaders left until the arrival of the Franciscans in 1620, Nazareth was a Muslim village with a mosque rising in its center. Muslims remained in the majority until long after the arrival of the Christians, whose numbers surpassed the Muslims in the early decades of the nineteenth century. Muslims again gained the majority in the 1960s as a result of the addition of Muslim refugees, the rural-to-urban migration of Muslim villagers, the sedentarization of some Muslim Bedouin families in the town, a higher birthrate than the declining rate among Christians, and a lower emigration rate than that of Christians.

Early drawings of the village show a landscape dominated by a minaret at the heart of the village, indicative of the strong Muslim presence. An illustration by Franciscan Brother Roger, published in 1664, shows to the rear of an imposing Latin convent the tall, square, stone minaret of a mosque. To the side of the minaret is a building with four arched doorways that must be the predecessor to the White Mosque, but is identified by Roger as the place where Muslim pilgrims lodge, suggesting perhaps a dual function of the building. An additional place of prayer for Muslims is located near the entrance to the convent (Bagatti 1969, 5). This is probably the monument of Sheikh Shahab al-Din, which is still used as a place of prayer today. Later artistic renderings of the village in 1839 by David Roberts show the minaret of the recently completed White Mosque as the dominant feature of the skyline. Today, first glances in this city where church steeples and large convents dot the landscape would seem to indicate that Nazareth was no longer a Muslim town. Closer inspection, however, finds many minarets hidden away in neighborhoods off the main road, homes decorated with palm branches in honor of family members undertaking the pilgrimage to Mecca, greengrocers whose shop walls are covered with posters of the Ka'ba in Mecca and the Dome of the Rock in Jerusalem, an increasing number of women who keep their heads covered with scarves, and radio broadcasts of the Friday sermon playing in sweetshops along Pope Paul VI Street, all of which mark an indeed strong Muslim presence in the town.

Nazareth's Muslim community is fairly homogeneous in that members are Sunni and for the most part all Arab. The community is also interspersed with a few Circassian Muslim families who have moved to Nazareth from one of the two Circassian villages located in northern Israel and with convert wives who have, for example, European-Christian or Israeli-Jewish backgrounds. Other distinctions within the community come from longtime Muslim families, the newer and in the beginning more prosperous Fahum and Zu'bi families, and more recent immigrants who are divided among the 1948 refugees, sedentarized Bedouin, and rural-to-urban migrants.

Numbered at between 36,000 to 42,000, the Muslims of Nazareth are now able to pray at any of eight main mosques. The oldest of the mosques is the White Mosque (al-Jami' al-Abiyad), located at the core of the old village area in what was known as the Muslim quarter, but is now more commonly known as the suq or market (the main entrance to the mosque complex borders the open-air produce and meat market). The White Mosque is unique in that it is the only one of the eight mosques to be called by the term *jami'* rather then *mesjid*. Jami' (which comes from the Arabic root word meaning "to gather") is used in reference to the Friday Mosque, which serves as the main gathering place for Muslims to hear the Friday sermon, as well as a place to gather for any or all of the five daily prayers. Mesjid (which comes from the Arabic root "to bow down," as in prayer), on the other hand, connotes a lesser status in that it serves primarily as a place for daily prayers. Nowadays all eight of Nazareth's mosques have Friday sermons so that the distinction between calling one a jami' and the others mesjid is one of former roles and tradition rather than current function.

According to a 6 September 1989 interview with 'Atif Fahum, the White Mosque belongs to the Fahum family waqf. This status is the result of orders in the latter part of the eighteenth century from Egyptian ruler Suleiman Pasha to Sheikh Abdallah al-Fahum, the high commissioner in Nazareth, to build a mosque in the village. The initial construction included a pulpit and an arcade porch, followed later by a minaret and additional rooms and walls, completed in 1804 (Mansur gives 1805–8 as construction dates). The sheikh served as the administrator of the mosque, and when he died in 1815 he was buried inside the mosque near the minaret. As a descendent of Abdallah, 'Atif serves as trustee of the family endowment, in addition to being the proprietor of the Fahum coffee store. The mosque was funded by Suleiman Pasha, who then bequeathed the trusteeship to the Fahum family in the form of a waqf. The revenues from the waqf, which also include rents from the offices now occupying the khan of the pasha at the entrance to Casa Nova Street, are used for the upkeep of the mosque and to join with the Ministry of Religion in paying the salary of the sheikh or imam. The mosque, with its cream-colored walls, green trim, and green dome, is busy each day as merchants, neighbors, and shoppers come to pray. Mohammad Jemal, who currently serves as the sheikh of the mosque, in a 24 May 1989 interview noted that on regular days, 100–200 people gather for the noon and afternoon prayers, while 2,000–3,000 gather for the Friday sermon.

As the oldest mosque in the city and as a result of efforts by the Fahum family, the White Mosque serves the Muslim community in a variety of ways. The mosque conducts religious classes for young men; upward of fifty gather here several days each week and every day during the fasting month of Ramadan to study Islam. The mosque is also the sponsor of the Muslim scout troop, with its 400 members of boys and girls ages nine to adult. The troop meets in a building adjacent to the mosque that was originally used as an Islamic school for boys. The mosque recently started sponsoring an annual contest during the month of Ramadan in which young men compete in answering questions about Islamic religion, history, and law. 'Atif Fahum noted that the purpose of the contest is "to encourage the youth to learn of good, noble, and historic matters" (al-Senara, 1 May 1987). As the Friday Mosque, the White Mosque is also selected on occasion to have its Friday sermon broadcast over Voice of Israel radio as part of its regular format.

The White Mosque served Nazareth's Muslim community until long after the Muslim community had outgrown it. With the expansion of the Muslim quarter into the Sharqiya (Eastern) quarter, it was decided that an additional mosque was needed to meet the needs of the large Muslim community. Land was selected in the flat, lower section of the Sharqiya quarter about fifty yards to the south of the Coptic Church. According to a 25 July 1989 interview with Salah Afifi, sheikh of the mosque, about two-thirds of the land was purchased from Mohammad Abu Ahmad, and the other third, which had been used as a watering place for livestock, was a gift from the municipality. Funding for the construction of the mosque came from donations from Muslims in Nazareth and the surrounding area (280,000 lira), from the Israeli government, whose contribution came from revenues obtained from Islamic waqf lands now controlled by the state (202,000 lira), from donations of building materials such as sand and rock (270,000 lira), and from the municipality (5,000 lira). Construction began in 1962; the completed Salam (peace) Mosque was dedicated on 20 December 1965. It was the first mosque to be built in Israel since the founding of the state.

The large, three-story mosque (the basement level houses an Islamic library), with its green dome, tall, slender minaret, and green and yellow windows, has in many respects taken over many of the roles previously performed by the White Mosque because of its larger size, easier access, and closer proximity to the largest concentration of Muslims in the city. A vacant lot located between the mosque and the Coptic Church (the owner of the lot) provides ample parking for the large crowds of Muslim faithful who gather for Friday sermons or to pray on feast days; it is also used as the site for annual carnivals held during the feasts to commemorate the birth of the prophet Mohammad and the opening of Mecca. In April 1989 it was estimated that over 10,000 Muslims gathered at the mosque and vacant lot for the festival celebrating the opening of Mecca, with many of the celebrants coming from surrounding villages (al-Senara, 28 April 1989). The mosque also serves as a gathering point for feast-day parades, a destination for 'Id al-Fitr (the feast at the end of Ramadan) marches, which originate at the outlying mosques, and as a rallying place for the Islamic political movement (figs. 14, 15).[1]

Even the large Salam Mosque could not accommodate the needs of all of Nazareth's Muslims, especially as new quarters with a high concentration of Muslims started to develop on the outskirts of the city beyond reasonable walking distance to the two mosques in the central city. Six new mosques have sprung up in the past two decades not only to meet the demand from the growing Muslim community, but also to accommodate the increased interest in Islam and a return to its teachings by many in the Muslim community. The first of these mosques to be built was the squat al-Hoda (right way) Mosque in the southern quarter of Jebel al-Daula, where most of the refugees from Mujeidil live. According to a 3 May 1989 interview with a suspicious Sheikh Mohammad, a graduate of the Hebron Islamic college, the mosque was built in 1968 with monies contributed from Nazareth's Muslim community. Mohammad Fahum indicated in a 28 June 1989 interview that

---

[1] The importance of the two central mosques is shown in part through the survey results in which 37 percent of the sixty-eight men who said they pray at a mosque indicated that they pray at the White Mosque; 31 percent pray at the Salam Mosque. The other five mosques averaged about 5 percent, with the Mosque of Omar attracting the largest percentage (9), and the Sadiq mosque the least (3).

Fig. 14. Salam Mosque, Basilica of the Annunciation, and Church of St. Joseph (square steeple)

the land for this mosque was donated by Mohammad Ali Nakhash, who lives next door to the mosque.

The next mosque built was the al-Nur (light) Mosque in Bir Abu-Jayish, the southernmost and most isolated quarter of Nazareth. An 11 May 1989 interview with Abu-Ali Rabi'a, one of six men gathered for noon prayers, revealed that the mosque was built in 1978 with monies contributed from the Islamic waqf in Jerusalem and from collections made on Fridays and holidays from local residents. He said that one or two hundred gather for Friday prayers and that on holidays, up to four hundred will gather inside and out. They come mainly from Bir Abu-Jayish and from Bir al-Amir, to the west across a vacant hillside.

In 1981 the Bilal Mosque was built in the lower Safafra quarter in what has now become known as the Bilal subquarter. The land was

Fig. 15. Bilal Mosque with unpaved streets

purchased from a neighboring family, and the mosque was built using contributions from Muslims in Nazareth and neighboring villages. A municipal announcement of the cornerstone-laying ceremony noted that the municipality contributed 25,000 lira toward construction costs, as well as providing a water meter and all the necessary sections of pipe for connecting the water, at a cost of 21,100 lira. The mosque sponsors weekly study sessions for neighborhood boys and girls and offers classes in Arabic, Hebrew, English, and the Quran. The mosque even provides a plastic book bag, with "Bilal Mosque" printed on it, for each pupil to carry books to and from the classes.

Just up the hill in the upper part of the Safafra quarter is the Mosque of Omar, built in 1982. In a 13 June 1989 interview, Selim Bihar, the muezzin at the mosque, explained that the land for the mosque was donated by the municipal government and that most of the money came from donations by local Muslims, with some coming from the Ministry of Religion. As is the case with all of the new mosques, donations for its construction were solicited from residents in the neighborhood, whether Muslim or Christian. One Greek Ortho- dox family living in the Upper Safafra quarter said that they also con- tributed to the construction of the mosque when representatives of the construction committee visited their home to ask for donations. The muezzin estimated that from fifty to seventy men gather on Fridays for prayers, and that the mosque is filled to overflowing on feast days. The evening prayer that followed the Tuesday interview was attended by many young men in their twenties who seemed to be enjoying the brotherhood and friendship of gathering together. Of the five new mosques, the Mosque of Omar has the most pleasing interior, complete with two levels and a carved wooden *minbar* (pulpit) and *mihrab* (prayer niche).

The Sadiq (the faithful) Mosque is located in the Jebel Hamuda quarter. Sheikh Ziyad, a native Nazarene who studied at the Qalqiliya Islamic college in the West Bank, explained in a 3 April 1989 interview that the mosque was built in 1983 on land purchased from a Muslim family in the neighborhood with monies contributed from Muslims in "all of Palestine." The sheikh further explained that Israel permitted no contributions from the outside to help in building what he estimated as a U.S.$50,000 project. He did not mention any help from the munic- ipality, but an article on the cornerstone-laying ceremony held on the first day of Ramadan in June 1983 related that Mayor Tawfiq Ziyad in- vited the committee in charge of building the mosque to come to the city offices "to accept what the municipality will offer as a participant in building the mosque." Donations were also collected from those who attended the ceremony (*al-Senara*, 10 June 1983). The mosque is perched on the upper slopes of the hill rising above the flat of the Garage quarter. Its basement is used as a recreation room where neigh- borhood youth come for Ping Pong, karate classes, and weight lifting. The mosque sponsors classes on Islam for the neighborhood boys.

The construction of these seven mosques gradually fulfilled the needs of every major concentration of Muslims except those living in the Krum quarter. In order to meet the needs of the 8,000 Muslims in this growing area, a council from the quarter in December 1987 submit- ted an application, signed by hundreds of citizens, to the municipality requesting that it allocate a section of government land in their quarter for the building of a mosque (*al-Senara*, 11 December 1987). As of 1994 the proposed al-Akhdar (Green) Mosque had yet to be built. Reasons varied as to why the mosque had not yet been built. One produce mer- chant suggested that monies collected had been misused by religious leaders in the quarter, while leaders of the Islamic movement suggested that the municipality refused to allocate a plot of land, partly because of its proximity to Christian sections in the eastern portion of the quarter. Whatever the reason, the residents of the Krum quarter are now able to travel to the new and relatively close Nebi Se'in Mosque for prayers.

On the summit of the western hill above the property of the Salesian brothers and next to the old reservoir is a mosque/tomb/monument known as Nebi (prophet) Se'in. It is located on waqf land that once included a much larger area, but has since been reduced in size through land sales (the Salesians purchased part of the land) and expropriations. The history of the building is shrouded in mystery. Mansur suggests that it was originally a high place or sacred grove where Canaanites would worship; that it was then adopted as a Jewish, then Christian, and finally Muslim holy place. Differing traditions suggest that it is the tomb of Ishmael, son of Abraham; or of Simeon, who held the baby Jesus on the day he was presented at the temple in Jerusalem; or of a holy man named Sa'id. 'Atif Fahum suggested in a 25 April 1994 interview that the structure was built during Ottoman times as a place of prayer (*musallan*) for Turkish soldiers stationed in Nazareth. He said that the Arabic meaning of se'in is "those who are going to pray" and that there has never been a prophet with the name of Se'in.

Mansur notes that both Christians and Muslims had a custom of making promises to God through the site and the holy person associated with it. A Muslim, for example, might promise to clean the tomb or take flowers to it if the request is granted. Christians, on the other hand, promise to cook and eat a special lentil dish, which is not presented or eaten at the tomb but is still associated with it. The current association of the tomb with Islam is noted through Mansur's description of the structure, which by 1914 was in ruins. Only the south wall, with a mihrab, still stood (Mansur 1924, 189–92).

In 1989, members of the Islamic Movement of Nazareth decided to restore the structure so that it could be used as a place of prayer. As volunteers from the movement gathered to lay the foundation for a minaret in September of that year, one of the workers explained that they were also restoring the building because its only use in recent years had been as a hangout for drug users and that the movement hoped to change that. Six months later, in March 1990, the scaffolding around the structure caught fire in what police say was arson, but with no known motive or suspects (*JP*, 7 March 1990).

Perhaps a possible motive for the arson stems from the controversy surrounding the restoration of the structure. According to a 25 April 1994 interview with former city planner Adib Daud, the Islamic

Movement never obtained permission to restore the structure and build the minaret. In planning commission meetings Daud, a Christian, urged denying approval by noting that according to Islamic law minarets and mosques should not be associated with places of burial. Neither the municipal commission nor the national government, under whose control the land remains, was willing to either grant or deny permission. Daud twice issued court orders to halt construction, but they were ignored. In retaliation for building without permission, the municipality refused to supply water or electricity. The now completed Nebi Se'in mosque, with its tall, slender minaret, outrivals the nearby Salesian Church for dominance on the western hilltop. One Christian indicated that he sees the newest addition to Nazareth's religious landscape as an attempt to symbolize the dominance of Islam by locating a mosque adjacent to a Christian church, as he suggests is practiced in other parts of the Islamic world.

In addition to these eight mosques, there are two monuments or tombs for Muslim saints in the central quarters of the town; each has room inside its small structure for a dozen or so people to pray.[2] The domed tomb of Sheikh Shahab al-Din is located on Casa Nova Street halfway between Pope Paul VI Street and the Roman Catholic Basilica of the Annunciation. A similar structure for Sheikh 'Amer al-Din can be found in the narrow streets of the Latin quarter above the Anglican Church.

Muslim waqf properties include two cemeteries, both of which existed in the early 1900s, as evidenced by their inclusion on Mansur's map and by their location in areas close to the original Muslim quarter. The older of the two is located to the east of the Greek Orthodox bishop's complex and north of the central market. Located within it is a monument to the forty martyrs, which according to Mansur is the remains of a church built to commemorate forty Christian soldiers martyred by the brother-in-law of Emperor Constantine which was destroyed after the Crusades (Mansur 1924, 188). Another tradition is that the monument was built to honor forty Muslims killed during the Crusades (Stendel 1966). The other cemetery, known as the western cemetery and having two separate parts, is located in the southern section of the Latin quarter to the north of the French hospital. It was

---

[2] The origins and purpose of these small structures are uncertain. Mansur (1924, 188) identifies them as either monuments or tombs. He suggests that they might have been built following the Crusades in honor of Muslim martyrs, or that they were built for wandering dervishes who had died while visiting in Nazareth. Currently the structures are identified by residents and municipal publications as tombs. 'Atif Fahum said in a 25 April 1994 interview that these two stuctures were tombs for the sons of the sister of Salah al-Din who were killed in battle during the Crusades.

identified by Mansur as the place of burial for "strangers," perhaps intended for the newer migrants to town. Today no such division is used.

Another waqf, located near the Salam Mosque, was donated to the mosque by an elderly woman and is intended to be used as a home for aged women. Plots of land located next to the two tombs in the central city are also considered waqfs, but according to Mohammad Fahum, these properties, along with all three tombs, were declared government land in 1948 when many members of the *majlis* (Islamic council) fled Nazareth, leaving no one to administer the waqf lands. These waqfs have not been under the control of the Islamic waqf since. Purchase of new lands for the Islamic community is currently underway or under proposal by two different groups representing the community. The properties will be discussed shortly, but first it is necessary to understand these two groups.

Unlike the Christian communities with their expansive hierarchies, many institutions, and outside monetary support, the Islamic community, as a result of the tenets of Islam, is very decentralized. Each Muslim community has at its head a sheikh or imam who officiates in matters such as leading prayers, giving the Friday sermon, and conducting marriages, but he answers to no superior. This means that in Nazareth there are eight sheikhs over eight mosques, but there is no higher authority to unite the several smaller communities, which are centered on their mosques, into a larger Muslim community with a central leadership. The lack of a higher authority means no guaranteed sources of outside income for building or for maintaining religious institutions like schools or hospitals. As a result, all the institutions in Nazareth are run either by Christian institutions or government organizations. Another impediment to the establishment of Islamic institutions has been the Arab-Israeli conflict, which has prevented wealthy Arab Islamic states from giving financial aid to Israeli Arab Muslims.

In recognition of the need to provide better and more Islamic-oriented services for the Muslim community, the Islamic Charitable League was established in 1981, the Islamic Cemetery Restoration Committee in 1987, and the Islamic Movement of Nazareth in 1988. The Charitable League was organized with the goal of supporting pious and charitable works and raising the cultural level in the city. It was financed through the collection of *zakat*, the Islamic alms tax, and other contributions. During its first year anniversary, the Charitable League anticipated using the collected revenues to build a center for religious, cultural, educational, and recreational activities, then to construct a secondary school and to assist in the purchase or renting of lands for the establishment of additional cultural and educational projects. The organization also planned to find a site for a new Muslim cemetery.

During its first year in operation, the league offered scholarships, distributed schoolbooks, clothes, and money to the needy, raised money, and visited the sick, including Israeli soldiers wounded in Lebanon (*al-Ittihad*, 17 August 1982; *al-Anba*,' 12 August 1982).

Activities by this organization declined over the years, with many of its goals being adopted by the two more recent Islamic organizations. However, in August 1992 the Charitable League reemerged to proclaim solidarity with the Muslims suffering in Bosnia-Hercegovina. The league organized a march through downtown Nazareth, attended by over 8,000 Muslims assembled from throughout the country, to protest the massacre of Muslims in Bosnia. The organization also collected over 160,000 sheqels for relief aid (*al-Senara*, 28 August 1992).

According to director Mohammad Fahum, the four-member Cemetery Committee's original function was to restore and maintain the cemeteries in the absence of a functioning waqf leadership, but the organization has also been used to petition the government to allocate land on the road to 'Illut for the building of a third Muslim cemetery, an Islamic library—which would be more extensive that the small libraries found in most of the mosques, a large meeting hall, and eventually an Islamic elementary school. Fahum noted that the Ministry of the Interior has granted approval for the project; committee members are now awaiting the city engineer's permission to build an access road.

The committee has also spearheaded the construction of a small mosque or musallan in the western cemetery. This structure has become an object of dispute. According to 'Atif Fahum, it is a violation of Islamic law to build a mosque in a cemetery. He submits that the structure should be called a musallan (place of prayer), which differs from a mosque in that funeral prayers said at a musallan do not require taking off shoes or prostration. Mohammad Fahum, on the other hand, believes that the structure, which he refers to as Mesjid al-Rauda (Garden Mosque), should be called a mosque because it is not built over any graves; its location is not in the cemetery, but to its side. 'Atif, who founded the Muslim Cemetery Committee and then later resigned, even went so far as to petition al-Azhar University in Cairo, which responded in September 1988 with two *fatwas* (religious decrees) saying that mosques in cemeteries are not allowed. He said that an agreement was made following the fatwas to call the building a musallan. Mohammad Fahum may have agreed in principle to call it a musallan, but he stills refers to it as a mosque, and even showed drawings for a planned minaret. Although it is considered a mosque by the Cemetery Committee, Fahum noted that there will never be a sheikh or imam appointed, and it will be used only for prayers. Mayor Ziyad laid the cornerstone of the disputed mosque, which the municipality helped finance. 'Atif views this as a way for Jebha to buy more Muslim votes, noting that whenever Jebha needs votes, they make sure they contribute to the building of a mosque or some other project beneficial to Muslims.

The Islamic Movement of Nazareth has also become involved in representing the Muslims of Nazareth, not only in politics—as will be discussed in chapter 6—but also in a variety of other matters. One of the first goals of the movement was to initiate a return to the teachings of Islam among the Muslim community of the city and to provide services and assistance for the community rather than always having to rely upon Christian or government institutions. To achieve these goals, member Mazen Mahzumi explained in a 18 May 1989 interview, the movement purchased 1,000 square meters near the Salam Mosque through contributions from Muslims throughout Israel, which they intend to use for building an Islamic hospital and an Islamic community center. The Islamic Movement has already established a small community center in the Bilal quarter called Nadi Risala. The modest structure is rented by the movement with money collected at the Bilal Mosque and is used for Quran study, karate, weight lifting, table tennis, and video watching. Children in the neighborhood even sport Nadi Risala T-shirts. More recently the movement has purchased the Bathgate Clinic building from the United Brethren. Located near the Greek Orthodox bishop's compound, the building now functions as an additional Islamic nadi.

The Islamic movement is not without dispute among the Muslim community. Some Muslims in Nazareth resent efforts by the movement to return all Muslims to the teachings of Islam, because they themselves may not believe, or may not want to follow, all of the teachings. Others resent the involvement of a religious movement in politics because they fear it will sour years of Muslim-Christian cooperation and coexistence, or because they support Jebha and fear that the party will lose its stronghold in the municipality. A Muslim student at the municipal high school admitted that he himself does not care to associate with supporters of the Islamic movement because of their strict adherence to Islam and their nonacceptance of his lack of adherence; as a result, many of his friends are Christian.

In a 24 July 1989 interview, one young man from the Safafra quarter who supports the Islamic political movement described the Muslim community in Nazareth as being composed of various groups (divided along lines similar to those of the Greek Orthodox split), some of which strive for a return to the fundamentals of Islam, while others are comfortable with moderation, being Muslims when it is convenient, or in name only. He explained that one of the fundamentalist groups is led by Sheikh Fathi, who during a long stint in prison, found religion. His group, according to one source, "are fans of Hamas," the fundamentalist movement in the West Bank and Gaza. A second group is the larger and more inclusive Islamic Movement, mentioned above.

A third, more moderate, group is led by Mohammad Darousha, a member of the Knesset. Members of this group are viewed by Fathi and his followers as not being religious Muslims. During the 1989 elections, several of the factions, including Fathi and the Islamic Movement, joined forces, not out of a common agenda, but out of opposition to Communist dominance. Like the Communist faction in the Orthodox Church, some Muslims are concerned that a return to fundamentalist religion might adversely affect the delicate balance between Christians and Muslims. The next few years will be an interesting challenge for the Muslim community of Nazareth as they seek to redefine what it means to be Muslim and how that affects intra-Muslim and Muslim-Christian relations.

As in the Christian community, a variety of things identify the Muslims and solidify them into a community. Obedience to the teachings of Islam is a good indication of how extensively Nazareth's Muslims actually adhere to their religion. Based upon the responses of 140 men and 157 women, the percentages listed in table 9 indicate a higher degree of religiosity among women than men, especially in terms of fasting and prayer. They also show that while claiming to be Muslim, a significant proportion of Muslims fail to heed one of the most basic tenants of Islam, praying five times each day.

While the percentages indicate some lack of observance among all Muslims, there is evidence that religiosity is on the rise. A survey conducted in 1965 asked twenty-five young Muslim men from Nazareth how often they prayed. Nine of the twenty-five indicated that they prayed at least on Fridays; the other fourteen did not pray ("Three Surveys of Israeli Arabs" 1965, 92). This 36 percent result is even lower

TABLE 9. Percentage of religious practice among Muslims in Nazareth, 1989

	Men (N = 140)	Women (N = 157)
Pray daily	42	54
Pray sometimes	3	5
Never pray	55	41
Fast for Ramadan	68	90
Pilgrimage to Mecca	10	13
Pilgrimage to Jerusalem	55	57

than the 1989 survey results, in which 45 percent of the male respondents indicated that they prayed. Although the 1965 sample was small, a comparison with the 1989 results suggests a gradual increase in religious observance among Muslims of Nazareth.

This return to religion is particularly evident among the young men of Nazareth, who make up a large percentage of those attending evening prayers, and who have been the primary catalysts and support for the new Islamic organizations. It can also be seen among the young women. In an interview on 9 May 1989 with Laurie Zu'bi, an English teacher at the municipal high school, she noted that only in the early 1980s did female Muslim students first start to wear head coverings at school, and that each year the number has increased, especially among the twelfth-grade girls, in anticipation of marriage.

The Islamic revival in Nazareth is part of a larger trend in the Islamic world. It is also the result of the reopening of contacts with Muslims in the West Bank, Gaza, and East Jerusalem following the 1967 war. This increased interaction has brought Nazareth's Muslims in contact with Muslims who have been educated in Islamic institutions, such as the two sheikhs currently serving in Nazareth who were educated at al-Azhar College in Gaza. Another example of this is the August 1989 visit by Muslim men from Gaza, Jerusalem, and several cities in the West Bank who spent several days each at the Nur, Hoda, Omar, and Bilal mosques. During their visit at the Bilal Mosque, they explained that their purpose in coming to Nazareth was to teach Islam and to strengthen the local Muslim community. The dozen men, dressed in long white *gallabiyas* and wearing knitted white skullcaps, slept on the floors of the mosques and held religious classes during the interim between the two evening prayers.

Unlike prayer or fasting, pilgrimage (*hajj*) to Mecca cannot be used as a gauge of religiosity because of several limitations. For some the limitation is financial. For others it has been a ban on travel by Israeli Muslims to Mecca during the years 1948–77. This ban was imposed by both Jordan and Saudi Arabia, which, in their ongoing confrontation with Israel, refused to allow anyone with an Israeli passport to enter. In 1978, the Israeli government finally succeeded in persuading Saudi Arabia and Jordan to accept pilgrims from Israel in an agreement by which Israel would issue travel documents to pilgrims rather than have them use passports. Then Jordan would issue another travel document to the pilgrims, which would allow them to enter Saudi Arabia. This procedure, deemed acceptable by Jordan and Saudi Arabia, resulted in more than 3,000 Israeli Muslims making the pilgrimage by bus via Jordan during the first year of restored pilgrimage rights (*JP*, 25 October 1978).

Since the ban was lifted many Muslims from Nazareth have been able to make the pilgrimage. Most make the pilgimage only once in their lives, but one sixty-three-year-old mother of eleven from Bir Abu-Jayish indicated in the survey that she and her husband made the pilgrimage together in 1978, 1979, 1980, and 1983, and that following the death of her husband she has continued to make the pilgrimage each year from 1986 to 1989. In a 14 June 1989 interview, Hajj Yahya, who serves as the vice chairman of the Committee of Pilgrims in Israel, and has made the pilgrimage five times—hence the title hajj—indicated that about 400 pilgrims from Nazareth journeyed to Mecca in 1978, and that since then 200–300 per year have joined with the 2,000–3,000 pilgrims from all of Israel.[3] In 1981, 120 pilgrims from Nazareth flew to Saudi Arabia, but in all of the other years they have taken a four-day journey by bus through Jordan and on to Medina and Mecca where they stayed for about three weeks. Since the first year, the largest group from Nazareth has been in 1988, when 343 joined the 4,988 pilgrims from Israel.

In order to make the pilgrimage, pilgrims must be at least thirty years old, receive the necessary vaccinations, be able to pay the required cost, which in 1989 was U.S.$569, and then be accepted in a complex application process. The pilgrim makes application first to the Ministry of the Interior, then to Hajj Yahya, and then to the Islamic waqf in Jenin in the West Bank, which forwards the applications to Jordan for the final approval. Then the application is returned to Hajj Yahya, who organizes the pilgrims into bus groups.

The number of pilgrims from Nazareth in 1989 was 277, with a large contingent going from the quarters of Bir Abu-Jayish and Fakhura, as evidenced by the dozen or more homes decorated with the traditional palm branches and flowers. These decorations are hung during the several-week absence of the pilgrims, and then lighted rooftop or backyard parties are held to celebrate the return.

These decorations for the pilgrimage are temporary Islamic markings, but most Muslim homes are decorated permanently with markings that are unique to Islam. Of the 161 Muslim households surveyed, 95 percent indicated that they had one or more religious items hanging inside or outside their houses. The most common of these were calligraphic representations of verses from the Quran—found in 86 percent of the households—followed by the verse which says, "In the name of God the merciful and the compassionate" in 62 percent of the homes, a picture of Jerusalem's Dome of the Rock in 50 percent of the homes,

[3] British records show that in 1945 only nine Muslims from Nazareth made the pilgrimage to Mecca (ISA 27, G/433/II, 2632).

and a picture of Mecca and the Ka'ba in 41 percent of the homes. Some of the homes hung these items outside above the entrance.

Religious decorations are also found in many Muslim-owned shops. For example, one produce shop in the Khanuq quarter has an entire wall covered with posters of Jerusalem and Mecca. The fact that most Muslim households, and many shops, readily identify themselves as Muslims by their religious decor indicates that, like many of the Christians, even though they may not actively practice their religion, they still find their identity within its bounds.

Members of Nazareth's Muslim community find unity as they pray and attend Friday sermons together, as they fast during the month of Ramadan, as they associate in neighborhoods—which in many instances are entirely Muslim—and as they join in celebration of Islamic feast days. The two main feasts are 'Id al-Fitr, a three-day celebration at the end of Ramadan, and 'Id al-Adha, or feast of the sacrifice, which is celebrated throughout the Islamic world in conjunction with the sacrifice of goats and sheep performed in Mecca during the annual pilgrimage. Like the Christian feast days, these holidays are noted for their special foods, for dressing up in new clothing, for prayers, and for visiting relatives, friends, and neighbors. In preparation for the 1989 celebration of 'Id al-Fitr, held that year on 6–8 May, Mohammad Butu from Bir al-Amir made ninety green flags decorated with the Muslim creed or *shahada*, which states: "There is no God but Allah, and Mohammad is His messenger." He said in a 3 May 1989 interview, as he hung the newly painted flags out to dry in his front yard, that the flags were to be used for an evening celebration of the feast in which Muslim men from the two southern mosques would parade northward converging at the main intersection, then proceed to the Sadiq Mosque to join more Muslim men, who would then all proceed to the Salam Mosque. At the mosque they would rally with other Muslims from the central quarters and those coming in a similar procession from the two northern mosques.

Green flags were used again on the eve before 'Id al-Adha, when a group of about thirty Muslim young men ages six to adult, led by a bearded man in his thirties, paraded through Upper Safafra at 10:30 P.M., waving the banners and chanting "Allahu Akhbar" (God is the greatest). The next morning, 13 July, members of the Muslim community gathered for early morning prayers at the mosques and then joined in a scout-led procession to the cemetery to honor the dead. Children were dressed in new clothes, green being the predominant color. That afternoon over three hundred of the Muslim scouts led a parade through town, starting near the White Mosque and parading past the Basilica of the Annunciation, along the main street and ending at the

TABLE 10. 1983 census comparisons between Muslims and Christians in Nazareth

Category	Muslims	Christians
Population	25,236	16,445
Average household size	5.7	4.4
Average number of children	3.9	2.7
Percentage with four or more children	52.0	27.7
Median age	17.1	22.8
Mean net monthly income (sheqels) in household whose head is employed	26,800	30,500
Percentage who own telephone	12.8	25.1
Percentage who own car	30.1	43.8
Percentage who own dwelling	83.7	76.0
Dwelling built before 1955	20.4	35.8
Dwelling built after 1974	30.1	22.6
Percentage with more than two persons per room	43.9	19.6
Average years of school completed, women	8.4	10.2
Average years of school completed, men	8.9	10.3

SOURCE: 1983 *Census of Israel*

Salam Mosque. They were joined by representative patrols of the Orthodox, Latin, Catholic, Sadaqa, and visiting German scouts.

There are distinct religious differences between the Muslim and Christian communities in Nazareth in the way they worship and celebrate holidays. There are also demographic differences. Data from the 1983 *Census of Israel* confirms some of these differences (table 10). In general, the Muslim population of Nazareth have larger families, lower incomes, and lower levels of education. A higher percentage of Muslims have built homes since 1974, a result of their lower median age, meaning more house-seeking newlywed couples and more recent immigration into the city. There is a gradual narrowing of differences in many of the categories as members of the Muslim community achieve higher educational levels and better paying jobs.

The Refugee Communities

Religion is the main source of communal identification for Nazarenes, but place of origin also influences how people identify themselves and their relationships with others. Of particular note, in Nazareth, are the refugees from three neighboring villages, Saffuriya, Mujeidil, and Ma'lul, who over the years have congregated in Nazareth into specific quarters. This congregating of 1948 refugees along communal lines is common throughout areas of refugee settlement, among both internal refugees in Israel and external refugees in the diaspora.

When writing about Palestinians living in refugee camps in Lebanon, Bassem Sirhan notes (1975, 101): "The inhabitants of the camps
are grouped around the Palestinian village from which they originated
and the extended family units are still the basis of social life. . . . This
pattern thus meant the transfer of whole Palestinian villages, districts,
or larger kin groupings more or less to the same residential areas in exile." Majid al-Haj writes of similar patterns among the internal
refugees. He describes how refugees initially sought places of asylum,
which often meant moving from one locale to another as the war pro-
gressed. Following the destructive events of 1948, the refugees gradually settled in locales they deemed safe, which were often close to their
former village—to which they were not allowed to return. For nearly a
decade the status of the refugees remained uncertain. Many hoped to be
allowed one day to return to their homes and lands. As that hope diminished, refugees sought a more stable situation and began to buy
land and houses in new locals (al-Haj 1988, 149–63).

One factor that influenced the settlement of refugees was economic opportunity. Shefar 'Am, for example, received a large number
of refugees who were attracted to its close proximity to the Haifa industrial area. A second drawing power was a desire to reunite "the fragmented (original) communities and kinship groups." Whereas common ancestors had for so long determined kinship, al-Haj suggests that
a new relationship "began to emerge between the community of origin
and the kinship groups" (al-Haj 1988, 159). This new relatedness was
based on a common village and not just a common great-grandfather.
In seeking to reunite this new form of kinship, the internal refugees actively sought out others from their former villages and if possible settled in the same place, often forming new neighborhoods. Once settled,
communal bonds were strengthened through friendship networks and
intermarriage. In addition, living in a new town with its already established family and religious ties meant that even after decades of residence, a "refugee feeling" continued to persist, which only served to
heighten the desire to settle near those with a similar history of flight,
expulsion, circumstances of landlessness, and longing for home (al-Haj
1988, 162).[4]

---

[4] The trauma that results from refugee life is illustrated in the results of an interesting study performed by Dr. Bishara Bisharat. His 1984 survey of 1,000 Nazareth
Arabs showed that blood pressure was higher among Greek Catholics than Greek Orthodox or Muslims (*JP*, 11 July 1985). In a 9 September 1989 interview, Dr. Bisharat explained that the study was conducted in Shekun al-Arab, a quarter in which many of
the Greek Catholic residents are 1948 refugees, while the Greek Orthodox and Muslims
in the quarter are native Nazarenes. He suggested that the Greek Catholic experience
of being uprooted had "biological as well as psychological effects on blood pressure,"
which along with poor eating habits, similar to those of Muslims, and a high-paced

When writing about the communities of Shefar 'Am, al-Haj notes that the internal refugees, rural Muslims, and Bedouin who came to the town after 1948 had the status of *gharib* (stranger):

> They had come to the town empty-handed and were forced to compete for the existing resources which were in the hands of the local population. Members of these groups developed a strong feeling of belonging to a minority which, on the one hand, wished to defend itself, but on the other, wanted to become integrated into the majority. These feelings were clearly reflected in their housing patterns and the composition of their neighborhoods. They lived close to one another in crowded buildings, and eventually created sub-districts within the heterogeneous districts of the town. (al-Haj 1987, 58)

This congregating into quarters or clusters according to village ties has occurred in villages and towns throughout the Galilee, Nazareth included. Whether it be the few Christian families from Tiberias, who have clustered in Shekun al-Arab, the several Muslim families from 'Indur who now live in the Sharqiya quarter, or the residents of the Safafra and Jebel al-Daula quarters, where it seems whole villages have been transposed, refugees still find communal identification based on places they left over forty years ago.

Saffuriya

The most notable of the refugee groups to gather in Nazareth are those from the village of Saffuriya, a village five miles to the northwest of Nazareth which in 1945 boasted a population of 4,320 Muslims and ten Christians (*Village Statistics* 1945). Most of the villagers fled during the attack and bombardments of July 1948; others were expelled in September 1948. Gradually, however, some returned to the village. Fearing that once these infiltrators were in place others would also return, the Israeli government moved in and expelled the remaining villagers in January 1949, trucking them to nearby Nazareth, 'Illut, Reina, and Kfar Kanna. Motivation for the expulsion also came from three kibbutzim in the region that wanted to add the farmlands of Saffuriya to their own agricultural communities. The land of Saffuriya was distributed to two kibbutzim in February 1949 and to a third later that year (Morris 1987, 241).

The village of Saffuriya, with its famous pomegranates, encircled the sides of a hill that was crowned with the ruins of an Ottoman fortress. Surrounding the fortress now are the recently excavated ruins of several millennia of habitation, including ancient Sepphoris, which,

---

Western lifestyle, all combine to make them the most susceptible to high blood pressure.

according to tradition, was the hometown of Anna the mother of Mary and served as the headquarters for Herod Antipas. The village was demolished soon after the final Arab residents were expelled, and pine trees were planted in its place. Today that hill remains forested, but piles of underbrush-covered building rocks, cactus hedges, and pomegranate trees still testify that the Arab village of Saffuriya once was. The agricultural lands and scattered farm homes of the Jewish moshav of Zippori now spread out from the base of the hill.

Unable to return to their homes, the villagers from Saffuriya opted for the next best thing. Gradually they began to settle on the northwestern slope of Nazareth's northern hill, facing not down into the basin of their new hometown, but rather out toward the lands and demolished homes they still claim. The first family to settle in what was to become known as the Safafra quarter was that of Saleh Selim Suleiman. He served as mayor of Saffuriya from 1922 to 1948. In a 27 August 1989 interview, his son, Abd al-Rahman Suleiman, who was six years old in 1948, explained how the Safafra quarter came to be. During the attack on the village, his family fled first to Kfar Manda, a village just north of Saffuriya, and then on to the village of Dahra. The three youngest of the children (now adults living in Lebanon, Syria, and Saudi Arabia) had been sent on ahead with grandparents to Lebanon, the intended destination for the rest of the family. The family never made it, because along the way the mukhtars of each village encouraged Saleh to remain. Finally he was approached by a priest sent from Nazareth, who said that the mukhtars and priests of the city, out of respect for the many *sulhas* (peace negotiations) he had conducted among feuding Nazarene families (Fahum and Zu'bi), asked that he not flee to Lebanon, but rather stay and continue to serve as a respected leader. Saleh agreed and went to live in Reina, first with a friend and then in a house abandoned during the war, where the family lived for the next ten years. During this time Saleh served a term in the Knesset, from 1955 to 1959 .

The Israeli government was eager to settle the problem of the internal refugees, who continued to demand that they be allowed to return to their lands and villages. The government proposed that each family be offered one of several land options in a currently inhabited Arab city or village in exchange for relinquishing title to their land in abandoned villages like Saffuriya. Saleh, who was sixty-five when he left Saffuriya, still had children to provide for and, without his lands, little means to provide for them. He therefore felt he had no choice but to accept the government's offer. In a 1955 exchange for what his son estimated to be 2,500–3,000 dunams, the family received 20 dunams of garden land in Saffuriya, 3 dunams of land in Nazareth to build homes on, and an unknown amount of money. The reason Saleh accepted the land in Nazareth, rather than in one of several other possible locales, is that from Nazareth he would be able to look out and see where Saffuriya once stood.

The land that Saleh accepted in Nazareth was British land set aside for public use that had reverted to Israeli government jurisdiction in 1948. The land extended westward from police headquarters toward where the Omar Mosque now stands. Abd al-Rahman noted that he advised his father not to accept the offer, but understands why he had to do it. Construction started on the home in Nazareth in 1956; the family moved in in 1958. It was the first home in the area.

According to Abd al-Rahman, about a hundred other families from Saffuriya accepted the government's land exchange offer in 1955, partly because of the example of the respected Saleh. Approximately thirty-five of the first families also received farmland in Saffuriya, but the government soon stopped that part of the bargain, and later acceptors received land only in Nazareth. Negotiations have continued, with some families making the trade and others holding onto their claim to former lands. The primary objectors to the land trade were the younger refugees who were still able to work and could therefore eventually save enough money to buy land and a home. Abd al-Rahman estimates that 25–30 percent of the families from Saffuriya accepted the government's offer.

Once a few families had built in the new section of Nazareth, others soon followed. Those who did not accept the government's offer bought land in the neighborhood, many from the Christian Awad family, who owned a large tract of land adjacent to the government land being offered to the refugees. The refugees came from other quarters in Nazareth and from the surrounding villages. Today, only a few families from Saffuriya are left in Reina—one of the original places of refuge; the others have all moved to Nazareth and its burgeoning Safafra quarter.[5] A Christian resident of the quarter relates how his neighbors, five brothers from Saffuriya, and their families who had been living in Akka, all moved to Nazareth ten years ago to be with others from their village.

The social nature of the Saffuriya community is illustrated by several factors. First is that so many of the Saffuriyans have gradually congregated in Nazareth, where Abd al-Rahman estimates there are now about 10,000 Nazarenes from Saffuriya (he said he could even

[5] The village of Kfar Manda, located to the north of the village site of Saffuriya, also has a large concentration of refugee families from Saffuriya who have congregated into seven clusters: four in the northwest section of the village, one in the southwest, and two on the eastern edge of the village (Mossa 1988, 80).

identify people from the village by their unique accent, primarily in the way they pronounce the letter *qaf*). Second is their continual identification with the village. A 1989 study on the social adjustment of the refugees from Saffuriya who are living in the Safafra quarter indicates that of sixty adults surveyed, 43 percent identified themselves as being from Saffuriya, 48 percent as being from Saffuriya but living in Nazareth, and only 8 percent as being from Nazareth.

Third is continued intermarriage with fellow Saffuriyans. The same survey indicated that of the married participants (76 percent of the sixty), 35 percent had married someone from the same *hamula* of Saffuriya, 43 percent had married a nonrelative from Saffuriya, 2 percent had married someone from Nazareth, and 18 percent had married someone from another village. The 78 percent who had married another person from Saffuriya helps to indicate the strong communal ties which have persisted since the fall of the village. However, when asked how important it was to marry someone from Saffuriya, only 25 percent said it was very important, while 45 percent indicated that it was not important at all.

Fourth is the friendship and living patterns which perpetuate a feeling of community for many. When asked where their best friend was from, 23 percent indicated the same hamula of Saffuriya, 28 percent other hamulas in Saffuriya, 13 percent Nazareth, and 35 percent a Nazareth-Saffuriya mixture. When asked about neighbor preference, 34 percent said they would prefer a neighbor from Saffuriya, 7 percent would prefer a neighbor from Nazareth, and 61 percent said it did not matter where the neighbor was from (Hasanin 1989).

No Saffuriya communal organizations exist, but there has been one attempt to create one. According to Abd al-Rahman, in 1960 young men from the village proposed the organization of a Safafra political party. Refugee groups in other villages were beginning to organize themselves politically, and some Saffuriyans in Nazareth wanted to do the same. However Saffuriyan members of the Communist party objected because they felt that the intercommunal nature of the communist party served all of the communities of Nazareth, and that if they organized a party based on a Muslim refugee quarter, then other factions in Nazareth would also organize, and Nazareth politics would be divided by religion and quarter. Abd al-Rahman currently serves as the number-three man on the Jebha list (where his refugee status helps to continue the broad base of Jebha) and as such is a member of the municipal council.

While no organizations exist, there are activities which serve to unite. Abd al-Rahman explained that families enjoy returning to the village site for picnics throughout the year, especially on the mornings of each of the two major Islamic feast days. During the group picnics on the two feast days, the elderly tell stories about the village, and women lead special songs, some of which are about Saffuriya. He estimates that about two hundred gather each year. They also return to the village each May to clean up the four cemeteries. In 1978, the moshav of Zippori wanted to destroy the cemeteries and use the land to cultivate roses. Former residents of Saffuriya held a news conference and protested with letters to the Ministry of Religion and even to the United Nations. When the destruction was about to begin, twenty young people from the Safafra quarter sat in front of the bulldozers, bringing a temporary halt to the work. Eventually the Ministry of Religion intervened and stopped the work permanently. The moshav offered to put up fences around the cemeteries, but never did. They did, however, make good on their promise to return headstones that had been removed. The fate of the cemeteries is still unresolved, but they have not yet been destroyed.

The inhabitants of the moshav of Zippori are mostly Jews from Romania who were assigned to the moshav by the government without their being aware that they were living on lands of a former Arab village. Abd al-Rahman is on friendly terms with the moshav residents, whom he knows through continued use of the farmland (now used to raise chickens) which his father retained in the 1955 exchange. He relates an interesting anecdote about the confusion of having an Arab Saffuriya and a Jewish Zippori. One day a friend of his, a refugee from Saffuriya, was standing at a bus stop in Nazareth where he struck up a conversation with a Jewish woman. He asked where she was from. She said: "Zippori." To which he replied: "If you are from Zippori then I am from Romania."

Mujeidil

The next largest and cohesive of the refugee communities are the people from Mujeidil, a village several miles southwest of Nazareth along the main road to Haifa that in 1945 had a population of 1,640 Muslims and 260 Christians. All that remains of the village today are the shell of the Greek Orthodox Church and a Roman Catholic church, which still functions under the control of the Franciscans in Nazareth. The Jewish town of Migdal Ha Emek now stands adjacent to where the village once stood.

The refugees from Mujeidil who fled to Nazareth ended up staying wherever they could. Many stayed in the abandoned barracks of the British Royal Engineers in the Garage quarter. Like the refugees from Saffuriya, the refugees from Mujeidil were offered land from the government in exchange for the deed to their lands in the village, but few of the Mujeidil refugees living in Nazareth accepted. Mohammad Nakhash, in a 7 September 1989 interview, said that when he and his family sought refuge in Nazareth, they lived for the first seven years in a vacant house in the Maidan quarter. Then he and his brother rented land from the Zu'bi family on a vacant hillside on the southern edges of town known as Jebel al-Daula (government hill), after the nearby British and then Israeli police/military installation. Mohammad explained that they were the first two families to live in the area. In the 1960s, the Zu'bi family started to sell their land, which at the time was still outside Nazareth's municipal boundaries. Mohammad and his brother bought their land, and gradually friends and relatives from the village, who had been living in scattered locations, also purchased land in Jebel al-Daula. Many of the first homes, including Mohammad's, were hastily built, cheap shanties called tanaks, after the tin siding used to build them. These crude homes have gradually been replaced by modern homes as the financial situation of families has improved. Today one lone tanak still stands in the quarter.

Mohammad noted that a score of houses in his immediate neighborhood belonged to relatives and estimated that about 90 percent of the residents in the quarter of Jebel al-Daula are from Mujeidil. Families from Mujeidil who accepted government offers were for the most part required to settle on land in Shefar 'Am. One family from Mujeidil who now live in the Jebel Hamuda quarter of Nazareth indicated in the survey that they had exchanged their 50 dunams in the village for one dunam in Nazareth. The Christian refugees from the village did not congregate with the Muslims, but rather remain scattered throughout town in homes they have built or purchased.

The neighboring quarter of Bir al-Amir also became a gathering point for the Muslim refugees from Mujeidil. A survey of a cluster of eight homes in the southwest portion of the quarter, which includes two pairs of brothers, reveals that in five of the eight homes, both the husband and wife are from Mujeidil, and in the other three homes one from each couple is from Mujeidil, one wife coming from Iksal and another from Dabburiya (both villages in the Jezreel valley), and one husband a refugee from the village of Yajur near Haifa. None of the couples are old enough to have been married before they fled in 1948, but five of the eight still married someone from the village. The oldest of the eight couples were both born in Mujeidil in 1936, meaning that they were twelve years old when their families came to Nazareth. Of the two youngest couples, both in their thirties, one is a mixed marriage and the other a marriage of children of Mujeidil refugees. Their families all took circuitous routes through one or several other quarters of Nazareth before finally settling permanently in Bir al-Amir.

The selection of the southern reaches of Nazareth as the site for home building and congregating is probably the result of its being available land, but it is interesting to note that the two quarters heavily populated with refugees from Mujeidil are the closest quarters in Nazareth to the site of the former village. However, unlike in the Safafra quarter, in the Bir al-Amir quarter, intervening hills obstruct the view of the village site.

While the Mujeidilans do not have any communal organizations, the fact that they join together at celebrations of Muslim holidays, prayers at the mosque, weddings, family gatherings, or just in evening visits with neighbors means that there is a continuation of an identity centered on a village that most of the younger generation now only know through the stories of parents or grandparents.

Ma'lul

When the refugees from Ma'lul, who also lived scattered throughout Nazareth, started looking for permanent places of residence, they ended up moving just beyond the municipal boundaries of Nazareth to the growing village of Yafa. Here they live in a quarter called Jebel Ma'luli (Ma'lul Hill). According to a 24 August 1989 interview with Yusef Bisharat, a Christian refugee from Ma'lul who now lives in the northern end of Jebel al-Daula, the first residents to live in the Ma'luli quarter of Yafa were refugees who had squatted there, first in tents and then in tanaks. The government asked them to move, but they refused. Eventually the government consented to give them the lands they were squatting on. With an initial core of people, other families from Ma'lul started to move from small rented homes in Nazareth to much needed larger homes they built in Yafa. This gathering did not take place until after the 1967 war. Until then, the refugees had harbored a hope that one day they might be able to return to the village. The war dashed those hopes, so they congregated in a quarter with fellow villagers. Some of the families settled on 400 square meters of land offered to the eldest son of each refugee family, while others refused to accept the government's land-trade offer and purchased land instead. Land was also offered for exchange in Reina and Kfar Kanna, but not in Nazareth.

In 1948, Ma'lul was a small village composed of 490 Muslims and 200 Christians. Yusef noted that relations between the two communities were "especially good" and that they lived in mixed neighborhoods. Today Christians and Muslims still live together in Jebel Ma'luli, most of the Muslim families having left Nazareth for Yafa. One of the few Muslim families that have remained in Nazareth is that of Abu Anwar, of the Krum quarter, who related in a 18 June 1989 interview that his two brothers and four sisters have all settled in Jebel Ma'luli. His father, who lives in Yafa just below Jebel Ma'luli, owned 60 dunams in the village. He has refused to settle with the government, seeing no need to do so now that all of his children own homes of their own. According to Yusef, only several dozen Christian families from Ma'lul still reside in Nazareth. The quarters the Christians from Ma'lul live in are the newer Christian or mixed neighborhoods, and in the suq, where five families remain in the houses they settled in shortly after the war.

Perhaps one of the reasons the Christians of Ma'lul and Mujeidil did not all congregate into quarters as their fellow Muslim villagers did is that their need for community identification was satisfied within the Christian communities of Nazareth, whereas the more loosely structured Muslim community may not have met the needs of the Muslim villagers, who then reverted to the more familiar village ties. While the Muslim community may have been weak at the time of the refugees' settlement, owing to family rather than religious cohesiveness, it has since grown in strength, partially as a result of Muslim refugees. In reference to a similar situation in Shefar 'Am, al-Haj (1985, 118) explains that "the influx of internal refugees (almost all of them Muslims), who had come as single families or as sections of clans, did much to strengthen the collective nature of the Muslim community at the expense of its clan character."

Cohesiveness is still maintained through intermarriage. Yusef said that his generation all married Ma'lulans, and that they encourage their children, now of marriageable age, to do the same, but not always with the desired results. It is also maintained through a yearly gathering. One elderly Christian refugee from Ma'lul who now lives in central Nazareth, on a visit to the village site, pointed out the now forested hillside where his village once stood, the shells of a mosque and Greek Orthodox and Greek Catholic churches, the rubble of former homes, and the kibbutz-cultivated lands in the valley that he once worked. He then related how his family gathers each year on Israel's Independence Day with several hundred other Ma'lulans for a picnic of protest. They all like to congregate on their own family lands. His family prefers the farmland in the valley near the still visible threshing floor and amid the trees he planted years ago.

Formative Communities

Communal ties are very strong, and as a result, the formation of new communities is a slow process. The refugees have been successful in transforming village ties into an urban community centered on quarters, and the Anglicans have been successful in making the transition from a foreign missionary church to an Arab church and community, but it has been a long process. The Baptists are just on the threshold of emerging as a full-fledged community, while several other newer Protestant churches are moving in that direction. Two other groups have also started to take on certain communal characteristics: the Arabs of Upper Nazareth and the Communists.

The Arabs of Upper Nazareth

The precarious position of Israeli Arabs as they try to find a balanced position on the fence dividing the macrocommunities of Israelis and Arabs is perhaps best exemplified by the Arabs who live in Upper Nazareth. These Arabs represent an extension of all the communities of Nazareth, but live within the municipal boundaries of the intended all-Jewish community of Upper Nazareth. When Upper Nazareth was founded in 1956, it was on Arab-owned land expropriated from its owners in Nazareth and several of the surrounding villages. As the city gradually expanded its landholdings, it pressed up against Arab quarters in the north, east, and south of Nazareth, to the point that several Arab homes in the northern Khanuq quarter, with its spectacular view down into Nazareth's basin and the Jezreel valley beyond, found themselves one day as residents of a Jewish Nazareth rather than Arab Nazareth.[6] These Arab families did not purposely opt to become residents of Upper Nazareth, but did so by default. Gradually this area attracted more home owners, who built there on family lands.

More recently a growing number of Nazareth families have chosen to live in scattered areas of Upper Nazareth, not out of any great desire to live in the predominantly Jewish community, but because of limited housing in Arab Nazareth. Young couples often find that the only available rental housing is in the large apartment complexes of Upper Nazareth. Many of these apartments are owned by Jews, who can purchase housing at subsidized prices because of Upper Nazareth's designation as a development town, but who prefer living in less isolated towns. They therefore move to the Haifa or Tel Aviv regions and rent their flats in Upper Nazareth to any takers, oftentimes to Arabs.

This gradual process of Arabs moving from crowded Nazareth, with its lack of housing, to Upper Nazareth, with its excess housing[7]

---

[6] Other Arab families in the Sharqiya and Jebel al-Daula quarters built on properties which were the natural extension of Arab quarters, but on land that legally belonged to Upper Nazareth. While officially residents of Upper Nazareth, the Arabs in these quarters are in limbo as to municipal standing. For the most part they are considered residents of Nazareth, where they still vote.

[7] At least until the beginning of the influx of Soviet Jews. A report in July 1990 indicated that in the first six months of that year, six hundred Soviet Jews moved into Upper Nazareth (*JP*, International Edition, week of 14 July 1990). These Soviet Jews join

has resulted in an Arab population of over 4,000 in the city of 28,000 (estimated at 15–18 percent). Arabs—from all of the Arab communities—live scattered throughout Upper Nazareth wherever they can find housing, but the majority live in what is known as the Hakramim quarter, which straddles the top of Nazareth's northern hill just above the Khanuq quarter. Here expensive single-family homes and long, green-tinted *shekunat* (apartments, plural of *shekun*) house about 1,500 Arabs in an all-Arab neighborhood that gradually merges with the more Jewish quarters to the east.[8]

These Arab residents of Upper Nazareth are still very tied to their communities in Nazareth. There are no churches or mosques in Upper Nazareth and there are no schools (other than a neighborhood kindergarten) in which Arabic is the major language of instruction. Arab students therefore must descend each day into Arab Nazareth for school, most of their parents doing the same for work (some, however, are employed in one of the many factories in Upper Nazareth). For weddings and worship they also return to Arab Nazareth to join with their communities. Still, they are citizens of Upper Nazareth, and as such pay municipal taxes, which not only help keep the well-planned city running but also go toward financing schools the Arab children do not use and even toward the Jewish Burial Society, which obviously is not used by the Arab communities, all of whom use the cemeteries of their respective communities in Nazareth.

For years the Arabs of Upper Nazareth paid these taxes, without having any form of representation within the municipality. Then, in anticipation of the February 1989 municipal elections, Arabs and some supportive Jews of Upper Nazareth organized the Coexistence, Peace, and Equality list with the intent to elect Arabs to the municipal council. Part of the reason behind the formation of this mostly Arab list was that the Arab neighborhood of Upper Nazareth lagged behind the Jewish areas in terms of municipal services. Salim Khouri, who helped organize the list, explained just before the election that the Hakramim neighborhood had not yet been connected to the municipal sewage lines, water lines were outmoded, and garbage collection and street cleaning were not regular services as in the rest of Upper Nazareth. (*JP*, 10 February 1989). The Arab-dominated list was successful in its first

---

with an already diverse array of immigrants, ranging from recently arrived Ethiopian Jews to Uruguayan Jews who came in search of better economic opportunities.

[8] In 1989, Upper Nazareth added a Sabbath wire (*eruv*), a single strand of wire strung on poles around the entire city so that Sabbath travel distances are not restricted. This wire bisects the Hakramim quarter, leaving out the all-Arab portions of the quarter and including only the areas where Jews and Arabs own adjacent homes.

election, winning one seat on the fifteen-member council. Council member Salim Khouri was reelected in the 1993 municipal elections.

The fact that Upper Nazareth's scattered Arab community was able to unite in demanding representation within a Jewish-dominated municipality has for the first time given the Arabs of Upper Nazareth an identity separate from Arab Nazareth, whose many communal ties continue to extend into Upper Nazareth. Community ties will continue to exist with Arab Nazareth, but a new community of Arab Upper Nazarenes is gradually emerging as Arabs join together on the political front, and as they continue to foster friendships with fellow Arab neighbors.

The Communists

Like the residents of Upper Nazareth, the Communist party is a mixture of all the communities of Nazareth. Over the years it has attracted members from all segments of Nazareth society, including Muslims, Christians, and refugees. While never claiming to be a community, the party has nonetheless taken on several communal forms. The headquarters building of the Communist party, known as Beit Sadaqa (house of friendship), includes a large meeting hall in the basement for political rallies and a small adjacent building used as a clubhouse for the Communist youth organization. The Communist party sponsors holiday celebrations that rival the most grandiose of religious celebrations. The May Day parade and rally attract thousands (many, however, are Communists bused in from surrounding villages) who parade up Pope Paul VI Street waving red banners, and then gather at a rally in front of Beit Sadaqa. Meanwhile youth are entertained by organized sporting events held at the nearby Greek Orthodox nadi. The Communist party also instills an intense loyalty among its supporters. This has been the source of several conflicts in Nazareth, as evidenced by the split in the Greek Orthodox community and the Islamic-Communist battle in the 1989 municipal elections.

One thing that prohibits a total allegiance to the Communist community is that they do not have the legal authority to marry or bury, so even the most ardent Communist must return to the community of his or her birth for such services. This has caused problems, particularly in the Latin community. Father Arturo noted that when the secretary of the Communist party wanted to get married, he approached the parish priest and requested a 5:00 P.M. wedding. Arturo told him that that time was already booked; the wedding would have to be at 1:00 P.M. The young man became angry at the priest. Arturo, who claimed he did not know the young man was Communist in the beginning, said that through his curt actions toward a priest he could tell he was not a believer. The young man then opted to marry in the Greek Orthodox Church, where his wife was a member. Arturo does not perform civil weddings, and if a Communist says he does not believe in God then he will not perform the marriage.

Suheil Diyab, a leader in the Communist party, said in a 3 May 1989 interview that at least six members of the party have left the Roman Catholic Church for the Greek Orthodox Church in order to get married. When he married in the Latin Church, it was in a three-minute ceremony without communion, the traditional red carpet, or music. Suheil had wanted a full religious ceremony, to show the people that he was not against religion, but his involvement in the Communist party resulted in the priest performing just the bare minimum.

When asked if he thought the Communists were a community, Suheil replied that the Communists are a community only in that they share a common aim of improving life for all of the Arabs in Nazareth. He said that the Communist party's objectives were "higher and broader" than those of the traditional communities of Nazareth and that Communists do not further the cause of any one group or community, but rather the whole Arab community. He acknowledged that all are "obliged by birth" to stay within their communities for the needed services and ceremonies, but maintained that the Communists are there by choice, noting that there are really very few pure communists in Nazareth, and hence most still feel an identification with their communities of birth.

The interesting mix of Communists with the various religious communities is illustrated by the 1988 ordination of Nazareth native Michel Sabah as Latin patriarch of Jerusalem by Pope John Paul II at the Vatican. Meeting the pope and attending the ceremony was communist mayor Tawfiq Ziyad (al-Ittihad, 8 January 1988). Ziyad is Muslim by birth and is married to a woman who is Greek Orthodox by birth. When asked shortly after his election as mayor in 1975 if he still practices any tenets of Islam, the mayor replied: "No. You see: I'm a Communist" (JP, 19 December 1975). Still, as mayor of a religious town, he traveled to Rome to meet the pope and offer support for a native son. The Communist party will probably never function as a typical community of Nazareth, but through the years it has provided a secular alternative for those who feel that religious leaders and communities have failed to provide the answers to or successfully meet the needs of their community members.

Community Origins and Dispersions

With the many migrations of Christians and Muslims in and out of Nazareth, it would be highly unlikely that any Nazarenes would descend from village inhabitants of Roman or Byzantine times. Mansur's 1926 history of Nazareth includes a large section on the families of Nazareth, their religions and sects, their origins, and their genealogies. He divides the residents of the town into ten Muslim families and 130 Christian families (which he refers to with the Arabic word *dar*, which literally means "house" but is used here in reference to hamulas or extended families). Of the ten Muslim families, four are identified as originating in the Hijaz region in Arabia (with one of those, the Qubtan family, coming specifically from Mecca), one from Nablus in Palestine, one from the Maghreb (northwest Africa), one from Egypt, one from a "city in Persia," one whose origin is not listed, and one identified as Kurd, and therefore presumably from Kurdistan.

Most of the Christian residents of the town come from the Levant: thirty-eight originated from Palestine, including eight from Shefar 'Am, seven from several of the villages surrounding Nazareth, six from Akka and five from Bethlehem; twenty-seven were identified as coming from Lebanon; seventeen from Syria, including twelve who came from the Huran region (southwestern Syria); seventeen came from what is today known as Jordan, primarily the cities of Salt and 'Ajlun; two families came from Egypt; and one each from Turkey and Italy. Several families came from unidentifiable villages, and about twenty had no place of origin listed; some of these are identified as new hamulas who in recent centuries have emerged in Nazareth when men were given nicknames like Abunuwara (father of the blossom, for a man who always wore a flower in his hat) and Diik (crow), which eventually developed into family names with an identity separate from the original hamula. Roman Catholics and Maronites are identified as coming primarily from Lebanon, while the Greek Orthodox and Greek Catholics are identified mostly with the Huran region.

Mansur identifies several reasons for the migration to Nazareth. The Muslim family of al-Ziyadna is reported to have left the Hijaz in 1690 because of a drought. Christians fled problems with Muslim Arabs in the Huran and sought employment opportunities in Nazareth. Mansur notes that most of the Muslim families settled in the village in the fourteenth century following the Crusades. Some Christians came during the middle of the fifteenth century, but most came in the middle of the seventeenth century after they were granted permission to settle there (Mansur 1924, 200–55). At the time of these migrations, Nazareth was only a small village controlled over time by several different Islamic empires in a region known as Greater Syria. The migrations were made in an area that had no national boundaries. This made it easy for families to migrate throughout the region in search of a better livelihood or more agreeable living conditions.

Having come from such a diverse array of Middle Eastern locales, naturally new residents would find unity and a sense of identification first with their own extended families, second with those who originate from the same place, and third with those who are of the same religion. Over the years these migrants evolved into the cohesive communities of Mansur's day and gradually adopted Nazareth as their home.

The adoption of Nazareth and Palestine as their home is shown in responses from the survey in which 40 percent of the 569 respondents identify Nazareth as the place where their family originates, 16 percent indicate that their families come from Palestine in general, and 29 percent identify a specific town or village in Palestine, dominated mostly by the refugee villages, from which their families originate. In other words, 484 (85 percent) of the respondents indicate that their families come from Palestine, the others identifying Lebanon (thirty-two), Syria (seventeen), Jordan (fourteen), Egypt (thirteen), Iraq (six), and one each from Algeria, Cuba, and Finland as places of origin. None of the Muslims mentioned Saudi Arabia or the Hijaz, even though Mansur identifies this region as one of the primary places of origin for Nazareth's Muslims. Perhaps Muslims from these families figure that six centuries is sufficient time to establish new roots.

The change of origin from Mansur's day to today is partly the result of Nazarenes now actually feeling a part of both a Nazarene and Palestinian community, and partly because they either do not know their origins, or do not want, for nationalistic reasons, to admit that their ancestors are not indigenous to Palestine or Nazareth.

Nazarenes not only originate from a variety of places, they have also scattered to a variety of places for a variety of reasons. Threat of conscription and the hope of economic betterment were causes for emigration in the early years of this century as Nazarenes chose to relocate, primarily in the Americas; employment opportunities drew Nazarenes to the coastal cities during the British Mandate and on through Israeli control; and the upheavals of 1948 caused Nazarenes and relatives of refugees who came to Nazareth to seek refuge in neighboring Arab states or in countries of Europe and North America.

Survey results show that 77 percent of the families indicated having close relatives who live elsewhere in Israel, including sixty-five families with relatives in Haifa, twenty-nine in Jerusalem (some listed it as part of Israel and others the West Bank), twenty-eight in Akka, eighteen in Shefar 'Am, seventeen in Jaffa–Tel Aviv, and sixteen each in neighboring Kfar Kanna and Yafa. In all, the survey families indicated relatives living in sixty-three different villages and cities in Israel. The West Bank and Gaza are home to relatives of 30 percent of those surveyed. They live in thirty-five locales, with Nablus (twenty-one families) and Ramallah and Jenin (seventeen each) having the most. Seventy-one percent indicated that they had relatives living in other Arab countries (78 percent of the Muslim households and 64 percent of the Christian households). Over a hundred families have relatives living in Jordan, primarily Irbid (some still in refugee camps) and Amman, followed by several dozen with relatives in Syria and Lebanon. Relatives also live in Kuwait, Egypt, Saudi Arabia, Iraq, United Arab Emirates, Libya, Bahrain, Qatar, and Yemen. Finally, 65 percent said that they have relatives living in non-Arab foreign countries (47 percent of the Muslim households and 82 percent of the Christian households). Over 40 percent of the survey families have relatives living in the United States. The top attraction is California (thirty-five), mostly in Los Angeles (sixteen), followed by Texas (twelve), Florida (seven), Chicago (six), Michigan (five), and sixteen other states and cities. Canada ranks second (thirty-six), mostly in Toronto (sixteen), followed by Australia (ten), Germany (ten), United Kingdom (ten), Italy (ten), and France (eight), with one or two having relatives in Switzerland, Austria, Netherlands, Denmark, Sweden, Yugoslavia, USSR, Dominican Republic, Turkey, Cyprus, and Pakistan.

When asked where they would emigrate, if given a choice, thirty-nine families indicated a preference to go to the United States, twenty-six to Europe, seventeen to Canada, seven to another Arab country, five to Australia, and three to the West Bank. Of those who indicated a dream destination, 58 percent acknowledged that they have relatives living there now. Ninety-two of the families would not even venture a response, saying they preferred to stay in Nazareth.

Christians are more eager to leave than Muslims, and among the Christians it is the young single men who most often want to leave, primarily because they see few opportunities in Nazareth and Israel for education, employment, and housing. One young Greek Orthodox man named Khalil explained in a 24 May 1989 interview that he had worked as an illegal immigrant in Los Angeles for eighteen months. Fearing arrest, he turned himself in to immigration officials who then had him deported. Since then he has tried unsuccessfully several different schemes to return. Once he applied as a persecuted Baptist seeking religious freedom, and a second time he said he needed to attend the baptism of a nephew where he was to be the godfather. Others enter legally either as students or on work visas.

Some of the migrants choose to marry non-Arabs, but many return to Nazareth to find a wife. During the summer of 1989, at least two young men, with ties to Nazareth and the Greek Orthodox community, returned from Toronto and Australia to find wives. Using the connections of family and friends, both were successful in finding brides willing to marry in the community church and then follow them to foreign lands. Time and distance can weaken the ties to Nazareth, but for most the ties remain strong, bolstered by annual trips home to Nazareth for family gatherings such as funerals or weddings. Ties are also maintained through phone calls and videotapes of baptism and marriage celebrations. Ties with relatives in Arab countries are harder to maintain, owing to travel restrictions. Some family members have not seen each other since separated in 1948, while others have been able to arrange meetings on neutral territory, most often in Europe.

Nazarenes not only maintain ties to Nazareth, they also nurture ties with Nazarenes in their new-found homes. Raghada Khouri, a Nazareth native who now lives in Los Angeles with her husband and children, related that Nazarenes living in the Los Angeles area gather each year for a party. About two hundred families, both Christian and Muslim, attended the 1989 gathering. This group of Los Angelenos–Nazarenes has also raised money for a dialysis machine to be donated to the Nazareth Hospital. Whether Muslim or Christian, American or Australian, Nazareth remains an integral part of their identity.

5
The Quarters of Nazareth

Historical Development

The diversity among the inhabitants of Nazareth is evidenced not only by its variety of communities as symbolized by its mosques and many different churches, but also by the way in which Nazarenes, like the inhabitants of other Middle Eastern cities, have chosen to congregate into quarters[1] based on like religion, family, or place of origin.

The names of the three original quarters—Latin (Roman Catholic), Rum (Greek Orthodox), and Muslim—illustrate the religious basis of Nazareth's quarters.[2] Beginning in the early nineteenth century, travelers, in writing about their visits to Nazareth, almost always mentioned the religious diversity of the city, but the first reference to religious quarters seems to have come in 1868 with the publication of Tobler's work on Nazareth, in which a map drawn by a missionary in Nazareth named Zeller shows three religious quarters (fig. 1).

The process by which these quarters arose can be understood partly by the location of houses of worship. In 1620 when Emir Fakr al-Din allowed the Franciscans to return to the then Muslim village, they established themselves at the site of the Annunciation on the southern edge of what was to become known as the Muslim quarter. No doubt the Christians who followed chose to settle not among the Muslims,

---

[1] There are several Arabic words meaning "quarter," as in a neighborhood or section of a city. In Nazareth the most common term was originally *hara* (*haret* in construct form) with *hiyy* being the more common usage today. Older quarters are still commonly referred to as hara, hence haret al-Rum or haret al-Sharqiya, while the newer quarters are more often called hiyy as in hiyy al-Safafra or hiyy Schneller. Both words are used interchangeably, hiyy being the more common term and the one used by the municipality and newspapers.

[2] Other Palestinian Arab cities are also divided into quarters based on family and religious ties. Tsimhoni (1983, 63) notes the religious quarters of Jerusalem and then writes: "Residence in the Christian centers in the West Bank was largely kept in separate quarters as well, divided and named after the major extended families. The cohesion of the family quarters in Ramallah and Bethlehem has been somewhat undermined since 1948 as the result of the expansion and settlement of refugees in these towns. Nevertheless, the inclination to reside within a Christian neighborhood has prevailed."

but on land either owned by the church, or at least close to the protection and assistance of the church.

The Roman Catholics were not the only Western-Rite group to
inhabit the Latin Quarter. Also living in the quarter were the Greek
Catholics, who had worshiped since 1771 in the synagogue-turned-
church located in the market at the edge of the quarter; the Maronites,
whose church was built in 1770; and a small number of Protestants,
whose church, dedicated in 1871, sits near the center of the Latin quarter. The Greek Orthodox chose to settle not around their church at
Mary's well, but rather on the side of the village closest to their church,
eventually adding a second chapel and other institutions within the
quarter. The map shows that the Rum quarter seems to be slowly expanding toward its church.

Proximity to places of worship seems to be one explanation for
the development of the religious quarters of Nazareth, especially in the
case of the Latin and Greek Churches of the Annunciation, which existed as holy places long before the return of Christians to Nazareth. It
is also true that religious institutions and churches were erected in the
midst of quarters after the quarters had been established. This seems to
be the case of the White Mosque constructed in 1804 and its undated
predecessor, built in the heart of the already populated Muslim village,
and the Coptic Church, which was constructed long after the Copts had
congregated into their quarter.

Another explanation is the desire of communities to live together. Thus Nakhleh Bishara in a 13 September 1989 interview noted
the "tribal mentality," by which each religious community preferred to
live with family and other members of the community and in close
proximity to their church. As is the case in modern-day Nazareth, his-
torically the immigrants to the village settled next to immediate or extended family members on family-owned land, on whatever land was
available to rent or buy, or close to others who had migrated from the
same region. If given a choice, Maronite immigrants from Lebanon
would no doubt prefer to live close to other Lebanese Maronites, and
Greek Orthodox from the Huran region in Syria would prefer to seek
out other Orthodox from Syria. Fu'ad Farah, in a 3 September 1989 interview, noted that because most Western-Rite Christians came to Nazareth from Lebanon, and the Orthodox from Syria and Jordan, the two
groups did not tend to mix very much, but rather settled near their
churches and family members. He noted that his Orthodox ancestors
settled in caves above the Orthodox Church instead of going to where
the Roman Catholics had settled. Intercommunal relations in Nazareth were for the most part cordial and without Christian-Muslim
conflict, as in Damascus, or Christian-Christian conflict, as in Jerusa-

lem; still the tradition of sectarian conflict in the region must have kept Nazareth's inhabitants, both old and new, a little suspicious of the others and therefore wanting to maintain some degree of separation from potential adversaries.

Throughout the nineteenth century there are increasing references to the quarters of Nazareth. Bartlett provides a map in his travel account of 1879 that is an updated and anglicized version of Tobler's map (Bartlett 1977, 483). He describes the three quarters of Nazareth as the Latin quarter on the west, where "the Latins and Maronites reside," the Rum quarter on the north, "occupied mainly by Greeks," and the Muslim quarter in the eastern part of town, which "is the smallest of the three" (Thomson 1882, 313).

Other than mention of the quarters, there is little description of them. One traveler, however, gives an interesting description of the Muslim quarter which might help in understanding why Christians did not, or perhaps could not, settle in the older Muslim part of town. Upon leaving the Latin Church of the Annunciation, James Kean tells the future pilgrim wishing to visit the home and workshop of Joseph located in the midst of the Muslim quarter to

> proceed up the town a little way, and then strike to the right into the neighborhood behind, or to the west of, the church. This is the Muslim quarter of the town. The houses here are but huts. They are so closely planted that mere footpaths divide them: it is as though a hundred monster beehives had been set down at random, space being at a premium. . . . Threading your way with careful steps among these hovels and rubbish heaps, you arrive at a door in a wall. . . . Inside the enclosure is a small chapel said to occupy the site of Joseph's workshop. (Kean 1894, 224)

This crowded condition in the Muslim quarter no doubt led to the eventual expansion of the quarter. With the newer Christian quarters to the north and west, the Muslim quarter naturally expanded to the south and east. The original Muslim quarter also suffered from the loss of land to the Franciscans, who in the decades before 1900 had gradually purchased Muslim homes and lands surrounding the Church of the Annunciation. When the first series of archaeological digs took place in 1900, the Franciscans were able to excavate in much of the area around the church where Muslim homes had once stood (Briand 1982, 69).

Scrimgeour (1913, 1–3) describes the Muslim quarter as being located on "the lower part of the opposite hill-side." The location of what was originally referred to as the Muslim quarter was now noted as "the neighbourhood of the bazaars, which includes the most densely populated quarter of the town." Like Tobler, he noted only three quarters:

"As in most Turkish towns, there are several quarters designated by the religious persuasion of the inhabitants of that section of town. Almost all of the members of the Greek Orthodox Church live in the east end, the Roman Catholics with their religious associates the Maronites and the Greek Catholics occupy the west, while a portion of the centre and the whole of the south is Moslem."

Scrimgeour's familiarity with Nazareth did not result in greater delineations of the quarters, even though other contemporary works on Nazareth indicate that more existed. Baedeker, in his 1912 guide to Palestine and Syria, mentions that the "various confessions have their own quarters"—the Latin quarter on the south, the Greek Orthodox quarter on the north and "in the centre the Mohammedan Haret el-Islam, with a mosque and the new government-building (Serai)." He writes that the other quarters "contain a mixed population," which, as his map indicates, include el-Khanuk behind the Orthodox Church; haret esh-Sharkiyeh (eastern) east of haret el-Islam, but still west of the main road; haret el-Hosh (courtyard or enclosed area) next to the Latin Church; haret el-Gharaba south of the Latin quarter; haret el-Surudshi west of the Latin quarter; haret ez-Zirub west of haret el-Surudshi above the Maronite Church and Mensa Christi Church; and haret el-Gharbiyeh (western) south of the Zirub and Surudshi quarters. The Gharbiyeh quarter is the only quarter singled out on the map as having a mixed population, which could mean a mixture of just Latins, Maronites, and Greek Catholics, or perhaps even Greek Orthodox and Muslims (Baedeker 1912, 247).

All these quarters and several more are identified just a few years later in As'ad Mansur's history of Nazareth. Mansur, a native of Nazareth, in describing its quarters notes that "Nazareth is divided into three large quarters [hiyy] according to denomination"; a footnote explains that this phenomenon happens in "most cases," but families from one denomination do live in quarters of another denomination. He uses the example of his parishioners, the Protestants or Anglicans, who mostly live in the Rum quarter, even though their church and most of their waqfs are in the Latin and the western Muslim quarters. Mansur goes on to explain that the three large quarters are then divided into smaller sections or quarters (hara), but that fixed borders or boundaries do not exist between the various subquarters (Mansur 1924, 12).

Mansur's 1914 map of Nazareth (fig. 4, depicting a much larger area than Tobler's map of 1868) shows the expanding three main quarters and the eighteen other subquarters. Mansur also describes in his text these quarters and their religious composition. In most cases, the quarters are divided along Muslim-Christian lines as indicated on the map, but in some areas, such as newly inhabited areas in the southern part of town near the junction of the roads to Afula and Haifa, they are described as having inhabitants from both religions (Mansur 1924, 9–11).

The Rum (Orthodox) quarter is shown as having enveloped the Orthodox Church of the Annunciation and expanded up the north and northeastern slopes. Seven of the subquarters mentioned are found within this quarter. Four of the quarters are known by family names: haret al-Qa'war, haret al-Hish, haret al-'Adini, and haret al-Farah. These family-oriented quarters are located in the older section of the Rum quarter. Haret al-'Ain (the well) is the area adjacent to Mary's well. Haret al-Khanuq (literally suffocation or diphtheria, but more likely a place of squeezing, as in the *wadi*, or ravine, that runs through this quarter) is the quarter directly behind the Orthodox Church leading up to the summit, where the road then proceeds on to Kfar Kanna and Tiberias. Haret al-'Araq (name attributed to houses, roads, or tunnels carved out of stone) is on the northern slope on the hill to the east of St. Margaret's orphanage.

Mansur (1924, 12) describes the Latin quarter (haret al-Latin) as being inhabited by "Latins, Catholics and Maronites," and growing up the western hills. Mansur lists eight subquarters within its area. Haret al-Zarub (Zirub in Baedeker), haret al-Yaminia, haret al-Sarujia (Surudshi in Baedeker), haret al-Shuwafia, and haret al-Mazazwa are all quarters with family names. In addition, there are haret al-Hawush (Hosh in Baedeker), located just south of the Latin Church; haret Deir al-Binat (Little Sister's Convent), west of the main road leading south out of town; and haret al-Maidan (field or open space), past the convent on the same side of the road.

The Muslim quarter (haret al-Muslimin) is shown expanding up the eastern hills of the basin. This eastern section of the Muslim quarter is described by Mansur as not having one house in it thirty years earlier and as now "a large quarter." In addition to the new haret al-Sharqiya to the east of the main road, the Muslim quarter also includes haret al-Jami' (mosque) surrounding the White Mosque, where the Muslim quarter originated, and haret al-Gharbia (western), which is south of the Casa Nova and Latin quarter and west of the main road leading up to the market area. Located in this quarter is the khan of the pasha, where visitors, along with their camels and donkeys, find lodging for the night. In Baedeker's map this quarter extends farther south and is called Gharaba, which is based on the same root as "western," but connotes "strangeness" or "stranger," perhaps as in a visitor to the town. At first glance it would seem that Baedeker mixed up the two words, but he also has a Gharbiyeh quarter in the western part of town which is not mentioned by Mansur, who identifies the sector as the Sarujia and Shuwafia quarters.

Much of the original Muslim quarter is included by Mansur as part of the Latin quarter. No doubt the crowded conditions described by Kean had prompted inhabitants of the Muslim quarter to look for a more suitable location. In an 8 May 1989 interview, Abu 'Ammar Salman, a current resident of the Sharqiya quarter, related that his grandfather had lived in the original Muslim quarter adjacent to the Latin Church, but in 1915 had sold the land to the Franciscans. The family then moved across the valley to the eastern hill, where their home was the largest and farthest up the hill, until further growth of the quarter in 1948.

Paul Range, in his small monograph on Nazareth based on 1918 research in the town, identifies eight quarters and the religion of each quarter's inhabitants as follows: only Muslims live in the Sharqiya quarter; Greek and Latin Christians and also Muslims live in the Ghar-biya quarter; Latin and Maronite Christians live in the Latin quarter; Maronite, Greek Catholic, and Latin Christians live in the Surudshi quarter; Muslims live in the Islam quarter; Greek Catholic, Greek Or-thodox, and Protestants live in the Rum quarter; and inhabitants of various denominations live in the Gharaba quarter and the Khanuq quarter. Range notes that in the days of G. Schumacher, who wrote about Nazareth in 1890, the town was more strictly segregated accord-ing to denomination (Range 1923, 18).

The three main quarters are also noted by Mehmet Temimi in 1933. He notes that the houses constructed in the Sharqiya quarter are built in the midst of gardens, with considerable space between some of the homes. The Rum quarter is described as having the best homes and best climate in Nazareth, and every house in the quarter has a small garden with apple, peach, and almond trees in the front surrounded by cactus hedges or separated from neighbors by a short fence or a road. The houses in the Latin quarter are described as being joined together. The two other quarters mentioned are the Islam quarter in the center of town near the mosque and the Maidan quarter, both of which are described as having a mixed population (Temimi 1933, 377).

A 1966 study of Nazareth that divides Nazareth into thirteen quarters, identified in Hebrew as shekun, introduces several new names, including the Safafra quarter in the northwest; the Hapoalim (worker's) quarter located to the west of the Maidan quarter, and now known by the Hebrew-Arabic mix of Shekun al-Arab; the Archbishop Hakim quarter (now Mitram) south of Shekun al-Arab; the Maslakh quarter south of the Sharqiya quarter; the 'Amara quarter south of Maidan; the Krum quarter north of Shekun al-Arab and west of the

Latin quarter; and Bir al-Amir in the southwest section of town along the road to Haifa. Also noted are the older quarters of Rum, Sharqiya, Latin, Suq, and Maidan (Baruch 1966). The Survey of Israel map of Nazareth published in 1974 shows only eleven quarters by name: Rum (Greek) Orthodox quarter, Waqk er-Rum (the Greek Orthodox waqf), Latin quarter, el-Batris quarter, Worker's quarter (Shekun al-Arab), Archbishop Hakim quarter, Bir el-Amir, Jebel ed-Daula, el-Janan, Eastern quarter, and Worker's quarter (in the Eastern quarter).

Present-Day Quarters

As illustrated in chapter 2, Nazareth has grown from a sleepy village of several thousand inhabitants in the nineteenth century to the largest Arab city in Israel with a population of around 60,000. This has resulted in a similar increase in the number of quarters from the original three, then twenty-one in Mansur, to upward of fifty quarters and subquarters today (fig. 16). While more recent maps and works on Nazareth continue to identify some of the quarters, survey and fieldwork in Nazareth have revealed many more, but perhaps still not all. The exact number of quarters is uncertain, for names are constantly falling in and out of usage, and some secondary names or subquarters may have been overlooked. For instance, one woman surveyed mentioned that before moving to the Schneller quarter she lived in the Volvo quarter, but did not describe where it was located. Perhaps she got her car factories mixed up and actually lived in the Dodge quarter, but she is Catholic, and the Dodge quarter has few if any Christian residents. The location or even existence of a Volvo quarter is still uncertain.

The following is a list of the known quarter and subquarter names, beginning with the original three and moving outward and clockwise.

The Suq (market) is located in the heart of the city. This quarter includes the labyrinth of shops, the market, and what was originally, but no longer, known as the Muslim quarter. It overlaps parts of the Latin and Rum quarters and includes within its area the smaller quarters of Jami' (the mosque), Barclays (centered on Barclay's Bank and the road named after it which leads north from the Church of St. Joseph toward the Rum quarter), and al-Sheikh, located to the north of the mosque where a cluster of Fahum family members live in an area named after their ancestor Sheikh Abdallah al-Fahum who built the White Mosque. Many of the residents in the suq live in homes that have been passed down from generation to generation. Nowadays, however, this process is changing as many newlywed couples opt to live out of the suq with its older, crowded family homes, preferring rather to move into new homes in newer quarters. As a result, the

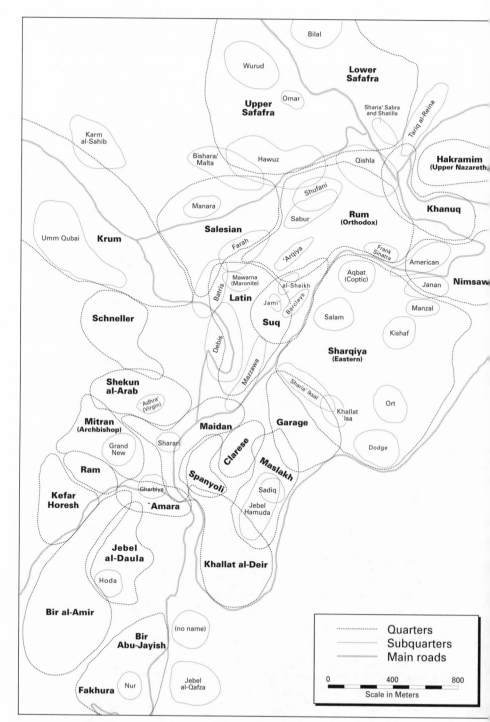

Fig. 16. The quarters of Nazareth

population of the suq gradually grows older. In the 1983 *Census of Israel*, the precinct which encompasses the suq had the highest median age of any of the twelve subquarters. Among all residents in the quarter, the average age was 23.4; among the Christian residents it was 26.3. On the other hand, the newer Safafra quarter had a median age of 16.4, and an even lower 15.9 among the Muslim inhabitants (*Census of Israel*, Population and Households no. 3, table 1).

The Latin quarter, still in its original location to the west of the suq and Basilica of the Annunciation, has lost many of the subquarter names from Mansur, but has maintained the Mazzawa (in Mansur written Mezazwa) quarter, which extends from the Galilee Hotel north to the Protestant Church. The tight-knit structure of Arab families helps in understanding why family-named quarters existed. The Mazzawa family, for example, during the British Mandate organized itself into a family association which sought to help poor members of the family, educate the youth, and strengthen the spirit of friendship (ISA 27-N632–2663). The Latin quarter has also added two more family-named quarters: Debis to the south of the Carmelite convent, and Batris to the north of the convent. One young man from the Debis family said that only three Debis families remain in the quarter that retains the Debis name, while twenty Debis families now live in Texas. One subquarter in the Latin quarter goes by two names: Mawarna (Maronite) or Naba' (spring). It surrounds the Maronite church and the now-dry spring that was located behind the church.

The Salesian quarter to the northwest of the city core could be considered an extension of the original Latin quarter. The Salesian Church of Jesus the Adolescent and vocational school dominate the summit of Jebel Nebi Se'in. Surrounding this large complex are a variety of residential areas with little cohesiveness other than that they all border the Salesian property. One of these areas on the back side of the hill is identified by one of its residents with a second name of the Manara (tower) quarter after a British watchtower that once stood nearby. He said that the municipality assigned this name to the new quarter beginning in 1976. This subquarter consists of only twelve houses—seven Muslim, two Greek Orthodox, two Greek Catholic, and one Maronite. Surrounding these homes are vacant lands owned by the Salesians.

The Rum (Orthodox) quarter to the northeast of the suq has kept the names of several of its original subquarters: 'Ain (well), 'Arqiya (in Mansur written 'Araq), and Farah or Jebel Farah (Mt. Farah), which, according to Ernest Farah in a 24 May 1989 interview, at one time extended from the suq up to the Salesian Church but now covers only the upper portion, as the Farah family has sold parts of its land closer to the suq. One of the reasons for the decline in size of the Farah quarter is the steady stream of emigration. According to Farah, fewer members of the Farah family now live in the quarter than before 1948. He said that there are now hundreds of Farahs in the United States and that every year a dozen or so more leave Nazareth for other countries; more want to leave, but are unable to get visas (figs. 17, 18).

Other areas that are found within the Rum quarter include Shufani (a family name), Sabur (cactus, presumably derived from cactus hedges which grew in the area), Frank Sinatra (after the youth center which he financed and came to dedicate, but which is now used as a Histadrut labor center), and Municipal Garden (after Nazareth's small and singular park). When asked the name of their quarters, several respondents in this area said they did not have a specific quarter name, but instead said they lived near the park or near the Frank Sinatra Center. If people in the neighborhood continue to refer to it as "near Frank Sinatra," the "near" may one day be dropped and Frank Sinatra may become the fourth person after the Virgin Mary, Archbishop Hakim, and Sheikh Abdallah to have a quarter named after him or her.

Several quarters might be considered extensions of the Rum quarter. Qishla (from the Turkish word for military barracks) is the hilltop area of homes surrounding what was an Ottoman police station, British district commissioner's residence, and now police headquarters

Fig. 17. Greek Orthodox quarter with Salesian Church of Jesus the Adolescent (top left), and St. Gabriel Hotel (former Franciscan Sisters' convent) (top right)

Fig. 18. Municipal garbage collector in the upper section of the Rum quarter

for the Northern District; Khanuq, which no longer refers to the section of the Rum quarter north of the church, is the name associated with the area located above the Rum quarter and below Upper Nazareth, including the uppermost portion of the main thoroughfare northward out of town. The American (Amerikani) quarter, to the east of the Rum quarter, derives its name from several Baptist families from the United States associated with the Baptist school who, along with several Arab Baptist families, both clergy and faculty, live in a Baptist cluster or quarter on land purchased by the Baptist Church. According to one resident the quarter's name came into common usage first by taxi drivers who, for lack of a better name to call the area to the east of the Rum quarter, started calling it the American quarter because of the two American families who lived there. The Baptist school in its earlier days was often referred to as the American school. This interchangeable usage of American and Baptist applies to the quarter, too. While it is most often called American, residents of Nazareth know that it is the area where a group of Baptists live.

To the east of the American quarter, where the main road begins to snake its way up and out of the northeastern terminus of the basin, is the Nimsawi (Austrian) quarter. Its name comes either from the Austrian hospital (now Italian Holy Family Hospital) located at the eastern edge of the quarter or, depending on whom you ask, from an Austrian doctor who lived in the area and worked at the hospital. During the beginning of this century this quarter developed as an affluent neighborhood mainly for friends of the Germans and Turks. A cemetery for WWI German soldiers is located in this quarter next to the hospital.

The Janan (garden) quarter straddles the Sharqiya and Nimsawi quarters. Of the eight homes surveyed in this quarter, five identified the quarter with the name of Nimsawi and three with the name Janan. Alternative names for those who called it Nimsawi included two listing Janan, one listing street number 721, and one listing Sharqiya quarter or Ain Umm al-Qasab (after a spring in the area). Two of the three who listed Janan as the name of the quarter identified Nimsawi as the secondary name. One resident, rather then use the term *hiyy* (quarter), used the Hebrew word *shekun*, which connotes an apartment building or a planned housing estate. Part of the quarter does look as if if it were a planned community, with its uniform houses and tree-lined walkways. The name may come from the developers of the shekun who wanted a pleasant-sounding name for marketing, as has been the case with other new housing areas; or perhaps the name comes from the gardens and orchards located here before the encroachment of houses.

The Sharqiya (Eastern) quarter has grown considerably since Mansur first depicted the Muslim quarter as shifting to the eastern hills of the Nazareth basin. Today it is the largest quarter in population and one of the largest in size. It might have expanded even further, as the quarters to the west have done, but its growth was restricted by the establishment of Upper Nazareth, whose border to the east of the quarter prevented growth up to the summit of Nazareth's eastern hills. As a result, much of the Muslim population of Nazareth who might have settled in the Sharqiya quarter are now living in the newer quarters to the south and north of the city.

Located within the Sharqiya quarter are several subquarters. Perhaps the most interesting is the Aqbat (Coptic) quarter in the northwest section. According to Munthir Qupti in a 21 August 1989 interview, the oldest house in the quarter is around a hundred years old, but most of the homes were built in the 1950s to accommodate the growing generation of Copts, which included Qupti's father. His father's home was one story high, but now his and other homes from the 1950s have added additional stories to make way for the succeeding generations. There are thirty-six Copt homes in the quarter, with no room for further expansion except for another story up. As a result, some Copt families are now moving to available housing in newer quarters. Since all of the Copts in Nazareth are descendents from one man and carry the family name of Qupti (Copti), the Coptic quarter is more correctly classified as a family-based quarter than a religious quarter, although in actuality it has characteristics of both. Muslims and other Christians who live adjacent to the cluster of Copt houses also refer to their quarter by the Copt name, the Sharqiya quarter being used with it interchangeably (figs. 19, 20).

Also within the Sharqiya quarter is the Manzal (apartment) quarter, which the Survey of Israel map labels as the Worker's quarter. This is a group of apartment buildings or shekunat built as low-income housing. They look as if they belong in Upper Nazareth with its many shekunat rather then in Nazareth's Sharqiya quarter, where single-unit and multiple-story homes are the norm. These were among the first apartment buildings built in Nazareth. The Kishaf (lookout point) quarter, like the Manara quarter, derives its name from one of the several British watchtowers that were positioned around Nazareth. One

Fig. 19. The Sharqiya quarter. Baptist school (lower left), Coptic Church (lower center), Salam Mosque (lower right), Government house (top center), Upper Nazareth (hilltops), Mt. Tabor (distance)

Fig. 20. Coptic quarter and church (foreground) Sharqiya quarter (rear)

resident noted that most of the families living in the quarter are refugees from Indur (biblical Endor), al-Hadatha, or al-Ghabiat. The Ort quarter is named after the nearby Ort-'Amal Secondary Vocational School. The Dodge quarter (originally called Krum Tiberias) is named after the one-time Ford factory (built to stimulate the economic development of Upper Nazareth), then Dodge factory, and now a government jeep factory, which sits to the south of the quarter across the main bypass road that serves as the boundary between the two Nazareths (fig. 21). Two of the homes located on or near what is now called Garage Street listed Shari' Iksal (Iksal Road) as an additional name for their quarter, with either Garage or Sharqiya quarter being the principal name. This name dates back to the time when the road to the village of Iksal, located below the precipice in the Jezreel valley, passed this way. Even though the name is still used, the road to Iksal now follows the main road south toward Afula and then branches when it reaches the valley floor. In a 25 April 1994 interview 'Atif Fahum indicated that the neighborhood surrounding his home along the old Iksal road is often referred to as Khallat 'Isa (Jesus). He indicated that *khallat* means a flat place surrounded by hills.

South of the Sharqiya quarter is the Garage quarter. Bounded by Garage Street on the north and Maslakh Street on the west, this pie-shaped section is the industrial area of Nazareth with its many garages and workshops. Also included in the quarter are the municipal secondary school and the quartered cemetery for the Copt and Western-Rite churches. This area was originally known as al-Bayadir (the threshing floor), because here was one of the few level places in the Nazareth basin where grain could be threshed. Though no threshing has taken place here for decades, older residents of Nazareth still describe this area by its former agricultural use rather than its present industrial use.

Southwest of the Garage quarter are several quarters surrounding the grounds and buildings of the hilltop cloistered convent of St. Clare and the adjacent Daughters of St. Anne home for the aged. The small quarter on the north of the hillside derives its name from the convent and is known as the Clarese quarter. To the north of this quarter is the former site of the convent of St. Clare, now used by the Don Guanella fathers as a school for the mentally handicapped. On the eastern slope of the hill is the Maslakh (slaughterhouse) quarter. It rises above Maslakh Street, which is now mostly industrial but at one time must have been the location of a slaughterhouse. Located within the Maslakh quarter is the area known as Jebel Hamuda (mount of the Hamuda family). Both names are used interchangeably for the hilltop section of this quarter. The southern portion of the hill and out onto the less populated flats where the Hypermarket is located is the area known as Khallat al-Deir (flat place of the convent). The western side

Fig. 21. Dodge quarter (middle left), government jeep plant (right), Upper Nazareth (rear)

of the hill is referred to as the Spanyoli quarter, after the Roman Catholic Spanyoli family (fig. 22).

Below the Spanyoli quarter on both sides of Pope Paul VI Street is the Maidan (open space, field, or arena) quarter. This quarter was at the southern edge of the city on Mansur's map when it was indeed an open place. The Survey of Palestine map shows homes along the western side of the main road, but indicates a football (soccer) ground along the eastern side. Today the Nazarene Church, a gas station, and Cinema Diana are located where the empty field, and then the playing field, were once located, but the name Maidan has continued to be used. A small section of the quarter is known by the Sharari family name. It straddles the beginning of a side road that follows a wadi up and west from the main road. Of the eight families surveyed in the Sharari quarter, all listed Maidan as the name of the quarter, with six listing Sharari as an additional name. However, one of the families, when asked if Sharari was another name for the quarter, emphatically said, "No!" The surveyor added in her notes that they were from the Yazbak family, another large, and perhaps rival, family in the neighborhood. Both of these families are Muslim.

Except for Khallat al-Deir and a few of the outermost subquarters in the Sharqiya quarter, all of the above-mentioned quarters were inhabited to some extent by 1948, a result of the natural growth pattern of Nazareth along the basin floor or up the hills from the original loca-

Fig. 22. Jebel Hamuda and the Maslakh quarters rising above the Garage quarter; Sadiq Mosque

tion on the lower western slope. These quarters, however, could not continue to accommodate Nazareth's natural growth or the 1948 refugees who, over the decades, gradually began moving out of their temporary quarters and looking for permanent housing. As a result, an interesting variety of new quarters continues to develop. Because of the 1956 establishment of Upper Nazareth to the east on expropriated Nazareth land, all the new quarters established since 1948 have been located on the southern, western, and northern hills.

At the extreme southern limit of Nazareth's municipal boundary, just before the switchbacking main road to Afula leaves the rocky hillside with its limited vegetation and passes into the pines reforested by the Jewish National Fund, lies a nameless cluster of fifteen homes of a Bedouin clan. According to an 11 May 1989 interview with Jemal, who was home on leave from serving with the Israeli Army in Gaza, the Bedouin settlement was established in about 1971 when his grandfather, his grandfather's brother, and their children bought the land from a Nazareth family. Before that they had lived in tents and migrated, but they decided to settle permanently in one place. Now they have a young olive orchard, terraced hillside gardens, and a herd of goats. Jemal comes from a family of twelve children. He studied at the Ort technical school in Nazareth. While the homes are on municipal land and have a Nazareth address (street number 113), they are not connected with municipal services, and they are so far south and almost hidden from view from the main road that they seem to function as a separate entity.

Several hundred yards north of this Bedouin cluster lie the southernmost quarters of Nazareth, Bir Abu-Jayish (well of someone, perhaps a famous leader, but the origin of the name is uncertain), and Fakhura (a pottery factory), where a small pottery factory once existed because of clay in the soil suitable for ceramics. The two names are used interchangeably, but Fakhura is generally attributed to the southern section, with Bir Abu-Jayish to the north. Resident George Qanazi', in a 26 April 1989 interview, explained that in the 1950s, neighboring Iksal expelled Bedouin who had settled in the village. These families (originally ten brothers from the Rabi'a tribe) then settled south of Nazareth on the road to Afula. Other reasons given for the growing sedentarization of the Galilee Bedouin include a lack of modern services and a lack of land in their former Bedouin settlements (Falah 1983, 3). The first Bedouin homes in the quarter were built without permits, but permits were later granted by the government after the fact. Fakhura is inhabited mostly by transplants from Nazareth who relocated here.

According to an enumeration of the Galilee Bedouin in non-Bedouin settlements in 1981, the 580 Bedouin living in Nazareth represented nine different families (Falah 1983, appendix 2). Based on the 1981 figures and a 1989 delineation of quarters drawn from an interview with Falah, the following numbers of Bedouin, listed by family name, live in Bir Abu-Jayish: Rabi'a, 99; Turkman, 60; Ghazalin, 41; Khawalid, 33; Hilf, 19; and Luhaib, 146 divided between Bir Abu-Jayish and Kefar Horesh. Falah noted that the 101 Bedouin of the Nu'aim family live on the road to Afula, but not in Bir Abu-Jayish, which means they are probably the isolated Bedouin cluster to the south of the quarter. The other families listed are 56 Masharikah in the Safafra quarter, and 23 Subaih in the Sharqiya quarter. While not known officially as such, Bir Abu-Jayish would certainly come closest to being Nazareth's only Bedouin quarter.

Situated on the southern slope of Jebel al-Daula, Fakhura and Bir Abu-Jayish command a fine view of the Jezreel valley. To the north of the quarters lie the Nazareth Gardens Hotel (a former Histadrut rest house) and a hilltop military post in what was once a British police station. Nestled behind pine woods and protective fences, these two compounds come under the jurisdiction of Upper Nazareth. They function as an exclave, but in reality are connected to Upper Nazareth by a narrow strip of land that runs just south of Khallat al-Deir. This island of Upper Nazareth land has served to isolate these quarters from the rest of Nazareth, and has prevented any development for approximately 400 meters along the road to Bir Abu-Jayish and Fakhura. The first homes to the south of the undeveloped strip are a group of about twenty houses north of Bir Abu-Jayish across from the hotel on the east side of the Afula road. According to the one family surveyed here, this neighborhood has yet to be named and is not considered to be a part of Bir Abu-Jayish. New homes to the south of this cluster were identified by a resident as Jebel al-Qafza (mount of the leap) after the nearby holy site.

To the west of Fakhura and Bir Abu-Jayish across an open hillside with a new elementary school at its northern end is the quarter of Bir al-Amir (spring of the Amir). This elongated quarter begins in the north at the Nazareth-Haifa road and then parallels the road as it turns southwestward, with the quarter following below it to the east in a wadi and then up the southwestern lower slopes of Jebel al-Daula. In 1945 this area included some orchards, a small cluster of several homes, and two springs, one with a pumping engine. Today it is a fast-growing neighborhood, where additional sewer lines and paved roads are added yearly, in a never-ending budget battle to keep up. Of the eleven households surveyed in this quarter, all were Muslim, and eighteen of the twenty-two parents were from refugee families. Family and village ties have obviously contributed to the communal nature of this section of the quarter. Bir al-Amir is known as predominantly refugee, but its refugee population is more mixed than the other two refugee quarters of Jebel al-Daula and Safafra.

To the northwest of Bir al-Amir sits the quarter of Jebel al-Daula (government hill) on the western slopes of the hill from which it gets its name. Along the eastern border of this quarter, the homes press right up against the fence of the military installation and rest house. During the Mandate, this area was also known as Jebel al-Daula, probably from the government police station perched atop the hill. Like Bir al-Amir, this area in 1945 consisted of orchards and uncultivated lands, with only a few homes in the northernmost section near the road to the police station. Then in the 1950s, families, mostly refugees from Mujeidil, gradually began moving in, first as renters and then as land and home owners. Today the quarter has its own mosque, and as mentioned above, its population consists mostly of refugees from Mujeidil. The survey results also indicate refugees from Ma'lul, Haifa, Saffuriya, and Dahi as well as native Nazarenes living in the quarter.

There are two smaller quarters on the northern slope of the government hill. The 'Amara (building) quarter takes its name from the large government building. A dozen or so homes were located here along the road to Haifa in 1945, so the name most likely comes from when the building was a British police station. Today it is a busy road with shops along both sides and needs a stoplight to facilitate the many cars turning south into Bir al-Amir and north into the Mitran quarter. According to the one household surveyed in the area to the north of the 'Amara quarter, the neighborhood is called the Gharbiya (western) quarter, not to be confused with the two other western quarters from earlier times whose names no longer persist.

To the west of Bir al-Amir and the road to Haifa sits the Kefar Horesh quarter, named after Kibbutz Kefar Ha Horesh (established during the Mandate), which borders Nazareth to the west. The road to the kibbutz winds up the hill through the quarter before entering the forested part of the kibbutz land. The road existed before the first houses of the quarter were built so the quarter adopted the name of the road that passes through it and the kibbutz that borders it. To its southwest, the quarter abuts the border of Yafa and its quarter known as Jebel Ma'luli, where many of the refugees from Ma'lul have settled.

A new subquarter, which extends into neighboring Yafa, has recently been developed in the Kefar Horesh quarter. In April 1986 the construction company of George Laham announced the beginning of construction on a new apartment complex which he proposed to name the Amal (hope) quarter. He even submitted a proposal to the municipalities of Nazareth and Yafa so the quarter could be known by the name of Amal. He said the name was chosen for lack of an already established name for the street or location (*al-Senara*, 4 April 1986)

The Ram or Mukhalis (Savior) quarter is north of Kefar Horesh. One of its names comes from the Ram construction company, the first company to build apartments in the quarter. The other name is obviously Christian and must be influenced by the nearby Mitran (Archbishop) quarter, which was developed by the Greek Catholics and has a school run by the Mukhalis (Salvatorian) Sisters. Today the quarter is made up of a score of white, four-story apartment buildings. According to an 8 August 1989 interview with contractor Mohammad Abd al-Qadar, his company built five apartment buildings (shekunat) for a total of seventy-two apartments in the quarter after the Ram company had finished construction of the first section of apartments. Qadar said the land in the quarter was government land and that the apartments are rented with the help of government loans. Of the families surveyed in the quarter, several offered explanations of why they are living there. One of the families said it was because there was no available land on which to build in Nazareth. A second family consisting of seven orphaned children and the aunt who is raising them obviously could not afford anything better. A third family lives there because the father is blind and his insurance pays for part of the apartment, which is managed by the government-related Amidar Company. This family said that all the families in its building receive government subsidies. Of the seven parties running in the Nazareth municipal election, this family gave the Labor party the highest rating. This unusual act owes perhaps to the fact that it is the Labor party that could help provide access to government-sponsored housing, not the Communist or Islamic parties (figs. 23, 24).

The Mitran (Archbishop) quarter, or Archbishop Hakim quarter, as it is identified on the Survey of Israel map, is a hilltop quarter to the north of the Ram quarter. Until the 1950s this area was vacant. Then, as related in a 17 May 1989 interview with Yusef Nakhleh, Archbishop Hakim started to buy land on the mountain in an effort to keep Arabs, and particularly the Greek Catholics, from emigrating by providing additional schools, a church, a seminary, and land for homes. Hakim bought the land over a span of years from 1951 to 1954. According to Nakhleh, the land where the Mukhalis school is now located was purchased from Greek Orthodox families; the land for the Convent of the Annunciation and the St. Joseph's seminary and secondary school, also known as the Mitran school, was acquired from Muslim families. In a different explanation, Antoine Farah, a retired teacher from the Mitran school, explained in a 5 September 1989 interview that the land Hakim bought from the government was land abandoned by Muslim land-

Fig. 23. The low-income, religiously mixed Ram quarter. White dome of the Greek Catholic convent chapel (top left)

Fig. 24. Mitran quarter with Greek Catholic Mitran high school (left), Salvatorian high school (right) and scout office (center left)

owners in 1948, and that part of the agreement with the government included Hakim deeding the rights to Greek Catholic land in abandoned villages in exchange for the land in Nazareth for his Greek Catholic complex.

This complex of convent, seminary, and two secondary schools— originally one for boys and the other for girls, but now both mixed— also includes a Catholic scout center and a Christian center. The land not used by the archbishop for Greek Catholic institutions was then sold, primarily to Greek Catholics. Nakhleh, for example, bought land near the Mitran school where a son and daughter have both built homes. In the block of eight homes surveyed in the quarter, all of which are Christian, four of the homes were purchased from the Muslim Shitaiwi family, who were willing to sell land on a monthly payment basis rather than the more usual all-at-once payment. This gave lower-income families a chance to buy their own homes. Of the eleven families surveyed in this quarter, five are Greek Catholic, three are Greek Orthodox, one is Roman Catholic (who said they bought the land from the Greek Catholic Church), and two are Muslim. The two Muslim families live lower down the hill, while the Christian families live on the road that skirts the Greek Catholic institutional complex. The mother of Michel Sabah, the Latin patriarch of Jerusalem, lives in this quarter.

One additional building project in the Mitran quarter is the Grand New Hotel, which dominates the hilltop with its panoramic view north toward the city center. This hotel was built as a joint venture between Hakim and the Tabar family. The land for the hotel was Tabar family land, but part of the financing was provided by the Greek Catholic Church, which, according to an 8 September 1989 interview with Rula Tabar, shares in the profits of the hotel. Those homes in the Mitran quarter that surround the hotel also refer to their quarter as the Grand New quarter.

On the next ridge to the north lies Shekun al-Arab (apartment of the Arabs) which is also called Shekun al-'Amal (worker's apartment) or the more complete Shekun 'Amal al-Arab. The history of this quarter begins in 1954 when a Roman Catholic priest from France named Paul Gauthier wanted to "extend the spiritual basis of an apostolic life" by spending time with the working class in order to "preach the Gospel to the poor and to establish the Church in the world of labour." Gauthier journeyed to Nazareth under the invitation of Archbishop Hakim. In Nazareth, Gauthier noted that the refugees who had come to Nazareth in 1948 and piled "into the Schools, the Casa Nova, the hovels, the caves, the stables, the henhouses and the pigsties" were still living in misery eight years later. In describing the living conditions in

Nazareth, Gauthier (1965, 101) noted: "One working-class family out of three lives with its seven or eight members in conditions often unworthy of human beings and always unhygienic, with the walls sweating with damp or running with infected water. The ikons and crucifixes hanging on the walls are often besmirched by water dripping from the cesspits of the houses built in terraces above. One family lives in a cave without light and almost without air, with the result that its children are half-blind."

In response to these poor living conditions, Gauthier founded the Fraternity of the Companions of Jesus the Carpenter to help the workers and the poor of Nazareth. The members of the fraternity formed a group of workers who investigated living conditions in Nazareth. They then wrote a report called *S.O.S. Nazareth!*, which they submitted to ecclesiastical, government, and trade-union leaders. These leaders agreed to help as they could, but met suspicion from the very workers who needed help. However, a group of thirteen men who needed work and a place for their families to live formed the first cooperative, which they named Shekun, or "The house." Gauthier relates that the fact that this first cooperative had as one of its members a priest gave confidence to the men and renewed their faith in themselves and in society.

The members had to raise two-fifths of the starting capital, while the trade unions and the government supplied the rest. This, however, prevented the very poor from participating. A Belgian priest, Father Warlomont, on a pilgrimage to Nazareth heard of the need and, upon his return to Belgium, sold his car and bought a cement mixer for the Shekun cooperative. He then solicited donations, which were used for long-term loans with little or no interest for the poorest of the workers to use. The cooperative system gained momentum, and by 1963 some 180 families had been rehoused. Of these families, thirty-one were unable to contribute anything except their poverty, while twenty others were able to contribute less than half of their required share. But through the long-term loans, the families were all able to gain housing (Gauthier 1965, 92–104).

The cornerstone for the housing project was laid in July 1958, with the first twenty-eight families moving into the fourteen one-story, two-family homes in June 1959. Each apartment cost 5,500 Israeli lira to build, with the government offering a long-term loan of IL 2,500, payable at 4 percent interest over twenty-five years, and the Histadrut (labor union) providing a loan of IL 1,000. The 70 dunams of land for the housing project were donated by the government (*JP*, 29 May 1959).

Amin Qudha explained in a 4 September 1989 interview that the urgency for housing prompted many to build even before services could be installed. He also noted that the quarter was not designed with modern services such as water, sewers, electricity, and roads in mind. This meant that in the beginning, sanitary conditions were not up to modern standards. Qudha blamed this problem on the government, which failed to appoint a civil engineer or provide other professional support in planning or installing the infrastructure. This neglect sharply contrasts with the building of Upper Nazareth, where only a few years later a modern community was built with full government supervision and with complete services in place before any of the apartments were built.

The original residents of Shekun al-Arab were for the most part Greek Catholic, owing to the sponsorship of Archbishop Hakim and Father Gauthier, who became Greek Catholic during his stay in Nazareth. Qudha explained that a committee headed by Hakim "would indirectly turn down Muslims saying all of the plots were full," but that later the Christian residents would sell their homes to Muslims because the two groups have always "lived together with brotherly relations." In defence of Hakim's actions, Qudha, a Greek Orthodox, explained that Hakim was acting out of loyalty to his own community; he was not against Muslims. In a 5 September interview, Antoine Farah explained that even though the selection committee preached equal opportunity for all, in actuality they preferred Christians. Farah is a Maronite from Ber'am who was given a chance to live in Shekun al-Arab by Hakim himself, but opted for a home in Safafra because he, like other villagers, preferred a more open, less crowded neighborhood.

Greek Catholic involvement in the quarter is evidenced by the shrine to the Virgin Mary located in the center of the quarter, which was built through donations from residents of the quarter. The area around the shrine is known as the al-'Adhra' (Virgin) quarter. The section of eight homes surveyed on the street just below the shrine are all Greek Catholic. In three of the families the husbands came to Nazareth in 1948 as refugees in their teens. Two came from Tiberias and one from Beisan. One of the Tiberian men is married to a woman who also came from Tiberias. This older part of the quarter is sometimes differentiated as the Lower Shekun al-Arab, with the new apartments further up the hill toward the abandoned Schneller orphanage called Upper Shekun al-Arab. The upper section is more mixed: five Roman Catholics, two Greek Catholics, two Greek Orthodox, and one Muslim family live in the group of eight houses surveyed.

Apartment living was a foreign concept to the Arabs of Nazareth. The traditional form of housing was a single-family home with children building above or beside the parents. Living in an apartment building with nonrelatives was not done. Perhaps the single most important factor in influencing Arabs to move into Shekun al-Arab and the subsequent housing projects was the lack of family homes or land to build on, as well as insufficient money. This resulted in low-income and landless refugees having few other choices for home ownership other than the less expensive shekunat. The Ministry of Housing did try to ameliorate Arab apprehensions by modifying the standard shekun format with such features as separate entrances and external stairs for each family, flat roofs for food-drying, laundry, and evening sitting, and space for the addition of rooms (For Better Living, 1964).

The original apartments were small: just two bedrooms, a tiny kitchen, a living room, and a bath. One Muslim resident of the quarter bought a shekun from a Christian family in 1967 for U.S.$12,000. The wife said that at that time, no other housing was available in Nazareth. When they moved in, the shekun was still its original small size, so they added two additional bedrooms and expanded the living room and kitchen. Most residents have done the same to the point that it is almost impossible to see that the duplexes were originally the same. The uppermost section of the quarter is mostly composed of two-story, multiunit apartment buildings that cannot be added on to. These do, however, have more floor space than the original apartments in the lower section of the quarter.

The Schneller quarter to the north of Shekun al-Arab takes its name from the hilltop orphanage built during Ottoman times by German Lutherans and identified on Mansur's map as the lone building on the hill. Since then it has been used by the military, but today lies abandoned; a sign attributes jurisdiction over the building and the surrounding land to the Ministry of Lands. Houses and apartments are going up right along the perimeter fence. Much of the area to the north and west of the orphanage and above the Mitran and Shekun al-Arab quarters and then down the back side of the hill up to the border of the kibbutz of Kefar Ha Horesh was originally planned by the Ministry of Housing as a residential area with 650 housing units (For Better Living, 1964). However, this plan never materialized because, according to a 13 August 1989 interview with city planner Adib Daud, the members of Kefar Ha Horesh objected to construction on the back side of the Schneller hill because it would be visible from the kibbutz.

Today, two distinct areas carry the Schneller name. One area lies adjacent to Shekun al-Arab on the middle of the eastern-facing slope and comprises two new apartment complexes. The lower group of apartment buildings is called hiyy Schneller, and the upper group hiyy Qimma (Summit) Schneller. Mohammad Abd al-Qadar, who developed hiyy Schneller and gave it its name, said in an 8 August 1989 interview that his company bought the land for the apartments from the government. His company, in a full-page newspaper advertisement, listed an 84-square-meter apartment for U.S.$41,000 and a 97-square-meter apartment for U.S.$44,000 (*al-Senara*, 26 July 1985). On the northern slope closer to the summit is the second area known as Schneller, consisting primarily of single-unit homes with only a few apartment buildings. This quarter is gradually encircling the hill in a counterclockwise direction.

To the north of the Schneller quarter and to the west of the Latin and Salesian quarters along the road to the village of 'Illut is the area known as Krum (vineyard, garden, orchard). The 1945 Survey of Palestine map identifies the area as Kurum en-Nasira (the vineyard of Nazareth), where there were indeed a few vineyards surrounded by larger olive and fruit orchards. The now abandoned Sisters of Nazareth convent was located amid the orchards as well as scattered homes and a cluster of homes called al-Manshiya. One man surveyed from this quarter explained that his father built their house in 1930, and it was one of the first in the area. Today most of the agriculture has been replaced by residential areas.

The quarter continues to expand toward Illut and up to the property of Kefar Ha Horesh. At its farthest extremity is a hill topped by a JNF (Jewish National Fund) fire-watch tower, an army transmitting tower, and a settlement of fifteen houses. According to a 6 September 1989 interview with one of the residents, in 1953 a Muslim family of refugees from Ma'lul bought the land from the Christian Awad family. The refugee family had eleven daughters and ten sons. All ten sons built homes on the land, and now their sons are building homes. It is interesting to note that this isolated cluster has electricity only because the government had to extend power lines to the hill for the transmitter. This family cluster is now separated from the rest of Krum by about 300 yards, but the quarter is slowly expanding to include it.

In the depression between the Schneller and Krum ridges lies a subquarter of Krum known as Umm Qubai (probably from *qabwa*, meaning a vault or arch, perhaps in reference to an old home built with arches). This name originally referred to the large area on the back side of the Nebi Se'in hill that included the smaller area known as Krum; but now the name has become more site-specific and most often refers to only a portion of the Krum quarter. Occasionally it is used interchangeably with Krum, but Krum seems to be the more dominant usage. A relatively new cluster of fifty homes on the northern side of the Krum ridge below the main road to 'Illut was identified by a resident as the Karm al-Sahib (garden or vineyard of the friend) quarter.

The Safafra quarter is located on the northwestern side of the northern hill along the road that leads to Shefar 'Am and the former site of the village of Saffuriya. The first residents of this quarter were

Fig. 25. Bilal subquarter of the Safafra quarter. Most residents of this quarter are originally from the village of Saffuriya, which once stood on the site of the forested hill in the distance (center left).

refugees from Saffuriya who in the late 1950s began to accept government compensation for the land they lost in the village. One Christian family who live in the quarter noted that they bought their land from a Muslim lawyer, who bought it from a Saffuriya refugee, who had exchanged his land in the village for the land in the quarter. The section of the quarter to the southwest of the main road is sometimes referred to as Safafra *fauq* (upper), while the northeastern section is called Safafra *taht* (lower). Lower Safafra is also occasionally called Tanak, after earlier homes built of inexpensive tin siding. These have since been replaced with more permanent cement and rock houses (figs. 25, 26).

The Tanak area of lower Safafra is also known as the Bilal quarter, after the green cupolaed Bilal Mosque at its center. Most of this section of Safafra is part of the village of Reina, but the water and sewer are provided by Nazareth, and the stongest ties are still toward Nazareth. Additional names cited in the survey for the area of Lower Safafra closest to Khanuq include Tariq al-Reina al-Qadima (the Old Reina Road), also known as Wadi al-Qantara (wadi of the Arch); and the Sabra and Shatilla Road, so called by its residents in memory of the 1982 massacre of Palestinians in these refugee camps in Beirut.

In Upper Safafra where it abuts the Salesian and Rum quarters is the subquarter known locally as Hawuz (reservoir) after the city reser-

Fig. 26. Lower Safafra quarter with the unpaved Sabra and Shatilla Road (left)

voir the quarter surrounds. Extending out from this quarter along the back side of Nebi Se'in hill is a new quarter referred to by local residents as either the Malta quarter (the name Malta may have been applied to the area by the British) or the more common Bishara quarter after the several Bishara families who first moved into the area. Further north on the outer limits of Upper Safafra is the new quarter of Wurud (roses or blossoms), another housing development named and built by the Qadar construction company. Qadar related in his 8 August 1989 interview that, like Schneller, the land for Wurud was purchased from the government. In the Wurud quarter he has built thirty shekunat in four buildings, and seventy houses; an additional seventy houses are planned. He said that the homes are purchased with the help of government loans payable over a thirty-year period in installments of NIS (New Israeli Sheqels) 300–400 (U.S.$150–200) per month.

The final quarter to be mentioned is really not a quarter, but it does serve as a place identifier. Sharia' (Street) Pope Paul VI, or Sharia' Raisa (Main Street), is used to identify the main road through town, particularly in the midsection dividing the Suq from the Sharqiya quarter. The inhabitants of the sections of the road in Maidan and Nimsawi also refer to their location with the street name, but they more often use the quarter name.

A summary of the origins of the quarter names shows the variety of factors that have been influential in their development and naming.

Those named after a religious group living in the quarter include Latin, Rum, Aqbat, and Mawarna. Quarters with a religious name, either a religious structure or person, include Clarese, Salesian, 'Adhra', Mitran, Mukhalis, and Bilal. Quarters named after a person include al-Sheikh, Mitran, 'Adhra', and Frank Sinatra. Those named after a family include Aqbat, Shufani, Bishara, Farah, Batris, Debis, Mazzawa, Spanyoli, Sharari, and Jebel Hamuda. Those named after a physical feature such as a spring, hill, or garden include Khanuq, Wadi, Qantara, Naba', Krum, Karm al-Sahib, Wurud, Sabur, Janan, Bir al-Amir, Bir Abu-Jayish, Jebel al-Daula, Jebel Hamuda, Jebel al-Qafza, Khallat al-Deir, Khallat Isa, and Maidan. Those named after a building or other physical structure include Kishaf, Manara, Manzal, Ort, Dodge, Garage, 'Amara, Grand New, Schneller, Hawuz, Qishla, Frank Sinatra, Barclays, 'Arqiya, Maslakh, Shekun al-Arab, Suq, Umm Qubai, and Fakhura. Those named after a place such as a country or village include American, Nimsawi, Safafra, Kefar Horesh, and perhaps Malta. And those named after a direction include Sharqiya and Gharbiya. In addition, several areas are known by actual street names, such as Pope Paul VI Street, Sabra and Shatilla Street, Old Reina Road, and Iksal Road; some residents on occasion give a street number as a place identifier. The most numerous sources of names are physical structures, often prominent buildings that are recognizable and whose name residents living nearby can use to describe the location of their home.

The names of some quarters indicate to a certain extent the human content of the quarter. The Rum quarter is mostly Greek Orthodox, the Aqbat quarter mostly Copt, and the Latin quarter mostly Western-Rite Christian, though in continually decreasing proportions; its subquarter, the Mawarna quarter, is now inhabited by relatively few Maronites. The Safafra quarter looks out on Saffuriya, straddles the road to Saffuriya, and is inhabited by a majority of former residents of Saffuriya. Family quarters like Farah, Shufani, and Spanyoli still indicate a presence of those families in the quarter, while in the Farah and Debis quarters, the percentage of family members living in the quarter has been diluted as families have moved and lands have been sold. In the case of these quarters, the name is not a guarantor of identifying the religion, family, or former habitation of a quarter's occupants, but it does give a good indication of the majority of residents' community affiliation.

The names of other quarters signify physical content. The Suq is just what it says it is—a market, as is the Garage primarily a neighborhood of garages and other industrial structures. Shekun al-Arab is likewise a quarter of apartments inhabited by Arabs, and the Manzal quarter has apartments, just as its name implies. However, quarters like Krum, Janan, and Wurud are no longer gardenlike, and in the case of the last two, may never have been. The land that is now Wurud was not and is not a place of roses and blossoms, except for a few springtime wildflowers that grace the vacant parcels of land in and around the quarter, along with the flowers that now adorn the newly planted yards.

Some quarter names have persisted, while over time others have fallen out of use. Evidence of the evolution of names comes from a 26 April 1994 visit with several members of the Islamic Movement of Nazareth. During the course of the conversation they referred several times to the Sadiq quarter. Further explanations revealed that within much of the Muslim community there is a growing tendency to call the areas surrounding mosques by the name of the mosque. Thus the area in the Jebel Hamuda quarter surrounding the Sadiq Mosque is now called the Sadiq quarter. Now added to the already established names of Bilal and Jami' will be the Sadiq, Hoda, Nur, Salam, and Omar quarters.

Communal Composition of Quarters

Since place-names give only a few clues to the communal composition of the quarters of Nazareth, it is necessary to look at other data to know to what extent religion and other communal bonds have continued to influence residential patterns, from the early days of three quarters with a high degree of segregation, to more than fifty quarters of Nazareth today.

One of the best sources is the residents themselves. Muslims know which of their neighbors are Christian, but not always by sect; and Christians know which neighbors are Muslim and which Christians are from what sect. In Bir al-Amir, Muslim families know that several clusters of Christian families live in the northern section of the quarter. In the northern section of Schneller, a Muslim mother was able to go down the street and identify the religion and sect of each household—six Muslims, three Greek Orthodox, and two Greek Catholics. She was also able to do the same with the eight apartments in the Ram apartment building where she formerly lived—three Muslims, three Roman Catholics, and one apartment where the husband was Muslim and his wife Roman Catholic (who presumably converted to Islam in order to get married according to Israeli law).

George Qanazi', a Greek Orthodox, noted in a 26 April 1989 interview that he knew of only four Christian families living in Fakhura and Bir Abu-Jayish. He moved his family from a home in the Rum quarter to a new house at the northern end of Bir Abu-Jayish in 1980. His family had owned the land for forty years and had divided it into lots for twelve homes. Now his wife's sister's family (also Greek Orthodox) and a Greek Catholic family have also built homes on neighboring lots. This small cluster of Christians are the only ones in Bir Abu-Jayish; one Greek Catholic family lives in Fakhura.

Postmen are also very skilled at identifying the religion of their postal patrons. One young postman assigned to the Safafra quarter indicated that he could identify the religion of each household, but was hesitant to do so because of the sensitivity of the subject of religion. Fu'ad Tuma, however, was more willing. He is one of the senior postmen in Nazareth, and it is now his duty to train new recruits on all of Nazareth's routes. In a city where street numbers exist only on maps and house numbers have been assigned, but never posted, mailmen are forced to know each household by name. This familiarity also brings a knowledge of religious affiliation. Accompanying Fu'ad on a mail delivery route across the Rum, Suq, and Latin quarters revealed an interesting pattern in which Muslims are now dominant in the central area of the suq and are scattered throughout the two adjacent Christian quarters, Orthodox families are still dominant in the section of the Rum quarter closest to the parish church, and residents from the three Western-Rite churches are still dominant in the upper reaches of the Latin quarter, as shown in figure 27. (The presence of a number before a letter on the map indicates that the house is multilevel and divided among the indicated number of families. For example, just below the Salesian church is a multistory home with six Maronite families living in it. Not all multifamily homes were identified as such by Tuma, but those identified give a good example of how relatives join together in building homes or add on to existing structures for succeeding generations.)

Clergy are also able to identify the quarters in which their parishioners live. Father Arturo in a 13 July 1989 interview identified the following quarters as having the main concentrations of Roman Catholics: Shekun al-Arab, Spanyoli, Krum, and the upper section of the Latin quarter near the Carmelite convent. Father Yusef, in a 31 August 1989 interview, named the quarters of Maronite families and their numbers as follows: Krum, 30; 'Amara near Hotel Nazareth, 10 (5 in one building); Mitran, 10; Ram, 10; Salesian below the church, 10 (6 of those families lived in one multistory home, as also indicated by Tuma); Safafra, 6 (all in the same neighborhood); Kefar Horesh, 5; Maidan, 5; Mawarna near the church, 5; Bilal, 3; Bir al-Amir, 3 (all in one building); Nimsawi, 3; Upper Nazareth, 3; Rum, 1; and Suq, 1. Archimandrite Shahada in a 31 August 1989 interview gave the following quarters and estimates of the number of Greek Catholic families: Shekun al-Arab and Mitran, 170; Maslakh, 50; Latin, 40; Krum, 40;

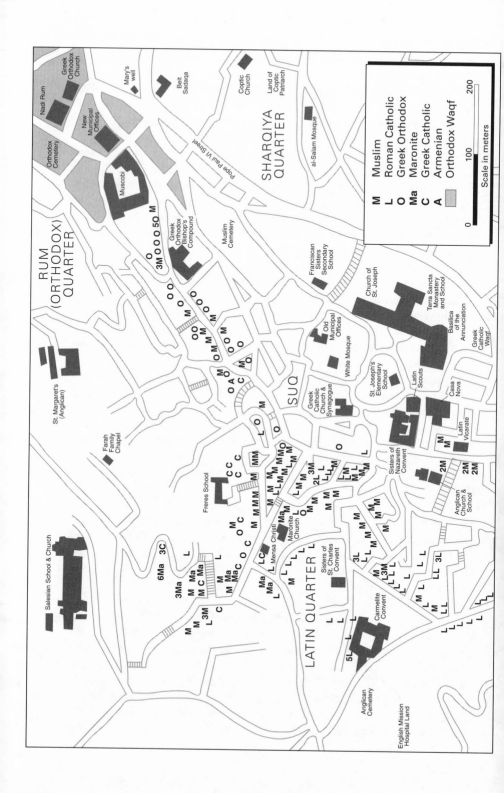

Spanyoli, 30–40; Rum, 30; Safafra, 25; Ram, 15; Nimsawi, 10; Kefar Horesh, 5; Sharqiya, 2–3; and Fakhura, 1.

Zahi Nasser, who serves as assistant pastor, indicated that the Anglican families live scattered throughout the Christian quarters of the town. Most are located singularly or in pairs, but there are three large clusters. Fourteen Anglican families live in the Protestant apartment building in the Rum quarter; eleven families from the Abu 'Assal (as in the name of the pastor) family live in a cluster just below the French hospital in the Maidan quarter; and five more Abu 'Assal families live in a group in the Latin quarter up the hill from the church.

It seems that every adult in town except for the very old or the recent arrivals knows that the Sharqiya quarter is almost entirely Muslim, that Jebel Hamuda, Fakhura, Bir Abu-Jayish, Umm Qubai, and Bir al-Amir are mostly Muslim, that Jebel al-Daula is mostly Muslim refugees from Mujeidil, that Safafra is mostly Muslim refugees from Saffuriya, that Rum, Nimsawi, and Khanuq are mostly Greek Orthodox, that Spanyoli is mostly Roman Catholic, that Aqbat is Coptic, that Mitran and Shekun al-Arab have the highest concentration of Greek Catholics, that a group of Baptist families live in the American quarter, and that Kefar Horesh, Ram, Schneller, Maidan, Krum, and Salesian are mixed quarters of Christians and Muslims.

The steeples and minarets of the town also help to identify the predominant religions in many of the quarters. The seven mosques in the Suq, Sharqiya, Jebel Hamuda, Fakhura, Jebel al-Daula, Upper Safafra, and Lower Safafra quarters are all located in areas with a high concentration of Muslims. The many Christian churches, convents, and institutions are all situated in areas with significant Christian populations. The churches in the heart of the Rum or Mitran quarters signify the presence of a high percentage of Greek Orthodox and Greek Catholics respectively, while the Maronite, Greek Catholic, and Roman Catholic churches in the Latin quarter indicate a former Christian quarter that is gradually becoming more mixed. The Salesian Church and Poor Clare convent indicate newer quarters, which may have started out with clusters of Christians, but have become mixed in many of their growing sections as both Christians and Muslims buy nearby property.

On a smaller scale, certain streets and homes also play a role in marking off the various Christian and Muslim areas. During the fasting month of Ramadan, banners quoting sura 2, verse 183, from the Quran admonishing Muslims to fast are strung across streets at the entrances of quarters. Of a more permanent nature are the religious markings placed on the outside of homes, which were identified by

surveyors on walks along all of the streets of Nazareth.[3] Only those religious markings that could be seen by passing pedestrians were noted
(fig. 28).

A variety of markers identify Muslim homes. The most common
is a Quranic verse saying *bismi Allah al-rahman al-rahim* (in the name
of God the merciful and the compassionate). These are most often
placed above the doors upon the completion of the house and usually
include the year of completion by both Gregorian and Islamic calendars. Of those dates, the oldest noted was 1957 on Garage Street, but
most are from the 1970s and 1980s, partly because of the housing boom,
but perhaps also because of a growing interest or identity with Islam in
recent years. The other common marking is a ceramic plaque with a
molding of the Dome of the Rock, often painted in bright reds, oranges,
and greens. These are more commonly found on new homes in the
newer quarters, perhaps an indication of a recent rise in nationalistic
feelings among the Arabs in that the Dome of the Rock is often used as
a symbol of Palestinian nationalism. A few houses have a crescent and
star above the door. One home on Maslakh Road near the municipal
secondary school has *hamdu li Allah* (praise to God) written above the
door, and a home in Fakhura has *rabb ahfiz hadha al-bait* (Lord protect
this house) above its door (figs. 29, 30).

The most common Christian marking is a statue of the Virgin
Mary. Such statues are commonly attributed to the Western-Rite
churches, but in Nazareth, the Eastern-Rite churches also honor Mary,
not just with traditional icons, but with statues as well. Some are simple, but others are very elaborate—Mary is housed inside a small
shrine or Christmas tree lights surround her. Crosses appear on about a
dozen homes, with Saint George above one door in the Grand New
quarter. Large, lighted letter M's for Mary are placed on roofs in August
to shine during the Feast of Mary. After the celebrations, some families
never quite get around to taking down the lighted decorations, so they
remain year round as a permanent marker on a handful of Christian
homes in Nazareth.

Several homes, both Christian and Muslim, have above their
doors the Arabic inscription *hadha min fadli rabby* (This is from the
grace of my Lord), obviously in recognition of and gratitude to God for

---

[3] The placing of such markings has stirred little attention from residents in
Nazareth. However, similar actions in India, where Hindu and Muslim communities
are at odds, have had disastrous results. When a Hindu merchant, whose stall was on
the outer wall of the central mosque, tried to hang a statue of Hanuman, the Hindu
monkey God, a crowd of cheering Hindus and angry Muslims erupted into two days of
riots in which seventeen people were injured and forty shops and houses were burned
(*Time*, 15 May 1989, 28).

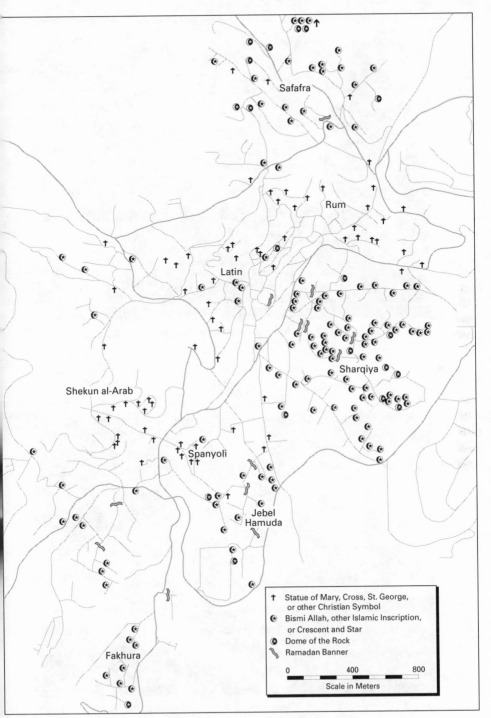

Fig. 28. Religious symbols on exteriors of houses

Fig. 29. Al-Hoda Mosque with Ramadan banner

Fig. 30. Dome of the Rock plaque above door to a house in the Sharqiya quarter

providing them with a home. One of these homes in upper Maidan near the Mitran quarter has a cross beside the saying to identify it as a Christian home, while in Schneller the saying was accompanied by a crescent and star. Two other homes feature the saying above their doors, but have no other markers to identify a specific religion. The one near Frank Sinatra was identified by a neighbor as Christian, while the one in Jebel al-Daula was in an all-Muslim neighborhood.

Except for Ram and other apartment complexes where doors are not visible from the street, the southern section of Bir al-Amir, and the westernmost section of Krum, these markings are found in every quarter and neighborhood. Sharqiya and the southern quarters have only Muslim markings; Safafra, Krum, and the Suq have more Muslim markings than Christian; Rum, Shekun al-Arab, and Mitran have all Christian markings; the rest of the quarters generally have both. Interesting patterns emerge on the map of exterior household religious symbols. These patterns are fine for the general picture of religious distribution, but the reality is much more complex and at times even patternless. For example, in the Spanyoli quarter, there is a Quranic verse above the door of one home and a year-round creche in the yard next door.

Predominantly Muslim quarters can also be identified by other outward signs. Here, many women wear traditional head coverings and robes. Some older Christian women also keep their heads covered with scarves, but they differ from the more traditional dress of the Muslim woman, which covers more of the head. Men are also seen wearing long white gallabiyas and white knitted skullcaps. There are, as a general rule, more children playing in the street and more laundry hanging on the lines, owing to the higher birthrate and larger families among Muslims. Homes of pilgrims to Mecca are decorated with palm branches, flowers, and strings of lights along patios and rooftops. During the Feast of 'Id al-Adha, when Muslims sacrifice sheep or goats, Muslim homes can be identified on occasion by the presence of sacrificial goats. For example, in upper Shekun al-Arab one apartment owner bought his goat a few days early and kept it tied up to his truck until the day of sacrifice. Christian quarters, by contrast, are identified by a lack of these Islamic characteristics, and from a few of their own identifying marks, such as occasional strings of lights at Christmas or fireworks for the Feast of Mary.

Quarter names, religious structures, and house decorations all help delineate the pattern of religious distribution in Nazareth, but they lack comprehensiveness. The 1983 census verifies those patterns of Christian-Muslim distribution with interesting results (fig. 31). The census bureau divides the municipality of Nazareth into four subquar-

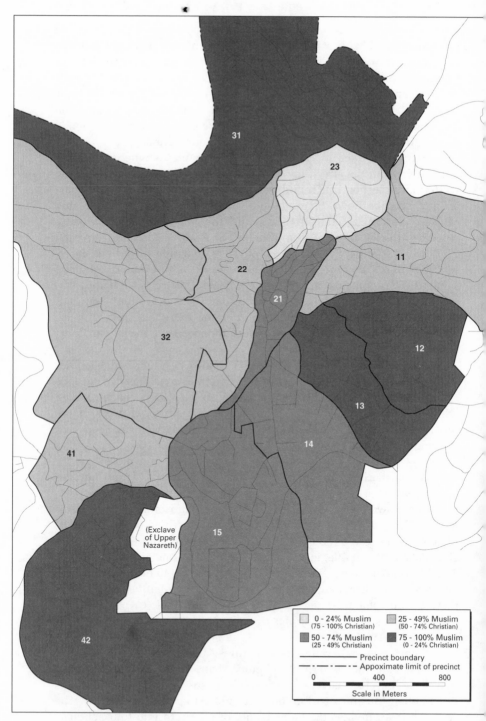

Fig. 31. Population of Nazareth by religion: 1983 census precincts

ters which are then divided into twelve smaller statistical areas. Table 11 shows the population of Nazareth in 1983 by religious grouping of Muslims, Christians, and Jews for the twelve sectors.

The most striking indication of residential segregation by religion is that Muslims compose 98.6 percent and 96.4 percent of the population in the two statistical areas located in the heart of the Sharqiya quarter (areas 13 and 12 respectively) and 90.8 percent of the population in the southern quarters of Bir al-Amir, Jebel al-Daula, Fakhura, and Bir Abu-Jayish (area 42), while Christians compose 83.9 percent of the population in one section (23) of the Rum quarter. Because the statistical areas do not always correspond to quarter areas, the results are sometimes diluted. In statistical area 11, which is 59.8 percent Christian, most of the Christians live north of the main road, while most of the Muslims live to its south. The few Christians to the south would be those along the main road, in the Janan quarter, and the Copts in their quarter. This fact is supported by the survey results. Of the thirty-three homes surveyed in statistical area 11, only six were Muslim and those six were all in the area south of the main road. The two clusters of eight homes located to the south of the main road, with four Muslims out of eight in the Aqbat quarter and one out of eight in the Janan quarter, are both on the periphery of the Sharqiya quarter in transitional zones and therefore do not adequately reflect the high proportion of Muslims that actually live in the southern section of area 11. All fourteen homes to the north of the road are Christian, and ten of those are

TABLE 11. Population by religion and census statistical area

Area	Muslim pop.	Percentage	Christian pop.	Percentage	Jewish pop.	Druze pop.	Total
11	1,393	39.8	2,093	59.8	11	0	3,497
12	3,026	96.4	113	3.6	0	0	3,139
13	2,867	98.6	36	1.2	6	0	2,909
14	847	71.7	335	28.3	0	0	1,182
15	2,424	62.4	1,455	37.5	3	0	3,882
21	858	59.3	585	40.5	2	0	1,445
22	1,249	33.8	2,434	65.9	3	6	3,692
23	450	16.1	2,344	83.9	0	0	2,794
31	3,563	77.1	1,051	22.8	2	1	4,617
32	2,476	41.5	3,483	58.4	7	0	5,966
41	1,696	44.9	2,073	54.9	5	3	3,777
42	4,387	90.8	443	9.2	3	0	4,833
Totals	25,236	60.5	16,445	39.4	42	10	41,733

SOURCE: *Census of Israel*, 1983, Census of Population and Housing no. 4, table 1

Greek Orthodox. One family in the Khanuq listed one of its four neighbors as being Muslim, but all the other homes in the northern section listed all four neighbors as being Christian.

A similar situation occurs in statistical area 15. Here Muslims compose 62.4 percent of the population, but smaller units would reveal an even higher percentage of Muslims in the Jebel Hamuda and Khallat al-Deir quarters, with a lower percentage in Maidan, Spanyoli, and Clarese quarters. Of the twenty-six homes surveyed in this area, fourteen of the fifteen Muslim families live south of the road circling the grounds of the convent in the quarters of Jebel Hamuda, Khallat al-Deir, and the nameless quarter on the road to Afula. One Christian family lives in the southern section in the homes just north of the Hypermarket. Conversely, one Muslim family lives in Spanyoli, the other ten families in the northern section being Christian—eight Roman Catholic and three Greek Catholic.

Statistical area 32, which is 58.4 percent Christian, is likewise more segregated than the census figures indicate. Most of the Christians in this part of town live in Shekun al-Arab and the eastern section of Krum, while the Muslims in general congregate in the western portion of Krum and the northern section of Schneller. One of the eighteen homes surveyed in Shekun al-Arab was Muslim, eleven of the seventeen Christian homes being Greek Catholic.

While some areas can be classified as predominantly Muslim or Christian, the house-to-house pattern shows that many neighborhoods of Nazareth are mixed, even though the quarter may be dominated by a majority of one religion (fig. 32). Of the twenty-five clusters of eight homes surveyed, seven were all Muslim (in Bir al-Amir, Bir Abu-Jayish, Jebel Hamuda, Krum, Bilal, and two in Sharqiya), and four were all Christian (in Grand New, Shekun al-Arab, Rum, and Shufani). The remaining fourteen were mixed in varying proportions. The mixing takes place as Christians and Muslims jointly move into areas like Ram or Wurud, or in a one-directional pattern, as Muslims move into traditional Christian quarters, while few Christians move into the quarters already established as Muslim.

A similar pattern of segregation and mixing is verified by Baruch in his 1966 study. For example, the Sharqiya quarter (20 percent of the population of Nazareth) is 97.2 percent Muslim, while the Khanuq quarter (10.7 percent of the population) is 84.9 percent Christian, and the Latin quarter and Suq (24.9 percent of the population) are 64.4 percent Christian (Baruch 1966, 378).

This interesting pattern of congregating and mixing is influenced by a variety of factors. The first is that in traditional Arab families the married sons usually remain in, above, or next to their parents' home.

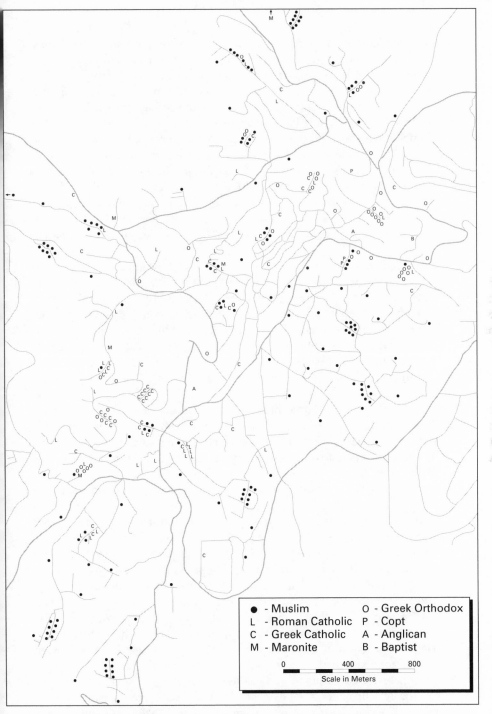

Fig. 32. Sample distribution of religious communities in Nazareth

Families will buy a parcel of land for a home and garden. As the family grows and sons marry, the garden land is then used for additional homes. A look at the settlement pattern from the 1946 Survey of Palestine shows scattered homes in the new neighborhoods surrounding the more compact central city that was the village of Mansur's day. Since then, the vacant lands, gardens, and orchards surrounding the homes have filled in as sons and grandsons have built homes on the family land, creating what are now compact, established quarters in which little change or movement takes place. The emergent pattern is one in which houses are often added on to, and in which old and new homes stand side by side as sons build next to parents and brothers next to brothers. A look at any quarter reveals a lower level of rock and older cement homes topped by upper floors of newer and newest cement.

Today, very few vacant lots still exist in the central Latin, Rum, or Suq quarters. The next ring of quarters, such as Maslakh or Maidan, is also filling in fast. The Sharqiya quarter has filled in considerably since 1945, but this quarter still has future homesites in its open lots, primarily in the upward sections, some of which are still planted with gardens and olive trees. Meanwhile, the outer ring of new quarters is going through the same process of families buying land and then filling them in with houses as the family grows, resulting in a gradual increase of population density.

Of the three hundred households surveyed, 40 percent of the families indicated that they live in the same quarter as the husband's parents, with 15 percent living in the same quarter as the wife's parents. While it is not known whether living in the same quarter indicates living next door to parents, it can be assumed that this is the situation in most cases. (The surveyor who covered the fifty-one households in and around Maidan, Spanyoli, Khallat al-Deir, and Maslakh reported that for all twenty-six cases in which a family indicated that they lived in the same quarter as the husband's parents, it meant that the couple lived next door to or on another level of the parent's house.) Of those who do not live in the same quarter as a parent, 12 percent indicated either the husband's or wife's parents' quarter as a preferable place to live.

Examples of this family clustering, and perhaps the foundation for future family-named quarters, include the Muslim family of Abu Daqa, who live in Khallat al-Deir. In a 29 August 1989 interview, Sa'id Abu Daqa explained that he and his seven brothers all live on neighboring lots on 10 dunams where the convent hill flattens toward the south. The brothers are all truck drivers who surround their homes with olive and fruit orchards. They have two sisters living in Reina, one in 'Illut, and one in another quarter of Nazareth, but the brothers have all stuck together. When asked if he planned to sell any of this land, Sa'id said that he was saving it all for his children to build on. In a 5 May 1989 interview, Mrs. Sa'id Hamad related that they have lived in their home to the northeast of the Ort school for forty years, and that their seven sons, three of whom are butchers, all live on the same side street, while the three daughters live elsewhere. One son lives on the lower level of the parent's home; the other six sons in their own individual homes.

Deputy mayor Suheil Fahum noted in a 12 July 1989 interview from his large, old, two-story home with its orange tile roof in the al-Sheikh quarter that many from the Fahum family have moved out of the original, but now crowded, family quarter where he still lives, and have congregated in seven new family clusters. Three of these clusters are located in the southern section of the Sharqiya quarter on or near the old Iksal Road, two are located in the Maslakh/Jebel Hamuda quarters, one is located in Khallat al-Deir, and an eighth Fahum family cluster is located at the entrance to the Jebel al-Daula quarter.[4]

This grouping together by family creates a very static housing market, for once a home is built, it usually remains in the family for generations. Hence the current residents of the Rum quarter are the descendents of the original Greek Orthodox land buyers and home builders. This phenomenon also means that, in general, Nazareth cannot be divided along class lines because in every family and religious quarter the affluent and poor live side by side. Only in some of the newer mixed quarters where family and religious cohesiveness is not maintained are there pockets of poor, as in the Ram apartments, or pockets of wealthy, primarily on the hilltop periphery. The central quarters are gradually turning into lower-income neighborhoods as more affluent families move up and out, but enough families have stayed put to maintain a mix of classes.

Because conversions between Christians and Muslims are almost nonexistent, family clustering results in religious clustering. Hence the Spanyoli quarter is mostly Roman Catholic, the Aqbat quarter is all Coptic at its core, and Jebel Hamuda is all Muslim. The concentration of the Fahum family in the al-Shiekh subquarter has helped it to main-

---

[4] Williams notes similar patterns in his study of a village in Lebanon where an initial visit in 1950 revealed isolated houses being built in outlying areas which "seemed to forebode the breakup of the extended family patrilocal residence patterns." When he returned fifteen years later "it was clear that kin had followed kin into the village outskirts, and the traditional clustering of houses of brothers and their children had been preserved in the new quarters, with some lineages maintaining two or more residential foci" (quoted in Prothro and Diyab 1974, 66).

tain its predominantly Muslim nature, with clans like the Bayatra giving the Sharqiya quarter its high concentration of Muslims. Throughout the town, relatives live next to relatives and thus Muslims live next to Muslims and Christians next to Christians.

Just as family cohesiveness developed religious quarters, so too did a common place of origin. As already noted, when the refugees came to Nazareth in 1948, they were scattered throughout the city in temporary housing. Gradually they started to rebuild their lives and to look for permanent housing. Some obtained land in certain parts of the city, such as Safafra, through exchanges with the government, while others saved money and bought their land. Amin Qudha explained in a 4 September 1989 interview that when the refugees began looking for land to buy, they "took into consideration their origins and their religion, not because they were against Christians, but because of the family and village ties that existed. Without intention they found themselves in separate quarters." While established on the basis of family and village ties, these quarters are also characteristically Muslim.

Land is a finite quantity in Nazareth and housing availability is very tight, so family, village, and religious cohesiveness cannot always be maintained in terms of house location. Scarcity of land has forced many in Nazareth to look beyond traditional residential patterns and accept housing wherever it can be obtained. Once the core quarters filled up, newly married children and newcomers had to find other housing, either in the new apartment complexes in quarters like Ram, Schneller, Manzal, or Wurud, in Upper Nazareth, or on new land purchased in the newer quarters like Safafra, Krum, or Bir al-Amir. For example, two Greek Orthodox brothers from an overflowing neighborhood in the Rum quarter bought land in Upper Safafra, where they constructed adjoining houses. One brother moved in on marrying, and the other, already married, brother lives in an Upper Nazareth apartment while he saves enough money to finish his side of the house. The lot behind the two brothers is owned by an uncle, who eventually plans to sell his home in the crowded, inaccessible-to-cars Suq and move to this more favorable locale.

This move from the older central city to newer quarters is illustrated in the 1983 census results which showed the northern and western sections of Nazareth (areas 31 and 32) to be the fastest growing, with an increase in population of 66.3 percent from 1972 to 1983 (table 12). The central, more crowded quarters of the Suq (area 21), Rum (area 23) and Latin (area 22) had a decrease in population, with the Suq having the highest net loss of 32.4 percent. The Muslim eastern (areas 12 and 13) and southern quarters (15, 41, and 42) witnessed significant increases in population. Also of note is the high population density in

TABLE 12. Population change and density by census statistical area, 1972–83

Statistical area and quarter	Area (sq. km.)	1972 pop.	1983 pop.	1972–83 % change	1972 density (per sq. km.)	1983 density (per sq. km.)
11 Nimsawi	0.612	3,129	3,497	+11.8	5,113	5,714
12 and 13	0.609	4,899	6,048	+23.5	8,044	
12 Sharqiya	0.293		3,139			10,713
13 Sharqiya	0.316		2,909			9,206
14 Garage	0.563	1,042	1,182	+13.4	1,851	2,099
15 Jebel Hamuda	0.783	2,863	3,883	+33.9	3,656	4,959
21 Suq	0.199	2,140	1,446	−32.4	10,754	7,266
22 Latin	0.448	4,296	3,692	−14.1	9,589	8,241
23 Rum	0.317	3,116	2,794	−10.3	9,830	8,814
31 and 32	6.340	6,366	10,586	+66.3	1,004	
31 Safafra	4.563		4,617			1,012
32 Krum	1.777		5,969			3,359
41 and 42	2.653	5,453	8,610	+57.9	2,055	
41 Mitran	0.412		3,777			9,167
42 Bir al-Amir	2.241		4,833			2,157

SOURCE: 1983 *Census of Israel*

areas 12 and 13 of the Sharqiya quarter, where large Muslim families live in compact family housing complexes that have filled in vacant lands and rooftops over the years; and in area 41, which includes the high-density, low-income Ram apartment complex.

Changes in quarter composition have also resulted when owners of large sections of land have sold portions of their property to the highest bidder regardless of religion. According to a 26 April 1989 interview with George Qanazi', this has happened when, for example, the Christian Tabar family sold land in Khallat al-Deir in the area surrounding the Hypermarket, and when the Muslim Fahum family sold land to the south of Maslakh. As a result, both of these areas are growing with a mixed Christian-Muslim population.

When asked from whom the land or home was purchased, 18 percent of the 290 respondents said it was bought from a family member, 17 percent said it was inherited, 5 percent bought from friends, and 43 percent bought from others. Of those Christians who bought homes from nonfamily members, 71 percent bought from fellow Christians and 29 percent from Muslims. For the Muslim homebuyers, 84 percent bought from Muslims and 16 percent from Christians. Among the three main Christian groups, a higher percentage of Greek Orthodox (27 percent) and Roman Catholics (24 percent) inherited or bought homes or land from family members than Muslims (15 percent) and Greek Catholics (12 percent), partially because the refugees of 1948 were primarily from the latter two groups and therefore had no established family roots in Nazareth.

Another factor influencing mixing is the desire to upgrade housing and location. The one-time Latin nature of the Latin quarter and the Greek Orthodox concentration in the older sections of the Rum quarter are slowly diminishing as Christians move out of the crowded central city and seek better housing on higher, more accessible land. Their homes in the central quarters are then sold or rented to others. A good example of this mixing is found in the eight houses surveyed in the Mawarna quarter just up the street from the Maronite Church. The religious mix of the residents includes one Maronite, one Roman Catholic, two Greek Catholic, and four Muslim families. The Maronite family said their home is over a hundred years old and that they have lived in it since 1952, when the husband was thirty-two years old and his wife twenty-two, probably the year they were married. One of the Greek Catholic families has lived in their hundred-plus-year-old home for ten years, which they rent from another Christian family. Their former home needed to be demolished and until a new one can be built they are living here because of the cheap rent. One Muslim family, the husband a refugee from Yajur, bought their seventy-six-year-old home in 1970 from a Christian family. Two Muslim couples, both in their thirties and each with five children, live in houses that were abandoned in 1948 by families who left Nazareth for the security of other countries, perhaps Maronites to Lebanon. These houses are now government property and are leased-to-own by the Muslim families, who have been living in their homes for six and nine years. What was once a predominantly Maronite Christian neighborhood is now fairly evenly mixed between Muslims and Christians.

The fact that proximity to family and available housing are much more influential than religious solidarity in determining the residential patterns in Nazareth is evident in the responses to the survey question asking what factors influenced them in choosing where to live (table 13). Because fourteen respondents listed up to four factors as influencing their choices, the frequencies exceed the 299 who responded, but the percentages are calculated from 299. The four factors of Parents' home, Above or next to parents, Close to relatives, and Family-owned land, when combined (minus three for the three respondents who listed two of these factors), total 128 households or 43 percent of those surveyed. The factors of Only thing affordable and Only thing available combined (minus nine for those who listed both) total 131 households, or 44 percent. These combined groupings of family ownership and ties,

TABLE 13. Factors influencing the selection of house location

Factors	Frequency	Percentage
Only thing available	93	31
Family-owned land	59	20
Favorable location	56	19
Only thing affordable	47	16
Originally home of parents	42	14
Above or next to parents	40	13
Close to friends	20	7
Close to relatives	10	3
Bought with government help	8	3
Close to neighbors of same religion	2	1
Exchanged for confiscated land	2	1
Renting, could not find a house	2	1
On main road, near center	2	1
Bought with church help	1	1
Near work	1	1
Close to church or mosque	0	0

and of affordability and availability, total 89 percent. Only two families listed nearness to coreligionists as a factor and in both cases this factor was one of three other influential factors, with parents' home and family-owned land also influencing the decision. Closeness to a place of worship had no acknowledged effect on location of a home.

While only two cited religion of neighbors as a deciding factor, there may be more who abstained from citing this factor because of the sensitivity of religious divisions in Nazareth. Few readily admit that they would prefer to live next to someone from the same religion or sect. Christians, now in the minority, are quick not to offend the Muslims of Nazareth and so do not acknowledge such a preference. Given a choice, however, Christians would prefer to live next to Christians and Muslims next to Muslims, if for no other reason than that they share a similar religion and culture.

Cultural differences can make living together awkward. For example, one Christian family in the Safafra quarter, who prefer to eat meals in the summer on the patio under the grape arbor, said that when eating pork they eat inside so as not to offend their Muslim neighbors. Proximity to a mosque can be a deterrent to Christians living in Muslim quarters primarily because the first call to prayer in the morning and the predawn reminder from the mosque during Ramadan to begin fasting prove nonconducive to sleep.

In spite of the friendships and willingness to accept, or at least tolerate, living in mixed quarters, segregationist attitudes still emerge on occasion. One Muslim family living in lower Shekun al-Arab noted that they bought their home from a Greek Catholic, who luckily was willing to sell to Muslims because otherwise they would never have been able to buy housing in the Greek Catholic-supervised shekun system. This may be true for the homes of lower Shekun al-Arab, where according to a group of local high-school students only four Muslim families now live, but the upper portion has included Muslims as well as Christians as residents from the beginning. One woman resident of the modern Panorama apartment building, which looks down on the Rum quarter from the Qishla quarter, said that three Greek Catholic brothers own the building and that Christians live in all twenty-two of the apartments. She said that if Muslims apply to buy an apartment, they are told there are no vacancies. She also said that when Christians buy apartments, they must sign a contract saying that the apartment will not be rented to Muslims.

A Christian woman living in Maidan, whose friendships with Muslims and Christians are based more on like interests, education, and socioeconomic standing than on religion, said that she would not sell her home to Muslims, out of respect for her Christian neighbors. She related how once, when two Christian brothers with side-by-side houses were feuding, one of the brothers threatened to sell his house to a Muslim. In another case, a land sale out of revenge actually went through. She said her Muslim neighbors bought land from a Christian family who sold their land to Muslims in order to punish rival family members.

A prominent member of the Greek Orthodox community said that it is important for Christians to live in Christian quarters so that their children are raised in a Christian environment, noting that the Jews survived because they lived separately in a ghetto system. He said Christians would no doubt prefer to live in new Christian quarters if they were made available. Similarly, a Christian resident of Safafra, who lives in a family cluster of four Christian homes among his Muslim neighbors, observed that "even today Christians love to live near Christians," but because the lands in the center of town in the traditional Christian quarters are expensive and are filling up, less affluent Christians along with the newcomers, refugees, and laborers have to buy land farther out in mixed neighborhoods. He also felt that people should respect their neighbors when selling homes and not sell to someone the neighboring families would prefer not to have as new neighbors.

While Christian living with Christian is his ideal, his attitude of living among Muslims is a positive one. He said that when he moved to Safafra in 1963, all of his friends wondered why he would do such a thing and predicted that he would have a hard time. He admitted that his family moved in with prejudicial feelings, which prompted them and their relative neighbor to build a fence around, but not between, their yards, making themselves into a Christian ghetto. Since then, he explained, the four Christian families have had no problems with their Muslim neighbors. The Muslim children respect him as an elder and mind what he says. His family delivers Easter cookies to their Muslim neighbors, as well as home-grown grapes. He said he bought the land because it was cheap and because it looked north to where he came from. "I was afraid of living here," he said, "but I have had no problems. We coexist well." Muslim residents do not seem as concerned about living among Christians as do the Christians among Muslims, and not all Christians hold views such as expressed above.

While these few examples indicate that religion is a consideration in determining where people live, most Nazarenes surveyed and interviewed did not mention religion as a factor influencing housing choice or neighbor preference. Amin Qudha expressed these common feelings when he explained that "Nazareth is reshaping itself" in that nowadays "people prefer, but don't seek, to have their neighbors at similar educational and economic standing," as opposed to preferring or seeking those of like religion. He said that when his family sold fifty plots of land in Safafra, they never considered a person's religion and that those buying land never asked about the religion of their potential neighbors.

Preference for Quarters and Quarter Functions

To many, the location of a quarter and its quality of life are more important factors than its religious composition. Because the quarters vary in location, density, accessibility, and human composition, some areas are preferred over others.

In the early 1960s a survey of Nazarenes revealed that 62 percent were satisfied with where they lived. When asked why, 57 percent indicated that it was because they owned their own homes, 30 percent because their homes were accessible, 10 percent because of favorable social surroundings. Only 1 percent cited a good economic environment, and 2 percent, low rent. Of the 33 percent who were not satisfied with where they lived, 81 percent said it was because their home was too small, 7 percent because the social surroundings were not favorable, 7 percent because of a poor economic environment, and 5 percent because of high rent. In regard to living in apartments, 42 percent said that they would be willing to live in an apartment, but 77 percent said they would prefer to live in a private house based on Arab traditional ways.

The Sharqiya quarter, with its Muslim majority, most strongly supported the traditional extended-family living arrangements; 44 percent, as opposed to only 4 percent in Krum and Safafra and 8 percent in Khanuq, preferred to live with extended family rather than in their own private homes. The 22 percent who said they would prefer a shekun did so because to them it was the only way out of living with, or next door to, family in the traditional way. Only 26 percent still thought favorably of newlyweds living with the husband's parents; 61 percent agreed that living close to parents was good. The quarters in the 1960s with the highest percentage of satisfaction among residents were Bir al-Amir at 79 percent and Shekun al-Arab at 76 percent. The least favorable sections of town were Krum and Safafra, then perceived as being too isolated and far away, with only 34 percent favorable responses. The other six sectors all had satisfactory responses, ranging from 58 to 66 percent (Baruch 1966).

Preferences have changed over the years. In the 1989 survey, when asked what their preferred place of residence would be, most of those surveyed said that they favored any place that is open, high, and quiet, or they gave the name of a quarter that has those attributes (table 14). One person living in the Sharari quarter commented in the survey that she preferred to live on the Mount of the Precipice south of town because no one lives there. Wurud and Safafra are areas that are high and relatively quiet, and command a beautiful view north toward the Upper Galilee and the Netofa valley; most of the homes are accessible by car. If these two areas are combined, then the northwestern section of Nazareth is the most desirable thanks to its favorable characteristics. The other most preferred quarters have a common factor of all being up and away from the center of the city, as opposed to the low preference Suq, Latin, and Garage quarters, or the crowded low-income apartments of Ram. Not all subquarters were identified as preferred spots, but the small Dodge quarter was preferred by three persons because it is on the upper edge of the Sharqiya quarter.

The notion that the grass is always greener on the other side of the fence or, as in the case of Nazareth, the topside of the hill, holds true for quarter preference. Based on a satisfaction scale of one to five, with one being very satisfied and five being very dissatisfied, survey results show a wide range of satisfaction; and the residents of those quarters most often selected as a preferred place to live are not always as content as outsiders might expect. Still, the four quarters with the highest degree of satisfaction fit the general list of optimal characteristics, including quiet, higher, and accessible. The highest ranked of the twenty-five blocks of eight is the Mitran quarter, with an average rating of 1.5, followed by Janan at 1.63, Ort at 1.88, and Wurud at 2.0. At the other end of the scale is Ram, which, like low-income housing complexes in other countries, seems to be the quarter in Nazareth where no one really wants to live. Of the eight families surveyed in the Ram block, five indicated that they were very dissatisfied with living conditions in their quarter, for an average of 4.13. The other low-ranking blocks are upper Shekun al-Arab, Spanyoli, and Jebel Hamuda, all with a 3.13 rating, and Bir Abu-Jayish, with 3.0. The rest range from 2.25 to 2.88. The average for all 298 respondents was a favorable 2.4. Of these 298, 18 percent gave a ranking of very satisfied, 43 percent were satisfied, 25 percent gave their quarter an average rating, 7 percent were dissatisfied, and 7 percent were very dissatisfied.

TABLE 14. Preference of quarters and quarter characteristics

Quarters:	Frequency
Rum	19
Mitran	18
Krum	17
Shekun al-Arab, Khanuq, Safafra	12
Wurud, Nimsawi	11
Salesian	9
American, Schneller	7
Bir al-Amir, Maidan	6
Spanyoli	5
Kefar Horesh	4
Latin, Dodge, Sharqiya, Umm Qubai, Jebel Hamuda, Khallat al-Deir	3
Maslakh, Clarese, Qishla, Bir Abu-Jayish	1
Suq, Garage, Jebel al-Daula, Janan, Aqbat, Ram, Fakhura	0
Other areas:	
A named village, city, or country other than Nazareth	19
Not in Nazareth	10
Upper Nazareth	3
Characteristics:	
Quiet	14
Open, high	13
Near main road	10

Many factors contribute to the wide range of satisfaction. The resident surveyed in the heart of the Garage quarter was naturally "not happy at all" with her house location. The only resident in Krum indicating dissatisfaction with living in his quarter might have based his opinion on the fact that until this year, the water flow to his home had been sporadic during the summer. Similarly, a resident of Bir al-Amir complained that sometimes the quarter has no running water for days at a time, the streets are not paved, and a sewer system has yet to be installed. In this case, however, the dissatisfaction was not necessarily with the quarter, but rather the municipality, which the resident accused of allocating funds only to fellow Jebha party members. Three brothers living in the older part of Safafra near Khanuq said that they moved from the center of town to their present location twenty years ago, and still their houses are not hooked up to sewer lines. One family at the entrance to the Garage quarter were very satisfied with their quarter, as were another family just east of the main road in the Sharqiya quarter. To them, living along or near the heavily congested roads of the central business district was not a detrimental factor.

The religious composition of a quarter does not seem to be an influential factor in determining satisfaction except perhaps in Jebel al-Daula. Here the block of eight homes include part of a small cluster of Christians—one of only a few groupings of Christians in the northern section of this mainly Muslim quarter. These eight families rated their quarter with an average of 2.25. Closer examination, however, shows that the three Muslim families all ranked their quarter with a very satisfied rating of one, while the two Greek Catholics gave it a neutral rating of three, and the three Roman Catholics split, two giving a rating of two and one giving a rating of five, or very dissatisfied. In this block, the Muslims were more satisfied than the Christians, but in the lower Safafra group of eight, which is also a quarter with a Muslim majority, survey rankings show that religion does not seem to be a deciding factor; nor does it seem to be with the Muslim families in the Christian-dominated 'Arqiya subquarter of the Rum quarter.

The functions of the many quarters can vary: some function as cohesive units in which there is a spirit of unity or closeness,[5] while others exist in name only, to describe the location of a home or business. In those quarters where a high concentration of one religion or

---

[5] In his study of quarters in the Moroccan town of Boujad, Eickelman (1974) suggests that "ideally the households of a *darb* [quarter] are considered to be bound together by multiple personal ties and by common interests" which he identifies as *qraba* (closeness). He notes how immigrant quarters seldom have the necessary closeness to be identified as a quarter and because these quarters lack notables to represent them they often are the last to acquire urban amenities of water, sewers, and roads.

sect centers around a church or mosque, the place of worship serves as a unifying factor for the quarter. In the Rum, Aqbat, Latin, and Mitran quarters, the churches function as places in which residents can gather together for baptisms, weddings, funerals, and religious holidays. An evening funeral at the Greek Orthodox Church will find men from throughout the quarter converging at the home of the deceased, and then escorting the coffin in a parade of men to the church, then to the nearby cemetery. Non-Orthodox friends and neighbors and Orthodox from other quarters of the city also participate, but since most of the participants are Orthodox from the Rum quarter, the residents of the quarter have a feeling of cohesiveness.

Feast days at the Coptic Church have the feeling of a neighborhood party. For the 21 August 1989 Feast of Mary, attendance at mass gradually increased during the evening service from just five at the 8:00 P.M. beginning, up to at least fifty-five toward the end of the service at 8:30, and then increasing to even more as other residents of the quarter joined the congregation outside for coffee, sweets, and fireworks. Likewise the shrine of Mary in Shekun al-Arab during the Feast of Mary celebration serves as a gathering point for residents of the quarter as they assemble to watch the parade, listen to speeches, and then mingle and visit while dodging firecrackers thrown by partying youth. Feast days at the less intimate Latin Basilica of the Annunciation, or at the Maronite and Greek Catholic churches, because of the more dispersed nature of the communities that once formed the nucleus of the Latin quarter, no longer serve to unite the quarter as much as to unite the community, as parishioners gather from throughout the city and not just from one quarter.

Mosques also serve as gathering points for quarter members each day at prayers, and even more so during feast days when, for example, thousands of Muslims from throughout the city and region gather together on the vacant land between the Coptic Church and Salam Mosque to celebrate the prophet Mohammad's birthday. Muslim quarters also demonstrate cohesiveness and cooperation, as they have organized and raised funds for the building of mosques in their quarters.

Some neighborhoods and quarters not centering on a place of worship also function as a unit as a result of home owners living together long enough for bonds to develop as children play or walk to school together, wives visit, and all gather in homes, gardens, or on rooftops for prewedding parties, or in homes to offer comfort during a death in the family. The newer, less permanent quarters lack the cohesiveness fostered by longtime proximity; their residents rely more on family or religious community ties than quarter ties, whereas in some quarters, family, religious, and quarter ties are all the same.

A lack of sewers served a unique means of joining together the residents of the Bilal quarter when in May and June 1988 they submitted, on two different occasions, open letters to the municipality first condemning the high sewer tax levied on both home and property in a quarter of low-income laborers and unemployed, and then requesting the installment of water and sewer lines (al-Senara, 27 May, 17 June 1988). Another section of the Safafra quarter near the main road north to Reina joined forces to petition the municipality that a road be built connecting their neighborhood with the main road. This letter was also published in the local paper and was signed by twenty-two heads of households (al-Senara, 21 July 1989).

Neighborhoods also unite when it comes to paving roads. According to a 7 September 1989 interview with Ahmad Ziyad, the mayor's brother, municipal ordinances require that the first paving of a road be paid for by the local residents. Mohammad Nakhash illustrated the point. He and his neighbors were having the road paved in front of their homes in the Bir al-Amir quarter. On the day of the interview, he and the men of his street had spent part of their evening surveying the progress of the day's work. He said that each family had to pay about U.S.$1,200 for the paving of the road; the municipality provided materials and manpower. He indicated that if they waited until the municipality had funds to finance the project, it would take years.

One quarter rallied together under more pleasant circumstances. In August 1983 the residents of Shekun al-Arab celebrated the thirty-fifth anniversary of the establishment of their quarter in conjunction with the Feast of Mary. There was the usual scout parade, houses and streets decorated with lights, and a celebration at the playground of the neighborhood club (al-Ittihad, 15 August 1983).

The names of the three original quarters and their mostly homogeneous religious concentrations suggest that religion was indeed an important factor in the formation of Nazareth's quarters. New quarter names, home and street religious decorations, voting patterns (as will be discussed in the next chapter), and residential patterns as determined from census data and fieldwork all indicate that religion has continued to influence where Nazarenes choose to live. Baruch noted in his study of Nazareth that "the development of neighborhoods in Nazareth was completely due to religious concentrations." He then goes on to clarify, as has been shown above, that additional factors influenced the religious composition of quarters, such as the influx of refugees in 1948, who had no choice but to live wherever they could; and that the older areas of town no longer had room for further development, which forced Christians and Muslims to mix in the new sectors of town (Baruch 1966, 325). Rapid growth and scarcity of land have indeed influenced the evolution of a less segregated Nazareth. The need for affordable housing and the desire to live in less crowded, more scenic, and more accessible housing has changed residential patterns. For most Nazarenes, availability and affordability are more important in residence selection than living in a neighborhood of coreligionists. As a result of these changing factors, many new quarters have been integrated from the beginning, while some of the older neighborhoods are becoming more integrated as longtime residents move to preferable locations, and newer residents, often from a lower class and a different religious community, move in.

An analysis of the ways in which Christian and Muslim Arabs in Nazareth live is but one way in which to understand better the complex relationship between the two communities. For centuries they have chosen to live apart, but now, often without a choice, they live together as friends and neighbors. Some prefer to hold on to old ways in which religion was the dividing line, while others are perfectly content living in mixed neighborhoods. The next chapter examines other factors that further demonstrate the unity and disunity of Nazareth's communities.

6

Community Relations

Even though the various religious and refugee communities of Nazareth have at times congregated into distinct homogeneous quarters,
many communities also maintain an identity as part of a larger community of Nazarenes and as parts of even larger communities of Israeli
Arabs, Palestinian Arabs, and just plain Arabs. As a result, each Nazarene possesses a complex array of loyalties, which can serve either to
unite or to divide. A common Palestinian heritage, Israeli citizenship,
and Arab culture serve to unite the citizens of Nazareth as a community seeking to better their city, improve their status as second-class citizens in Israel, support Palestinian nationalism in the West Bank and
Gaza, or enjoy a common Arab culture.[1] However, at the same time,
Christian-Christian differences, Muslim-Christian differences, as well
as rural-urban, and refugee-native differences can divide. This chapter
looks at how these complex loyalties to a variety of communities have
influenced relationships of cooperation and conflict among the people
of Nazareth; these help explain the feelings that influence some to be
willing to live in integrated neighborhoods, while others still prefer to
remain within community clusters.

By way of introduction, results from the survey give a general
overview of how Nazarenes view the complex issue of Christian-
Muslim relations. When asked about Christian-Muslim relationships
in Nazareth, 83 percent of the 299 respondents indicated that relations
were positive, 14 percent gave relations a neutral rating, and only 3 per-

[1] Nineteen years of separation under different forms of government have resulted
in noticeable differences for the Palestinian community. Lutfi and Vida Mashour, editors of the Arabic weekly *al-Senara*, noted that Israeli Arab society tends to be "closed
and introverted, obsessed with keeping its identity under years of military government," while Palestinian society in Vida's hometown of Bethlehem is (or at least was)
"more open, cosmopolitan and at ease with its environment." Lutfi said that his generation of Israeli Arabs were influenced by their "struggle to continue existing as Arabs in
their land," which, according to Vida created a very different society than that which
she had known growing up in Bethlehem. She said that when she came to Nazareth
she noticed that "relations between people were very close"; she felt as if "Nazareth
was a large village, and something of a ghetto" (*JP Magazine*, 12 June 1987, 5).

cent gave relations a negative rating (table 15). When asked if Christian-Muslim relations were improving, 35 percent said they were improving, 39 percent said they were staying the same, and 26 percent said they were getting worse. Sixty-nine respondents identified factors they felt were influencing relations. On the positive side, 6 percent said that relations were good and that Christians and Muslims were brothers, while on the negative side the majority of people cited politics (16 percent) and more specifically the new Islamic party (51 percent) as adversely influencing interreligious relations. The negative influence of religious fanaticism was identified as a problem by 14 percent of the sixty-nine people, economic and cultural differences by 4 percent, the murder of Selim Nusseri by 4 percent, with segregation, a Muslim majority, and the state trying to divide us, each being identified by 1 percent.

From comments added to the survey, one Muslim man from Shekun al-Arab said that relations are good, and that because of the Intifada they are getting better as all Arabs join together in opposition to Israel's occupation. Similarly, a Muslim man from the Bilal quarter suggested that Christian-Muslim relations in Nazareth are better than any other place because the two peoples have the same destiny and face the same difficulties in that both are discriminated against in Israel. However a Muslim woman from Krum said relations are getting worse because of the political and financial situation. She said that all the people think only about themselves. A Roman Catholic man from the Maidan quarter commented during the survey that "Christian-Muslim relations are bad and getting worse because people treat others differently based on what religion they are."

When analyzed according to religion, Muslims in general are more optimistic than Christians, and within the Christian community, Greek Orthodox respondents have a more favorable view of Christian-Muslim relations than Roman Catholics (see table 15). A majority of Muslims, 51 percent, said relations are improving; only 12 percent indicated that they are worsening. Christians gave almost opposite responses, only 16 percent saying relations are improving and 42 saying they are worsening. Thirty-three Christians and two Muslims (51 percent) identified the Islamic movement as influencing the decline in relations. In less condemning terms, six Muslims and five Christians (14 percent) cited politics, and seven Muslims and three Christians (16 percent) cited religious fanaticism. These three factors of the Islamic movement, politics, and religious fanaticism refer totally or in part to the rise of the Islamic Movement in Nazareth, which obviously has residents concerned, particularly the Christians, but also Muslims. When these three factors are combined, 81 percent of the sixty-nine

TABLE 15. Percentage ranking of Christian-Muslim relations by religion

	Very good	Good	Neutral	Bad	Very Bad
Muslims (160)	44.4	45.6	7.5	2.5	0.0
Christians (139)	12.2	62.5	21.5	2.1	1.4
Greek Orthodox (49)	20.4	57.1	20.4	0.0	2.0
Roman Catholics (37)	5.4	54.1	32.4	5.4	2.7
Greek Catholics (42)	9.5	71.4	16.7	2.4	0.0
Other Christians (11)	9.1	81.8	9.1	0.0	0.0
Nazarenes (299)	29.4	53.5	14.0	2.3	0.7

people who ventured an explanation of why relations are improving or not improving referred to the increasingly combustible mix of religion and politics in Nazareth. Of the four who responded in the positive that Christians and Muslims are brothers, all were Muslim.

Some people found responding to questions about relations difficult, not only because of the sensitive nature of the subject, but also, as one Greek Catholic woman from the Latin quarter observed, because relationships in certain areas and with certain people can be improving while at the same time others can be worsening. She and a Greek Catholic man from Krum both said that it depends on the situation. A Muslim woman who lives in lower Safafra also indicated that it was hard to categorize Christian-Muslim relations for the whole city when, in reality, relations vary from quarter to quarter, some quarters having good interreligious relations and others not. Since it is difficult to make generalized statements about relations and to categorize attitudes and causes into neat compartments, let us now look at both the positive and negative sides of intercommunal relations in Nazareth.

Unity among Communities

When residents of Nazareth were surveyed or interviewed about community relations, the most common answer from the notable to the ordinary was "we are all brothers." For example, Saif al-Din al-Zu'bi, a Muslim from a prominent Nazareth family who was a member of Israel's first Knesset and who served as mayor of Nazareth on and off for twelve years between 1956 and 1975, wrote in his memoirs: "Our belief is that Christians and Muslims in Nazareth are family and brothers, formed from one body" (al-Zu'bi 1987, 207). Father Nathaniel Shahada, the Greek Catholic parish priest, when asked in a newspaper interview about relations between Christians and Muslims in Nazareth, replied that "relations are good to the utmost," adding that the citizens of Nazareth are proud of this relationship which joins the parts as one (al-Fajr, 23 August 1985). Greek Orthodox priest Father Barnaba explained in a 23 August 1989 interview that on both sides "there are very wise men who are working for good relations between the two communities." He added: "I don't say they are angels, but the relationship between Christians and Muslims in Nazareth is much better than anywhere else."

Bilal and Ayad, teenage Muslim boys from the Krum quarter, when asked if their neighborhood was Christian or Muslim, both replied that "it was just Arab," and that they were "all brothers." Similarly, three Christian young men, just out of high school, from the same quarter expressed that Muslims and Christians are brothers. A Muslim family from the Sharari quarter noted during the survey that the Muslims and Christians living in their quarter "are family." The surveyor assigned to the Sharqiya quarter noted that in many of the interviews, when asked about religion, the residents' common response was "Why do you ask about religion? We are all Arabs."

One of the reasons for this bond of brotherhood is the common culture shared by Nazarenes, as explained by Samih Rizik, a Christian, during a 15 March 1989 interview. He noted that the two groups both offer the same hospitality, enjoy doing the same dances, celebrate marriage in similar fashions, and value the custom of protecting women. He went on to explain that in addition to a common culture, they also share in education and services. Food provides many instances of a common culture, including the same date-filled cookies served for Easter and 'Id al-Fitr and the same half-moon-shaped pancakes filled with walnuts, cinnamon, and sugar and then fried in clarified butter served for Epiphany and during Ramadan. This common cuisine also includes Arab staples like olives, pita bread, yoghurt-like *leban*, *hummous*, mutton, and coffee. Only the Islamic prohibition on pork and alcoholic drinks—the Nazareth favorite being *'araq*, an anise-flavored liquor which the Christians drink mixed with water—distinguishes the culinary preferences of the two groups. In addition to food, there is a common language in which the pronunciation and vocabulary of Nazareth varies from that of even neighboring villages.

The common bond associated with living in Israel as an Arab minority among Jews also unites the people of Nazareth. For Independence Day, a day on which most Israeli Jews fly the flag, the only flags to be seen in Nazareth are on government buildings and the government-related Bank Leumi and Mashbir department store. Nazareth's Arabs are united in their boycott of the national holiday. One young Muslim man from the Safafra quarter said that Christians and Muslims are not enemies, but they have a common enemy in the Israeli Jews. As a sign of solidarity and in protest of Israeli policies which divide the Arab community along religious lines, the citizens of Nazareth were encouraged during the 1982 census to answer the question about religion with neither "Christian" nor "Muslim," but with "Arab." Participation by Nazarenes of all communities in May Day rallies with placards calling for "two states for two peoples," in marches protesting discriminatory action by police against Nazareth fans at the Nahariya soccer game, in day-long strikes on Land Day, and in bank burning and stone throwing in outrage at the 20 May 1990 killing of seven day laborers from Gaza in Rishon Lezion by an Israeli man dressed in an army uniform all signal the unity that arises out of shared feelings of frustration for Arabs living in Israel.

Friendship also provides a unifying bond. Samih Rizik, who lives in an affluent Arab neighborhood annexed to Upper Nazareth, noted that a Muslim family moved in next door, and that they have become friends based on a common economic and educational level. He then explained that class distinctions determine friendships more than do religious differences. He also explained that when he was a young man growing up in Nazareth, his parents encouraged him to have Muslim as well as Christian friends so that he would learn positive characteristics attributed to Muslims, such as aggressiveness and the ability to curse at appropriate times.

One Greek Catholic family in Krum, in an effort to show their good relations with their Muslim neighbors, offered to hurry next door and bring their daughter's friend, who, they were proud to announce, kept her head covered in a scarf according to Islamic practice. Banker Riyad Debini, in a 2 September 1989 interview, explained that at the final party hosted by the groom prior to his July 1989 wedding, five hundred friends and relatives gathered at the Greek Orthodox community center. Among those guests were about a hundred Muslim friends from work and school, as well as bank customers. Even his Jewish boss came and danced with the groom.

In'am Zu'bi, a Muslim and wife of the former Mayor, in a 15 July 1989 interview, related that since childhood, both where she first lived in the Latin quarter and then in the Sharqiya quarter, 95 percent of her friends have been Christian. She said she would go to church with childhood friends, and she still attends churches for weddings. Acknowledging that a broad mind and a good education have helped in her acceptance of Christians, she expressed that her "personal relations are very warm with Christians." She commented that even among the less educated there is "no suspicion or distrust toward the other group," but rather some people choose to live a very closed life and do not bother to extend their circles of friendship.

Two young Christian men, while working on their car in front of their upper Safafra home, explained that politics is the only problem between religious groups in Nazareth, and that that has been the case only since the rise of an Islamic party. They both had just mentioned that they had friends who were Muslim when two young Muslim men walked up and greeted the two Christian men with a warm *marhaba shabab* (hello, fellow young men) and then proceeded to talk about soccer. Shibly, a young Muslim man from the lower Safafra quarter, in a 7 July 1989 interview commented that while he was a student at the Terra Sancta school, Christian friends taught him how to work, so he considers Christians as brothers. He admitted, however, that since graduating from school he has had little contact with his Christian friends. He said that in everyday life there is no differentiation between Muslims and Christians in that people do not consider religious differences; the two groups have more in common than not.

Two Christian sisters who live on the upper edge of the Khanuq quarter and who helped with the survey were hesitant to venture into the Safafra quarter because of its predominantly Muslim composition, so they were assigned the Rum and Krum areas, which have a good mix of Christians and Muslims. Following the completion of the surveys, these two college students announced their surprise that they had been better received in the Muslim homes, and that for the most part the Muslims they interviewed were friendlier than the Christians.

One of the men of Nazareth who strongly advocate the idea of Christian-Muslim brotherhood is Sim'an Arslan, a merchant, leader in the Islamic scout troop, muezzin of the White Mosque, and a hajj. During my 11 November 1988 visit to his shop to buy an umbrella, he and his wife, who had her hair wrapped in a scarf, explained that one of their three children attended the nearby Protestant elementary school. When asked it they were Protestant, Sim'an replied that it was not good to ask a person's religion in Nazareth because they are all Arab. To prove his point he moved out into the market, just up the street from the Greek Catholic church and started pointing out the mix of shops owned by Christian Arabs and Muslim Arabs. The only hint that he was Muslim was a pennant for the Islamic scouts tucked in a back corner of his shop and possibly the scarf on his wife's head. During a second visit on 10 August 1989, when I knew he was Muslim from having seen him march with the Muslim scouts for the 'Id al-Adha parade, he talked about Christian-Muslim relationships in Nazareth. He said that it is "foolish" to say there are Christians and Muslims, for all pray to God, and "God wants us to live together in peace as one family, including the Jews." To promote his espousal of unity among the religious groups of Nazareth, each year during Ramadan he invites eighteen civic and religious leaders to his home for a meal surrounding a large table built especially for such occasions. Representatives at the dinner are evenly matched, with nine Christian religious leaders from each of the main denominations, and nine Muslim notables. Sim'an was educated at the Freres Christian school, and his children are now attending Christian schools. He said his fourteen-year-old son gets nervous when asked his religion because his parents have always taught him that there are no Christians and no Muslims, just people who love God.

The extent of Christian-Muslim friendship is illustrated by survey results in which 88 percent of 139 Christians surveyed indicated that they have friends who are Muslim. Broken down by sect, 100 percent of the Maronites, Copts, Anglicans, and Baptists—eleven persons total— 89 percent of Roman Catholics, 88 percent of Greek Orthodox, and 83 percent of Greek Catholics indicated that they have friends who are Muslim. Of those who have Muslim friends, 75 percent of the Christians said they visit these friends in their homes and 74 percent of their Muslim friends come to visit them in their own homes. Of the 160 Muslims surveyed, 92 percent indicated that they have friends who are Christian. Of those who have Christian friends, 80 percent of the Muslims said they visit these friends in their homes, and 80 percent of the Christian friends visit them in their own homes. The frequency of these visits was not asked, but some of the respondents noted during the survey that visits to their other-religion friends were less than frequent, sometimes only yearly for holidays or special occasions, while others visited with other-religion neighbors quite regularly (fig. 33).

The respondents were also asked where these friends lived. The diversity of answers was surprising. There was no set friendship pattern or network. Muslims visited their Christian friends in all quarters, as did the Christians, many of whom indicated that they visited Muslim friends in the strongly Islamic Sharqiya quarter. This mixing of friendship networks is partly the result of the mixed schools, markets, jobs, and neighborhoods where friendships with members of other communities can develop. When asked if the friends are from work, school, the neighborhood, or elsewhere, the most common answer from both groups was work (144 responses), followed by neighbors (121), school (69), and elsewhere (23). Many indicated that they had met their other-religion friends at several different places.

Religiosity seems to have little influence on intercommunal friendships. Among both Christian and Muslim men and women, those who attend church regularly or pray regularly were just as likely to have friends from the other religious group as those who were less devout in their religious practices. For example, among the Muslim men, 96 percent of those who pray regularly and 95 percent of those who never pray indicate that they have Christian friends. Among

Fig. 33. Muslim and Christian neighbors and friends in the Hakramim quarter of Upper Nazareth

Christian women, 96 percent of those who attend church regularly, 81 percent of those who attend for special occasions only, and 92 percent of those who never attend report having friends who are Muslim.

Both religions teach love and respect for others. Anglican Zahi Nasser in a 22 May 1989 interview explained that "true Christians and true Muslims can live together without problems"; he is concerned only with "artificial Muslims who live by the letter of the law and not the spirit."

Mutual participation in religious traditions and festivals further demonstrates the brotherhood that exists among Christians and Muslims in Nazareth. Speaking at the thirty-fifth anniversary celebration of the establishment of Shekun al-Arab during the Feast of Mary, Mayor Tawfiq Ziyad said that "the feast of each sect in Nazareth is a feast for all sects in the city" (*al-Ittihad*, 15 August 1983). This is best illustrated by the practice of scout groups from the various sects marching for both Christian and Muslim feast days.[2] Scout groups in Nazareth are spon-

---

[2] This practice is not unique to Nazareth, although at other times and in different places the intent of the processions and scout participation have differed. During Ottoman times the large Palm Sunday procession by Christians down the Mount of Olives into Jerusalem "served local Christians as a means of publicly expressing themselves as Christians in a Muslim land." Nowadays, however, the procession has taken on a whole new meaning: Muslims cheer on the procession as a way of expressing the

sored by the Greek Orthodox, Roman Catholic, Greek Catholic, and Maronite churches, the White Mosque, and the independent Sadaqa (friendship) scouts, who originally were also a Greek Catholic troop.

Most of the troops are fairly homogeneous, partly as a result of scout participation in religious holidays, but some have members from other sects. The Maronite scouts recently admitted a Muslim boy to their troop. He lives in the Maronite quarter and has several Maronite friends who are members of the troop. The Sadaqa scouts are the most integrated of the troops. According to a 10 September 1989 interview with Sadaqa scout leader Samir Qandalfat, his troop of about 120 scouts has approximately the following representation from Nazareth's religious groups: 25 Muslims, 20 Greek Catholics, 15 Greek Orthodox, 15 Copts, 10 Roman Catholics, and 5 Maronites. He said the Sadaqa troop was organized in 1956 as part of the Greek Catholic scout organization and that it split from the Catholic troop over a disagreement on troop membership. Some leaders rejected a proposal to admit non-Greek Catholics as scout leaders or as members of the troop, while those who organized the Sadaqa troop felt that scouting should be open to youth from all of Nazareth's sects. The troop meets near Mary's well in a waqf building of the Greek Catholic bishop in Haifa, while the parent troop, still primarily Greek Catholic, meets in a hall next to the synagogue church. Both are affiliated with the Catholic scout organization and both march for religious holidays at the two Greek Catholic churches in town. Samir confessed that he attends church only when his troop marches. The troops sponsored by the Western-Rite churches include members from the other Western-Rite churches, while the Orthodox and Muslim troops remain the most homogeneous.

For Christian feast days like Palm Sunday, Good Friday, or the Feast of the Annunciation, each scout troop marches for its own individual church. For the Palm Sunday procession each troop marches either before or after mass in a procession of scouts who carry palm branches. The Orthodox troop with their bagpipe band marches around the block of the Orthodox Church; the Latin scouts, accompanied by the cadence of drums and the blats of two bugles, parade up Casa Nova Street to the courtyard of their large basilica; the Greek Catholic scouts, also with drums and bugles, wind through the narrow streets of the suq, passing in front of the Latin Church and then back to their church in the heart of the market; the Sadaqa scouts march around the Greek Catholic Church of St. Joseph, located adjacent to the Mitran school;

---

rights of Palestinians to "perform the Palestinian cultural traditions of the land they claim." In Beit Sahour, Christian and Muslim scouts march together for both Greek and Latin Christmas days, but such mingling is not permitted in Bethlehem, where the Christmas Eve procession is tightly controlled by the church (Bowman 1986, 16).

and the Maronite scouts, with a marching band of brass and woodwind instruments, march through the Latin quarter near the Maronite Church. On Christmas Eve (24 December, according to the Western-Rite calendar), all the Christian troops join with the Muslim troop and march from the chapel of the Virgin in Shekun al-Arab through town to the Basilica of the Annunciation. Similarly on the Feast of Mary in mid-August all of the troops (no Roman Catholic scouts for the 1989 parade) participate in a parade down through Shekun al-Arab to the small chapel dedicated to Mary. For the Muslim Feast of 'Id al-Adha, most of the Christian troops join with the Muslim troop for a parade from the White Mosque past the Basilica of the Annunciation, down Pope Paul VI Street, and into the Sharqiya quarter, where they end at a rally in front of the Salam Mosque. For the 14 July 1989 'Id al-Adha parade, 361 of the 400-strong contingent of Muslim scouts marched. They were joined by representative patrols of the Orthodox (without bagpipes), Greek Catholic (with the best-sounding bugles), Roman Catholic, and for the first time by a somber-looking troop of Roman Catholic scouts from West Germany (fig. 34).

At the rally held at the end of the 'Id al-Adha parade in 1989, Majid 'Atallah from the Catholic Scout Center addressed the gathered crowd by offering congratulations from all of the troops and expressing "hope that this get together and cooperation be an example to be followed by every citizen in all places and relations" (*al-Senara*, 12 July

Fig. 34. Muslim scout troop banner followed by flags of participating Christian troops during 'Id al-Adha parade

1989). When the Muslim scouts participate in the Feast of Mary parade, leader Sim'an Arslan joins with Greek Catholic leaders in addressing the crowd and in offering words of congratulations and support for the spirit of brotherhood that prevails at such gatherings. The Christmas march is followed by a gathering at Cinema Diana, sponsored by the municipality, in which leaders from all of Nazareth's denominations gather together.

The participation in religious feast days by the several religious groups is a symbolic act which Nazarenes take pride in, because it shows cooperation among the various groups. Still there are problems. Sim'an Arslan complained in a 31 August 1989 interview that the Maronite scouts never participate in the 'Id al-Adha parade. He gives an invitation each year to the Maronite scout leader, but never receives a response. He said that two years earlier the Maronites had invited the Muslim scouts to come and visit their summer camp in the woods near Saffuriya. The Muslim scouts went, but later when they extended a similar invitation to the Maronites, they did not reciprocate with a visit.

From the Maronite side, Father Yusef noted in a 31 August 1989 interview that the Maronites do not march for 'Id al-Adha because they are never invited. He suggested that perhaps when the Maronite scouts once failed to march in the Muslim-sponsored parade, further invitations were not extended. When I told Sim'an what Father Yusef had said, he related that the invitation was given to the Maronite scout leader and that perhaps he was the one who was not willing to participate, rather than Father Yusef, who might never have been shown an invitation. Sim'am also expressed his disappointment in the fact that twice he had invited Father Yusef to his Ramadan dinner, without ever receiving a response. The small rift between Muslim and Maronite was noted during a 31 August 1989 visit with another leader of the Islamic scouts at their clubhouse, initially built as a Quran school for boys (*kutab*) and located adjacent to the White Mosque. The leader commented that Maronites in Nazareth have tendencies like those in Lebanon, meaning that in neither place do the best of feelings exist between the two groups.[3] Brotherhood can be shown through simple

[3] Tsimhoni suggests that Christian-Muslim relations in Palestine during the British Mandate differed from the volatile relations in Lebanon because "unlike the Maronites of Mount Lebanon, the Christians of Palestine had become culturally and socially assimilated to the surrounding Muslim society" (Tsimhoni 1984, 186). While the Maronite scouts have not always chosen to march on Muslim holidays, the integration of the Maronite community of Nazareth into the larger Arab community and their association with the Muslim community is evidenced by the integration of the Maronites into many of the mixed and even predominantly Muslim quarters and by the frequent use by Muslims of Maronite religious ceremonies.

things like scout parades, but animosity can also develop over trivial things, such as not marching in a scout parade.

Participation in scout marches is but one of many ways in which the religious communities show their mutual respect toward each other and join in sharing a common religious heritage. When Pope Paul VI visited Nazareth in January 1964, Christians from all communities, as well as Muslims, lined the streets to welcome him. Muslim and Christian councilmen even voted to name the main street in honor of the pope; only the three Communist council members abstained (*JP*, 5, 6 January 1964). When Michel Sabah visited his hometown of Nazareth for the first time following his ordination as Latin patriarch of Jerusalem, Muslim and Christian scouts and religious leaders from all communities joined to welcome him (*al-Ittihad*, 1 April 1988).

In the hometown of Mary and Jesus, Christians and Muslims all find a common bond in honoring Nazareth's two most famous residents. Like the Bible, the Quran teaches of the birth of Jesus ('Isa), revered as a prophet in Islam, to Mary the virgin. Pictures of Mary are found not only in most Christian homes, but also on occasion in Muslim homes. Two of the Muslim families surveyed indicated that they had a picture of Mary hanging in their house. One of these homes in the Sharqiya quarter, owned by a widow who said she prays daily, fasts, and has been to Mecca, has a picture of Mary on the wall, along with a picture of the Dome of the Rock and calligraphy of verses from the Quran. Faisal, a Muslim refugee from the village of Qumia who owns a produce shop located at the beginning of Garage Street, has hanging on the back wall a framed Quranic verse in gold letters with black backing centered between an ornate painting of the Virgin Mary and a large poster of Clint Eastwood (fig. 35). He said he displays the two religious images because "Muslims and Christians are brothers." Another produce shop at the top of the Khanuq has only a picture of Mary hanging in the shop. It is owned by a Muslim family from Mujeidil who spoke of their high respect for Mary.

Father Paul Gauthier wrote of this adoration of Mary, explaining that while Islam venerates Jesus and Mary, "the Moslems who live in Nazareth go farther (though it isn't orthodox on their part!) and venerate her icon and join with the crowd which flocks from church to church on 15 August singing 'Holy Mary, protect us!'" He went on to relate that some Muslims knew the Bible better than the Quran, and that they pray Christian prayers (Gauthier 1965, 94). Young men who live in Shekun al-Arab told of one Muslim woman they know who joins with Christian women each evening during May in prayer at the shrine of Mary. Muslim boys in the Bilal quarter, most of whom have

Fig. 35. Muslim merchant with picture of Mary and
calligraphy of a Quranic verse

parents or grandparents who came from Saffuriya, referred to their ancestral village as a holy place because of the convent built there in
honor of Anna the mother of Mary. Muslims can also be seen at Christian churches on feast days, not participating in the service but milling
around outside with the many Christians who are more interested in
the social aspect of the celebration than the sacred.

Mary's well is the site of a long-standing tradition in which
henna-red crosses, or even crescents as observed on one occasion, are
painted on the limestone walls of the well, in gratitude for blessings received. According to Fu'ad Farah in a 3 September 1989 interview,
Muslim and Christian residents of Nazareth will make a vow to God
(*nedher*) with a promise that if, for instance, a child is made well, they
will go to Mary's well and paint henna crosses on it. He explained that

Muslims in particular like to do this because they believe very strongly in Mary. Henna is usually used by brides as a decorative ornament, but according to Farah, grateful people also like to use it to decorate the fountain of the Virgin.

Christians will also fulfill their vows by making contributions at church or, as explained by Farah, performing some other sacred act. His grandson, for example, was taken to the Maronite church by his Roman Catholic daughter to be dressed in the robes of the Maronite Saint Maroun because a Greek Orthodox relative had made a sacred vow concerning the child which required that the boy be dressed in the robes of the saint for several months. Kamil Asfur told how his father, a Greek Orthodox merchant from Nazareth who operated a shop in Haifa, promised to have his youngest son baptized a Roman Catholic in gratitude for the shelter offered for several weeks by the Latin Church in Haifa during the 1948 war, and for the help of the priest who guarded his store while he returned to his family in Nazareth. When the store was looted and then taken over by Jewish soldiers, the priest gave Kamil's father a shop owned by the church which the Asfur family continues to use. When the youngest son was three he was baptized in the Carmelite Church in Haifa. While never baptized as a Greek Orthodox, he was raised as one.

The making of vows that require participating in Christian rites and customs is readily acknowledged as being practiced by Muslims. Abed Fahum explained that his nephew was dressed in priest robes by his parents for the first year of his life in gratitude for being blessed with a son. Umm Jemal, a Muslim from the Schneller quarter, in an 11 August 1989 interview related that following the birth of her son Jemal she was unable to bear children for twelve years. Finally, she prayed to God and promised that if she was blessed with another child she would have the child baptized. A year later she gave birth to twin boys. She took the boys, accompanied by a Roman Catholic friend, to the Maronite Church, where they were baptized (she has photos to prove it), in fulfillment of her vow. The baptism was done out of gratitude; the sons, however, are being raised as Muslims. Father Yusef of the Maronite Church explained in a 31 August 1989 interview that Muslim children brought to his church as part of a vow are baptized with water, but not confirmed with oil. Before the ceremony, he asks the parents whether they want the child to become Christian, to which all have replied in the negative. In addition to baptism, he explained that others promise to dress their children in the habit of Saint Anthony of Egypt, so they come to the church on the saint's day to be dressed in the habit. Even newlywed Muslim couples will come on St. Anthony's day because they believe in him and want his benediction on their marriage.

Father Barnaba, in a 23 August 1989 interview, related that the Greek Orthodox Church often baptizes Muslim boys and occasionally Muslim girls as fulfillment of vows made by parents. He said that baptism was a common practice, as was the bringing of offerings of money, oil, candles, and incense. The Muslim children, he said, are baptized only with water, but not with the spirit, which would make them a Christian. Father Barnaba estimated that in the past eight years, he had baptized fifteen Muslim children. The Muslim families come with "full respect for the church." In times past he described how Muslim and Christian families would honor vows by bringing sheep to slaughter at the church entrance and then giving the meat to the poor.

The high regard for Mary and Jesus extends even into the mosques, where, for example, during Greek Orthodox Christmas, Sheikh Mohammad, the imam of the White Mosque, delivered the Friday sermon in remembrance of the birth of Jesus and the fraternity that exists between the two religions. He stressed that tolerance and brotherhood are what constitute the memory of Christmas (al-Senara, 16 January 1987).

While most of the religious participation is one-way, as a result of Islamic belief in Jesus and Mary, Christians too are known to have shown an interest in Islam. One Christian family noted that they contributed money to help build the Omar Mosque in their quarter, not out of any devotion to Islam, but out of support for their Muslim neighbors. The tiles in the small mosque built in the western Muslim cemetery were a donation from Christian Samir Awad, whom cemetery supervisor Mohammad Fahum, in a 28 June 1989 interview, referred to as a "man of faith."

For two consecutive years, some Christian students at Middle School B in Nazareth have joined in fasting with fellow Muslim students as a sign of their willingness to join with their companions in "carrying the burden of the fast." During the fasting month of Ramadan, the administration of the school sponsors a special breaking of the fast for participating Muslim and Christian students, preceded by an artistic program. The purpose of this celebration, as explained by the principal, is to strengthen the solidarity that exists among all the sects of the city. Attending the 1989 program were two Christian priests and representatives from the Islamic Movement (al-Senara, 28 April 1989).

Nazareth's educational system has also provided a means for the various religious communities to mix. This mix of Muslims and Christians of all sects encourages associations and friendships among the communities. Each morning, children with their distinct school uniforms and colors can be seen weaving paths throughout the city, en route from every quarter to every school via public buses, a parent's car, or on foot up and down the hills. Typical of the mixing are the students from the Hakramim neighborhood of Upper Nazareth who scatter each morning to most of Nazareth's schools, including two Greek Orthodox brothers to the municipal high school, a Muslim girl to St. Joseph's, three Roman Catholic brothers to the Baptist school, and several Muslim and Christian boys who travel across town to the Mitran school. From the surveys the lack of any pattern to schooling becomes evident. A Muslim family from the Ort quarter had their three children graduate from the Municipal, Ort, and Franciscan high schools. One Orthodox family in the Rum quarter has sent one of its sons to the municipal high school, two other sons to the Ort technical school, one daughter to St. Joseph's, and another to the Franciscan School for girls. A Muslim family in upper Safafra sent all five of its children to St. Joseph's school in the Nimsawi quarter.

Christian religious institutions have long provided for the education needs of Nazareth.[4] Today there are ten private elementary schools, operated by the Baptists, Protestant Church, Salvatorian Sisters, the Greek Catholic Church (two schools, grades K–3 and 4–12), Sisters of St. Joseph, Franciscan Sisters, Franciscan Brothers at Terra Sancta, Salesian Brothers, and Salesian Sisters. Most of these schools are kindergarten through eighth grade; 1988–89 total enrollment was 4,781. These schools are all integrated, but as in the case of the secondary schools, some are more mixed than others. The municipality operates thirteen elementary schools (K–6) with a 1988–89 total enrollment of 5,559. Most of these schools are relatively new and therefore are located beyond the city core. The overcrowding and inadequate facilities of schools in Israel's Arab sector has long been a problem. For example, until the completion of a school in 1989, the students in Bir Abu-Jayish and Fakhura met in rented rooms and houses scattered throughout their quarters. The three public middle schools (grades 7–9) had a 1988–89 enrollment of 2,156.

The high schools in Nazareth are listed in table 16. The municipality runs the large municipal high school and the Ort technical school, both of which have a student body composed mostly of Mus-

---

[4] Nazareth schools also serve the educational needs of many students from surrounding villages, where educational facilities can be extremely lacking or nonexistent. At the Ort technical school, 114 of the 639 students come from villages. Sister Mary at St. Joseph's school estimates that about 40 percent of the students come from the surrounding villages, some needing to leave their homes each morning at 5:00 A.M. in order to catch taxis (Israeli buses do not run on Sabbaths or Jewish holidays, so the students cannot rely on them for transportation). Until recently many of the schools also housed boarders, but as schools in the villages have improved, most have discontinued the service. Only the Salvatorian Sisters, which at one time had up to fifty boarders, still accept boarders—only six girls in the upper four classes.

lims, the majority of Christians at the Ort school being Greek Orthodox. The Christian schools are all mixed, the Baptist school having the highest percentage of Christian students, at 84 percent, and the Franciscan-run Terra Sancta the lowest, at 39 percent. The two Greek Catholic schools naturally have the highest percentage of Greek Catholic students. Terra Sancta and St. Joseph's, as Roman Catholic schools, have more Roman Catholic students than other Christian sects, but in the

TABLE 16. Religion of high-school students grades 9–12

School	Mus.	Chr.	G.O.	G.C.	R.C.	Mar.	Ang.	Other*	Total
Salesian (Latin)	120	207	84	56	53	8	4	2	327
% of total students	37	63	26	17	16	2	1	1	
% of Christians			41	27	26	4	2	1	
Terra Sancta (Latin)	161	104	34	29	36	3	2	0	265
% of total students	61	39	13	11	14	1	1	0	
% of Christians			33	28	35	3	2	0	
St. Joseph's (Latin)	167	157	49	46	52	7	3	0	324
% of total students	52	48	15	14	16	2	1	0	
% of Christians			31	29	33	4	2	0	
Franciscan** (Latin)	134	151	26	13	16	2	3	0	285
% of total students	47	53						0	
% of Christians			43	22	27	3	5	0	
Salvatorian (G.C.)	46	145	32	70	37	5	1	0	191
% of total students	24	76	17	37	19	3	1	0	
% of Christians			22	48	26	3	1	0	
Mitran (G.C.)	200	299	112	119	44	19	3	2	499
% of total students	40	60	22	24	9	4	1	1	
% of Christians			38	40	15	6	1	1	
Baptist	48	259							307
% of total students	16	84							
Ort (Public)	525	114							639
% of total students	82	18							
Municipal† (Public)	751	40							791
% of total students	95	5							

*Includes 1 Copt and 1 Armenian at Salesian and 1 Syrian Orthodox and 1 Armenian at Mitran.

**The numbers and percentages for the Christian sects were available only for grades 11 and 12.

†The totals and percentages for Christians and Muslims are estimates of the principal. Student information for each school was provided by the principal of that school.

Roman Catholic Salesian Technical School for boys, which has a special carpentry program, and in the Franciscan girls' schools Greek Orthodox students are the predominate Christian group primarily because the Greek Orthodox do not operate schools.

While mixing is practiced at all of the schools, there are still accusations of Christian schools discriminating against Muslims. Laurie Zu'bi, a U.S.-born and now Israeli Jewish woman married to a Muslim who teaches English at the secondary school, in a 9 May 1989 interview explained that originally the municipal high school was about 50 percent Christian, but that then schools like Mitran were built and they began to "pick and choose the best students from the government school." Now the school is about 90 percent Muslim. In her son's class there are only six Christians out of forty students. 'Abed Ghanim, the principal at the municipal secondary school, in a 24 May 1989 interview commented that the Christian schools are playing a negative role in the educational system of the town and are undermining the peaceful coexistence of Christians and Muslims. They do this, he said, by hiring mostly Christian faculty and staff, favoring students from their own denomination, ignoring entrance test scores—which he sees as just a front—and then accepting other students from more affluent families, who are usually Christians. He explained that the Christian schools teach ideas and attitudes which serve further to divide the communities of Nazareth. In addition, by restricting Muslim enrollment and favoring Christians and the more affluent, the schools, which, as instruments of the church are supposed to promote harmony, only serve to increase religious and social differences. The principal cited the Greek Catholic Mar Elias school in I'bilin, run by Father Elias Chacour, unlike the Mitran school, run by Father Emile Shufani, as a positive example of how a Christian school can be operated so that it is a positive influence in a community by offering education to all segments of society and employing both Muslims and Christians. He then accused the Baptist, Mitran, and St. Joseph's schools of being the worst offenders in Nazareth. He concluded by saying that Christians are indeed "segregating themselves through their schools."

Christian educational leaders are quick to explain just the opposite. They note how, during the seventh grade, Christian schools give an exam to all students wishing to enter. Those students with the highest test scores and those with older siblings already enrolled are given top priority. While this system seems fair and unbiased, it naturally selects students who have attended the better Christian elementary schools and discriminates against those who attend less adequate public schools or do not have the financial resources. While statistically this system seems to favor Christians over Muslims, in reality it favors better educated children from affluent families who, for the most part, also happen to be Christian.

The assertion that Christian schools do not hire many Muslims has a basis. Father Quirico Calella, principal of Terra Sancta, on 25 May 1989 noted that all thirty-five of the staff at his school are Christian, the majority being Roman Catholics or former Roman Catholics who have converted in order to marry someone from another sect. The one Muslim teacher employed at the school had retired the year before. Emil Shufani, in an 11 July 1989 interview, commented that six of the forty-two teachers at the Mitran school are Muslim.

During that same interview, Shufani expressed his opinion that the principal of the municipal secondary school has a negative attitude toward the Christian schools because his school has lower test results, and poorer facilities. He did, however, admit that lower-income Muslim families with more children to educate than the typical Christian family cannot afford Christian schools. He said that even Greek Catholics are not given preference over any other religious group at the Mitran school. Shufani noted that the problem was one of "geographical divisions," in that Muslim children attend public schools in their neighborhoods, while Christian children attend private schools in their neighborhoods. When the time comes for seventh-grade testing, the Christians do better as a result of having attended the better Christian elementary schools and are advanced to the Christian high schools, while the Muslim students are left to choose between the Ort or the municipal high school.

In regard to Christian-Muslim relations at his school, Father Shufani noted that they have never had any problems. "We respect the Muslim students and everyone feels at home here." Evidence of this is five young men from Shekun al-Arab, all of whom graduated in 1989 from the Mitran school. They are good friends in spite of their religious diversity: Greek Orthodox, Maronite, Greek Catholic (two), and Muslim. Shufani also noted that none of the Muslim girls wear head coverings at school, that they wear short pants for physical activities, and that all but two have participated in swimming activities. Christian religious instruction is held once a week, but Muslims are not required to attend; however, some of the Muslim students, as in other Christian schools, do attend the class as well as the monthly liturgy. When a ninety-minute prayer meeting was held during a field trip to Mt. Carmel, Shufani explained that the Muslim students wanted to come too. To encourage good relations, the school "insists that there is more in common than differences" between Muslims and Christians. Shufani noted that the percentage of Muslim students is now higher than when the school opened in 1956 because more Muslims are applying, owing to the high scholastic level of the school and because Muslims also want their children to have a good education and to improve their situation. He was proud to announce that 85 percent of the students from Mitran go on to university and that a Muslim girl from the first class of girls admitted in 1978 studied medicine in Jerusalem and is now a practicing physician.

Sister Margaret Ann, the principal of the Salvatorian Sisters school—a K–12 school located just west of the Mitran school, which was originally a school for girls, but began accepting boys three years ago—explained that two or three hundred students take the eighth-grade entrance exam each year, but only seventy of those can be accepted. Before, it was on a first-come, first-served basis, but now the students must take the exam and fill out an application form. Most students accepted are from the neighborhood, which is mostly Christian, and have additional family members attending the school. She said there are no rules for accepting students, but if two students have the same qualifications, the school will prefer the Greek Catholic. If the student is a Muslim with an older sibling already enrolled, it prefers that student. Religion class is required up to grade six, and then becomes optional. Until 1988, a religion class on Islam was offered for Muslim students, but according to Sister Margaret, when an Islamic group started to pressure the Ministry of Religion to compel Christian schools to offer classes on Islam, those few schools that did offer classes decided to drop them. When asked about intercommunal problems she cited occcasional minor incidents. One such occurred during the first day of school in 1988 when a teacher overheard one Christian tell another not to sit in a certain seat because it was next to a Muslim.

At St. Joseph's secondary school, the Christian students attend religion class twice a week and study from a text provided by the Latin patriarchate. Sister Mary, the principal, in an 18 May 1989 interview explained that Muslim students are free to go to the library or other classes during the religion class, but Muslim students do participate in the Christmas program. At the Baptist school, principal Emil Nusir in an 18 May 1989 interview explained that all students at the Baptist school are expected to attend the once-a-week religion class in which the Bible and general Christian principles are taught. So far, he said, no students have refused to attend. One graduate of the Baptist school tells a different story. Rawiya Abu Hanna, an Anglican, in an 8 August 1989 interview, related that in 1983 during her eighth-grade year, a Muslim classmate attending the Baptist school for the first time as an incoming high-school student asked if she might be excused from religion class. The teacher refused permission, so the student began tearing up the Bible in class. This action, however, failed to waive the requirement, so she stayed the year, attended religion class, and then transferred the following year to the Mitran school, where religion class attendance is not required of Muslims.

The dual educational system of Nazareth, in which a better funded and better equipped private system of Christian schools competes with a struggling public system, is bound to have problems. Because of the partially segregated school system, these problems are often viewed as religious, but they are more a result of socioeconomic differences in which the poorer, less-educated majority of Muslims and a relative few Christians attend the public schools and the more affluent Christians and some Muslims attend the private Christian schools. While this system may divide along class lines, it also unites within classes as students develop friendships with classmates from all quarters and all communities.

These friendship extend beyond the high school years. In a 10 June 1989 interview with Rawiya Abu Hanna, she listed the sects of students in seven dormitory apartments at Hebrew University occupied primarily by Nazarenes. While Christians formed the majority in all but one of the apartments, Christians and Muslims lived together in all seven of the apartments. These mixed groups were brought together through friendships from Nazareth school days, or from studying the same subject at the university. One apartment of three women included a Christian and Muslim who became friends at the Baptist school, and a second Muslim who studied at the Mitran school and became friends with the Christian student through university classes. Another apartment of coeds included three friends from the Mitran school, a Muslim, a Roman Catholic, and a Protestant; a fourth roommate was Maronite. A group of male students included two Greek Orthodox friends who both studied at the Baptist school. The two other roommates, a Roman Catholic and a Muslim, were law student friends of one of the Orthodox students.

Mixing of communities also takes place in the marketplace (fig. 36). On any given day, Muslims, Christians, Druze, Jews, and foreigners can be seen throughout the market. A Christian-owned frame shop on Barclays Street displays pictures to be sold and pictures customers have brought in to be framed which include Mary, the Last Supper, the Dome of the Rock, Quranic verses, and Gemal Abdel Nasser. Hajj Yahya enjoys long visits with Greek Orthodox priests and other Christians in his coffee bean shop. While some trades are dominated by certain religious groups, like the Muslim butcher, produce, and sweet shops, there is no religious pattern to the location of shops in the suq or along the main streets. A walk up Pope Paul VI Street during the Friday sermon radio broadcast finds the voice of the imam emanat-

Fig. 36. Nazareth's central produce market in the Suq

ing from a leap-frog pattern of shops. Only in those quarters with a high concentration of one religion are all the local shops run by families of the same religion.

When asked where they go to shop for clothing, 60 percent of those surveyed specified that religion was not an influence in determining where they shopped, while only one person indicated that she prefers to go to a merchant from her own religion. The primary influences were price (50 percent) and quality (46 percent). For food shopping, a similar pattern emerges, with 59 percent indicating that religion does not determine their choice of shops. Two people cited religion as an influence, one preferring merchants from the same religion and the other from the same sect. Percentages of responses for other influencing factors include price (44 percent) quality (38 percent), proximity (28 percent), central location (16 percent), and relatives (2 percent).[5] One Christian woman suggested that this nondenominational pattern of shopping is beginning to change as a result of the rise of the Islamic

[5] Nakhleh noted similar patterns in his study of Rameh. He writes that shopping patterns are influenced along sectarian lines when the choices are limited to one each from a sect. For example, Rameh has two clothing stores, located next door to each other. One is owned by a Christian and the other by a Druze. Most Christians patronize the Christian merchant, and most Druze the Druze shop. However, when there is more of a choice, as in food stores, then "neighborship, or propinquity, is more a common factor to all than other principles, such as kinship or sectarian affiliation" (Nakhleh 1973, 237).

party, in that "Christians have started to hate the Muslims and to not shop in their stores."

Religion plays a much greater role in the selection of dentists and insurance agents than of merchants. These two professions were used to help ascertain the degree of community solidarity, because the dentists and insurance representatives are still chosen by the individual and not assigned by the government, as are doctors in the clinics. When asked the religion of their dentists, 51 percent of 109 Muslims indicated that they go to a Muslim dentist; the remainder go to a Christian dentist. For the Christians, 94 percent of 110 indicated that they go to a Christian dentist. Seventeen respondents said that they do not go to a specific dentist and another seventeen, mainly Muslims, indicated going to a combination of Muslims, Christians, and Jews. With regard to insurance agents, 78 percent of 82 Muslims go to a Muslim agent, with 91 percent of the 88 Christian respondents indicating that they go to a Christian agent. One respondent insisted on saying that his insurance agent was "Arab," not Christian or Muslim, while another refused even to answer the question.

Religion is certainly a factor in determining selection of dentists and insurance agents, but the figures may be misleading, because respondents often indicated that while the professionals may have been from the same religion, they were selected because they were a relative or in some cases a friend or neighbor who just happened to be from the same religion.[6] Others noted to the surveyors that while the religion was the same, it was not the deciding factor, as in the case of one Muslim family who go to a Christian insurance agent and a Muslim dentist and said that religion was not a deciding factor. Still the fact that such an overwhelming percentage of Christians patronize only Christians indicates the present, but amicable, distance that still exists between the two groups.

Disunity among Communities

Mixed quarters, schools, market, and workplaces, as well as friendship patterns and shared cultural and religious beliefs, all help to unify the Arabs of Nazareth and give support to the well-worn phrase that they are brothers. In addition to these centripetal forces there are opposing centrifugal forces, like the recent increase of communal involvement in politics, which do indeed pull apart and seek to disunify. Religious differences have given each community its own special set of character-

---

[6] Family rather than religious solidarity was also a major factor in shopping patterns at the beginning of the century. Scrimgeour writes of shopping in the bazaars that it "is always considered desirable, if at all possible, to deal with a relative" (Scrimgeour 1913, 46).

istics. While most of these differences cause no conflict, they can contribute to ill feelings if only because they prevent the two main communities from ever becoming as one.

Evidence of lingering divisions is illustrated by a few comments from citizens of Nazareth. One Christian woman who studied at the Franciscan school as a girl more than forty-five years ago related how her grandmother would always warn her as she went to school not to go beyond the school and descend the stairs into the Sharqiya quarter. Although Muslim members of the Fahum family lived next door to them in the suq, the grandmother was not comfortable with her going into the main Muslim section. A Christian woman who lives in an apartment building in Ram along with four Muslim and five other Christian families, when asked in a 28 July 1989 interview if there are problems between Muslims and Christians in her neighborhood, responded by saying "There are very many." She then explained that the Muslim families have too many children, the children are not well mannered, and she does not feel safe in her apartment and so always locks the doors.

One Christian man described how hatred and suspicion are spoken of in the homes long after the inciting events have happened. He told of his many years on the municipal council as a representative of the Jebha party working to better Nazareth, and how all of the good performed has now been rejected by the Islamic party. This man said that he will tell his children and they will tell their children of how the Muslims rejected his positive efforts by wanting to do it themselves. In a conversation with two Christian women, one feared that within several years, Christian women would also be required to wear long sleeves and other modest attire as a result of the growing influence of the Islamic movement, while the other woman said it would never happen because within Islam there are adherents who do not agree with such policies.

While many admitted problems and divisions, few if any were willing to discuss communal relations or to be specific about what actually propagates the rift. One exception was a prominent Greek Orthodox man who in a September 1989 interview talked openly about Christian-Muslim relations. He said that "at one time people didn't think about whether or not you were Christian or Muslim; our nationalistic feelings united us"; now, however, the "Muslims are controlling everything," and the Christians are shrinking back and "becoming second-rate citizens." He explained that commerce, education, finance, and medicine were once all Christian-controlled, but that now Christians feel as if they are losing ground. He noted that the decline of Christian prominence began in Bethlehem in 1948, but did not begin in

Nazareth until the 1970s. According to him, it is an economic, social, and political problem in which the Muslims have "the votes, the money, the education, the power, and the land." Christians once had all of these, along with the support of the government, but now even the government backs the Muslims because they have larger numbers to offer. He explained that the *Mapai* political party always had one Druze, one Muslim, and one Christian included on its election lists, but now the Christian candidate has been dropped because the Christians are small in numbers and are internally divided, so not worth the energy to win their support. When Christians talk among themselves, the man asserted, they talk about things like Muslims controlling all the shops in the market, although the Christians do nothing about it. In his opinion, the Muslims are working to gain power, and the weakened Christians are doing nothing because they are afraid that if they bring up the issue of Muslim dominance, they will break up the Christian-Muslim unity and arouse the temper of the Muslims. "We are expecting trouble, it is beginning to boil," he lamented in regard to Christian-Muslim relations. "Christians don't resent Muslims for gaining education and jobs, but this limits the opportunities for Christians." At one time Muslims thought they needed the Christians, he went on to say, so they tried to establish good relations and the Christians complied, but now the Muslims feel as if they do not need the Christians. As a result of these changes and the rise of the Islamic party, "there is deep suspicion now," and worry about the future of the children. He said that Nazareth has lost its Christian atmosphere and has become increasingly Muslim, like Jenin and Nablus.

The feelings of this man are more concerns for the future of Christians than they are fears about Muslim domination in Nazareth. If the Christian churches were not stagnating or even on the decline, then perhaps his concern with Islamic growth and influence would abate. But since it is the Muslims who are progressing at the expense of Christians, religion naturally becomes the standard by which lines of animosity are drawn.

He also explained that part of the problem is caused by the rapid expansion of Nazareth, in that one encounters an increasing number of strangers, and that makes it harder to have congenial relations. Mundhir Qupti, a resident of the Aqbat quarter, made a similar observation in a 21 August 1989 interview. He explained that his parent's generation had close relationships with their Muslim neighbors, visiting them in their homes and attending their weddings. The Copts and Muslims in the Aqbat neighborhood still have good relations, but now among the younger generation there is no time for involved friendships, just a hello in passing. He said that even among Coptic extended families, there is less unity as people become more materialistic and more occupied with work.

Intermarriage between Christians and Muslims can, by the standards of some people, be an indicator of positive relations between the two groups, in that they are joining together. But for the most part the dearth of interreligious marriages and the rejection experienced by those who participate in them are evidence that there are limits to the bonds of friendship proclaimed as existing between Muslim and Christian. One Christian man questioned, "If there is nothing wrong between Christians and Muslims, then why isn't there intermarriage?" The practice of interreligious marriages is not necessarily new, but it is still not a common occurrence. According to a 28 July 1989 interview with Mohammad Fahum of Nazareth's Islamic court, conversions from Christianity to Islam in Nazareth are such a sensitive issue that those wishing to do so go to either Haifa or Akka's court to register. Records from those courts show that from 1982 to 1989, nine interreligious marriages were performed at the Haifa court for couples from Nazareth and four in the Akka court. When these marriages do occur, few of the couples return to live in Nazareth. The Nazareth court recorded during the same period thirty-two Christians and nine Jews who converted to Islam for the purpose of marriage. None of these were from Nazareth, but most were from the surrounding villages of Kfar Kanna, 'Eilabun, Maghar, and Turan.[7] While most of the marriages are Christian women to Muslim men, Father Barnaba remembers baptizing two Muslim men so they could marry Orthodox women, adding that now they go to neither mosque nor church. He noted that unfortunately, there is no required teaching of doctrine prior to the conversion and marriage. This topic is a sensitive one, for differences do separate the two communities, and loyalties are strong enough that they cause strain between the two groups when intermarriage does take place, just as they did for many years between the various Christian sects.[8]

[7] One couple from Nazareth, he a Muslim by birth and she a European Christian, related how when they got married, the wife, in accordance with Israeli law, had to convert to Islam. This meant that on the day of the marriage she had to confess the *shahada* (Islamic creed) to the Muslim *qadi* (judge). The husband said he laughed out loud when she recited the creed because she said it so fast and funnily. At the time she was wearing a cross and a short-sleeved dress. When the qadi asked her to remove the cross, she refused, saying that it was her choice to decide what she wore. After he performed the wedding the qadi told the Muslim husband that he would see him soon, meaning that he fully expected that a divorce would soon follow. Now the husband is a Christian.

[8] This fear of Christian-Muslim marriages has its effect on male-female relations. One of the Christian women who helped with the survey introduced me to a young Muslim man who could also help. They were both students at Haifa University

Strong historical divisions also prevent many conversions, and as a result, those who do convert for reasons other than marriage usually do so in secret or else risk being ostracized from their families and cultural community. One man, who describes himself as a Muslim who believes in Christ and prefers to be known as a believer rather than a Christian, in an August 1989 interview said that his Muslim family was unaccepting of his change at first. One brother even called him a *kafir* (unbeliever, infidel), but an uncle came to his defense by saying that Christians also worship God and that is good. Now, because his family have heard him and his wife pray, seen them attend church each week and observed their positive attributes, they accept the change. He said that every three or four months the strong Muslim Christian believers meet together in secret. During the last meeting, he said, there were twelve from the region, with about five or six from Nazareth. "There are many more believers, but we don't invite them to our meetings because we can't trust them." He noted that the believers are in a sensitive position, and a knowledge of their beliefs could be damaging.

When a newspaper article in 1949 reported on Nazareth's Easter celebration, the Jewish author noted in attendance the "large numbers of Arabs newly converted to Christianity from the Moslem faith"; whereas "in the past the city had over 6,000 Moslems," they now "number only 2,000" (*JP*, 18 April 1949). The religious leaders from the five main Christian communities in Nazareth replied in a letter to the editor refuting the author's statement as the "figment of a fertile imagination"; they stressed that "not a single Moslem has been converted to Christianity since the Israeli occupation, while, during the Mandatory regime, conversions were so rare as to make the term 'large numbers' totally false" (*JP*, 11 May 1949). Christians and Muslims may find common bonds in the worship of Mary or a common belief in Jesus, but when it comes to intermarriage or conversion, they are still very separate communities.

Few, if any, of the causes for disunity among the communities actually result in any form of intercommunal conflict. There is much suspicion and talk, but when push comes to shove, there is little action, for it would be difficult to live in Nazareth while always at odds with members of the other community. Still, on occasion, conflicts do happen, and religious differences become the undeserving scapegoat. In the early 1950s there was a skirmish in Nazareth involving Greek Catholic scouts and Muslims. The initial headline read: "Christians

---

and had become friends there, but I was cautioned by the woman never to mention this Muslim male friend around her parents, who would not approve of such a friendship.

and Moslems clash in Nazareth." That article and later ones indicate that a troop of young Greek Catholic scouts from Shefar 'Am were in Nazareth on 5 April 1952 to participate in a special Sunday mass officiated by Archbishop Hakim and broadcast over Israeli radio. During the service, while the scouts were waiting to participate in the religious procession, a local boy threw a stone at the scouts and fled. The scoutmaster pursued the boy toward the White Mosque into what reports called an ambush. There a fight erupted between the two groups. One elderly Muslim man, an onlooker, was injured in the fight and died two days later. A curfew was imposed on the city until charges could be sorted out and tempers calmed.

While Christians and Muslims were the combatants, the final reports saw it as a political battle, albeit from opposing views. The Communist-controlled paper *Kol Ha'am* accused Archbishop Hakim—who was noted for his strong anti-Communist feelings—of using his group of gangsters to disrupt the progressive and peace-loving elements of Nazareth. Hakim and all other newspaper accounts, however, saw the incident as an act perpetrated by the Communists against their rival, Hakim. Hakim said it was Communists who were lying in ambush near the mosque, where they attacked the scoutmaster with a barrage of stones, and then his scouts and assistants as they rushed in to help. Hakim said the man who died was trying to mediate the conflict. Muslim and Christian leaders met shortly after the fight, agreeing that the matter should go no further. By September a *sulha* (peace agreement) had been negotiated between the Catholic scouts and the family of the Muslim man who died; the scouts were banned from marching in Nazareth's main street for a year (*JP*, 17, 18 April, 16 September, 15 October, 1952).

More recently, nonreligious violence has also been attributed by some to Muslim-Christian rivalry. On 10 June 1989, thirteen-year-old Selim Nusseri, while visiting with his father at a friend's home near Mary's well, went to a nearby store to buy cigarettes for his father. En route, he was brutally murdered. His body was found that evening under a fig tree in a vacant lot of the Greek Catholic waqf near the municipal park. One suspect, 'Arab Mahrum, was arrested two days later and three other suspects were arrested within two weeks. According to the police inspector, the boy was robbed of thirty-four sheqels (less than twenty cents). The inspector said that the four suspects were known to the police and had previous criminal convictions. One article noted that Mahrum was a known drug user (*JP*, 12 June; *al-Senara*, 16, 23 June 1989). The official accounts link the motive to drugs, surmising that the suspects either needed money for drugs or acted under the influence of drugs. The municipal park and the waqf lot with their protective trees

were known hangouts for Nazareth's drug users, but have since been
cleaned up by their owners, and concealing shrubs and walls removed.

While drugs seemed to be the cause, the fact that Selim was Greek
Orthodox and the suspects Muslim created increased suspicion between
the two communities. One perceptive Christian explained that even
though the murderers were drug dealers and should be labeled as such,
they were most often labeled as Muslims. An Orthodox woman from
upper Safafra saw it as another example of tensions between Christians
and Muslims, perhaps because her thirteen-year-old son has had some
difficulties with Muslim boys in their neighborhood. A priest noted
that suspicions were aroused among Christians following the murder,
Christians saying that only Muslims would do such a thing. Another
priest said that the drug problem in Nazareth is "ninety percent Muslim." When asked what he viewed the cause of the murder to be, he
said that inwardly he thinks it could be both reasons, drugs and religion. Perhaps "the Muslims killed the Christian boy as part of a religious conflict or because they were on drugs and were bad people, or
maybe they weren't in their right mind, or are narrow-minded people
who don't think about what they are doing, or maybe they killed the
boy because they feel persecuted or have had a bad experience with
Christians." When finished with his explanation he quickly added, "I
have many friends that are Muslim."

Because of the heightened tension following the murder, leaders
of the Islamic movement distributed an official statement throughout
the town on a green leaflet in which they condemned the brutal attack
and asked that the criminals be brought to justice. They said that all
families of Nazareth felt as if they had lost a son. They concluded with
a prayer that the Nusseri family would find solace from their loss. Two
days later, the Islamic Cemetery Restoration Committee also issued a
leaflet, entitled "The Treachery, the Patience, the Forgiveness," in
which they too condemned the brutal incident and called upon religious and community leaders to join together in protecting the security, peace, and tranquility of Nazareth. The leaflet included words of
comfort from the Quran, sura 2, verses 155–56, which read "Glad tid-
ings to those who patiently persevere, Who say, when afflicted with
calamity: 'To God we belong, and to Him is our return.'" A memorial
rally for Selim was held a few days after his murder. Hundreds of
Nazarenes slowly paraded up Main Street to a memorial service held
in front of Mary's well. Leading the procession were civic and religious
leaders from all of Nazareth's sects and parties (fig. 37).

It is incidents such as this murder that prompted Mayor Saif al-
Din al-Zu'bi to write in his memoirs that when conflicts do arise between Muslims and Christians, it is important to remember that such

Fig. 37. Municipal and religious notables during memorial parade for slain Selim Nusseri. Franciscan Priest Arturo is third from the left, Mayor Ziyad is to the nun's left, and Coptic priest Sidrak is in the black robe and cap.

events are rare, they can be easily contained, the "water can return to its course quickly and judiciously," and they are caused by "evil, insolent hands" whose goal is to "fish in turbid waters" and weaken the strong relations between all the sons of Nazareth. He writes of the centuries of cooperation between the two groups, noting that religious leaders still cooperate to eradicate enmity by "joining the flags of peace and spreading faith and mutual trust between all citizens." He goes on to say that "the ripples from feuds and clashes between individuals from the two sects are interpreted by some biased persons and beneficiaries as if they were a sectarian dispute" (al-Zu'bi 1987, 206–7).

Politics and Religion

The communities of Nazareth and the quarters they inhabit have created patterns of segregation and interaction, of clustering and of mixing together. Nakhleh Bishara in a 13 September 1989 interview explained that the tribal mentality which influenced the establishment of religious-based quarters and affected living patterns and patterns of speech is still prevalent today, but he suggested that the framework has changed. Whereas religion was the original frame of reference for the tribal mentality among Christians, today it is framed according to political parties. He suggested that as Christians become more secular, reli-

gion is no longer as binding, so allegiance has shifted away from a religious identification toward political allegiances. This may be the case
for some Nazarenes, in that they identify with a political group rather
than a religious community, but for others, community identification
transposes to political identification and the result is religious-based
political parties. While the 1989 rise of the Islamic party is the best example of such phenomena, the mixing of politics and religion goes
back to both Ottoman and Mandate times.[9]

During Ottoman rule, the mayor of Nazareth was elected every
three years in a system that alternated between a Muslim and Christian
mayor. The two other elected officials were representatives of the
Christian and Muslim courts (Scrimgeour 1913, 98). The first known
instance of communal conflict over municipal representation occurred
in 1924 when the death of the mayor resulted in a dispute between the
two communities over who should be appointed the successor (Porath
1974, 303).

When municipal elections were held in 1934, elected members of
the municipal council included three Greek Orthodox, two Roman
Catholics, and two Muslims. In 1942 Najib Bathish, one of the Roman
Catholic members of the council, passed away, and Habib Khoury, a
Greek Catholic, was appointed to take his place. On 22 May 1944 Habib
Khoury died, leaving a vacancy in the council. This prompted the
Greek Catholic community of Nazareth to petition the mayor to appoint a successor from their community. But H. F. Davies, the assistant
district commissioner in Nazareth, wrote on 10 August to the district
commissioner that he could not find anyone whom he considered
"suitable" from the Greek Catholic community to recommend as councilor and instead recommended that Nayif Bathish, a Roman Catholic,
be appointed to take Khoury's place "in view of the fact that religion
has had no bearing on the elections of the council in 1934." With that
recommendation, the district commissioner recommended Bathish's
appointment on 14 August. Meanwhile, 110 members of the Greek
Catholic community signed a petition, which they sent to Archbishop
Hakim, requesting that he "approach the authorities concerned to preserve our right of representation at the municipality so that one of our
community will be selected to fill the gap." Hakim forwarded the petition, along with his own letter to the commissioner, on 9 September,
in which he expressed his surprise that a Roman Catholic had already
been appointed and questioned whether "due regard" had been given
to the "claims and merit" of the candidates from the Greek Catholic
community. The commissioner wrote back five days later informing

---

[9] For an overview of Arab politics within Israel since 1967 see Landau 1993.

the archbishop that "the municipal corporations ordinance makes no provision for representation of the council being decided by communities." He went on to explain that with all of the communities and sects in Palestine, it would be "quite impossible to form any type of local government if each separate community who at an election happened to have a member elected as a member of the council would thereby create a right to always have a member of its community as member of the council." He concluded by saying that the Greek Catholic community of Nazareth was "quite wrong in assuming that it has any right to have a member of the Municipal Council nominated or elected as their special representative" (ISA, Nazareth Municipal Membership, 27-N/79/1–2657).

The desire for community representation was manifest again during the first municipal elections as part of the State of Israel in 1954, when most of Nazareth's religious communities organized their own lists of candidates for municipal council and mayor, in opposition to the already established Communist party. The Communist party has its roots in the nineteenth-century establishment of Nazareth's first high school, called Muscobi, by the Russians—the designated guardians of Orthodox Christianity in the Holy Land. This school educated many of those who became leaders in Nazareth during the first part of the twentieth century. The school dissolved following the Russian revolution, but strong attachments to Russia endured. Most of the students at the school were Greek Orthodox, which helps to explain the continued involvement and predominance of Orthodox Christians in the communist party. When the Russians left, many of the Christian Arabs joined with Jewish immigrants from Eastern Europe to form the first Communist cell in Palestine (Mansour 1975).[10]

The Communist party in Nazareth showed its strength during the 1951 Knesset elections when it received over 40 percent of the votes, even though one report "put the number of real Communists at below 20" (JP, 3 March 1954). While strongly supported as a non-Zionist party in the national elections, at the local level, in preparation for Nazareth's first municipal election within the State of Israel, the Communist party experienced opposition organized by the various communities. The Greek Catholics were reportedly the first group to meet and discuss involvement in the municipal election, followed shortly by the Greek Orthodox community, which decided to operate as a group. This was viewed as a setback by the Communists, who had hoped for greater support from the Greek Orthodox community (JP, 18

---

[10] For a historical summary of the Communist party in Israel and Arab involvement in the party, see for example chapter 7 in Merhav 1980.

January 1954). Soon a variety of religious and family-based parties were organized, including three Muslim parties divided on hamula lines, two Greek Orthodox parties, and a united party of the Western-Rite churches. These parties campaigned with similar platforms of improving education and public services and tackling unemployment, while the Communist platform addressed national problems of abolishing the military government and concluding peace with the Arabs. Local needs ranked much lower on their platform list. In the weeks preceding the election, the courtyard of the Orthodox Church, Communist party headquarters, and other meeting places were used as arenas to accuse the opposing parties of cooperating with the authorities of Israel during and after the war. These accusations pitted religious party against Communist party but not sect against sect. Police reinforcements were even sent to Nazareth because of the expected clash between Muslims and Communists (*JP*, 8, 11 April 1954). Of the Communist candidates, the first person on the list was a Muslim; the other top contenders for a seat on the council were Greek Orthodox men. Two women were included much lower down on the list (*JP*, 18 March 1954).

Of the 9,501 eligible voters, 7,973 (83.9 percent) voted in the 17 April 1954 municipal elections to elect fifteen councilors from among eighty-seven candidates from eight lists. The voters included fifteen Jews, who reportedly voted for the Orthodox list; veiled women from the Sharqiya quarter, some of whom lacked photographs in their identity books and therefore were not required to identify themselves; and cloistered nuns, who were allowed by their Mother Superior to venture out to vote when a request to establish a polling booth in the convent was denied (*JP*, 19 April 1954). According to records kept by Jebha recorder Amin Qudha, the Communist party received 38.4 percent of the votes and six seats on the council. The *al-Ahliya* party, made up of a coalition of the Western-Rite churches, received 23.8 percent of the votes and three seats on the council. The Islamiya party, headed by the Fahum and Zu'bi families, received 12.4 percent of the votes and two council seats. The other two Muslim parties, *Hiyy Sharqiya* (Eastern quarter) and *al-Huda*, received 5.5 percent and 5.2 percent of the vote respectively and gained one seat each on the council. The two Orthodox parties, *al-Mustaqilla* and *al-Orthodox*, received 6.5 percent and 4.9 percent respectively and gained one seat each on the council. The *Mapam* party, a national Zionist party, received 3.4 percent of the vote, not enough for a seat.

One report suggested that the Mapam candidate received the votes of some of the 100 Copts who, by an oversight, were not included in the Western-Rite Church list. While communities sponsored their own lists, there was not total allegiance. Of the 3,800 eligible Muslim voters, only 1,800 voted for one of the three Islamic parties; and of the 3,000 eligible Orthodox voters, only 900 voted for one of the two Orthodox lists; while of the 2,300 Western-Rite voters, 1,800 voted for their church list. Many Muslim and Christians voted for the Communist party, not out of any political belief in communism, but rather "in protest against the backward way in which town affairs have been managed by heads of families and communities." The feeling of many who voted against their community lists and for the Communists was that the Communists "could do no worse than these old-fashioned elements and should be given a chance to carry out their many promises" (JP, 14 April 1954).

Other reasons for the success of the Communists include a report that the Communists threatened any who did not vote for them with a charge of collaboration. The Communists said that they would relay the names of the collaborators across the border, which might then endanger family members living in Jordan and Lebanon. The journalist then noted that such threats were particularly effective with the Christians, who "had always felt that their Moslem brothers tolerated them with difficulty and deemed it more secure to outdo them in their nationalism." Another report suggested that the non-Communists had hoped that the family and sectarian lists, rather than party-based lists, would unite the citizens against the Communists, but because the influence of the family heads and clergy had "suffered an enormous drop," the non-Communist lists failed to attract the desired votes. The report noted that community organizations, particularly Orthodox and Muslim, had ceased to attract the youth, who were looking for other venues of activity which their own communities were unable to provide. The split in the Greek Orthodox community between the Greek hierarchy and those who supported their list, and the breakaway Arab members and their list (al-Mustaqilla), along with the lack of leadership in the community of Israeli Muslims, created a vacuum into which the communists stepped, "cleverly exploiting hidden and open splits and feuds" (JP, 22 April 1954).

Tensions between Communists and non-Communists continued after the elections. In June, the meeting place of the Communist Youth Organization was broken into, presumably by anti-Communists, followed by fights in the streets between Communist councilors on their way to a council session and anti-Communists (JP, 18, 22 June 1954). Later that month a vendor of the Communist weekly al-Ittihad was beaten and stabbed, necessitating extra police patrols to prevent more fighting (JP, 27 June 1954). Then in July, members of the Zu'bi family reportedly attacked Communists selling al-Ittihad (JP, 25 July 1954).

In the meantime, negotiations were under way to form a coalition government and select a mayor. Yakub Farah of the independent Orthodox party and the three members from the Catholic party, at the urging of Archbishop Hakim, proposed that the nine non-Communist councilors form a unity government and elect the mayor. The Communist party was also courting councilors in the hopes that it could gather enough support for a coalition (*JP*, 19 April 1954). By July, various blocs emerged. One bloc was made up of three Muslim councilors, Fahum, Zu'bi, and Kasim; a second was composed of Muslim councilor Kang and the three Catholic councilors, with the two Greek Orthodox councilors, Farah and Amin Jarjura forming the third bloc (*JP*, 4 July 1954). Finally, after months of negotiations, a coalition was formed, and Amin Jarjura of the Orthodox party was elected as mayor, with the votes of himself, the four Muslims and the three Catholics against the six votes of the Communists and Yakub Farah of the independent Orthodox party, who had agreed to be the Communist's candidate for mayor (*JP*, 16 July 1954).

The results widened the rift between the Communist and non-Communist factions, resulting in actual fistfights in the council chamber a few years later. It began when the Communist party called for a day-long strike in memory of the anniversary of the Kfar Kassem massacre in which forty-three Israeli Arabs were killed by an Israeli Army unit. In answer to the call, several secondary school boys skipped classes for a day. This prompted the mayor to issue a leaflet calling on parents not to allow their children to skip school for political reasons. During the next council meeting, an argument erupted over the mayor's warning, and four Communist councilors attacked Yakub Farah, obviously no longer in alliance with the Communists. Muslim councilor Fahum came to Farah's aid. After the fight, in which shirts were torn and spectacles broken, the Communist councilors accused their colleagues of being "traitors" and of betraying the interests of the Arabs. The next day the fighting continued when Farah was assaulted in his grocery store by several men with Communist connections, including relatives of Communist councilor Khoury. Three attempts at a sulha were rejected by Farah, who continued to blame the Communists for starting the incident (*JP*, 3, 4, 5, 19 November 1957). While religion was a definite factor in the formation of political lists, it was not the cause of the occasional conflicts or ongoing rivalry in the political arena. These conflicts were purely political, as the Communists and their opponents struggled for control.

The role of religious communities in the formation of local political lists gradually declined over the years. In the four elections spanning the years 1959–70, the Communist party continued to win the most seats, but never a majority, thus enabling the opposing lists to form coalitions in selecting non-Communist mayors.[11]

By 1974, the religious-based parties had all but disappeared. Meanwhile, the Communist party joined forces with a newly organized group of students who had become politically active in Arab rights at Haifa University, a group of university graduates, and a group of merchants to form the Democratic Front of Nazareth, or just plain Jebha (front). Jebha is run by a majlis (council) of sixty-seven members—twenty from the Communists, twenty from the merchants, twenty for the university graduates, and seven from the university students. The bureau of seventeen and secretariat of seven members are also divided in roughly the same proportions among the four groups. With this broad coalition, Jebha won 66.7 percent of the vote and eleven of seventeen council seats in the 1975 elections. This majority in the council then elected Tawfiq Ziyad, a well-known protest poet, as Nazareth's first Communist mayor.

Two main factors contributed to the ascendance of the communists and Jebha. First, the Arabs of Nazareth finally decided to express their true concerns as a suppressed minority, and it was the Communist party that had always been willing to act as their voice. Following the 1975 Jebha victory, Moshe Dayan, in an interview with the Hebrew daily *Ha'aretz*, noted that many of the Arabs in Israel did not support the government because they "did not become Israelis of their own free will." Their opposition toward the government, however, was suppressed because they "were afraid of an angry reaction of some kind if

[11] The 1959 election saw the narrowing of Islamic lists to two and Orthodox lists to one, and a restructuring of the Western churches into two lists, both formed by joining smaller, mostly family-based parties. The Communist party won its record low of only three seats on the council, four seats going to the two Western Church lists, four to the two Islamic lists, one to the Orthodox, and the other three to two other parties with Muslim councilmen. Saif al-Din al-Zu'bi, the Mapan councilman, was elected as mayor with a coalition of the four Catholics, the Greek Orthodox and Mapam (a Muslim) councilors, and four Muslim councilors. Later the four Muslims from the Huda and Sharqiya lists also joined the coalition, leaving only the three Communists outside (*JP*, 7 February 1960).

In the 1965 elections, the Communist party won seven of the seats, the Labor-affiliated party won five, a Roman Catholic–oriented party won two, and Mapam won one seat; six other parties, some of which were religious-based, gained no seats. The new mayor, Abdul Aziz Zu'bi, was elected through a coalition of his party, Mapam, and the Communists, but was forced to resign ninety days later owing to noncooperation from the seven alignment-affiliated councilmen (*JP*, 22 December 1965, 22 March 1966). The next year the Communists won six, the Labor affiliate four, Mapam two, and the Islamic, Greek Catholic, and Roman Catholic lists each one seat. In the 1970 election, the Communists led once again with seven seats, followed by the Labor affiliate with five seats, the National Religious party with two, and Mapam, and two other new parties with one each.

they expressed views against the government of Israel." As a result, they "voted and acted not in accordance with their true aspirations, but rather in accordance with their daily needs," which required that they act "through the framework of established parties, party agents or other interests" (*Ha'aretz*, 19 December 1975, in *Journal of Palestine Studies* 5 [Spring/Summer 1976]: 178).

For years the Arabs of Israel supported non-Arab parties, not out of support for platforms, but in order to survive. It was through party affiliation that many favors like housing and jobs were won. One of the lingering examples of this system is the National Religious party (*Mifdal*), an odd mix of Arabs and Orthodox Jews supported by the Mazzawa family. The minister of the interior most often comes from the National Religious party, and it is through this ministry that housing and hunting permits are issued. One Greek Orthodox man said that he and others support this party not out of any identification with the party ideology, but because, for hunters who like to hunt wild boar in the Golan Heights and Galilee, support for the Mazzawa family ensures getting the hard-to-obtain permits.

Second, in addition to finally breaking from the Zionist-oriented parties in order to make known their national aspirations, the Communists gained support because of problems at the local level. As suggested in an editorial in the Hebrew press, "the voters of Nazareth penalized the parties that have run the municipality so incompetently and inefficiently in the last few years" (*Davar*, 11 December 1975, in *Journal of Palestine Studies* 5 (Spring/Summer 1976): 178). One Israeli writer observed that the change in the local government of Israel "proved that government by protection, intimidation, handouts, and sheer corruption had become impossible" (Peled 1976, 36).

In the 1983 elections Jebha retained its momentum, gaining 65.1 percent of the votes and eleven council seats. Its main opposition was the Taqadumia (Progressive) list, which won four council seats. The other two seats went to the Jewish National Religious party and the labor-affiliated party. An analysis of voting patterns (fig. 38) shows Jebha receiving strong support in precincts located in both Muslim and Christian neighborhoods. Qudha's records show a high of 85.7 percent for Jebha in precinct 35 in the very Muslim upper portion of the Sharqiya quarter, the next highest precinct being number 8/1 in the mostly Greek Orthodox upper sector of the Rum quarter, with 81.4 percent of the votes going to Jebha. The precinct with the lowest support for Jebha was number 39 in the Spanyoli and Clarese quarters, with only 39.8 percent. This section of town has a high population of Mazzawa family members, and because of this the precinct showed the highest support (30.6 percent) for the Orthodox Jewish party. Taqadumia received its

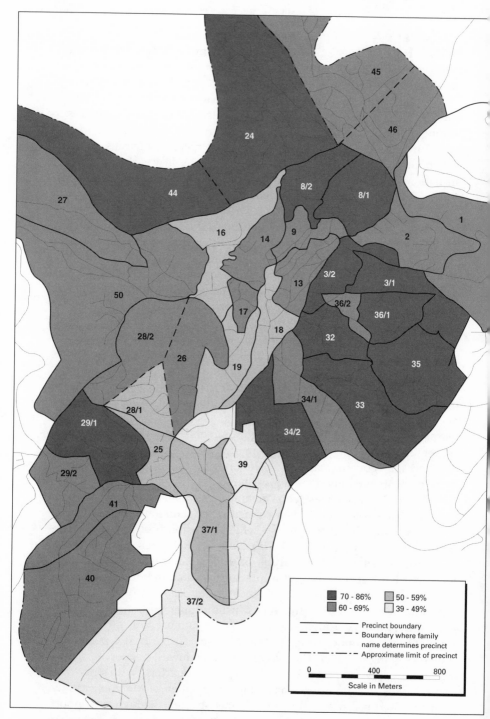

Fig. 38. 1983 Nazareth municipal election, percentage vote by precinct: Jebha list

high of 32.8 percent of the votes in precinct 37/2 (now 38) in the Maslakh quarter. Jebha received over 50 percent of the votes in all but these two precincts. The nonsectarian support of Jebha is plainly evident.

The major nonsectarian parties have always tried to maintain a balance among the Christian sects and Muslims by running candidates from all of the religious communities. In addition, all parties try to run candidates from a wide representation of quarters and families. Jebha also tries to provide a mix of representatives from the Communists, merchants, and academics. Table 17 shows the diversity of religions and locations in the selection of candidates from the Jebha list for both the 1983 and 1989 elections and for the Taqadumia list for the 1989 election. For the 1989 election, Jebha reorganized its list by moving several Muslim candidates higher up on the list in order to offset the strong draw of the Islamic list. In 1983, the top eleven candidates from Jebha were elected and in 1989 the top ten were elected. Only the top two from Taqadumia were elected in 1989.

This system has for the most part worked to ensure an acceptable mix of Christians and Muslims on the city council. According to names supplied from municipal records with their religions identified by

TABLE 17. Religion and quarter of candidates for the Jebha and Taqadumia election lists

1983 Jebha list	1989 Jebha list	1989 Taqadumia list
1. Muslim, Sharqiya	1. Muslim, Sharqiya	1. Muslim, Sharqiya
2. Greek Orthodox, Rum	2. Greek Orthodox, Rum	2. Greek Orthodox,
3. Muslim, Safafra	3. Muslim, Safafra	Municipal Park
4. Roman Catholic,	4. Roman Catholic,	3. Greek Catholic,
Jebel al-Daula	Jebel al-Daula	Maslakh
5. Greek Catholic, Mitran	5. Muslim, Suq	4. Muslim, Maidan
6. Greek Orthodox, Rum	6. Greek Catholic, Mitran	5. Muslim, Nimsawi
7. Muslim, Sharqiya	7. Muslim, Sharqiya	6. Greek Orthodox, Rum
8. Church of Christ, Krum	8. Muslim, Bir al-Amir	7. Muslim, Latin
9. Roman Catholic, Bir	9. Greek Orthodox, Rum	8. Copt, Aqbat
al-Amir	(a woman)	9. Muslim, Sharqiya
10. Muslim, Maslakh	10. Muslim/Bedouin,	10. Maronite, Maidan
11. Muslim/Bedouin,	Fakhura	
Fakhura	11. Church of Christ, Krum	
13. Greek Orthodox, Rum	12. Roman Catholic,	
(a woman)	Bir al-Amir	
14. Muslim, Jebel al-Daula	13. Muslim, Sharqiya	
15. Greek Orthodox,	14. Greek Orthodox,	
Maslakh	Maslakh	
	15. Muslim, Sharqiya	

municipal employee Khalid 'Atiya in an 11 September 1989 interview, the seventeen-man council was composed of eight Muslims and nine Christians in 1976, nine Muslims and eight Christians in 1979, ten Muslims and seven Christians in 1983, and seven Muslims and ten Christians in 1986. The 1989 election, with the advent of the Islamic party, shifted the balance toward a definite Muslim majority of thirteen Muslims and six Christians. Muslims have always been well represented on the municipal council and in the office of mayor. While their growing numbers warrant an even larger share of representation on the council, the Islamic list was created in 1989 not out of a desire to increase Muslim representation or to overthrow any perceived Christian dominance. It was a political move to challenge the rule of Jebha, and more specifically the Communists who control Jebha. Old lines of contention were once again drawn, pitting Muslims against communists. As the Muslim-Communist rivalry commenced, Christian concern of Islamic dominance escalated latent fears among many into open animosity and even feelings of hostility.

In August 1988 the Islamic Movement announced from Umm al-Fahm that they planned to enter the 1989 municipal elections in all Arab villages and cities (al-Senara, 26 August 1988). Then in October, flyers were distributed throughout Nazareth calling on residents to vote according to their beliefs and conscience in the national election and not to boycott the national elections as they had been encouraged to do in the past. The leaflet also announced that the Islamic Movement planned to run in the upcoming municipal elections (JP, 13 October 1988).

The Islamic Movement of Nazareth has its roots in the Islamic Movement of Israel, which began in the second half of the 1970s in the villages of the region known as the Triangle. Reasons for its start there include the influence of the resurgence of Islam throughout the Muslim world, access to the Islamic holy places in Jerusalem, the granting of permission for Israeli Muslims to make the pilgrimage to Mecca beginning in 1978, and the 1967 occupation of the West Bank and Gaza, which opened the doors to contact with devout Muslims from the territories who had studied Islam in local and regional schools and who shared their publications, libraries, ideas, and devotion with the Muslim citizens of Israel who had been isolated from the Arab and Muslim world since 1948 (JP, 22 March 1989). In addition, the Arabs of the Triangle were all Muslims with long-established family and political ties with the Arabs of the adjacent West Bank. Galilee, on the other hand, populated by Christian and Muslim Arabs, was not as traditional as the Triangle, and was the center of Arab support for the Communist party. As a result, the rise of the Islamic movement did not gain momentum there until the 1980s (Paz 1990).

The decline of Arab support for Zionist parties, supplanted by the emergence of a variety of parties with an Arab platform, also paved the way for an Islamic party. In the beginning the Communist party was the only party that sufficiently represented Arab political objectives, but it was dominated primarily by Christians and Jews. The only Islamic-related function of the party was a General Islamic Committee, whose objective was to try to return the assets from the Islamic waqfs to the Muslim population. By failing to address the growing needs of the Muslim sector, the Communist party lost its chance to continue as the primary representative of the Muslim Arabs (Paz 1990).

Reuven Paz defines the Islamic movement as a "religious social movement," "distinct from Muslim societies in Egypt or the Palestinians' Islamic Jihad" in that it endeavored to "build a popular movement from below, resting on the broadest possible base, . . . with a preference for Islamic social justice over the ritualistic precepts of the Islamic creed" (Paz 1990, 20). The Islamic party in the Triangle and particularly Umm al-Fahm therefore gained support by striving to meet the needs of the neglected Arab community in Israel. It sought to do this without seeking state funding or protesting the lack thereof. This meant embarking on self-help programs in which municipal services were extended to new neighborhoods, roads repaired or paved, youth centers built, clinic and kindergartens opened, and bus stops constructed with women's and men's sides. Sheikh Abdallah Darwish, the spiritual leader of the Islamic movement, noted that "if the state is not ready to help us, we shall help ourselves" (*JP*, 22 March 1989).

This spirit of self-help took longer to spread into the Galilee, partly because the Islamic movements in the two main Arab sectors of Israel were not of the same mold. With no real national organization to coordinate projects, platforms, and ideologies, the Islamic movements emerged with differences. Based on an analysis of their publications, the Umm al-Fahm movement was more politically motivated, while the Nazareth-based group depicted stronger religious feelings "without the political overtones discernable in their colleagues' writings" (Paz 1990, 22).

Even within the Nazareth movement there are differing opinions on what exactly the Islamic movement is. *Harakat Islamia* (Islamic Movement) in Nazareth is defined as a movement that is not politically but religiously motivated, in that it wants the Muslims of Nazareth to become more religious. In addition, it wants to improve living conditions in all of the quarters of Nazareth and to improve the life of Muslims in the city by building schools, hospitals, community centers, and more mosques. To many there is no difference between being a Muslim and being a member of Harakat Islamia, for both stress the importance of living the tenants of Islam and of working for the well-being of the community. Mazen Mahzumi, one of the leaders of the Islamic list and an elected representative of that list on the municipal council, noted in a 7 September 1989 interview that "all of the Muslims of Nazareth are Harakat Islamia, maybe ninety-eight percent." To him the Islamic movement and the community of Muslims were one and the same. This means that even those Muslims who are not religious and do not want to be involved in an Islamic movement are included as members of the movement by nature of their simply being Muslim. While he did not specify why the other 2 percent were not included as members, it most likely refers to those who have become true Communists in the atheistic sense of the word, or perhaps those few who have converted to Christianity.

Within the fold of Harakat Islamia lies *Qa'ima Islamia* (Islamic list). To some, this is simply the local manifestation of the national Islamic movement, while to others it is the political arm of the movement which seeks to better Nazareth as a whole, as well as its community of Muslims, through involvement in the political process. One resident of the Eastern quarter named Walid said: "I am from Harakat Islamia. I am a Muslim, that's it. I am not from Qa'ima Islamia." Perhaps he was a supporter of another party and resented the implication that his being Muslim should mean that he supports the political movement of Islam.

The Islamic list functions as a local political party and campaigns for voters, just as Jebha or Labor does. Within the Israeli electoral system each political party or list uses a letter or combination of letters to serve as its symbol throughout the campaign, and then within the voting booth, where voters vote by selecting the alphabetic symbol of their preferred party. The Islamic list of Nazareth purposely selected the Arabic letters *Ya-Sin* (Y-S) as their symbol because these two letters are the title of sura 36 in the Quran. Jebha uses the Arabic *Jim-Dal* (J-D), Taqadumia the letter *Fa* (F), the Labor party the letters *Alif-Mim-Ta* (A-M-T), which in Hebrew means truth, and the National Religious party *Ba'* (B). These Arabic letters are used at the municipal level by Arabic-speaking voters. Parties that are also national parties use corresponding Hebrew letters along with the Arabic in national elections. When Nazarenes refer to the Islamic movement or the Islamic list, they often use the Islamic list's voting symbol and call the Islamic political, social, and religious movements by the short, easy, and all-encompassing Ya-Sin (pronounced "ya-seen").

There are a variety of reasons for the rise of an Islamic movement in Nazareth. Mazen Mahzumi indicated that the movement hoped to improve services for Muslims in the city, with goals to construct in the near future a building on land purchased near the Salam Mosque to house a press office, a holy hall, and offices for Muslim doctors and engineers. In addition, the movement hopes eventually to build an Islamic hospital, secondary school, and college—like the Islamic College in Gaza. They would also like to promote volunteerism, as in the Jebha-sponsored work camp each August, which would help both Christians and Muslims. One difference is that women would be given more suitable work that does not require them to work in plain sight on the roads, as they do during the Jebha camp. These goals are an attempt to provide an Islamic alternative to the many Christian institutions and schools in town and make up for the lack of municipal institutions.

Another way in which the movement felt it could improve the lot of Muslims and their Christian brothers in Nazareth was to run against the Communist-influenced Jebha party. While many Muslims had originally embraced Jebha, growing dissatisfaction with the lack of services and the apparent neglect of Muslims and their neighborhoods also served to propel the Islamic movement into the political arena. For example, Shibly, a campaign worker for the Islamic list, explained on election day that the primary reason for Muslims creating their own party was their frustration with the long-time dominance of Jebha. He related how during a previous fasting month of Ramadan, Muslims had hung banners with Quranic verses across streets in the Muslim quarters, only to have them removed by municipal workers. The Muslims, feeling disappointed, petitioned the municipality for an answer. According to Shibly, no answer was given, and it was only later that they learned of the municipal code requiring a permit to hang banners. Even though during the next Ramadan permits were obtained and banners were hung throughout the town, Muslims use this as an example of why the Muslims decided to take on city hall. Shibly also noted that the Communists had made verbal attacks against Islam, God, religion, and their imam.

That same day, a visit with three young men in their twenties revealed further disgust with Jebha. Two of the young men, whose car was decorated with Islamic list posters, called Mayor Ziyad a kafir (heathen or unbeliever) because he was not a practicing Muslim and because he was a "drunk." They also accused their friend of being a kafir because he, as a Muslim, supported Jebha. The two explained that the improvements in Nazareth were not the doings of Jebha, but rather those of the foreign Christian churches. When the two young men used harsh profanity in reference to Jebha, their friend from Jebha accused them of hypocrisy, becasue they professed piety and support for the Islamic movement, and yet they profaned.

This dislike for Jebha also stemmed from the fact that most Muslims in Nazareth lived in the newer neighborhoods on the outskirts of town where sewer lines had not yet been extended and roads not yet paved. They felt that municipal funds were going toward projects that benefited only the loyal supporters of Jebha. One year before the election, the residents of the Safafra quarter wrote an open letter to the mayor protesting the levying of a high sewer tax to be used to extend the line into their neighborhood. They noted that the residents of the quarter were poor laborers or unemployed who were unable to meet such demands. They wondered how the money in the municipal budget had been used and what had been done with the loans and grants from the government (*al-Senara*, 27 May 1988) (fig. 39).

Two months later, the residents of the Safafra quarter published a second open letter to the mayor, signed by at least twenty-seven residents. In it they suggested that the most important concern of the mayor should be "the sewer and garbage our children swim in, or the rats which scare the cats, or the flying insects which can be overwhelming at times." They then sarcastically offered to forgive the mayor if he was not able to attend to these important matters because of more pressing needs, like supporting the revolution in Afghanistan or attacking the Islamic movement in Nazareth. They suggested that if the mayor was ever at his office or in Nazareth, he would see the "wretchedness" of the town in which garbage is collected only once a

Fig. 39. Sewer installation in the Sharqiya quarter

month, streetlights remain broken, and residents use perfume to cover the stench of the open sewers which flow in the streets where children play. These items, they said, are trivial compared to important concerns like erecting a hundred-thousand-dollar statue of Hagar in the town park which "looks like an ape and is used as a public urinal," holding a celebration in honor of the October Revolution, or hosting a banquet "during the height of Ramadan (with alcoholic beverages, of course!)" They concluded by asking that sewer and water lines be installed soon, rather than at the intended completion date in three or four years (*al-Senara*, 17 June 1988).

Islamic list councilman Mazen Mahzumi, in a 27 April 1989 interview, said that there had been no justice for the Muslims of Nazareth until now because of the Communist control of the municipality. He accused mayor Tawfiq Ziyad of being a Muslim in name only, of always being drunk, of turning Nazareth from a religious city into a kafir city, and of giving more help and money to the churches and followers of his party than to Muslims, many of whom had supported the mayor in previous elections because he was a Muslim. Mazen prefers a mayor who would help both Christians and Muslims. He said he would prefer that deputy mayor Ramiz Jerayseh, a Christian, be mayor, as opposed to Ziyad. He stressed that the Islamic list was organized in opposition to the Communists and not against the Christians, noting that Christians and Muslims believe in God, but Communists do not.

Suheil Diyab, a member of the Communist party who serves as the party secretary, described his view of the Islamic-Communist contest in Nazareth during a 3 May 1989 interview from his third-floor office at Jebha headquarters in the Communist-owned building called Beit Sadaqa. He described the Islamic movement as a "political movement in religious wrapping." According to Diyab, there are many reasons for the rise of the movement.

First, he noted the high rate of unemployment in Nazareth, at about 24 percent, as well as the general economic and political problems experienced by Arabs in Israel. These problems, he said, cause people to "connect with mystic thoughts," or in other words, to return to religion and the mosque as a solution to their problems. Second, Diyab noted the rise of Hamas in the occupied territories, and the influence they have wielded on the Islamic movement inside Israel. He accused the Israeli government of supporting the movement in order to undermine the power of the Communists and leftists, who call for two states for two peoples—an acceptable peace proposal. He then accused Israel of supporting the Islamic movement, which proposes an Islamic state for all of Palestine, because Israel knows such a solution is impossible and will therefore never result in Israel having to give up

part of the territory it now controls (this view of an Islamic state controlling all the land is more representative of the views of Hamas than
the Islamic movement inside Israel).

Third, he explained that the movement is a movement "organized solely against Jebha," and that the cooperative social works they
perform are only to gain support. He explained that, unlike Jebha, the
Islamic party is not working on national issues like a solution to the
Palestine problem, land confiscations, or equality, and as a result it
would lose out on political issues, although because of poor municipal
services in Nazareth, the party has a platform and a cause. While the
party may succeed at the local level, Diyab sees its level of influence as
limited, because the Muslims are part of a mixed Christian-Muslim
population who are connected nationally and not religiously; thus
Muslims can never achieve the power and influence of the Islamic parties in Jordan or Egypt.

In a 3 May 1989 interview, several members of the Far family,
who are also members of Jebha, expressed concern over the rise of the
Islamic party. They noted that while the Islamic party distributed a
handbill condemning the suppression of Islam in the USSR and Soviet
actions against Muslims in Afghanistan, they wrote nothing about Israeli actions on the Temple Mount/Haram al-Sharif in Jerusalem. To
the Far family, this condemnation of Soviet/Communist actions but
not of Israeli actions is clear evidence that the Islamic list is supported
by the government of Israel as a deterrent to the power of the communists in Israel. The family explained that they are not against Muslims,
but that they oppose the involvement of religion in politics or fanaticism in any religion. They saw those who voted for the Islamic party as
"simple-minded and easily persuaded."

Campaigning for the election came in many forms. Posters were
scattered throughout town on walls, buildings, poles, and cars (fig. 40).
Newspapers and leaflets were distributed by parties describing platforms and, in the case of Jebha, illustrating through photographs and
the written word all that they, through their leadership, had done for
the betterment of Nazareth. Supporters held rallies at election headquarters and throughout the quarters at the homes of neighborhood
representatives; they made house-to-house visits and advertised in the
local newspapers; and debate and discussion continued among Nazarenes in their workplaces, neighborhoods, and homes. One supporter
of Jebha, a Christian, when asked on the street about the Islamic movement, spoke negatively of the movement but only in a hushed voice.
Christian young men when referring to the movement would often
pull down from their chins as if pulling at a beard, the likes of which
now adorn the faces of many of the more fervent Muslims.

Another form of campaigning was described in a 6 April 1989 interview with psychologist Sami Debini, whose brother George was the number six candidate for city council from the Taqadumia party. He described the "spoken propaganda" used by Jebha: teams were sent out to visit in the homes of Christians and there suggest that the Islamic movement, if successful, would begin to prohibit alcohol and to enforce Islamic dress standards, as had been done in Iran. They would then offer the services of Jebha in protecting the Christians from the Islamic movement. Debini then stressed that "Jebha is the threat to Christians and not the Islamic movement," citing Communist control of the Greek Orthodox bishop, priests, and council as an example of their adverse influence. In defence of the Islamic movement, he noted how during the campaign they had visited with members of the Christian clergy to reassure them that theirs was not an anti-Christian movement and had published an article which offered Easter greetings to the Christians of Nazareth. He said he believes in their hand of fellowship and sees Jebha as feeling threatened, and therefore resorting to various means to weaken their opponent by trying to exploit Christian-Muslim differences. Several Jebha officials, when asked about the "spoken propaganda" to scare the Christians into supporting Jebha, denied the allegations of Debini.

Before the election, the Islamic list campaigned by distributing handbills, running notices in the local newspapers, and publishing

Fig. 40. Campaign posters of mayoral candidates from Jebha (top center), Islamic list (left), and Taqadumia (center)

their own newspaper, called *Ya-Sin*. Articles in the weekly newspaper denounced charges of "racial and religious bigotry and conspiracy against the unity of the people" and then countered the charge that "Islam is against Christianity," with a reminder that Muslims follow the tenets "To you, your religion and to us, our religion, . . . there is no compulsion in religion, . . . he who harms a Dhimmi [non-Muslim] harms me and who harms me harms God" (*al-Senara*, 13 January 1989). The front-page headline in the first edition of the party newspaper said: "Nazareth resounds: Yes to the Ways of the Prophets, Yes to the Unity of Its Inhabitants, No to Atheism, Promiscuity, and to Those Who Spread Mutual Conflict." From the headline alone it is obvious that the movement was trying to calm the fears of Christians by mentioning all the prophets, most of whom are common to both Christianity and Islam, and not just the prophet Mohammad. The article accused the mayor of spreading lies that the Islamic movement was racist, that the movement would turn Nazareth into a second Beirut, and that Jebha was the only way to save Nazareth from this expected calamity. The article went on to explain how the leaders of the Islamic movement had met with leaders of the Christian community and reassured them that that such lies would adversely affect the brotherhood of Nazareth. During the meeting, Christian leaders explained that their community was not weak and did not need Jebha's protection. The article also explained that Islam and Christianity are both revealed religions and therefore have much in common, while communism and religion have nothing in common (*Ya-Sin*, 24 February 1989).

The rise of the Islamic list in Nazareth became a reality on 28 February 1989, when in the municipal elections, the Islamic list surprised most residents of the town by receiving 30 percent of the 21,950 votes cast, good for six seats on the nineteen-seat municipal council (table 18). When compared with results of the 25 October 1983 election, Jebha's support showed a significant decline from 65 percent to 51 percent. Taqadumia was the other loser to the Islamic list.

An analysis of the election results, in which 76 percent of the electorate voted, shows that the Islamic list received the highest percentage of votes in those precincts that were located in predominantly Muslim quarters (fig. 41). Precinct 49 in the Bir al-Amir quarter had the highest percentage of votes for the Islamic list. This quarter, on the southern edge of town, is where many Muslim refugees from the nearby village of Mujeidil have put down new roots. Twenty-three percent of the votes went to the Jebha list. In the 1983 census the subdistrict that included this precinct showed that 90 percent of its residents were Muslim, which indicates that not all Muslims voted for the Islamic list. Precincts 45 and 46 in the lower Safafra neighborhood also registered

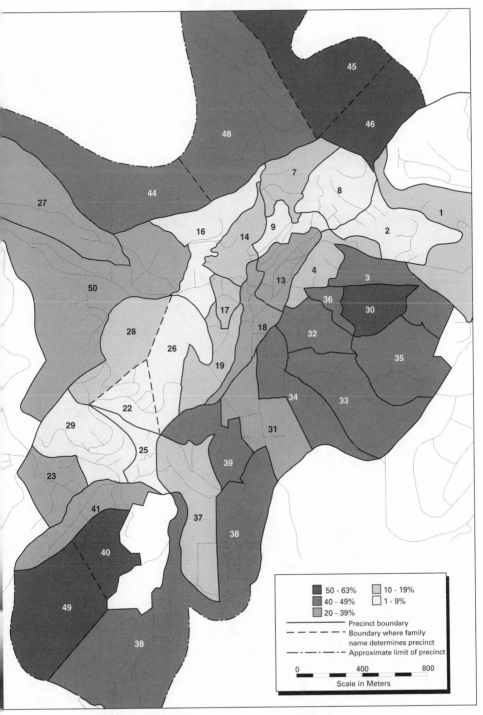

Fig. 41. 1989 Nazareth municipal election, percentage vote by precinct:
Islamic list

TABLE 18. 1983, 1989, and 1993 municipal election results

Party	1983 Votes	1983 %	1983 Seats	1989 Votes	1989 %	1989 Seats	1994 Votes	1994 %	1994 Seats
Jebha list	11,688	65.1	11	11,141	50.8	10	13,424	56.4	11
Taqadumia (Progressive)	3,734	20.8	4	1,769	8.1	2			
NRP (Jewish)	1,001	5.6	1	1,028	4.7	1	1,270	5.3	1
Labor	1,245	6.9	1	506	2.3	0			
Mapam	287	1.6	0						
Islamic list				6,593	30.0	6	1,532	6.4	1
Arab Democratic				485	2.2	0	978	4.1	1
Sons of Village				428	1.9	0	1,030	4.3	1
Risala list							3,789	15.9	3
Sons of Nazareth							1,346	5.7	1
Independent Islamic Bloc							450	1.9	0
Totals	17,955		17	21,950		19	23,819		19

high support for the Islamic list, with 55 and 57 percent of the votes, respectively. In the Safafra quarter, Muslims make up 77 percent of the population. These two quarters, composed primarily of refugees and newcomers to Nazareth and a strong majority of Muslims, are only now seeing roads paved and sewer lines hooked up. The seven precincts in the Sharqiya quarter all gave the Islamic list over 40 percent of their votes, the highest percentage of 57 percent being in precinct 30 at the center of the quarter. The two census subdistricts that generally correspond with these seven precincts are 98.5 percent and 96.4 percent Muslim. As in the other quarters showing strong support for the Islamic list, these precincts included many Jebha supporters, some of the precincts being almost evenly divided between the two main parties.

Jebha's universal support found its strongest constituency in those quarters with the highest percentage of Christians (fig. 42). Precinct 8 in the heart of the Rum quarter gave 82 percent of its votes to Jebha, 12 percent to Taqadumia, and only 1 percent (seven votes) to the Islamic list. Two adjacent precincts in the quarter tallied 71 and 73 percent for Jebha, with 4 and 9 percent respectively for the Islamic list. The fact that each precinct recorded votes for the Islamic list helps to show how scattered Muslims have become in Nazareth.

That the Islamic list was not supported by all Muslims in Nazareth was evidenced also by the lighted campaign symbols that deco-

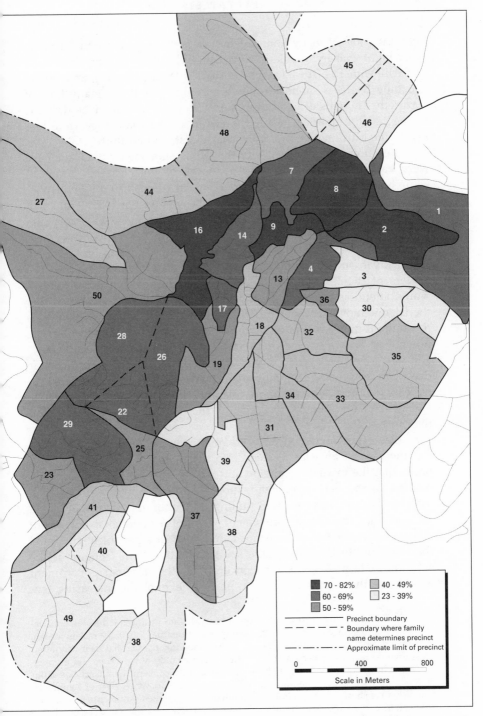

Fig. 42. 1989 Nazareth municipal election, percentage vote by precinct: Jebha list

rated the roofs of many homes. For several months before the election, every night, Nazareth took on a Christmaslike air as red Jim-Dals (J-Ds) and Alif-Mim-Tas (A-M-Ts), green Ya-Sins (Y-Ss), Fas (Fs), and 'Ains , and blue Bas (Bs) shone throughout the basin and the many hills of Nazareth. The reds of Jebha were found in every quarter, including the strong Muslim quarters, while the greens of the Islamic list were limited to the Muslim quarters of the south, east, and north (fig. 43).

Reactions to and reasons for the strong showing by the Islamic list were varied. Pastor Riyah Abu al-'Assal, of the Nazareth Anglican Church and Taqadumia party leadership, mentioned in a 9 September 1989 interview that on election night he visited the Islamic election center near the Salam mosque. Party members came to escort him there. At the victory celebration, the leaders of the Islamic Movement assured the pastor that they supported Muslim-Christian brotherhood. When Riyah spoke, he too emphasized the need for brotherhood. The leaders of the Islamic list had hoped that invited Christian leaders would attend as a sign of cooperation and friendship. Riyah noted that the Islamic movement was in Israel to stay, as evidenced by their wins throughout the Arab municipalities. He suggested that the Islamic movement was a "wave of fundamentalism that comes and goes," adding, "I am not worried; my relationship [with them] is cordial." He described how within the movement there are those who are more fanatical and those who are more tolerant, cooperative, and intellectual; and their victory should be used for "the betterment of Nazareth and the cause of Palestine."[12]

One priest suggested that perhaps it was the government that had put the idea of an Islamic party into the minds of Muslims. He also noted that the mixing of religion and politics is dangerous; such a mix has led to the decline of civilizations. Another prominent Christian saw the Islamic movement as pulling the communities further apart. He said that the Islamic movement was not a nationalist movement and therefore the Christian Arabs could not feel a part of it. He noted that their motto is "Islam is the solution" rather than "religion is the solution." He also expressed concern that the national government would use the rise of the Islamic party to exploit the increasing ten-

---

[12] The entry and surprising success of the Muslim Brotherhood in the national elections in Jordan in 1989 brought similar responses from the Christian Arabs in Jordan. Many were concerned about the Islamists' strong showing, fearing that their newfound power would result in a ban on alcohol, greater segregation of the sexes, and more Islamic teachings in the schools. Others expressed little concern. One Christian commented: "As a Christian from the Middle East I have no fears whatsoever of genuine Islam. What we should be careful of are distorted or exaggerated sentiments that impose restrictions reflecting social traditions rather than religious dictates" (*Salt Lake Tribune*, 13 November 1989).

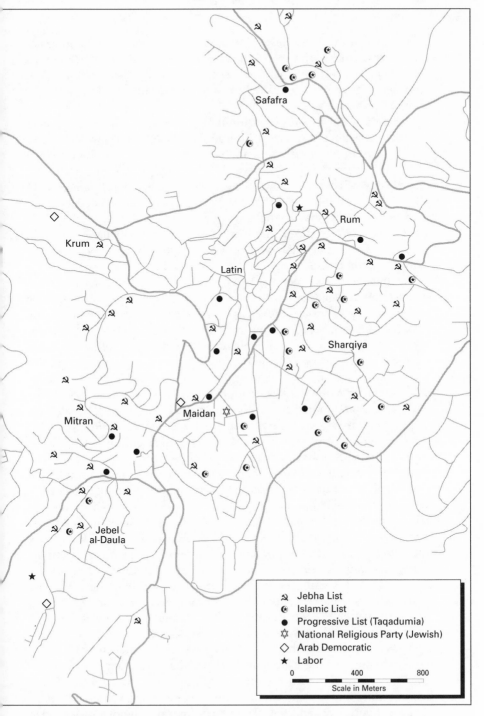

Fig. 43. Distribution of lighted party symbols for the 1989 municipal election

sions between the two groups. He felt that as of now, the Communists were the only ones with the strength and resources to stand against the Islamic movement, but that increased support for the Christian communities from abroad could help restore the declining Christian presence in Nazareth.

Samir Rok, an official with the Ministry of the Interior who works on elections, explained in a 30 April 1989 interview that more adult voters in Nazareth are Christian than Muslim, but many of the Christians chose not to vote because all of the party's candidates for mayor were Muslim. Antoine Shaheen, of the Labor party, lamented in a 7 March 1989 interview that his party had not succeeded because Christians saw Jebha as the only viable opposition to the Islamic Movement. He advocated that Christians also leave Jebha and form a Christian-Democratic alliance, which would then have direct dialogue with the Islamic Movement.

After-the-fact reflections by former and present Jebha members suggested that Jebha had unknowingly helped in the rise of the Islamic movement by ignoring the refugee/Muslim neighborhoods on the outskirts of town. Riyad Debini, who at one time worked with the academic section in Jebha, in a 2 September 1989 interview told of repeated warnings by members of the Jebha council of a rising wave of religious opposition to Jebha; in order to counter the swell, Jebha needed to be more involved with the residents of the newer neighborhoods. The leaders of Jebha ignored the warnings and failed to go into Bir al-Amir or Safafra quarters, saying it was just the government trying to divide the Arabs. As a result, the residents of these quarters turned to the Islamic movement. Johny Jahshan, who represented the merchant section of Jebha and who was their number-eleven man for municipal council, in a 5 July 1989 interview also suggested that the Islamic movement succeeded partially because Jebha was not rooted in the new neighborhoods on the periphery, even though they thought they were. He also felt that the Islamic movement succeeded because of the lack of municipal services in peripheral neighborhoods, the influence of outside events, and the efforts of the government to divide the Arabs.

Abd al-Rahman, the number-three councilman elected from Jebha, who is from a prominent Muslim refugee family in the Safafra quarter, explained that Muslims in his neighborhood voted for the Islamic list because they were poor and uneducated, and thought that religion would solve all their problems. Two young men had told him they had voted for the Islamic list because they had been caught up in the "hurricane." He said that if asked, people in the new neighborhoods would have to admit that improvements had been made in their neighborhoods, and that they voted only for religious reasons. He feels that this euphoria over religious solutions to political problems will eventually dwindle.

Christian concern stems partly from the fact that for the first time in memory, this once-dominant community might have to submit to rule by the Muslim community. For centuries, both communities were ruled by outsiders—Ottoman Turks, the British, and then the Israeli military; the Christians generally had the upper hand, but never complete control. As outside control gradually decreased, local rule came under the direction of Christian/Muslim coalitions, Zionist-affiliated parties, and then the multicommunal Communists, but never just Christians or Muslims. Now that the Communists are weakened and the Islamic movement is on the rise, the lack of a strong ruling power has created heightened tension.

Al-Haj (1985, 131) noted similar occurrences in Shefar 'Am, where, following the 1948 war, the elimination of economic interdependence and Christian hegemony resulted in "increasingly fierce" intercommunal conflicts. However, "the recent establishment of Muslim hegemony heralded a new era of continuous stability." He summarized that communal conflict increases as hegemony decreases, and that as long as there is a clear focus of power, relations will remain stable. This hypothesis suggests that Nazareth is headed for continued political upheaval until the Islamic party either gains outright control or the Communists regain hegemony; it is highly unlikely that a Christian party will rise to power.

The Islamic Movement has continued to be active in municipal affairs since the election. In November 1989, the movement won six seats out of twenty-one on the Nazareth Worker's Council (Landau 1993, 161). The movement has also sought to make good on its promises. Money has been raised for the Islamic center, to be built near the main mosque; a neighborhood youth center has been established in a rented building in the Safafra quarter; food and clothing have been distributed to the poor during Ramadan; and a protest rally has been held. The May 1989 protest was over a proposed increased in municipal taxes; and it included a parade through town past the municipal building, marchers waving the green banners of Islam, and then on past the Basilica of the Annunciation, where chants of "Allahu akhbar" (God is the greatest) competed with bells inviting parishioners to evening mass for Mary (fig. 44).

Members of the movement have been quick to visit both Muslims and Christians during times of mourning. When a Greek Orthodox woman and her three children were killed in a car accident, leaders of the Islamic Movement came to offer condolences. Likewise, when Selim Nusseri was murdered by Muslim young men, the Islamic

Fig. 44. Islamic Movement march to protest a tax increase

Movement distributed leaflets condemning the crime, calling for justice to be met and offering condolences to the family.

One Christian family from the Safafra quarter related that soon after the elections, representatives from the Islamic movement visited
their home to alleviate their fears, to let them know that they are not
against Christians, and to offer any help if needed. The national leader
of the Islamic movement, Sheikh Darwish, even visited Christian
leaders in Nazareth shortly after the election to reassure them, to stress
that Christians and Muslims had long struggled together as brothers in
a common cause and "to thwart all attempts of those powers which
strive to agitate sectarian pride among the Palestinians inside Israel."
He noted in a second newspaper interview that he would share his
bread with his "non-Muslim, Arab, Palestinian brethren," and that he
would also share in both their joys and sorrows. He quoted the prophet

Mohammad, "He who hurts a dhimmi, hurts me," and then added that any "Muslim who looks at a Christian with racist feelings has no religion" (*al-Senara*, 17 March, 8 April 1989).

The six men from the Islamic list who sat on the municipal council from 1989 to 1993 were not trained politicians. Of their known occupations, three were builders, one a mechanic, and one an unemployed builder. That they were able to receive 30 percent of the vote at their first entrance into the political arena is indeed amazing. One Christian warned following the 1989 election that now that they had succeeded once, all it would take was better organization and the addition of more qualified candidates, and they might one day be able to control the municipality. That control of the municipality has yet to happen. In fact results of the November 1993 election indicate that the Islamic movement has splintered and its political power has weakened.

Suheil Diyab indicated in a 26 April 1994 interview that the first signs of schism occurred in 1991 over differences of opinion as to how to administer the hajj registration revenues and whether or not to join in coalition with Jebha in municipal development projects. Eventually three parties emerged out of the once united Islamic movement. At the core of the split was a difference of opinion over relations between Nazareth's Islamic movement and broader-based Islamic movements. Qa'ima Islamia, headed by Mazen Mahzumi, is an independent Islamic list which functions only at the municipal level and seeks to maintain its independence from outside influences. While, according to a 22 April 1994 interview with leader Salman Abu Ahmad, *Qa'ima Risala* (the message list)—also known as Harekat Islamia—is part of the Islamic movements in Israel and throughout the Islamic world. It seeks to promote the status of Muslims at local, national, and international levels. It also hopes to provide a more educated list of candidates to represent Nazareth's Muslims. The third and least successful party— the Independent Islamic Bloc, was formed by former council member Omar Sharara, who seems to be more interested in leading his own party than professing any specific ideology or loyalty.

Qa'ima Risala was the most successful of the three Islamic parties, gaining 15.9 percent of the votes and three seats on the municipal council. Qa'ima Islamia received only 6.4 percent of the votes, good for only one seat on the council. Mazen Mahzumi noted in a 26 April 1994 interview that one of the reasons Qa'ima Risala outperformed his party is that it received additional financing from outside Islamic sources and because it is supported by some of Nazareth's larger, more established Muslim families. His party, on the other hand, is locally funded and supported by less influential and smaller families, many of whom are refugees.

The big winner in the 1993 municipal elections was the still influential Jebha, winning 56.4 percent of the votes and a majority of
eleven seats on the council. Tawfiq Ziyad was also reelected as mayor,[13]
with 62.5 percent of the votes. Jebha member Suheil Diyab, who serves
as one of two deputy mayors, attributes his party's success to several factors, not only that recent political and economic improvements have
weakened calls for change by Muslims, but also that Jebha represents all
of Nazareth's communities. Jebha member Johny Jahshan added in a
26 April 1994 interview that Jebha's success could also be attributed to
the lack of any other alternative party for Christians and to the fact that
the municipality, under Jebha control and learning from past mistakes,
had begun to emphasize development in peripheral quarters by building more schools, paving more roads, and installing more services.
Also influential was that one-time rival Taqadumia failed to participate in the elections after attempts to form a broad-based coalition with
several other parties, including Labor and Meretz, failed.

With the breakup and decline of the Islamic movement, Christians in Nazareth are breathing somewhat easier than in 1989. They
still worry about possible Islamic dominance, but they now realize that
many Muslims, like Christians, recognize that religion is not the solution for Nazareth's political needs. As long as the Islamic parties stick
to improving municipal services and bettering all sectors of Nazareth,
the Christians will be tolerant. But at the first sign of enforced Islamic
principles or at the first threat of any kind to the already dwindling
Christian presence in Nazareth, the Christians might retaliate by organizing a rival Christian party which would escalate the battle from political to religious. In regard to this potentially divisive situation an editorial gave an appropriate warning to the many segments of Nazareth:
"There is no existence for our people except in the totality of all its patriotic and responsible sects, movements, and parties and there will
never be an existence for us if the fire of sectarianism ignites in one of
our parts" (al-Senara, 3 March 1989).

The entrance of Islamic parties into Nazareth's politics has been
peaceful and beneficial. It has helped to include the new Muslims in
the political process and alleviated the alienation they have long en-

[13]Mayor Ziyad was killed in a 5 July 1994 head-on collision as he was returning
from the welcome ceremony for PLO chief Yasser Arafat in Jericho (NYT, 6 July 1994).
Jebha then nominated Ramiz Jerayseh, a Christian who had been serving as deputy
mayor, to fill out the remainder of the four-year term. The Jebha-dominated council
ratified the Jebha nomination of Jerayseh. Jerayseh is respected among Nazarenes and
has played a visible role in the city for many years, often acting in behalf of Mayor
Ziyad as he attended to duties in the Knesset or the Communist party. This change in
leadership might have a calming effect on Nazareth's political tensions and serve to
lessen the concerns of its Christian community.

dured. It has also forced Jebha and the Communists to reevaluate their role in Nazareth and hopefully has made them more sensitive to trying to serve all segments of the society. Nazareth's problems, like those of all Arab municipalities in Israel, are challenging. Overcoming those challenges will require the cooperation of all its communities and all its parties.

7

Conclusion

Nazareth's communal composition has been significantly influenced by its location in the hills of Galilee, in a land called Holy, Israel, and Palestine, and in a region of the world identified with such terms as the Fertile Crescent, Levant, Middle East, Arab, and Islamic. To its holy sites, protective hills, and fertile basin, located just beyond several major transportation routes and in the middle of a strategic and worshiped land, have come a variety of peoples with multiple identities. These identities are based on several different characteristics including ethnicity, nationality, religion, politics, and place of origin, and they have varying labels: Arab, Israeli, Palestinian, Muslim, Christian, Orthodox, Latin, Catholic, Maronite, Copt, Communist, and refugee.

As in other places inhabited by mixed groups, Nazareth has known communal conflict and contention, but most of the conflicts have been the result of outsiders fighting for control, not just of Nazareth, but of all the land. Local conflicts by actual Nazarenes have been more sporadic and have not always been communal in nature, even though noncommunal disputes, such as those in the political arena, are often attributed to communal differences. Several factors have helped to ensure that the combustible mix of peoples in Nazareth has not exploded. First, within its diversity Nazareth has also found unity. Muslims and Christians join together within the larger community of Arabs; Communists and Islamists find common aspirations in being Palestinian; and refugee and resident share desires to earn an income, own homes, and live amid family and friends.

Second, communities have often joined forces in opposition to adversaries. The Arab communities of the Middle East have long joined in trying to throw off the control of outsiders, whether they be Christian crusaders, Muslim Turks, or British and French imperialists. More recently, the unifying foe has been the State of Israel. This has placed Israeli Arabs in a precarious situation, for they are citizens of Israel as well as Arabs who resent the creation of a Jewish state on what they consider to be Arab lands. Slowly they are learning to balance the two identities as they work within the Israeli system to bring about their goals. Part of the popularity of the Communist party is based on its being for many years one of the few legitimate venues in which Israeli Arabs have been able to work toward peaceful change.

Third, common religious beliefs and mutual respect strengthen ties. All Nazarenes, Christian and Muslim, pray to Allah, Arabic for God. They also revere as holy the city's two most famous residents—Jesus and Mary—which brings together the two communities for holidays that honor the two. Teachings of Mohammad that admonish Muslims to respect people of the book—Jews and Christians—along with teachings of Jesus to love your neighbor have had a positive impact on Nazarenes. The well-worn phase that speaks of brotherhood is truly believed.

Fourth, the separation of religion and politics has, until recently, alleviated significant strain on communal relations. Nazareth has been able to avoid the problems of its Levantine neighbor Lebanon, where the Christian-Muslim rift has become institutionalized in the form of political parties and militias divided along communal lines. Jebha, Taqadumia, Labor, and other political parties have been able to transcend sectarian divisions and provide a common ground for members of all communities.

Fifth, for many Nazarenes cooperation is the product of a long established status quo in which residents of all communities realize that if Nazareth is to maintain its peaceful coexistence, tolerance and civility need to be maintained. For this reason Christians are hesitant to form Christian-based parties and many Muslims reject the Islamic parties. Nazarenes of all communities consciously make decisions based on whether or not it will upset the precarious, but lasting, balance.

Finally, separation into quarters helps to maintain accommodation among communities. As in other cities of the region, the peoples of Nazareth found that living in segregated communal clusters not only strengthened community cohesiveness, but also helped to keep conflict to a minimum. This segregation manifests itself in the formation of separate quarters based on communal allegiance. The causes for such segregation were varied and have changed over time. Islamic influences, in which minority communities traditionally lived in quarters in order to facilitate tax collection and the providing of community services, stimulated the growth of ethnic and religious quarters throughout the Islamic realm. As Christians moved to the Muslim village of Nazareth, they no doubt perpetuated these patterns, which continued to persist under the influence of the Ottoman millet system. Memories of Christian-Muslim conflict during the Crusades and knowledge of ongoing problems in other parts of the region kept suspicions high and also encouraged separation. Close proximity to the protection and sustenance provided by the Franciscan monastery at the site of the Annunciation influenced the congregating of Western-Rite Christians into what would become known as the Latin quarter. Similar factors of family cohesiveness, common origins, proximity to their site of the Annunciation and the ongoing feud between Eastern and Western Christianity motivated the Greek Orthodox to gather into the Rum quarter.

Later quarters developed along these and other lines. Family cohesiveness was the main factor in the formation of the Christian Coptic quarter, in which the descendents of one Egyptian Christian gradually filled in a large tract of family land; and Muslim quarters like Jebel Hamuda and al-Sheikh, in which successive generations continue to live in, above, or next to the parent home. The Greek Catholic Mitran and lower Shekun al-Arab quarters developed because church leaders helped in the purchase of land and in the obtaining of loans to build homes. Refugee quarters of Safafra, Jebel al-Daula, and Bir al-Amir emerged as predominantly Muslim quarters when village ties attracted scattered families, unable to return to former homes, to build next to fellow villagers. In the case of the Safafra quarter, land trades with the government also stimulated congregation, in that the land the government offered was restricted to certain locales.

No single reason can explain entirely the development of communal quarters in Nazareth. Islamic attitudes toward minorities; Ottoman laws that governed through the separation of communities; fear of conflict; proximity to holy sites and places of worship; protection, provision, employment, and land provided by religious institutions; and the desire to be with community members, extended families, immigrants from the same region, city, or village, or fellow refugees from the same village all worked together to form the quarters in Nazareth.

These residential patterns of segregation have persisted to this day, but new patterns are emerging under the influence of different factors. Gone are the ruling powers of Islam and Istanbul, which so influenced the formation of traditional Islamic cities and their quarters. Gone too are large tracts of family-owned land waiting to be filled in by successive generations. Gone is the need to live next to protective monasteries or a desire to live near places of worship. Going are the need and desire to live with family and community as improved communication, transportation, and even the demise of strong family ties have motivated some to break with tradition and live beyond established bounds. With the influx of landless migrants and refugees and with many landholding families slowly running out of building property, many Nazarenes must now buy land wherever it is available and affordable. New apartment complexes and housing developments attract residents from all of Nazareth's communities and from all of its quarters, as do hilltop and peripheral neighborhoods, which invite a mix of people who are tired of living in crowded, older, inaccessible sections of town.

The changing quarters of Nazareth indicate a growing change among its communities. Whereas religion was once the identifying mark of a person, today's Nazarenes append religion to other equally important identifying factors. For many, to be Arab, Palestinian, and Israeli, as well as a member of a political party, is just as influential in defining who they are as being Muslim, Latin, or Orthodox, for it is as Israeli Arabs that they join together, Christians and Muslims, in their ongoing quest to be treated as equals in a Jewish state, and it is within the political system that this quest is realized. Bonds of brotherhood have emerged from this common opposition. This oft-mentioned brotherhood has also continued to develop as education and employment have become increasingly integrated, and as commerce has continued to serve as the main meeting and mingling place for Nazarenes. Proximity in politics, jobs, schools, shops, parades, and playgrounds has helped to ease increased proximity in place of residence. When families look for available land, religion of the neighbors is seldom an issue, for they probably already have friends and acquaintances from that community.

The evolution of Nazareth's communities and quarters is by no means complete. It is a process constantly subject to change. Peaceful relations and the beginnings of integrated neighborhoods could all change in the future, just as they have in the past, depending on such factors as the influence of outside rulers or perceived threats to communal existence. Singular events have had and will continue to have long-lasting effects. Positive influences on relations have included a variety of events and actions. Promised protection from Muslim rulers when they granted permission for Christians to settle in Nazareth ensured that relations throughout much of the sixteenth and seventeenth centuries were amicable. The decision of Christian communities to sanction intercommunal marriages with the wife always entering the sect of her husband has significantly ameliorated tensions among Christian communities. The creation of a Jewish state of Israel instead of an Arab state of Palestine necessitated that Christians and Muslims join forces. If the land of Palestine had remained Arab, then perhaps the Christians and Muslims of Nazareth would be experiencing conflicts similar to those of Lebanon's religious communities.

There are also negative influences and events. Inter-Christian rivalries over conversions and intermarriages have subsided, but disputes over joint cemetery use and joint holiday celebrations continue to divide the Christian communities. The linking of communal conflict with nonsectarian feuds is also a problem. Many squabbles in Nazareth identified as either Christian-Christian conflict or Muslim-Christian conflict are in actuality family feuds, economic disputes, or political confrontations. Perhaps the most potentially divisive action has been the formation of an Islamic political movement, which has put a strain on relations and could have significant impact in the future, depending on what course of action the movement takes.

If the Islamic movement goes beyond its promoted polices of merely acting in opposition to the Communists and of striving to better life for all communities in Nazareth, then perhaps a Christian-Muslim conflict might emerge in Nazareth. This could happen if concerned Christians organize themselves politically to offset the rising power of the Islamic movement, but as long as Nazareth remains a part of Israel, this is not likely to happen. It is in Israel's interest both to weaken the strength of the Communist party and to keep Christians and Muslims at odds, thereby weakening the Arab minority, but it is not in its interest to have the two communities in conflict or to have a powerful Islamic movement ruling in Arab municipalities. For now, the Islamic movement is not a threat to communal relations. It has created concern and heightened suspicion, but Christians and Muslims are still friends and neighbors. The next few elections, however, might bring a change. If the Islamic movement gains in power or if the Christian residents of Nazareth feel that their status and position in the city have eroded too far or are too threatened, then perhaps they will create their own religious-based party. The volatile combination of Christian and Muslim political parties could then spill over into other arenas, and communal conflict could emerge. The result would be the abandonment of mixed neighborhoods and increased emigration of Christians.

The experience of Nazareth's communities shows that accommodation is possible in a region of conflict, but that conflict is always a threat. Nazareth's challenge is to learn from its past and continue to recognize that in spite of differences and strong communal loyalties, paths of moderation and accommodation have been paved. The quarters of Nazareth are symbolic of all that is Nazareth. They represent the divisions that exist between the communities in the creation and continuation of segregated quarters based along communal and family lines. They represent the challenges facing a growing Nazareth in which sewer and water lines remain only plans and where refugees from the 1948 war have had to rebuild their lives and homes on new lands. They represent change in which new quarters house families from all of Nazareth's communities. Hope springs from these quarters, for it is here that members of the Muslim, Orthodox, Latin, Catholic, Maronite, Copt, Anglican, and refugee communities have congregated and where coexistence is practiced every day.

Bibliography

Abu al-'Assal, Riyah. 1971. *Al-Yubil al-Mi'awiy.* Nazareth: al-Hakim Press.

Abu-Lughod, Janet. 1987. "The Islamic City: Historic Myth, Islamic Essence, and Contemporary Relevance." *International Journal of Middle Eastern Studies* 19 (May): 155–76.

Agnew, John A., John Mercer, and David E. Sopher, eds. 1984. *The City in Cultural Context.* Boston: Allen and Unwin.

Annuaire de l'Eglise Catholique en Terre Sainte. 1993. Jerusalem: Franciscan Printing Press.

Ashworth, John. 1869. *Walks in Canaan.* Manchester: Tubbs and Brook.

Ateek, Naim Stifan. 1989. *Justice, and Only Justice.* Maryknoll, N.Y.: Orbis Books.

Baedeker, Karl. 1912. *Palestine and Syria.* Leipzig: Karl Baedeker.

Bagatti, Bellarmino. 1969. *Excavations in Nazareth.* Vol. 1. Jerusalem: Franciscan Printing Press.

———. 1984. *Gli Scavi di Nazaret.* Vol. 2. Jerusalem: Franciscan Printing Press.

Bar-Gal, Yoram, and Arnon Soffer. 1981. *Geographical Changes in the Traditional Arab Villages in Northern Israel.* Durham: University of Durham Centre for Middle Eastern and Islamic Studies, Occasional Papers Series no. 9.

Bartlett, Samuel Colcord. 1977. *From Egypt to Palestine.* 1879. Reprint, New York: Arno Press.

Baruch, Nissim. 1966. *Development of the City of Nazareth and Ways for Its Economic Prosperity.* Jerusalem: Office of Arab Affairs. (In Hebrew)

Ben-Arieh, Yehoshua. 1975. "The Growth of Jerusalem in the Nineteenth Century." *Annals of the Association of American Geographers* 65 (June): 252–69.

Benvenisti, Meron. 1970. *The Crusaders in the Holy Land.* Jerusalem: Israel Universities Press.

Betts, Robert. 1978. *Christians in the Arab East.* Athens: Lycabettus Press.

al-Bishara. 1985–90. Nazareth: The al-Nour Society.

Boal, Frederick. 1976. "Ethnic Residential Segregation." In *Spatial Processes and Form,* ed. D. T. Herbert and R. J. Johnston. London: John Wiley and Sons.

Bowman, Glenn. 1986. "Unholy Struggle on Holy Ground." *Anthropology Today* 2 (June): 14–17.

Briand, Jean. 1982. *The Judeo-Christian Church of Nazareth.* Translated by Mildred Deuel. Jerusalem: Franciscan Printing Press.

Browne, J. Ross. 1868. *Yusef; or The Journey of the Frangi: A Crusade in the East.* New York: Harper and Brothers.

Burckhardt, John Lewis. 1822. *Travels in Syria and the Holy Land.* London: John Murray.

Carrouges, Michel. 1956. *Soldier of the Spirit: The Life of Charles de Foucauld.* Translated by Marie-Christine Hellin. New York: G. P. Putnam's Sons.

Carse, Raphael. 1985. *The Arab Christian Communities of Israel.* Jerusalem: Israel Interfaith Association.

Census of Israel. 1961, 1972, 1983. Jerusalem: Government of Israel.

Census of Palestine. 1922, 1931. Jerusalem: British Mandate Administration.

Chacour, Elias. 1992. *We Belong to the Land.* New York: Harper Collins.

Chitham, E. J. 1986. *The Coptic Community in Egypt: Spatial and Social Change.* Durham: University of Durham Centre for Middle Eastern and Islamic Studies, Occasional Papers Series no. 32.

Colbi, Saul P. 1988. *A History of the Christian Presence in the Holy Land.* Lanham: University Press of America.

Conder, Claude R. 1878. *Tent Work in Palestine.* London: Richard Bently and Sons.

Cragg, Kenneth. 1991. *The Arab Christian: A History in the Middle East.* Louisville, Ky.: Westminister/John Knox Press.

Davison, Roderic H. 1954. "Turkish Attitudes Concerning Christian-Muslim Equality in the Nineteenth Century." *American Historical Review* 59 (July): 844–64.

Efrat, Elisha. 1976. *Towns and Urbanization in Israel.* Israel: Achiasaf Publishing House.

Ehlers, Eckhart. 1992. "The City of the Islamic Middle East." *Colloquium Geographicum* 22: 89–107.

Eickelman, Dale. 1974. "Is There an Islamic City? The Making of a Quarter in a Moroccan Town." *International Journal of Middle East Studies* 5: 274–94.

Eldar, Yishai. 1990. "Greek Patriarchate Suspends Ecumenical Dialogue." *Christian Life in Israel,* no. 31 (Winter 1989/90): 3.

English, Paul W. 1967. "Nationalism, Secularism, and the Zoroastrians of Kirman: The Impact of Modern Forces on an Ancient Middle Eastern Minority." In *Cultural Geography: Selected Readings.* ed. Fred E. Dohrs and Lawerence M. Sommers. New York: Thomas Y. Crowall Co.

———. 1973. "Geographical Perspectives on the Middle East: The Passing of the Ecological Trilogy." In *Geographers Abroad: Essays on the Problems and Prospects of Research in Foreign Areas,* ed. Marvin W. Mikesell. Chicago: University of Chicago Department of Geography Research Paper no. 152.

Falah, Ghazi. 1983. *Patterns of Spontaneous Bedouin Settlement in Galilee.* Durham: University of Durham Department of Geography, Occasional Publications, n.s. no. 18.

al-Fusuh al-Majid. 1988–89. Nazareth: Greek Orthodox Community Council.

For Better Living. 1964. Tel Aviv: Ministry of Housing, State of Israel.

Freese, Jacob R. 1869. *The Old World: Palestine, Syria, and Asia Minor.* Philadelphia: J. B. Lippincott.

Friedman, Saul S. 1982. *Land of Dust: Palestine at the Turn of the Century.* Washington, D.C.: University Press of America.

Gauthier, Paul. 1965. *Christ, the Church and the Poor.* Translated by Edward Fitzgerald. Westminister, Md.: Newman Press.

Goitein, S. D. 1971. *A Mediterranean Society: The Jewish Communities of the Arab World as Portrayed in the Documents of the Cairo Geniza,* vol. 2, *The Community.* Berkeley: University of California Press.

Greenshields, Thomas H. 1980. "'Quarters' and Ethnicity." In *The Changing Middle Eastern City,* ed. G. H. Blake and R. I. Lawless. London: Croon Helm.

———. 1981. "The Settlement of Armenian Refugees in Syria and Lebanon, 1915–1939." In *Change and Development in the Middle East,* ed. John I. Clark and Howard Bowen-Jones. London: Methuen.

Grunebaum, Gustav von. 1955. "The Structure of the Muslim Town." In *Islam: Essays in the Nature and Growth of a Cultural Tradition*. American Anthropological Association, memoir no. 81. Ann Arbor: American Anthropological Association.

Gulick, John. 1967. *Tripoli: A Modern Arab City*. Cambridge, Mass.: Harvard University Press.

al-Haj, Majid. 1985. "Ethnic Relations in an Arab Town in Israel." In *Studies in Israeli Ethnicity: After the Ingathering*, ed. Alex Weingrod. New York: Gordon and Breach Science Publishers.

_____. 1987. *Social Change and Family Processes: Arab Communities in Shefar-'Am*. Boulder: Westview Press.

_____. 1988. "The Arab Internal Refugees in Israel: The Emergence of a Minority within a Minority." *Immigrants and Minorities* 7 (July): 149–65.

al-Haj, Majid, and Henry Rosenfeld. 1990. *Arab Local Government in Israel*. Boulder: Westview Press.

Hasanin, Fadili. 1989. "Social Adjustment of Refugees from Saffuriya." Photocopy.

Hoade, Eugene. 1984. *Guide to the Holy Land*. Jerusalem: Franciscan Printing Press.

Hofman, John E., and Sami Debbiny. 1970. "Religious Affiliation and Ethnic Identity." *Psychological Reports* 26: 1014.

Hofman, John E., et al. 1988. *Arab-Jewish Relations in Israel*. Bristol, Ind.: Wyndham Hall Press.

Hollis, Christopher, and Ronald Brownrigg. 1969. *Holy Places*. New York: Frederick Praeger Publishers.

Hopkins, I. W. J. 1971. "The Four Quarters of Jerusalem." *Palestine Exploration Quarterly* 103: 68–84.

Institute for Arab-Jewish Affairs. *Arabs in Israel*, vol. 1 (8), 26 March 1991. Tel Aviv: IAJA.

IPAC. 1988. *Nazareth: Strategy for Economic Development*, part A. Haifa: IPAC.

James, Montague R. 1924. *The Apocryphal New Testament*. Oxford: Claredon Press.

Jiryis, Sabri. 1976. *The Arabs in Israel*. New York: Monthly Review Press.

Joseph, John. 1983. *Muslim-Christian Relations and Inter-Christian Rivalries in the Middle East*. Albany: State University of New York Press.

Joseph, Suad, and Barbara Pillsbury, eds. 1978. *Muslim-Christian Conflicts: Economic, Political, and Social Origins*. Boulder: Westview Press.

Jowett, William. 1827. *Christian Researches in the Holy Land in 1823*. Philadelphia: American Sunday School Union.

Kamen, Charles S. 1987. "After the Catastrophe I: The Arabs in Israel, 1948–51." *Middle Eastern Studies* 23 (October): 453–95.

_____. 1988. "After the Catastrophe II: The Arabs in Israel, 1948–1951." *Middle Eastern Studies* 24 (January): 68–109.

Kana'na, Mahmud abd al-Qadr. 1964. *Tarikh al-Nasira*. Nazareth: Hakim Printing.

Kark, Ruth. 1981. "The Traditional Middle Eastern City: The Cases of Jerusalem and Jaffa in the Nineteenth Century." *Zeitschrift des Dt. Palastina-Vereins* 97. 1: 94–108.

Kean, James. 1894. *Among the Holy Places*. London: T. Fisher Unwin.

Khalidi, Raja. 1988. *The Arab Economy in Israel: The Dynamics of a Region's Development*. London: Croom Helm.

Kipnis, Baruch A., and Izhak Schnell. 1978. "Changes in the Distribution of Arabs in Mixed Jewish-Arab Cities." *Economic Geography* 54 (October): 168–80.

Landau, Jacob M. 1993. *The Arab Minority in Israel, 1967–1991: Political Aspects*. Oxford: Clarendon Press.

Lapidus, Ira M. 1973. "The Evolution of Muslim Urban Society." *Comparative Studies in Society and History* 15 (January): 21–50.

Le Hardy, Gaston. 1905. *Histoire de Nazareth et des ses sanctuaires.* Paris: Librairie Victor LeCoffre.

Lewis, Bernard. 1965. "Nazareth in the Sixteenth Century, According to the Ottoman Tapu Registers." In *Arabic and Islamic Studies in Honor of Hamilton A. R. Gibb,* ed. George Makdisi. Leiden: E. J. Brill.

Livio, Jean-Bernard. 1982. "Les Fouilles chez les Religieuses de Nazareth." *Le Monde de la Bible* 16.

Ludwig, Gumbert. 1986. *The Basilica in Nazareth.* Munich: Commissariat of the Holy Land.

Lustick, Ian. 1989. "The Political Road to Binationalism: Arabs in Jewish Politics." In *The Emergence of a Binational State,* ed. Ilan Peleg and Ofira Seliktar. Boulder: Westview Press.

Maalouf, Amin. 1984. *The Crusades through Arab Eyes.* New York: Schocken Books.

Mansour, Atallah. 1975. *Waiting for the Dawn: An Autobiography.* London: Seeker and Warsburg.

———. 1988. "The Arab Citizens: Israelis or Palestinians?" In *The Impact of the Six-Day War,* ed. Stephen J. Roth. London: MacMillan Press.

Mansur, As'ad. 1924. *Tarikh al-Nasira.* Cairo: al-Hilal Publishing Co.

Ma'oz, Moshe. 1982. "Communal Conflicts in Ottoman Syria during the Reform Era: The Role of Political and Economic Factors." In *Christians and Jews in the Ottoman Empire,* vol. 2, ed. Benjamin Braude and Bernard Lewis. New York: Holmes and Meier Publishers.

Masterman, Ernest W. Gurney. 1909. *Studies in Galilee.* Chicago: University of Chicago Press.

McCarthy, Justin. 1990. *The Population of Palestine.* New York: Columbia University Press.

Meistermann, Barnabe. 1923. *New Guide to the Holy Land.* London: Burns and Oates.

Merhav, Peretz. 1980. *The Israeli Left.* San Diego: A. S. Barnes and Company.

Morony, Michael. 1974. "Religious Communities in Late Sasanian and Early Muslim Iraq." *Journal of the Economic and Social History of the Orient* 17, no. 2: 113–35.

Morris, Benny. 1987. *The Birth of the Palestinian Refugee Problem, 1947–1949.* Cambridge: Cambridge University Press.

Mossa, Hassan. 1988. *The Geographical Distribution of Arab Homeland Refugees in the Galilee Region.* MA thesis, University of Haifa.

Murphy-O'Connor, Jerome. 1986. *The Holy Land.* Oxford: Oxford University Press.

Nakhleh, Khalil Abdullah. 1973. *Shifting Patterns of Conflict in Selected Arab Villages in Israel.* Ph.D. diss., Indiana University.

Nazareth Today. 1969. Translated by Gerard Bushell. Jerusalem: Franciscan Printing Press.

Nazzal, Nafez. 1978. *The Palestinian Exodus from Galilee, 1948.* Beirut: Institute for Palestine Studies.

Newman, David, and Juval Portugali. 1987. "Israeli-Palestinian Relations as Reflected in the Scientific Literature." *Progress in Human Geography* 11 (September): 3, 315–32.

Newman, J. P. 1876. *From Dan to Beersheba.* New York: Harper and Brothers.

Newton, Frances. 1948. *Fifty Years in Palestine.* Wrotham, England: Coldharbour Press.

Niccolo of Poggibonsi. 1945. *A Voyage Beyond the Seas (1346–1350).* Translated by T. Bellorini and E. Hoade. Jerusalem: Franciscan Press.

Palumbo, Michael. 1987. *The Palestinian Catastrophe*. London: Faber and Faber.

Paz, Reuven. 1990. "The Islamic Movement in Israel and the Municipal Election of 1989." *Jerusalem Quarterly* 53: 3–26.

Peled, Mattityahu. 1976. "The Cure for Nazareth." *New Outlook* 19 (January): 35–38.

Pena, Ignazio. 1986. "The Christians of Nazareth." *Holy Land* 6 (Spring 1986): 11–16.

Peretz, Don. 1958. *Israel and the Palestine Arabs*. Washington, D.C.: Middle East Institute.

Porath, Yehoshua. 1974. *The Emergence of the Palestinian-Arab National Movement, 1918–1929*. London: Frank Cass.

_____. 1977. *The Palestinian Arab National Movement, 1929–1939*. London: Frank Cass.

Prothro, Edwin Terry, and Lutfy Najib Diaab. 1974. *Changing Family Patterns in the Arab East*. Beirut: American University of Beirut.

Range, Paul. 1923. *Nazareth*. Leipzig: J. C. Hinrichs'sche Buchhandlung.

Robinson, Edward. 1970. *Biblical Researches in Palestine and the Adjacent Region, vol. 2, A Journal of Travels in the Years 1838 and 1852*. Jerusalem: Universitas Booksellers.

Romann, Michael, and Alex Weingrod. 1991. *Living Together Separately: Arabs and Jews in Contemporary Jerusalem*. Princeton, N.J.: Princeton University Press.

Rosenfeld, Henry. 1988. "Nazareth and Upper Nazareth in the Political Economy of Israel." In *Arab-Jewish Relations in Israel*, ed. John E. Hofman et al. Bristol, Ind.: Wyndham Hall Press.

Rubin, Morton. 1974. *The Walls of Acre: Intergroup Relations and Urban Development in Israel*. New York: Holt, Reinhart and Winston.

Salibi, Kamal S. 1968. "The 1860 Upheaval in Damascus. . . ." In *Beginnings of Modernization in the Middle East*, ed. William R. Polk and Richard L. Chambers, 185–202. Chicago: University of Chicago Press.

_____. 1988. "Tribal Origins of the Religious Sects in the Arab East." In *Toward a Viable Lebanon*, ed. Halim Barakat, 15–26. London: Croom Helm.

Samuel, Edwin. 1970. *A Lifetime in Jerusalem*. London: Abelard-Schuman.

Schaff, Philip. 1977. *Through Bible Lands*. 1878. Reprint, New York: Arno Press.

Schwarz, Walter. 1959. *The Arabs in Israel*. London: Faber and Faber.

Scrimgeour, Frederic John. 1913. *Nazareth of To-Day*. Edinburgh: William Green and Sons.

Segev, Tom. 1986. *1949: The First Israelis*. New York: Free Press.

Shilhav, Yosseph. 1983. "Communal Conflict in Jerusalem: The Spread of Ultra-Orthodox Neighborhoods." In *Pluralism and Political Geography*, ed. Nurit Kliot and Stanley Waterman. London: Croon Helm.

Sirhan, Bassem. 1975. "Palestinian Refugee Life in Lebanon." *Journal of Palestine Studies* 4 (Winter 1975): 91–107.

Smith, George A., et al. 1977. *Correspondence of Palestine Tourists*. 1875. Reprint, New York: Arno Press.

Smith, George Adam. 1966. *The Historical Geography of the Holy Land*. 1894. Reprint, London: Fontana Library.

Smooha, Sammy. 1978. *Israel: Pluralism and Conflict*. Berkeley: Univerisity of California Press.

_____. 1989. *Arabs and Jews in Israel*. Boulder: Westview Press.

Smooha, Sammy, and Ora Cibulski. 1987. *Social Research on Arabs in Israel, 1948–1976*. Haifa: University of Haifa.

Stanley, Arthur Penrhyn. 1895. *Sinai and Palestine.* New York: A. C. Armstrong and Son.

Stendel, Ori. 1966. *Nazareth in the Past and Present.* Jerusalem: School of Tourism. (In Hebrew)

_____. 1973. "Nazareth: Its Development in the State of Israel." *Christian News from Israel* 24, no. 1: 5–10.

Suriano, Francesco. 1949. *Treatise on the Holy Land.* Translated by T. Bellorini and E. Hoade. Jerusalem: Franciscan Press.

Temimi, Mehmet R. 1933. *Wilaya Beirut, al-Qisim al-Janub.* Beirut: al-Aqbal Publishers.

Thomson, William M. 1882. *The Land and the Book: Central Palestine and Phoenicia.* New York: Harper and Brothers.

"Three Surveys of Israeli Arabs." *Hamizrah Hehadash* 15 (1–2): 85–94.

Tobler, Titus. 1868. *Nazareth in Palastina.* Berlin: G. Reimer.

Treves, Frederick. 1913. *The Land That Is Desolate.* London: Smith, Elder and Co.

Tsimhoni, Daphne. 1983. "Demographic Trends of the Christian Population in Jerusalem and the West Bank 1948–1978." *Middle East Journal* 37 (Winter): 54–64.

_____. 1984a. "The Armenians and the Syrians: Ethno-Religious Communities in Jerusalem." *Middle Eastern Studies* 20 (July): 352–69.

_____. 1984b. "The Status of the Arab Christians under the British Mandate in Palestine." *Middle Eastern Studies* 20 (October): 166–92.

_____. 1986. "Continuity and Change in Communal Autonomy: The Christian Communal Organizations in Jerusalem 1948–80." *Middle Eastern Studies* 22 (July): 398–417.

_____. 1993. *Christian Communities in Jerusalem and the West Bank since 1948.* Westport, Conn.: Praeger.

Twain, Mark. 1966. *The Innocents Abroad.* New York: New American Library.

Village Statistics. 1945. Government of Palestine.

Von Suchem, Ludolph. 1895. Translated by Aubrey Stewart. *Description of the Holy Land.* London: Palestine Pilgrims' Text Society.

Walker, Franklin. 1974. *Irreverent Pilgrims.* Seattle: University of Washington Press.

Waterman, Stanley. 1985. "Not Just Milk and Honey—Now a Way of Life: Israeli Human Geography since the Six-Day War." *Progress in Human Geography* 9 (June): 194–234.

Whittingham, George N. 1921. *The Home of Fadeless Splendour; or, Palestine of Today.* London: Hutchinson and Co.

Wilkinson, John, ed. 1988. *Jerusalem Pilgrimage 1099–1185.* London: Hakluyt Society.

Wright, Thomas, ed. 1848. *Early Travels in Palestine.* London: Henry G. Bohn.

Yiftachel, Oren. 1992. *Planning a Mixed Region: The Political Geography of Arab-Jewish Relations in the Galilee.* Aldershot, England: Avebury.

al-Zu'bi, Saif al-Din. 1987. *Shahid 'Ayan.* Shefa 'Amr: Dar al-Mashriq.

Index

The University of Chicago
GEOGRAPHY RESEARCH PAPERS
(Lithographed, 6 x 9 inches)

Titles in Print

127. GOHEEN, PETER G. *Victorian Toronto, 1850 to 1900: Pattern and Process of Growth.* 1970. xiii + 278 pp.

131. NEILS, ELAINE M. *Reservation to City: Indian Migration and Federal Relocation.* 1971. x + 198 pp.

132. MOLINE, NORMAN T. *Mobility and the Small Town, 1900–1930.* 1971. ix + 169 pp.

133. SCHWIND, PAUL J. *Migration and Regional Development in the United States, 1950–1960.* 1971. x + 170 pp.

134. PYLE, GERALD F. *Heart Disease, Cancer and Stroke in Chicago: A Geographical Analysis with Facilities, Plans for 1980.* 1971. ix + 292 pp.

136. BUTZER, KARL W. *Recent History of an Ethiopian Delta: The Omo River and the Level of Lake Rudolf.* 1971. xvi + 184 pp.

139. McMANIS, DOUGLAS R. *European Impressions of the New England Coast, 1497–1620.* 1972. viii + 147 pp.

142. PLATT, RUTHERFORD H. *The Open Space Decision Process: Spatial Allocation of Costs and Benefits.* 1972. xi + 189 pp.

143. GOLANT, STEPHEN M. *The Residential Location and Spatial Behavior of the Elderly: A Canadian Example.* 1972. xv + 226 pp.

144. PANNELL, CLIFTON W. *T'ai-Chung, T'ai-wan: Structure and Function.* 1973. xii + 200 pp.

145. LANKFORD, PHILIP M. *Regional Incomes in the United States, 1929–1967: Level, Distribution, Stability, and Growth.* 1972. x + 137 pp.

148. JOHNSON, DOUGLAS L. *Jabal al-Akhdar, Cyrenaica: An Historical Geography of Settlement and Livelihood.* 1973. xii + 240 pp.

149. YEUNG, YUE-MAN. *National Development Policy and Urban Transformation in Singapore: A Study of Public Housing and the Marketing System.* 1973. x + 204 pp.

150. HALL, FRED L. *Location Criteria for High Schools: Student Transportation and Racial Integration.* 1973. xii + 156 pp.

151. ROSENBERG, TERRY J. *Residence, Employment, and Mobility of Puerto Ricans in New York City.* 1974. xi + 230 pp.

152. MIKESELL, MARVIN W., ed. *Geographers Abroad: Essays on the Problems and Prospects of Research in Foreign Areas.* 1973. ix + 296 pp.

154. WACHT, WALTER F. *The Domestic Air Transportation Network of the United States.* 1974. ix + 98 pp.

160. MEYER, JUDITH W. *Diffusion of an American Montessori Education.* 1975. xi + 97 pp.

162. LAMB, RICHARD F. *Metropolitan Impacts on Rural America.* 1975. xii + 196 pp.

163. FEDOR, THOMAS STANLEY. *Patterns of Urban Growth in the Russian Empire during the Nineteenth Century.* 1975. xxv + 245 pp.

164. HARRIS, CHAUNCY D. *Guide to Geographical Bibliographies and Reference Works in Russian or on the Soviet Union.* 1975. xviii + 478 pp.

165. JONES, DONALD W. *Migration and Urban Unemployment in Dualistic Economic Development.* 1975. x + 174 pp.

166. BEDNARZ, ROBERT S. *The Effect of Air Pollution on Property Value in Chicago.* 1975. viii + 111 pp.

167. HANNEMANN, MANFRED. *The Diffusion of the Reformation in Southwestern Germany, 1518–1534.* 1975. ix + 235 pp.

168. SUBLETT, MICHAEL D. *Farmers on the Road: Interfarm Migration and the Farming of Noncontiguous Lands in Three Midwestern Townships. 1939–1969.* 1975. xiii + 214 pp.

169. STETZER, DONALD FOSTER. *Special Districts in Cook County: Toward a Geography of Local Government.* 1975. xi + 177 pp.

172. COHEN, YEHOSHUA S., and BRIAN J. L. BERRY. *Spatial Components of Manufacturing Change.* 1975. vi + 262 pp.

173. HAYES, CHARLES R. *The Dispersed City: The Case of Piedmont, North Carolina.* 1976. ix + 157 pp.

174. CARGO, DOUGLAS B. *Solid Wastes: Factors Influencing Generation Rates.* 1977. 100 pp.

176. MORGAN, DAVID J. *Patterns of Population Distribution: A Residential Preference Model and Its Dynamic.* 1978. xiii + 200 pp.

177. STOKES, HOUSTON H.; DONALD W. JONES; and HUGH M. NEUBURGER. *Unemployment and Adjustment in the Labor Market: A Comparison between the Regional and National Responses.* 1975. ix + 125 pp.

181. GOODWIN, GARY C. *Cherokees in Transition: A Study of Changing Culture and Environment Prior to 1775.* 1977. ix + 207 pp.

183. HAIGH, MARTIN J. *The Evolution of Slopes on Artificial Landforms, Blaenavon, U.K.* 1978. xiv + 293 pp.

184. FINK, L. DEE. *Listening to the Learner: An Exploratory Study of Personal Meaning in College Geography Courses.* 1977. ix + 186 pp.

185. HELGREN, DAVID M. *Rivers of Diamonds: An Alluvial History of the Lower Vaal Basin, South Africa.* 1979. xix + 389 pp.

186. BUTZER, KARL W., ed. *Dimensions of Human Geography: Essays on Some Familiar and Neglected Themes.* 1978. vii + 190 pp.

187. MITSUHASHI, SETSUKO. *Japanese Commodity Flows.* 1978. x + 172 pp.

188. CARIS, SUSAN L. *Community Attitudes toward Pollution.* 1978. xii + 211 pp.

189. REES, PHILIP M. *Residential Patterns in American Cities: 1960.* 1979. xvi + 405 pp.

190. KANNE, EDWARD A. *Fresh Food for Nicosia.* 1979. x + 106 pp.

192. KIRCHNER, JOHN A. *Sugar and Seasonal Labor Migration: The Case of Tucumán, Argentina.* 1980. xii + 174 pp.

194. HARRIS, CHAUNCY D. *Annotated World List of Selected Current Geographical Serials, Fourth Edition. 1980.* 1980. iv + 165 pp.

196. LEUNG, CHI-KEUNG, and NORTON S. GINSBURG, eds. *China: Urbanizations and National Development.* 1980. ix + 283 pp.

197. DAICHES, SOL. *People in Distress: A Geographical Perspective on Psychological Well-being.* 1981. xiv + 199 pp.

198. JOHNSON, JOSEPH T. *Location and Trade Theory: Industrial Location, Comparative Advantage, and the Geographic Pattern of Production in the United States.* 1981. xi + 107 pp.

199–200. STEVENSON, ARTHUR J. *The New York–Newark Air Freight System.* 1982. xvi + 440 pp.

201. LICATE, JACK A. *Creation of a Mexican Landscape: Territorial Organization and Settlement in the Eastern Puebla Basin, 1520–1605.* 1981. x + 143 pp.

202. RUDZITIS, GUNDARS. *Residential Location Determinants of the Older Population.* 1982. x + 117 pp.

204. DAHMANN, DONALD C. *Locals and Cosmopolitans: Patterns of Spatial Mobility during the Transition from Youth to Early Adulthood.* 1982. xiii + 146 pp.

206. HARRIS, CHAUNCY D. *Bibliography of Geography. Part II: Regional. Volume 1. The United States of America.* 1984. viii + 178 pp.

207–208. WHEATLEY, PAUL. *Nagara and Commandery: Origins of the Southeast Asian Urban Traditions.* 1983. xv + 472 pp.

209. SAARINEN, THOMAS F.; DAVID SEAMON; and JAMES L. SELL, eds. *Environmental Perception and Behavior: An Inventory and Prospect.* 1984. x + 263 pp.

210. WESCOAT, JAMES L., JR. *Integrated Water Development: Water Use and Conservation Practice in Western Colorado.* 1984. xi + 239 pp.

211. DEMKO, GEORGE J., and ROLAND J. FUCHS, eds. *Geographical Studies on the Soviet Union: Essays in Honor of Chauncy D. Harris.* 1984. vii + 294 pp.

212. HOLMES, ROLAND C. *Irrigation in Southern Peru: The Chili Basin.* 1986. ix + 199 pp.

213. EDMONDS, RICHARD LOUIS. *Northern Frontiers of Qing China and Tokugawa Japan: A Comparative Study of Frontier Policy.* 1985. xi + 209 pp.

214. FREEMAN, DONALD B., and GLEN B. NORCLIFFE. *Rural Enterprise in Kenya: Development and Spatial Organization of the Nonfarm Sector.* 1985. xiv + 180 pp.

215. COHEN, YEHOSHUA S., and AMNON SHINAR. *Neighborhoods and Friendship Networks: A Study of Three Residential Neighborhoods in Jerusalem.* 1985. ix + 137 pp.

216. OBERMEYER, NANCY J. *Bureaucrats, Clients, and Geography: The Bailly Nuclear Power Plant Battle in Northern Indiana.* 1989. x + 135 pp.

217–218. CONZEN, MICHAEL P., ed. *World Patterns of Modern Urban Change: Essays in Honor of Chauncy D. Harris.* 1986. x + 479 pp.

219. KOMOGUCHI, YOSHIMI. *Agricultural Systems in the Tamil Nadu: A Case Study of Peruvalanallur Village.* 1986. xvi + 175 pp.

220. GINSBURG, NORTON; JAMES OSBORN; and GRANT BLANK. *Geographic Perspectives on the Wealth of Nations.* 1986. ix + 133 pp.

221. BAYLSON, JOSHUA C. *Territorial Allocation by Imperial Rivalry: The Human Legacy in the Near East.* 1987. xi + 138 pp.

222. DORN, MARILYN APRIL. *The Administrative Partitioning of Costa Rica: Politics and Planners in the 1970s.* 1989. xi + 126 pp.

223. ASTROTH, JOSEPH H., JR. *Understanding Peasant Agriculture: An Integrated Land-Use Model for the Punjab.* 1990. xiii + 173 pp.

224. PLATT, RUTHERFORD H.; SHEILA G. PELCZARSKI; and BARBARA K. BURBANK, eds. *Cities on the Beach: Management Issues of Developed Coastal Barriers.* 1987. vii + 324 pp.

225. LATZ, GIL. *Agricultural Development in Japan: The Land Improvement District in Concept and Practice.* 1989. viii + 135 pp.

226. GRITZNER, JEFFREY A. *The West African Sahel: Human Agency and Environmental Change.* 1988. xii + 170 pp.

227. MURPHY, ALEXANDER B. *The Regional Dynamics of Language Differentiation in Belgium: A Study in Cultural-Political Geography.* 1988. xiii + 249 pp.

228–229. BISHOP, BARRY C. *Karnali under Stress: Livelihood Strategies and Seasonal Rhythms in a Changing Nepal Himalaya.* 1990. xviii + 460 pp.

230. MUELLER-WILLE, CHRISTOPHER. *Natural Landscape Amenities and Suburban Growth: Metropolitan Chicago, 1970–1980.* 1990. xi + 153 pp.

231. WILKINSON, M. JUSTIN. *Paleoenvironments in the Namib Desert: The Lower Tumas Basin in the Late Cenozoic.* 1990. xv + 196 pp.

232. DUBOIS, RANDOM. *Soil Erosion in a Coastal River Basin: A Case Study from the Philippines.* 1990. xii + 138 pp.

233. PALM, RISA, AND MICHAEL E. HODGSON. *After a California Earthquake: Attitude and Behavior Change.* 1992. xii + 130 pp.

234. KUMMER, DAVID M. *Deforestation in the Postwar Philippines.* 1992. xviii + 179 pp.

235. CONZEN, MICHAEL P., THOMAS A. RUMNEY, AND GRAEME WYNN. *A Scholar's Guide to Geographical Writing on the American and Canadian Past.* 1993. xiii + 751 pp.

236. COHEN, SHAUL EPHRAIM. *The Politics of Planting: Israeli-Palestinian Competition for Control of Land in the Jerusalem Periphery.* 1993. xiv + 203 pp.

237. EMMETT, CHAD F. *Beyond the Basilica: Christians and Muslims in Nazareth.* 1994. xix + 303 pp.